Helping Your Kids Cope with Divorce the Sandcastles™ Way

Helping Your Kids Cope with Divorce the Sandcastles™ Way

M. Gary Neuman

CREATOR OF THE NATIONALLY RENOWNED SANDCASTLES™ PROGRAM

with
Patricia Romanowski

TIMES 𝕿 BOOKS

RANDOM HOUSE

The families and individuals who appear throughout this book in "case histories," examples, and the question-and-answer sections are the fictional creations of the coauthors, written specifically to illustrate typical divorce-related issues and situations. No "case history," example, or question-and-answer is in any way based on any real person known to either of the coauthors, nor on any person or case M. Gary Neuman has encountered through his private therapy practice, the Sandcastles Program, or any other professional or private situation. Any resemblance between the characters in this book and any persons, living or dead, is purely coincidental.

Sandcastles is a trademark of M. Gary Neuman.

Copyright © 1998 by G.K.N. Corporation
All rights reserved under International and Pan-American Copyright Conventions.
Published in the United States by Times Books, a division of Random House, Inc.,
New York, and simultaneously in Canada by Random House of Canada Limited,
Toronto.

Library of Congress Cataloging-in-Publication Data
Neuman, M. Gary.
Helping your kids cope with divorce the Sandcastles way / M. Gary Neuman, with
Patricia Romanowski. — 1st ed.
p.   cm.
Includes index.
ISBN 0-8129-2902-0 (hardcover : alk. paper)
1. Children of divorced parents—United States—Psychology.   2. Divorced
parents—United States—Psychology.   3. Divorce—United States—Psychological
aspects.   I. Romanowski, Patricia.   II. Title.
HQ777.5.N48   1998
306.89—dc21   97-26653

Random House website address: www.randomhouse.com
Printed in the United States of America

9 8 7 6 5 4 3 2

First Edition

Interior design by Robert Bull Design

To my parents, David and Celia,
for always being there with love
To my wife, Melisa,
in celebration of our love, laughter, respect, and magic

Acknowledgments

Countless people have helped me on my road to helping others. To each, I express the deepest gratitude and the understanding that they have a share in the good this book may produce.

I wish to acknowledge and thank those professionals who provided their invaluable expertise to the realization of this book:

Patricia Romanowski, whose organization and research skills are so superb it's scary. Her professional approach provided great ideas on every front. She is a gifted writer and editor, a student of human nature, and an outstanding individual. I thank her for her friendship and dedication to this book. Thanks as well to her husband, Philip Bashe, and their son, Justin, for their friendship.

Sarah Lazin, my agent, whose vision and knowledge were wonderful to lean on. I am extremely grateful to her for making so much possible.

To those at Times Books who made themselves available and took the time to explain and guide me through every step of the process, my heartfelt thanks and appreciation. Editor Betsy Rapoport welcomed this project, and throughout has shared her wit, insight, endless effort, and excellent suggestions; her assistant, John Rambow, handled countless details, great and small. Copy chief Nancy Inglis helped hold me to deadlines, and copy editor Susan Betz improved the almost-finished manuscript with sound suggestions. Publicist Mary Beth Roche has given me the benefit of her energy, suggestions, and time. Wanda Chappell has shown great dedication to this project from the start, and Peter Bernstein has provided invaluable direction.

Among those who have helped me in so many ways with their advice and guidance, I thank:

Jill Simons-Smith, a gifted psychotherapist and skilled clinician. Her innovation and creativity were invaluable to this book and many of the activities. I thank her for countless hours of effort and wonderful ideas and suggestions.

Hindi Klein, Psy.D., for her professional insight and expertise as well as her generous gifts of time and energy in reviewing the Sandcastles Program and the chapters herein on child development.

E. Jean Carroll, whose talent I respect and from whose kindness I benefited.

Edward Reitman, Ph.D., for his friendship and the time he spent reviewing the Sandcastles Program.

Malka Lichter Zacharawitz, Ph.D., for her time and helpful suggestions regarding the art and play therapy chapter of this book.

The success of the Sandcastles Program would not have been possible without the support of the judges across the country who have mandated the program, the administrators and teachers who provide the program, and members of the media, who have covered the program and the issues it addresses with care and sensitivity.

On a very personal note, I offer my heartfelt appreciation of these very special people in my life:

My wife, Melisa, who teaches me every day more about love, understanding, and parenting. With her love, enthusiasm, ideas, and inspiration, I have been able to follow my dreams and enjoy the ride every step of the way. Words could never express what she means to me.

My parents, David and Celia Neuman, whose extraordinary ability to love and support continue to be a catalyst for my own comfort in the world and in my work. They have always been and continue to be there for me unconditionally. My thanks to them for all that they have enabled me to do.

My parents-in-law, Stuart and Rochelle Simons, who have loved me as a son and on whose warmth, wisdom, and laughter I have come to depend. They are two of my closest friends and much of my ability to pursue my endeavors is due to their time and effort.

My brother Craig Neuman, CPA, for his gift of time and advice. Thanks for returning a brother's call at the drop of a hat.

Jeff Neuman, Steve Neuman, Rich Neuman, and David Smith, for brotherly advice, love, and enthusiasm beyond belief.

Fred Rogers, for his grace and inspiration.

Allan Rosenthal, Esq., for his friendship and guidance.

Vicky Lansky, for her help and time in the beginning, the middle, and last week.

Kiki Bochi, for her assistance in starting and expanding my column.

Jon Gordon, whose confidence in me and friendship has always been appreciated.

To Eduardo Rasco, Marc Burns, Bonnie, Adam Kaplan, Jerome Hollo, Rabbi Glixman, Rabbi Zweig, the much-missed Rabbi Shapiro, and Mitchell Kaplan for their ongoing assistance.

Alfred Jonas, M.D., for his genuine kindness in helping me to become a therapist with respect for the process and the people it helps. His integrity, ethics, modesty, and generosity are unparalleled.

And, of course, my five wonderful children: Yehuda, Esther, Michael, Chaim Pesachia, and Daniel. Each of them adds immeasurably to my life and who I am. They bring me joy and pride beyond imagination, and my love for them is endless. Their warmth, character, and love of life continue to teach me about the infinite possibilities we have, both as people and as parents. They have taught me more than they will ever know, and much of that knowledge is written into this book.

To the One who makes everything possible.

To my precious children and all the children of our world—

I know what's important now.
I haven't used a bathroom in peace for years
I've taxied children to violin, swimming, baseball,
    hockey, piano, parties
I've run through the streets drenched with sweat, holding
    the back of a child's bicycle
I've jumped with sheer joy when I let go and saw that
    bike continue on its own
I've had children's songs race through my mind for hours
    at a time
I've romantically danced with my wife to Barney tunes
I've built castles, pizza, tunnels, and mud pies at the
    beach
I've pushed a swing a million times
I've cupped the small, warm fingers of my child in my
    hand
I've crept into my children's rooms to watch them sleep
I've found my shoes fifty feet from where I left them,
    filled with little men, pennies, and tissues
I've made my children cry and have cried for them
I've read the same story no less than a thousand times
I've dressed moving targets
I've checked for monsters under beds and in closets
I've spent nights with bottles, medicines, sheet changes
    after accidents, diapers, and hugging scared children after
    nightmares
I've changed over three thousand diapers
I've gotten goose bumps while watching the smiling
    faces of my children

I've stayed in the most luxurious hotels alone, dying to
     get back home
I've prayed . . . a lot
Now, don't get me wrong. There have been moments when
I've dreamt of luxuriating baths and exquisite sleep with
     a quiet, long breakfast while reading a whole dry newspaper
I've remembered having money in my pocket
I've longed to be bored
I've wished that kid would stop poking me in my sleep
But I am a parent, see, and I know what's important now.

—Gary Neuman

Contents

Helping
Your Kids
Cope with Divorce
the Sandcastles™ Way

Introduction

Parenting After Divorce

Sometimes divorce is good. Sometimes divorce is bad. But the thing it always does is cause your life to change.
—Boy, fifteen

No more fighting and screaming allowed,
Because after the divorce, the problems will fly away on a cloud.
—Girl, thirteen

Why do couples divorce? Usually because one or both partners believe that ending the marriage will free them to create happier, emotionally healthier lives for themselves and their children. Yet it seems that everywhere you look today, the idea that a child of divorce can grow up to be as happy, well adjusted, confident, and accomplished as any other is met with skepticism. Your own confidence in yourself and in your child may falter when you encounter the negative stereotypes, the frightening statistics, and the doomy predictions of divorce studies.

Free to love. *Children of divorce need and deserve permission to love both of their parents, as this seventeen-year-old boy illustrates.*

All loving parents want the best for their children. We do everything humanly possible to provide for them, to enrich their lives, and to make them feel loved. Perhaps now more than ever, you are acutely conscious of wanting to give your child all the love, support, and guidance he needs, but suddenly everything seems harder and more complicated. You and your family are not alone. For more than half of all American children, divorce is a fact of life.[1]

How parents handle their divorce determines a lot about how their children will fare, both today and tomorrow. That sounds like a big responsibility, and it is. But it is also an incredible opportunity, for no one—no psychologist, member of the clergy, teacher, friend, or relative—shares with your child the extraordinary relationship you two have. No one knows your child better than you do, and no one is in a better position to give him the security, guidance, structure, and support he needs now. You may not be a child development expert, but you are something much better: a concerned, conscientious, and loving parent who's willing to learn how to help your child. With your help, your child will not only be shielded from unnecessary pain and confusion surrounding divorce, he will grow and thrive. One day he will be able to look back on his childhood as a loving, joyful time touched by divorce, not a once-blissful state ruined forever by divorce.

FACING THE FUTURE TOGETHER

The legal dissolution of a marriage is not a single, isolated event but a long-term series of gains and losses, breakthroughs and setbacks, calm and crisis. Years, even decades, after the final decree is signed, divorce will be a factor in your life, something to be considered when your son decides which of you should accompany him to visit college campuses or your daughter plans the seating at her wedding reception.

For adults, divorce can represent an escape from an unhappy or abusive situation, a new world of challenges and possibilities, a tragic disappointment, a fresh start. Parents may become so absorbed in the emotional, legal, and personal issues of divorce, they may not realize how differently their children view the changes in their lives. Even in the best of situations, divorce can endure as the defining moment of their lives. Exactly what that will mean for your child will be determined not so much by the simple fact you have divorced, but by how you choose to handle the issues and challenges that lie ahead.

How CHILDREN EXPERIENCE DIVORCE

Dear Mom,
Why did you divorce with Dad? All he said was, "The room is a mess," but it was my fault.
—Boy, nine

A nine-year-old who concludes he caused his parents to break up and believes so for a year has spent more than a tenth of his life bearing this painful "secret." If you're thirty, imagine spending three years convinced that you were the cause of some tragic event. Then imagine yourself in a magical land where time moves more slowly. There, you are too afraid to tell anyone how you feel, because you believe you are the only person in that whole world this has ever happened to. In this special place, all the information and support we adults depend on (therapy, self-help books, support groups, good friends who've been through it, magazine articles, television programs) do not exist, because no one thinks you need them. And one other thing: You have absolutely no control over your own life. Welcome to childhood.

If there is ever a time when parents need to see the world through a child's eyes, this is it. As the director of the Sandcastles Program for children of divorce (see page 8) and a therapist in private practice, I always strive to view each child's world as he sees and experiences it. Clearly, divorce is a family problem, but this book is predominantly about children: how divorce affects them, how they feel about it, and how parents and other concerned adults can help them. This book will not tell you whether or not you and your ex should reconcile, the fine points of disputing a custody agreement, or how to force your child's other parent to do things your way. There are countless books, peer support groups, lawyers, and therapists you can turn to for help in resolving your personal divorce-related issues. What this book will give you is the insight and the practical advice to help your child cope with and under-

WHERE DO THE PESSIMISTIC PREDICTIONS COME FROM?

While the fact that children suffer from divorce continually makes fresh headlines, the skyrocketing divorce rate is not a recent phenomenon. After a sudden surge following World War II, the rate stabilized through the 1950s, then in 1960 began a consistent rise that began to level off in the mid-to late 1980s.[2]

Despite this, the full impact of divorce on families and on children in particular is still a relatively new field of study. Certainly the subject deserves our attention, but the vast majority of what we hear and read about the results of these studies leaves parents feeling anxious, discouraged, and overwhelmed. In part, that's because the expert who admits that children vary greatly in their response to divorce simply does not attract the same attention as the one who predicts that more than half of all children of divorce will grow up profoundly troubled.

The truth is, we are still in the process of learning about children and divorce, and most of the studies include children who are not involved in a support program or receiving psychotherapy. Every study has its limitations, and every expert has his biases. For example, some of the most often cited studies involved fewer than one hundred families. Others were restricted to studying a single aspect of divorce (the role that having divorced parents might play on unwed teenage motherhood) or a specific group of children (such as those already identified as troubled). One of the best-kept secrets about studies in psychology and sociology is that fair-minded authors often balance persuasive statistics with an examination of other possible factors and a call for further research. In other words, little of what we learn from the media is complete, final, or considered by the experts to be written in stone.

Parents should always remember that a study can only tell us what happened to someone else. It cannot predict how *your* child will be affected by divorce.

stand, to the best of his ability, the myriad changes and problems divorce throws his way.

Divorce is extremely stressful, but we usually regard stress as an adult problem. Children of divorce also experience high levels of stress but lack the coping skills and opportunities adults depend on. Your child can't just take the car and go work out at the gym, go shopping, or commiserate with sympathetic friends over a good bottle of wine. Unlike Mom and Dad, he takes little consolation in believing that ultimately divorce is the "right" thing, nor does he necessarily look forward to life after the separation as being better (not even in some cases of violence or abuse).

It is impossible to predict how your child will react to divorce, and when she does, we don't always understand what her reaction means. Twelve-year-old Phoebe, whom everyone praises for being "so grown-up" and "handling it so well," may actually be more adversely affected by divorce than her six-year-old brother, Danny, who throws tantrums, disrupts the class, and cries every night because he misses Daddy. Both Phoebe and Danny are typical children of divorce; both feel a sense of alienation, loss, and grief. Youngsters like Phoebe, who do not express their emotions, may feel even more alienated and misunderstood. They may deal with their pain by acting out in unacceptable, destructive, and self-defeating ways. They may harbor unrealistic fantasies (that their parents will reunite) or irrational, guilt-inducing fears (that they "caused" the divorce). Danny, on the other hand, is probably doing a little better in the sense that he is expressing his emotions and sending his parents the message that he needs help with his pain. The problem is that he needs to learn to do so in an appropriate, acceptable manner.

All children need a parent's guidance and love to find the acceptance and resolution they must achieve to continue growing. You cannot hope to lead your child on this journey until you know how he feels and thinks. And you can't do that unless you are communicating consistently and creatively.

COMMUNICATION AS AN EXPRESSION OF LOVE

Dear Dad,
Thanks for trying to make me feel better. You told me straight out what was going on and without hurting me.
—Girl, seventeen

I can almost hear you saying, "Communicate? That's what everyone keeps telling me to do, but it's not that simple." As a parent of five, I know that even when experts spell out what I should do—be a good listener, ask questions, and so on—they often neglect to say exactly *how*. Asking your kids direct questions like "How do you feel about our divorce?" is practically guaranteed to shut down communication altogether. And when children feel torn between Mom and Dad, as most do, they can be even less forthcoming. Remember: A child who refuses to talk is defending himself against emotions that seem overwhelming to him. It is not that he "doesn't want to talk"; he does. He just isn't sure how to let the feelings out *and* protect himself at the same time.

To really work, communication must flow two ways. Communicating with children is not always easy under the best of circumstances, and divorced parents often have trouble for other reasons. Of all the hardships and tragedies that can possibly befall our children, divorce can be the hardest for us to discuss with them. It's usually the only one we feel we have "caused," even if indirectly. And it's never easy to hear what your child has on her mind when you feel somewhat responsible for her unhappiness and pain. Additionally, when sensitive topics parents feel strongly about do arise, they may not be prepared to discuss them in a neutral, supportive way.

Divorce complicates the job of parenting. You may be very angry with your ex-spouse or feel threatened by your child's relationships with step- or half siblings and a stepparent. You may know what you would like to say to your child, but then become paralyzed by the fear of saying the "wrong" thing. Perhaps you find it too painful to acknowledge how

WHAT IS THE SANDCASTLES PROGRAM?

The Sandcastles Program is a three-and-a-half-hour, onetime group session for children of divorce between the ages of six and seventeen. The last half hour includes the children's parents and focuses on improving communication between them. The program was first instituted in Miami-Dade County, Florida, and is now mandatory there and in over a dozen other jurisdictions throughout the country. In these counties, no final divorce decree will be granted any couple whose minor children do not participate in the Sandcastles Program.

As a result of meeting with peers who are going through a similar experience, kids usually emerge with a newfound sense of confidence, hope, and community. They realize that they are not alone, that it is normal to feel anxious, angry, sad, and confused. Sandcastles uses a range of innovative techniques designed to help children

- develop self-expression and problem-solving skills,
- learn appropriate means of expressing anger and other intense emotions,
- reach a better understanding of the reality of divorce,
- recognize their own unique qualities and strengths.

Each child receives an age-appropriate workbook, which he or she fills out anonymously. Kids are invited to draw pictures, write poems, compose letters to their parents, answer questions about their divorce experience, and more. The writings and art used throughout this book have been selected from approximately six thousand completed workbooks. (The italicized material in the excerpts are the questions and instructions from the workbooks.) In addition to writing and drawing, the participants are guided in such activities as role-playing, discussion, and interviewing fellow group members. In the last half hour, parents together with their children learn techniques for interacting and expressing their feelings about divorce. At the end of each session, participants complete a written evaluation of their Sandcastles experience, as do their parents, in a followup questionnaire completed afterward.

much your child misses your ex-spouse or you are too demoralized to admit that your own behavior (such as criticizing your child's other parent) hurts your child.

Many parents feel utterly confused and helpless when, for example, their independent kindergartner regresses to bed-wetting and thumb sucking, their preadolescent turns into a sullen, mercurial stranger, and their teenager slams the bedroom door and cranks up the music. "I try to talk to them," parents often say, "but we just don't seem to connect anymore." For these parents, divorce not only dissolves the bonds of marriage, it threatens to drive their children away emotionally as well.

It's typical of divorced parents to feel helpless, isolated, and ravaged, at least once in a while. You may feel you are not as competent a parent as you were before. If you are the residential (or custodial) parent, you may feel overwhelmed by suddenly having to be "two parents in one." If you are the nonresidential parent, you may worry that you aren't seeing your kids enough, and when you do, you're trying too hard to make every moment together "special." And, as if things aren't tough enough already, you may have noticed changes in your child's behavior and attitude and wondered, *What is he really thinking? How can I help?*

You are not alone. As a rabbi, a family therapist, and the architect of the Sandcastles Program—an innovative, nationally recognized support and educational group experience designed to meet the needs of children of divorce—I have seen firsthand the devastation divorce can wreak on a young person's sense of himself and the world. At the same time, I have also known the joy and immense satisfaction of seeing the techniques and philosophy of the Sandcastles Program help kids and their parents understand themselves, each other, and divorce.

This book is based on what I've learned and observed from more than twenty thousand children and their parents who have participated in the Sandcastles Program. In addition to working with hundreds of families outside the Program, I have collected and studied over six thousand Sandcastles workbooks and program participants' written evaluations. The workbook responses and figures cited throughout this book are based on a closer examination of over one thousand workbooks that were selected at random.

I chose the name "Sandcastles" for the program on which this book is based because the image of a child carefully molding his new "home" of sand to replace the old one swept away by turbulent water captures the difficult quest every child of divorce must complete in order to grow up emotionally healthy and equal to life's future challenges.

THE LONG-TERM EFFECTS OF DIVORCE: CHILDREN AT RISK

> I love you, you love me,
> Why can't we be a happy family?
> —Girl, ten

The overwhelming majority of children of divorce feel sad, confused, angry, guilty, and conflicted. When these feelings are not expressed and dealt with in a healthy, productive way, they endure and taint children's views of themselves and of others. This is why, decades after the fact, most adult children of divorce view it as the most devastating event of their childhoods, if not their lives. How well a child copes with her family's transition and its far-ranging implications will be a—if not *the*—major influence on several important aspects of her life, including the ability to forge and sustain loving relationships and be a good parent herself.

As you hold your sobbing child or prepare for another family holiday that seems somehow incomplete, you may wonder if your child will ever be happy again. You may worry that your divorce has set the stage for your child's dropping out of school and experiencing chronic depression, alcohol or drug abuse, low self-esteem, and problematic future relationships. It's important to remember two key points. One, children whose parents do not divorce also share these problems. And two, because the study of children and divorce is relatively new, kids who do experience these negative outcomes may in part reflect a previous lack of awareness of divorce-related problems and intervention to help children deal with them.

We rarely confront these issues until a problem develops, only to discover its root stretching back to a childhood event or unresolved emotional issue. The lesson here is pretty clear: For all parents, but for parents of divorce especially, the future really is now. Understanding how children experience divorce will help you identify and address problems early on.

A time of trepidation. *As this eleven-year-old girl shows, children of divorce often feel confused about what has happened to their families and what the future holds.*

CHARTING YOUR FAMILY'S NEW COURSE

Conscientious parents are understandably troubled by these pessimistic projections, as I believe we all should be. But they tell only part of the story. *The truth is, children can and do live happily after divorce.* Unquestionably, families who encourage love, trust, and open communication are better prepared to meet the challenges than those who do not. On the journey of life, divorce is often a surprise detour off the "scenic route" of our dreams. Sooner or later, you will reach your destination. The crucial question is how. For parents who heed the warnings, keep moving ahead, these dark projections represent blinking caution signs, not the end of the road.

You are your child's first and most influential teacher, his protector, and his guide. You can read a thousand books, see your family therapist daily, and spend every evening with a support group. But nothing has the power to help you and your child as much as your coming to terms with what has happened and resolving to move ahead and grow. We plan for tomorrow—for vacations, for college—and we prepare for our children in the event tragedy befalls us. We immunize our children against diseases and protect them from harm as much as we can (or as much as they allow). If we want our children to thrive in the wake of divorce, we must think proactively and preventively. We have the opportunity to model behavior, teach coping and communication skills, and shelter our children with our love and support. We cannot change the fact that divorce forced us onto this bumpy

---

WHAT WOULD YOU DO DIFFERENTLY?

We ask children in the Sandcastles Program, *What do you think you would do differently than, or the same as, your parents when you are older and have a family?*

I will be faithful to my wife, make her seem like she's the Queen of England, buy her flowers every month, just to remind her that I love her.

    —Boy, fourteen

I will probably end up getting divorced just like my mom, seeing how she got divorced twice already.

    —Girl, fourteen

I won't get married without solving the problems that I have before I get married.

    —Boy, fifteen

I don't know. I'll probably do the same things, like a divorce.

    —Boy, fifteen

I guess I won't get married, because I don't have to do this twice!

    —Girl, nineteen

I would get married when I'm older than my parents were. I would think that if I did, I would be more mature than they were.

    —Girl, thirteen

HOW TO BUILD A COPARENTING RELATIONSHIP
(EVEN WHEN YOU THINK YOU CAN'T)

Here is a comment I've heard too many times to count—in therapy, in workshops, from people I meet while traveling: "Now that I'm divorced, my therapist keeps lecturing me on the value of coparenting. While I can see why it's best for our children, and I would do anything for them, the truth is my ex and I simply cannot maintain even a civil relationship. The whole reason we got divorced is that we couldn't agree on things, including raising our kids. And now we're expected to magically agree or risk our kids growing up with serious problems. The upshot is I feel like I'm less of a parent and that my children are doomed forever because my ex and I cannot be in the same room together. What's the solution?"

As I've said before, divorce often presents us with problems that have no clear-cut solutions. For many families, the best, most realistic course is learning how to cope. The promotion of coparenting—in which each parent has roughly equal input and involvement—as an ideal relationship for families of divorce has had several positive effects, namely keeping both parents actively engaged in a child's life. Yet there are many divorced couples for whom coparenting is simply not a viable, realistic option, for whom the pressure to coparent often results in even more conflict. For all the positive benefits of coparenting, among divorced couples a solid, low- or no-conflict relationship soon after divorce seems to be the exception, not the rule.

While divorce may seem to solve one problem, it often creates others. Conflict between ex-spouses is, perhaps understandably, all too common. With the marriage ended, ex-spouses often lack the incentive to work toward compromise. You may be reading this, thinking, *If we could have communicated and cooperated before, we wouldn't have divorced in the first place,* and you're right. But keep in mind that just because the two of you couldn't make one type of relationship (a marriage) work, that does not mean that you cannot be successful in a different one, coparenting.

Most parents do want to do what's best for their kids, but the intense emotions of divorce cloud their views. In rare cases, both exes dig in their heels and refuse to give an inch on anything, no matter how trivial. More often, however, one parent is willing to give in and overlook the other's bad behavior, for a while. After a few arguments, some insults, and a few times "forgetting" to pick up the kids, the more coopera-

tive parent just gives up and gives in to what our children would call the dark side: "What's the difference what I do? He'll never change." The next thing you know, Mom is slamming down the phone every time Dad calls to wish Jenny happy birthday, and Dad keeps "forgetting" to get Carlos back home in time for Sunday dinner at Grandmother's.

It's important for parents to view their coparenting venture in both the long and the short term. The fact is fewer divorced couples have respectful, cooperative relationships in the immediate wake of divorce. If this is where you find yourself, know that you are not alone, and you may want to take extra care to avoid conflict. However, before you decide that this is how it will always be and that there's no point in extending yourself, you should also know that, after a few years, that situation usually changes. While divorced spouses may not consider each other buddies, most do manage to establish a civil if not cordial relationship, if only for the sake of their children. Doing this may require you to separate your personal issues with your ex from those that involve your children. It may also require you to compromise a little more than you might like at times, to bite your tongue, and to hold your anger. Always remember, however, that you have a clear and worthwhile goal: your child's ability to grow through this divorce.

✔ *Redefine your relationship.* If you cannot view your ex as a friend, think of him as your business partner and your child as your business. Many business partners are not good friends, yet their common goal allows them to respect each other's strengths and overlook each other's shortcomings.

✔ *Choose your battles wisely.* Differences in your parenting styles tend to become more pronounced—and the incentive to compromise less compelling—after divorce. Recognize the control you do have over your child while at the same time learning to accept what you cannot control. (See chapter 12.)

✔ *Respect your ex's relationship with your child.* No one has yet discovered the one "right" way to be a parent. Respect and stay out of your child's unique relationship with your ex (assuming it is not an abusive situation), just as you would wish your ex not to interfere with your relationship with your child. (See chapters 12 and 13.)

✔ *When you have good cause to be concerned about your ex's parenting behavior, discuss it in a nonthreatening manner.* Pepper your conversation liberally with expressions like:

"Perhaps just consider . . ." (as opposed to "You should . . .")

"Obviously, it's up to you . . ." (as opposed to "I think you ought to . . .")

"In case this is helpful . . ." (as opposed to "The way I do things . . .")

"It may not work for you, but here's something that worked for me . . ." (as opposed to "Try it this way . . .")

"Of course, you can figure out your own solutions, but here's an idea if you want to consider it . . ." (as opposed to "Here's the solution . . .")

Before you open your mouth or dial the number, resolve to resist the impulse to call names, explode in anger, or shut down communication completely. If your ex will not listen to you, consider asking a friend, family member, or someone your ex respects to speak on your behalf. This might upset your ex, so be sure your point is important and that there is a reasonable chance that the behavior will change. If your ex has ever abused your child—emotionally, physically, or sexually—or you have reason to suspect he or she may be doing so now, you have an obligation to contact authorities (e.g., pediatrician, psychotherapist, police, attorney, public abuse investigative bureau) and take the proper steps to protect your child. (See page 297.)

✔ *Go out of your way to ensure that your ex is included in your child's life.* Be sure your ex is notified as early as possible of upcoming school events (see box "The Importance of School," page 51), extracurricular activities, and other important occasions in your child's life. Even the most recalcitrant parents have a hard time remaining angry and bitter with an ex who makes an apparent effort to keep them in the loop.

✔ *Try not to fight, and especially never in front of your child.* It's important to realize that, for most children, the one good thing to come out of divorce is the end of their parents' fighting. In our Sandcastles Survey (see page 419), 35.2 percent of eight- to ten-year-olds completed the sentence "*I am sad when . . .*" with "parents fight." Over 30 percent gave the same response to the sentence "*I cry when . . .*" For most older children in the Survey, divorce brings a dramatic drop in parental conflict. Over 70 percent of eleven- to thirteen-year-olds and 74.3 percent of fourteen- to seventeen-year-olds said that their parents "argued a lot" before the divorce. After divorce, however, only 32 percent of eleven- to thirteen-year-olds and approximately 38 percent of fourteen- to seventeen-year-olds said their parents still fought. Although you will probably disagree with your ex, stop short of arguing, if you can. Remember that every time you two fight, your child is drawn back to the most painful moments of her past. For her sake, be smart enough to walk away or hang up the phone (cordially, of course) if you sense your or your ex's anger escalating or the line of discussion beginning to fall into an old familiar rut that you know will end badly. Say, "I want to talk about this more, but I need to think things out first," and call a time-out.

✔ *Be flexible.* Life heeds no schedule, not even the one the court may have hammered out for visitation. Everyone has to swap weekend visits now and then or request a special visit because Grandpa is in town from Italy only those three days. Work with your ex to accommodate these changes. (See chapter 12.)

✔ *Remember that "coparenting" is not always synonymous with "equal parenting."* Maybe your ex isn't as emotionally involved with your children as you think she should be; maybe he doesn't do all those "dad" things your father did. Does that make your ex a "bad" parent? No. As you may know from your own childhood, even in happy, intact families, one parent often dominates in terms of being the emotional one or the "psychological" parent—the one a child turns to for support, advice, and nurturing. Be that parent for your child, even if your ex cannot, and he will thrive.

✔ *When making a decision about your child, think first:* What is in my child's best interest? Too often one ex says no simply because the other is saying yes. Recognize and learn to separate your personal issues with your ex from what is best for your child. If you have trouble doing this, then seek help from understanding but reasonable family, friends, clergy, or a therapist. (See the box "Deciding on Therapy," page 189.) On the journey to help your child grow through divorce, learn to leave your own baggage at home.

road, but we can learn the new rules of the road and improve the odds for our children and ourselves.

From the moment you became a parent, you have been helping your children learn to cope with disappointment and loss. Whether it was explaining why Zippy the hamster died, why your son wasn't chosen for the team, or why your daughter could not have that hundred-dollar dress, you've probably been through this drill a thousand times. Of course, the scripts for those scenes were already written because they're "normal," "typical," "everyday" events. You probably viewed those painful episodes as part of your child's difficult but inevitable work of growing up. Divorce is no different. Given its largely negative connotation, it may sound odd to even suggest that the experience may have positive aspects. But it can if you make it so.

The thousands of responses Sandcastles participants offer to the question *What do you think you would you do differently than, or the same as, your parents . . . ?* make clear that kids learn hundreds of lessons from divorce. They can't help but learn about conflict, sadness, and loss. But by maintaining open communication with your child, you can also ensure that he learns about resolution, love, and hope; about admitting mistakes and moving on; about accepting himself and trusting others, no matter what happened to your marriage.

Unfortunately, many parents are locked into assuming that the only "wisdom" divorce can confer is negative, bleak, and soul crushing: Love can hurt. One of the best-kept secrets about divorce is that you can craft from it invaluable, lasting lessons for your children about courage, independence, and self-esteem. We expect children to grow by learning from their mistakes. Divorce gives them the chance to learn from ours as well.

THE NEW FACTS OF LIFE

I believe that one reason parents and children of divorce feel so helpless is that the society at large has not quite reconciled to the reality of divorce. I firmly believe that every couple should strive to repair and develop a marriage of happiness. But that is not always possible, and once a couple has decided to divorce, everyone should accept their decision.

While couples usually have sound, valid, and compelling reasons for seeking divorce, we don't ordinarily think of divorce as a good thing. As a society, we seem reluctant to do or say things that can be interpreted as condoning divorce. You would scoff at someone who suggested you were encouraging illness by getting your child medical treatment, yet some people act as if anything done to help families in crisis just "gives them the idea that divorce is simple" and "encourages" them to seek this alleged "easy way out." It's beyond the scope of this book to address why these ideas persist. Suffice it to say, they are pervasive and color our attitudes toward divorced families.

If you were to explain to someone that little Joni was misbehaving because her father had recently died, there would be an outpouring of sympathy for her. To lose a parent to death in childhood is an unquestionable tragedy with which we can sympathize. If, on the other hand, Joni is a child of divorce, the unspoken response is more on the order of "So what else is new? Get in line," to "Don't give it too much attention. She'll get over it sooner or later." Lacking positive role models, traditions, or widespread social support, divorced parents feel lost and confused, and the children suffer. A widower who must raise his children alone is praised for being an exceptional parent. A divorced parent, however, gets little recognition for accomplishing an equally difficult feat. Why? Perhaps because somewhere deep down, many people still believe that divorce is a choice, something people bring upon themselves, and so they get what they deserve.

The divorced family and its related family constellations—the single-parent family, the stepfamily, the blended family—are still viewed as less valid than the two- (ideally biological) parent nuclear family. The divorced family is still considered an aberration. The power of these beliefs is reflected in everything from the dearth of divorce-related peer support groups for children of divorce to the arduous, often needlessly painful years of

THE HARD FACTS ABOUT DIVORCE

In the United States, one in every two marriages ends in divorce, and two-thirds of these families include minor children. As a result, every year approximately one million new kids become "children of divorce." More prevalent than drug abuse, teenage pregnancy, or the death of a parent, divorce is the most common problem facing kids today. Only about 40 percent of those born in the mid-1980s can expect to grow up in a home with both biological parents present, a trend the U.S. Census Bureau predicts will continue into the next century. Currently, approximately 37 percent of all American children live with a divorced parent. Experts project that before reaching eighteen, approximately one quarter to 35 percent of American children will spend some time in a stepfamily; two-thirds of these children will have step- or half siblings. Compared to children from maritally "intact" homes (i.e., both biological parents), children of divorce have higher rates of depression, sexual acting out, substance abuse, conduct disorders, problems with school, and delinquent behavior. Statistically, they are more likely to marry earlier and divorce than children from "intact" families.[3]

legal wrangling children witness and of which they too often become the object.

Despite having joined the biggest "club" in the nation, children of divorce still feel they are different and often believe no one really understands them. They worry that their family is not as good as or is less than an intact two-parent family. Teenagers commonly express the fear that they have "inherited" their parents' fate and that their future relationships will end badly, too. At a time when children must learn to trust themselves, their world, and their ability to form positive, healthy relationships, these feelings can be devastating.

TIME FOR A CHANGE

I believe that kids need and deserve a lot better. The first step we should take as parents, teachers, and concerned adults is to change our thinking about divorce. We need to realize and to begin acting as if we believe that divorce is an appropriate option for a troubled couple who cannot resolve their differences. In fact, many studies have determined that children living in high-conflict but "intact" families grow up with more problems than children from low-conflict, divorced families.

We must stop regarding new family structures—single parent, step-, and blended—as somehow inferior and support these families for what they are: real families, too. We owe it to our children and to ourselves to acknowledge the positive lessons that can emerge from divorce and to communicate with our children so that those lessons can be learned.

I'm always fascinated that we can look back on even the most dire tragedy and see it as a catalyst for emotional growth, yet fail to view divorce in the same light as, say, a parent's death or some other uncontrollable event. Until we separate social, largely theoretical attitudes toward the institution of divorce from our feelings toward those who must experience it, we force families already struggling to rebuild their lives and reshape their dreams to bear an additional burden. In doing so, we punish the children by increasing their alienation and diminishing their self-esteem.

YOUR CHILD'S GREATEST ASSET: YOU

Roses are red, violets are blue,
I love my mom and dad,
I know they love me, too.
— Girl, thirteen

At the risk of repeating myself, I will say what every parent must believe: No one has a better chance of helping your child than you do. Only within the security of your love and understanding can your child find the safety and freedom to learn, to grow, and to make mistakes. One cruel irony is that divorce heaps upon families new problems while limiting their ability to cope. At a time when children most need attention and emotional support, you may be preoccupied with your own emotional issues. Just when children need to spend more time with their parents, your new work commitments or living arrangements may leave you with even *less* time, energy, and patience. And when kids most need the comfort and stability of familiar surroundings and routines, your family may be forced into new circumstances that disrupt them.

Parents who keep the line of communication open and humming, who acknowledge their children's feelings and help them master their divorce experience, do more than improve their child's chances of future happiness. Simply by facilitating that process, they create an environment in which their children will be comfortable discussing other important issues. These parents reduce the chances that unresolved divorce-related issues will create future problems. And by just remaining in touch with your child, you relieve yourself and your family of the stress of misunderstanding, shutting down, and losing each other.

This is not to say it is always an easy process. It's not unusual for a therapist to feel that a child who has begun expressing his emotions and speaking his mind has made an important breakthrough. To some parents, however, this new openness is a Pandora's box. "It was much easier when he was quieter about the divorce," the mother of twelve-year-old Elliot says. "Now he gets upset and says that he's angry about the divorce, or disappointed in his father and me because we couldn't make it work—things that I'd really rather not hear, to be honest. Before, I didn't have to stop and talk to him or deal with what he was feeling. I almost convinced myself sometimes that he was really handling it well. Now it's right there. I've got to deal with it, and it's a lot more work."

Parenting does require energy and time-consuming work when you do it right. But what parents like Elliot's mother tend to overlook is the time, energy, and emotion they expend on the effects of *not* dealing with their kids' true feelings. A few weeks after Elliot began expressing his feelings, his mother noticed some interesting changes: fewer arguments about housework and homework, a better attitude at school, and a renewed interest in his friendships and hobbies. "Okay, so I spend more time talking to Elliot, but I'm spending less time fighting with him about his messy room or getting calls from his teacher. The time I spend with Elliot now I view not as spent or wasted, but invested, and we have the 'returns' to show for it."

When children blame themselves. *Many children of divorce, such as this twelve-year-old girl, suspect or believe that they are to blame for their parents' breaking up, yet relatively few find a way to say it directly.*

THE SANDCASTLES APPROACH: THROUGH A CHILD'S EYES

Children embrace beliefs and harbor fears that we cannot imagine. As a young child, I was certain that my parents forbade my brothers and me to stick our hands out the car window because the resulting shift in weight would cause the car to tip over. How did I know? I'd seen it happen to Fred Flintstone.

No matter what their age, children of divorce have a limited capacity to understand exactly what is happening, what they are feeling, and why. That, however, does not stop them from forcing together a "big picture" from the few puzzle pieces they have. Children are driven to explain the world to themselves, to make the story complete, and they will find imaginary causes and affix unrealistic blame to themselves if that's what it takes to complete the puzzle. I will never forget the ten-year-old boy who "confessed": "I know why my parents broke up. My dad was always telling me I was playing Nintendo too much, and I guess he finally just couldn't take it." Because this boy's parents knew the divorce was not their son's fault, it never occurred to them that he would believe it was.

What they, like most parents, do not always understand is how their child's perspective so differs from their own. Based on the information this boy had and what he understood of the world, all the pieces of his version fit. You can only imagine what must have gone through this poor boy's mind every time he heard his parents argue, or the day his father moved out, or his mother went back to work.

The key to the Sandcastles Program and to this book is learning to create an environment conducive to effective and honest communication by entering your child's world. To adults, "communication" means "talking." Kids, however, often lack the emotional and intellectual maturity to express themselves through words alone. For them, each day provides myriad opportunities for self-expression: Through activities such as playing, drawing, writing, baking, and building, children offer their innermost thoughts and feelings to the world. They simply can't help it. It's up to parents to learn to recognize and understand the seemingly hidden true meanings in their child's words and actions. This book will show you how.

Parents are often troubled by their child's sudden changes in attitude, behavior, even personality. Behavior that parents find surprising and out of character for their children is, when understood through the eyes of the child, and in the context of divorce, completely logical. I recall one mother who was shocked when her young son, Jimmy, set a fire in their home. What most people would consider a malicious act had an oddly "logical" reasoning behind it: As Jimmy later explained, "If our house burned down, we'd all have to go live with Daddy. Then we could all be together again."

Like most children, Jimmy has an enormous though often underappreciated capacity for problem-solving. One of our Sandcastles groups included a six-year-old girl named Lisa who had begun cutting off her hair and the hair of all her dolls. Her parents found her behavior baffling, and Lisa wasn't talking. She brought a doll to the group, who "talked" to another doll, held by the group leader.

"You cut your hair," the group leader's doll observed.

"Yes, I cut my hair," Lisa's doll replied. "I'm a boy."

"You don't look like a boy."

"I *am* a boy," Lisa's doll insisted.

"Do you want to be a boy?" the leader's doll asked.

"Yeah," Lisa's doll answered firmly. "Because boys don't cry, and I don't want to cry. My brother doesn't cry, and I don't want to cry anymore!"

There was the answer. Knowing this, the group leader replied, "Lisa, it sounds like you're very sad. We all feel pain sometimes. But, you know, not crying doesn't mean that you don't feel

---

IN THEIR OWN WORDS

What I feel is sad mad puzzled sad sad happy out of shape and great sad.

    —Girl, six

I'm afraid that my mom will get married again and will not love me.

    —Girl, nine

The divorce has actually made me stronger.

    —Girl, fourteen

Dear Mom,

I understand why you separate from my father, but do not separate from us.

    —Boy, sixteen

I felt that I caused the divorce.

    —Boy, twelve

Dear Mom,

I love you so much and Dad too. But I have a question for you. Why are you and Dad getting a divorce? That's what I am afraid about. Because I've been wanting to ask you, but I just didn't know how to start telling you.

    —Girl, nine

hurt. Some people, like your brother, may feel a lot of hurt but not feel like crying. If you feel like crying, that's okay."

Both Jimmy and Lisa had done their best to put their "puzzles" together. In the absence of direct parental involvement and communication, their misconceptions were the answers they got, the misguided stories they might have been telling themselves for years to come.

How This Book Works

My purpose in writing this book was not to turn parents into substitute therapists, burden you with a glossary of psychobabble, or give you those wonderfully guilt-inducing lists of things to do. If all you get from this book is a greater understanding of how your child may be experiencing divorce and a heightened awareness of possible issues, you will have made great strides toward improving your child's prospects. These probably sound like vague, general goals, and in a sense they are. What follows describes neither a program nor a prescription but a *process,* a new way of looking at your child and understanding his world. Unfortunately, you are powerless to prevent your ex-spouse from missing visitations and powerless to shield your daughter from her pain when it happens. But you do have the power to help her learn to experience and express her feelings in a healthy way, to come through these rejections with her self-esteem intact and her security in your love and support reaffirmed.

This book was designed to help, whether you read it from cover to cover, focus on specific chapters, or scan short sections on your most pressing crisis. You'll find information covering a range of issues common to divorce, from how to tell your child that Mom and Dad are breaking up, to helping him learn to live as part of a stepfamily. The book also covers the impact of divorce on children from birth to early adulthood. You'll learn how to recognize and help your child deal with the feelings and issues common to divorce.

Incorporated throughout the text are samples of children's artwork and writings from the Sandcastles Program, which provide a revealing child's-eye view. Very often we at Sandcastles find that it is only through such indirect means of expression as writing and drawing that children reveal their deepest fears and fervent hopes. If you look at any creative work your child has done in the wake of divorce, you will probably find clues to his true thoughts and feelings. Chapter 2 will discuss typical responses to the various stages and issues of divorce, the most common ways kids express them, and how you can find greater understanding through your child's art, writing, and play.

HEARTWORK, NOT HOMEWORK: THE ACTIVITIES

If you're like most parents, you've probably paged through these pages, spotted the activity sections (though titled "Things 2 Do," many can involve more participants), and thought, *Oh, no. Homework!* Believe me, I understand. As mentioned previously, this book is written to be helpful even if you never introduce any of the activities to your child. However, I do urge you to look at them again and consider trying at least a few.

These are not assignments that must be "completed" or games with winners and losers, right answers and wrong. Perhaps it's best to think of them as structured play. Most of them are variations on activities children and families engage in every day: reading and telling stories, cooking and baking, games played in the car, and role-playing games. For example, you might play word-association games while driving to and from school, time you spend with your children anyway.

Although the directions usually assume one child does the activities, most of them can be used with a group of children, whether they're siblings, cousins, or friends. The cornerstone of the Sandcastles Program is the benefit children receive by simply being able to discuss their experiences with other children. They learn that they are not alone in their feelings. If your child's social circle includes other children of divorce, invite them to join activities and discuss their experiences. Remember: There is safety in numbers. One good technique is to have a small group of children share an age-appropriate book about divorce. Letting them take turns reading, a page each, will enhance their ability to emote and give voice to their feelings. Once they close the book, they

♡ WHILE YOU WERE OUT ♡

I was thinking of you

Date _____ Time _____

I want to tell you that I:

♡ want to spend more time   ♡ love you

♡ miss you   ♡ want to say thanks

♡ was thinking of you   ♡ wish you a nice day

♡ am happy that you're my child/parent

☐ Urgent   ☐ Need to talk soon

Message

_____

_____

_____

_____

PURPOSE: Children love to receive notes: packed in with lunch, posted on the fridge, left on the pillow. By creating a standard note form like the one above (or copying this one), you and your child can quickly and easily leave notes for each other. This type of form also gives a child an easy way to indicate a need to talk.

POETRY

Write a poem once a week about your love for your child and keep a journal listing some nice things your child did that week. Present it to your child at the end of each week.

PURPOSE: This lets your child know you are thinking about her even when you are not together. It is a lovely way of getting the message across to your child how much you love and appreciate her. It also helps you focus on your child's positive traits.

probably will begin discussing divorce with no prompting from you.

Again, even if you don't try any of the activities, take a moment to look through them. Since so many are based on things your child probably does already, they might offer a new way of looking at what she does in her play.

Obviously, parents cannot re-create the Sandcastles group experience, which entails groups of six to ten children and a trained leader engaging in a range of activities, including role-playing, workbooks, and artwork. However, I have developed a number of activities and techniques tailored to achieve the same goals at home.

FINALLY

Roses are red, violets are blue,
We are happy, just like you.
We go to a movie, before we get snoozy, and watch a cartoony
Life is good, can't you see?
We are happy,
Why wouldn't we be?
 —Boy, thirteen

There is no such thing as an ideal family or a perfect parent. You do not have to have all the answers or solve every single problem to be a good parent. Sometimes just expressing your concern, acknowledging your child's feelings, and showing that you do understand can inspire an immediate and profound change in your child's behavior and attitude. Getting down on the floor to play with a younger child, going with your eleven-year-old to see the movie he wants to see, cutting short your phone conversation to listen to your teen—these are small yet important ways of telling your child that he is your first priority, that he deserves your full attention, and that you are there to help. Again and again I've seen that children often hold the answers to their problems and behaviors. They really do want to be understood. You can discover the keys that unlock the answers.

CHAPTER 1

How Children Experience Divorce

I think that divorce is like splitting an apple. One piece goes away and the other one stays.
—Boy, twelve

I am afraid that my parents will forget about me when they start a new life.
—Girl, ten

WHAT WE LEARN FROM CHILDHOOD

For kids, one of the most challenging aspects of divorce is that it happens when they *are* kids. Even if this is your first divorce, it's probably not your first life crisis. Through facing disappointment and loss, you've probably learned something about life, change, and your own resilience. For most children, however, the feelings divorce inspires are not only intense and confusing, they are brand-new.

We talk of "families in crisis" and "changing families," and while these are certainly apt descriptions, we must remember that each family member experiences divorce differently. For example, you and your ex-spouse are your daughter's parents, but her relationship with each of you is unique. Or siblings may feel differently about each parent and why the divorce came about.

Childhood is more than a developmental stage or a way station between birth and adulthood. It is a state of being, rife with contradictions and full of wonder. Many of us look back on childhood as the proverbial best of times and worst of times. It shapes not only who we are but determines our capacity to continue growing long after we have "grown up."

CHILDHOOD TEACHES US THE SKILLS OF LIFE

It may sound contradictory, but we are not shaped as much by our actual experiences as how we are taught to respond to them. For example, Charmaine, whose father is a compulsive liar, may grow up believing that lying is acceptable and follow in his footsteps. With the proper guidance, strong self-esteem, and other counterbalancing influences (a stable mother, siblings, school, religion, friends), she is just as likely to grow up abhorring lies and become a woman of impeccable honesty and honor.

Or take another instance, where ten-year-old Jason slinks off the softball field after fumbling the game-winning pop fly. Whether he runs home wailing "I'm such a loser!" or tells his coach and teammates "I'm really sorry, but I know I can do better next time" depends on the behavior he models from others, his self-image, and what previous experiences like this have taught him. The disappointment is about the same in either case. What is different is how Jason interprets that disappointment. Is it one more item in the demoralizing, self-defeating inventory he believes defines him? Or is it an unfortunate but temporary event that he can feel responsible for but not defined by?

CHILDHOOD SETS THE "EMOTIONAL COMPASS" FOR LIFE

How do children see themselves? What do they expect from life? What do they believe they deserve? Our childhood experiences shape our self-image and precondition us to accept or reject beliefs and situations. If we are raised by people who value us, who show us that we are lovable and loved, who make it possible for us to feel happiness, trust, accomplishment, and pride in ourselves, we will regard this as normal and right. We will feel comfortable being loved and valued; we will seek out situations that give us opportunity for growth and mastery. We will believe we deserve happiness, and we will demand happiness from our lives.

If, on the other hand, we are raised by people who neglect us, who show us that we are not lovable and not loved, we will be set upon the trail of life with a faulty compass. Our emotional "true north" will not be north at all. If we have had limited experiences with happiness, trust, accomplishment, few opportunities to feel proud of ourselves, we will view these as normal. When given the chance to be loved, valued, accomplished, and happy, we may reflexively reject the opportunity because it doesn't feel "right." While we ultimately may seek and find success in love and work, it will require a great deal of awareness and determination.

For better or worse, children usually grow up seeking people and situations that reinforce and restate the basic premises they grew up with. Those raised to feel deserving of happiness will seek it out throughout life. Those raised to feel undeserving will be drawn to experiences and people who ensure they stay "on course." As parents, we draw the maps, set the compass, and point the way our children will follow, in terms of basic attitude and outlook, if nothing else. Too often it seems that the only time parental influence figures in the child development equation is when something goes wrong. In raising children, however, we are also granted countless opportunities to make things go right.

T H I N G S **2** D O

THE PERSON OF THE MOMENT

Set aside a short time when you and the children are together, at breakfast or while driving somewhere local, for example. Choose one family member as the Person of the Moment. Everyone says his name aloud, then all take turns saying one positive thing about that person. If there are only two players, you each say several things about the Person of the Moment. You can take turns being the Person.

Variation: Another version of this activity is to have everyone say something positive about each person in the family.

PURPOSE: This activity promotes self-esteem, allows siblings to focus on one another's positive traits, and develops the habit of complimenting others. It also allows the Person of the Moment to become comfortable hearing praise and appreciating himself.

THE ART OF DISCIPLINE

Most parents view discipline as a necessary but difficult part of raising children. For many divorced parents—whose time, patience, and energy are often taxed to the limit—discipline problems are even more complex. The two key points to remember about behavior and discipline are these:

1. *Discipline is good for children.* They need limits and can grow up feeling loved, safe, and secure only when they know someone who cares about them is in charge and controlling their environment. Without discipline, children simply cannot learn self-control.

2. *All behavior, including misbehavior, is an expression of emotion or need.* The behavior that usually prompts disciplinary action is a child's way of saying "I'm angry," "I'm hurt," or "I need attention."

The big question for divorced parents, for all parents, is how to enforce the limits and discourage misbehavior while at the same time recognizing and deciphering the true message behind it. When nine-year-old Eric begins routinely hitting other kids at school and becoming uncharacteristically aggressive, the message he's sending might be no different than if he walked up to his mother and said, "I'm so angry Dad left that I feel like beating up everyone I see." Discipline alone might stop the behavior, but it can never help you discover its true cause. Of course, all kids act up now and then by eating all the candy bars in the house, refusing to do their chores, or "forgetting" to do their homework. Smart parents separate the occasional transgression from misbehavior that is persistent, repeated, or uncharacteristic of their child. While the acts are similar, there is a world of difference between the youngster who talks back to you in a moment of anger and one who is constantly speaking to you in a belligerent, sarcastic, or angry tone; between the child who accidentally comes home with a playmate's toy and one who chronically steals from all of his friends. If your child is old enough to discuss the problem, open the conversation with "I've noticed you've been very upset with me lately. It's okay to feel that way, but let's talk about it instead of your doing things that make me upset and result in consequences for you." Remember to use the play, drawings, and activities suggested throughout this book to broaden your understanding of the issues that might prompt your child to act out. The most effective way of changing unacceptable behavior in the long run is to

- understand its message and help your child express himself in a more acceptable manner and

- make any changes that will help your child deal with the root of his issue.

For example, Mom stops answering the phone during dinner when she realizes that her young son annoys her while she's talking because this is the only time each day he can have uninterrupted time with her. She also role-plays with him in appropriate ways to help him express his feelings.

Ideally, the methods described below will save you from doing the all-too-common—and ultimately ineffective—things angry parents often do. Yelling, hitting, calling your child names, making him feel guilty, or criticizing him intensely rarely change a child's behavior. What they *are* very effective at doing is damaging a child's self-image, provoking even more anger and resentment, and kicking off a new cycle of misbehavior. Try to avoid these things, if possible.

That said, also remember that unacceptable behavior is unacceptable, regardless of its cause. For younger children, time-out is a very popular, practical, and effective approach. A child sits in a designated place for a brief period (most experts suggest one minute for every year of age). Older children can be sent to their rooms. The message of time-out is clear to even the youngest (those over two): "You need to get yourself under control and behave in an acceptable way. When you're able to do that, you may rejoin us."

Applying logical, or natural, consequences is another effective tactic. Remember, discipline and punishment are not the same thing. When a child is disciplined, the message we should send is not "You're a bad person," but "You have behaved in an unacceptable manner." Logical consequences are quite effective, because children soon realize that it is their behavior that determines the consequences. If, for example, a child fails a test, the natural consequence would be that he must study an additional half hour every school night. If she throws a fit every time you walk past the toy store, restrict her outings for a while; if your teenage son carelessly loses his keys, he should be responsible for having a new set made. By the same token, positive behaviors result in positive consequences. (See also the box "Techniques for Dealing with Anger," page 37.)

FAMILY IS THE GREENHOUSE WHERE CHILDHOOD GROWS

To experience childhood is to live in a constant state of becoming, of moving—sometimes rapidly, sometimes imperceptibly—toward who we will be. When we stop to consider them, even the most typical of childhood accomplishments—from learning to walk to making friends to trying out for the team—are acts of courage and of wonder, steps along the way to a sense of self.

While this is a journey each child makes for himself, it is not one he undertakes alone. He thrives on his parents' guidance and constant reassurance that he is lovable and loved. He also draws on the realization that he is part of a larger entity, a family, and that his family values him, loves him, and protects him. We all feel a need to belong, and there is no greater, more profound sense of belonging than that which comes from feeling that we are an important, integral part of a loving family.

WHAT FAMILY TEACHES US

I don't want my mother to get a divorce because I love my dad and mom. I wish they could be together again, because I want to live happily ever after.

—Gender, age unknown

Out of the picture. *By this age, most children can allocate the appropriate space for what they plan to draw. The fact that this eight-year-old girl seems to have run out of room and has to draw her brother outside the frame suggests she may be struggling to redefine exactly who remains in her family after divorce. Note the inclusion of Grandmother and Grandfather and the exclusion of Father.*

Roses are red, violets are blue
A pretty flower that is shining in the sky,
I know that's my family.
    —Boy, nine

One reason divorce often hits kids so hard is that it strikes at the very foundation of their world. Children of divorce commonly reason, *If one parent can leave, so can the other.* They worry that when their parents divorce, grandparents and other extended family members on one side or another may stop loving them. Some even question whether or not their parents will still be their parents. Children of all ages need to feel secure in their world, to know that what was there yesterday and is here today will be there tomorrow, too. Without having confidence that there is a secure base to which he can always return, a child cannot venture out—physically, emotionally, or socially.

Family is a child's whole world. No one outside it is as powerful, as wonderful, or as real as the people to whom he feels that he truly belongs. In the eyes of babies and preschoolers, parents are truly the entire

The great divide. *A twelve-year-old boy graphically illustrates a child's view of parents as two parts of one parental unit rather than as two individuals who are linked by parenthood.*

universe; there is literally little else. Even as children grow older and begin to pull away and even rebel, they continue to define themselves in terms of their family.

To children, family is an intrinsic part of who they are. If their parents are warm, caring, and respectful, even very young children grow up believing that they themselves have those qualities, too. And while each parent views him- or herself as half of a partnership, most children perceive their parents as two parts of a single entity, more as a single mom-and-dad than a mom and a dad. Since it is that entity from which their family was created, it is no wonder that they view their parents' breakup as the end of something crucially important.

CHILDREN, CHANGE, AND STRESS

Dear Mom,
I cannot hear more lies and fighting. And I feel sad, confused.
   —Girl, eight

My family is having problems. But I am mad and just want to run away from this thing and get it over with, because I am sick of it. I just want a good life.
   —Girl, ten

We never outgrow our need to feel secure. We are notoriously averse to change, and even positive, happy life events, like being promoted, getting married, and moving into a new home, induce stress. How we experience change is often determined by how much control we believe we have. Children have none. Even for children whose parents divorce in the best of circumstances, the irrefutable fact is that however you define family today, it is not what it was before, and that alone can make children feel insecure, unsure, and anxious.

Parents must be careful to reassure their children:

- They *always* will be part of a family.
- A family is defined by people loving and caring for one another, no matter where or with whom they live. Even though some family members do not all live in the same house (for instance, grandparents and aunts

THE ART OF COMMUNICATING WITH CHILDREN

✔ *Children want—and need—to talk.*

✔ *Any time can be a good time to talk. Some of the best communication occurs while you and your child are doing something else: riding in the car, weeding the garden, preparing dinner. Don't wait only for "special" moments.*

✔ *But also set up special times when your child has your undivided attention, especially to broach a serious topic. One such occasion is when you announce your plans to separate.*

✔ *Put yourself in your child's shoes. Before you speak, remember for a moment what it was like to be her age. Imagine how you would feel if you were in the situation she is in now.*

✔ *Remember: Most communication is nonverbal. Touch your child while you talk, smile if appropriate, make eye contact, keep an open stance (legs and arms "open," not folded or crossed), and maintain an even, relaxed tone of voice.*

✔ *Let your child know you hear and understand what he is saying by mirroring or paraphrasing his statements back to him.*

> JERRY: I looked around. Tom's parents were both at the meet; Helen's parents were there.
> MOM: You felt like you were the only one who didn't have both parents there.

✔ *Respond to your child in a way that gives him the words for his feelings. Do this even if he does not express his feelings directly himself.*

> JERRY: I can't believe I only got a crummy 80 after all the studying I did!
> DAD: It sounds like you feel frustrated after putting in all that time and effort.

> MARY: You didn't even tell me you were going away for the weekend.
> MOM: It sounds like you felt very betrayed [or "scared," if it's a young child].

and uncles), they are still family; that's how it will be with your family now, since parents will be living separately.

• Their parents will continue to love them; divorce changes the feelings between Mom and Dad only (assuming there will still be regular contact between both parents and the children).

• You will be there to help your children whenever they need you, and together you will get through this difficult time. If your ex will not be in touch with your child in the foreseeable future, speak only for yourself. You might say, "I'll always be here for you, and my feelings have not changed."

As important as these reassurances are, they alone are not enough. Children need to see these beliefs demonstrated in their daily life. Yes, it is important to talk about these things, to reassure and comfort your child. But for most kids, an unexpected heartfelt hug, a loving note tucked into a lunch box, or a surprise dinner out on a school night say "I'll always be here for you" better than words.

A NGER: THE MISUNDERSTOOD EMOTION

Dear Dad,
I am incredibly mad at you for what you have done to us. Why did you have to lie? Why did you do this to us? If you love me, why did you lie?
— Girl, ten

Rose are red, violets are green,
I look at my family and just want to SCREEM!
— Girl, ten

Dear Dad,
I'm still mad at you, but I do not show it. You know what you have done to us. It hurt us very bad. I felt like doing something I should not have done, but this is how you made me feel.
— Boy, twelve

Parents must understand how their children think and feel, but that can be difficult for even the most conscientious among us. We are so focused on a child's *behavior* that we too often take at face value what she says and does to be true expressions of how she really feels. Children show a range of emotional responses to divorce, but anger—expressed as rage, withdrawal, depression—is almost universal. They may be angry at parents for failing to protect them from the divorce. *After all, you're bigger and stronger,* they may reason. *Why can't you make Daddy come back . . . make Mommy happy again . . . try again . . . be nicer to each other . . . drink less?* They may also be angry that the divorce causes them to feel other powerful and frightening emotions: fear, sadness, confusion, loss, doubt, and hurt.

Despite its bad reputation, anger can often be a healthy emotion. It allows us to express pent-up feelings, blow off steam, endure high levels of stress and frustration. It can inspire us to take action for good. It can alert us to danger and prompt us to protect ourselves. Our real problem with anger is how we experience and express it. Usually we get only as angry as our surroundings will allow, and, as children, what we are allowed often runs to one extreme or another. On one side are parents who totally stifle anger, which can cause a child's sadness or frustration to be turned inward, resulting in withdrawal, depression (or a "numbing down" of feelings), and indifference. On the other are those who openly invite anger without establishing boundaries, resulting in a child who loses self-control and lacks the ability to cope with challenging situations.

Further complicating the picture is how we express and perceive anger. When we do express anger, we often disguise it under the cloak of

A brewing storm. *"Draw a picture of your family" elicits a typical family portrait. However, when asked, "Draw a picture of how you feel when you think about your family," this ten-year-old girl drew "A Storm": a dark, fierce storm with black clouds against a brown sky filled with sharp, yellow lightning bolts and large light-blue raindrops. In the Sandcastles workbook, she described her reaction to the news of her parents' divorce as "shocked, sad, confused, angry, scared, depressed, surprised, unsure, sorry."*

BLOWUP

Get a balloon (helium is best), and have your child use a marker to draw a face on it, preferably one showing how she feels. If you'd like, you can discuss how she feels ("Those pointy teeth make it seem like your balloon might be angry") or not, depending on how your child feels. Then give your child the option of keeping the balloon, letting it go, or popping it (by pinching it or stomping on it).

Variation: Bubble-type packing material is great for releasing tension. (Have you ever seen anyone who can resist squeezing each little bubble to death?) If you have recently relocated, you probably have plenty of the stuff on hand. You can take turns saying what you'd like to pop: "I'd like to pop this stupid divorce!" "I'd like to pop sharing a bedroom with Sis." And so on.

PURPOSE: This helps you see how your child is feeling and helps her to literally release some of her anger or sadness.

"I'M ANGRY!"

For children eight and above: Sit down and calmly ask your child to list things that she is angry about, and you list things that you are angry about. Try to guess aloud what the other has written before you share your lists. Then make a star next to the ones you can change or do something about and discuss what cannot be changed as well. Obviously, parents' lists should not express hostility toward the other parent.

PURPOSE: Since anger is a normal and healthy feeling, parents want to assist children in learning proper ways to identify anger, express it to a parent in a healthy way, and think about possible solutions.

another issue. A child unable to say "I am very angry about the divorce" can opt for a more comfortable, indirect expression: withdraw into silence, put on a false happy face, or lash out, shouting, "I hate you!" Most parents would find any of these situations difficult, but when you may be angry yourself about a range of issues (including how the divorce is affecting your child), it's harder to keep your cool. Finally, most of us would rather avoid another person's anger altogether, especially if we suspect or know that we are in some way responsible for it.

Somewhere in this morass is a balance that accommodates healthy expression. It just takes some patience, a little detective work, and tenacity to find. When we use our "emotional X-ray vision" to see the real feeling lurking under the emotional "disguise," we can respond appropriately and constructively. If, however, we rise to the decoy bait, we not only find ourselves hooked to the wrong line of argument, we also miss a chance to help our child work through his anger and learn how to deal with it effectively.

ANGRY JACKET AND HAT

Help your child decorate a jacket or hat to represent her images of anger. Let her suggest colors or shapes that spell "mad" to her. Tell your child to put it on whenever she wants to send the message that she is angry or hurt. This can cue you that it's time to talk to your child about her pain.

PURPOSE: It is difficult for young children to appropriately express anger. This activity will help them learn to calmly approach their anger and find healthy avenues to discuss it.

Let's take a scenario familiar to many divorced parents. Nora nicely asks her nine-year-old son, Brandon, to clean up his toy raceway, unleashing an angry torrent of toy-tossing and screaming. "I hate you, Mom! I want to go live with Daddy. He has no stupid rules in his house!" There are a number of ways Nora might respond, including the classics:

• *The "I don't want to deal with your anger" response.* "Go to your room! Don't you ever talk to me like that again!" Effect: Brandon stomps off to his room, slams the door, and he and Mom spend the next two days tiptoeing around each other without ever discussing what's really bothering Brandon.

• *The "I'm taking your anger personally" response.* "You inconsiderate brat! After all I've done for you! Your father does squat for you, but go ahead—call him. He and his girlfriend won't want you anyway." Effect: Brandon runs out in tears, then gives Mom the silent treatment for the next few days, as she apologizes profusely for everything she said without ever discussing what's really bothering Brandon.

• *The "I'm rising to the decoy bait" response.* "We have rules in this house, and that mess is going to be cleaned up by the time I count to ten. Now get going!" Effect: Brandon throws a few more cars at the wall, *then* runs out of the room, and Nora adds "disobedience" to the list of misbehavior Brandon will have to answer for later, without ever knowing what's really bothering him.

There is a better way:

> Nora draws a deep breath and says, "Boy, you seem angry lately. You must be really upset inside."
>
> "You bet I am! You said I could see Daddy anytime I wanted, and now you say it's not his turn to have me, so I have to stay here this weekend."
>
> "Oh, so you feel I've lied a little and changed my tune about you and your father?"

TECHNIQUES FOR DEALING WITH ANGER

✔ *Teach your child the words he needs to express his anger. Help him create angry statements, like "I am angry that..."*

✔ *If your child is very young, designate an "angry hat" or other piece of clothing she can put on when she feels angry to signal that she needs to talk.*

✔ *With older children, agree on a secret code word or hand signal to express his anger and need to talk.*

✔ *Use "noncharged" language.* Compare "You seem a little upset at me for..." to "You're angry at me. I can tell." The first response, said lovingly, invites the child to share his feelings with you. In contrast, the second statement has the ring of an accusation, implies that the child is wrong to be angry, and sends the message that there's nothing more to say on the subject.

✔ *Speak very slowly and deliberately, and encourage your child to do the same.*

✔ *Empathize.* Tell your child you would feel hurt or angry if you were in her shoes. This validates your child's feelings and lets her know that you would understand. It's a great invitation to talk further.

✔ *Don't let anger excuse otherwise unacceptable behavior.* Hitting, cursing, biting, throwing objects, and screaming are not acceptable forms of behavior or expression. If your child expresses her anger—no matter how valid—in an unacceptable manner, you must (1) state firmly that the behavior will not be tolerated; (2) state the consequences if the behavior continues or recurs (for example, time-out, loss of privileges, being sent to her room); (3) carry through with consequences when necessary.

When Brandon's twelve-year-old sister, Elise, began cursing and throwing her schoolbooks after learning her father wouldn't be attending her orchestra recital, her mother, Nora, empathized with her daughter while at the same time making it clear that her behavior was unacceptable: "I see why you're very angry, and I want to talk about it. But you need to talk with me without cursing and throwing things. Or you can go to your room and let me know when you're ready to discuss this calmly." Elise stormed off, but emerged an hour later ready to talk.

See also these activities: "Blowup" and "I'm Angry!" (page 35), and "Angry Jacket and Hat" (page 36).

"Yes," Brandon answers softly, then begins crying. "I stay here during the whole week, and I don't see why I can't see him on weekends."

"I understand that you miss your dad, Brandon. But during the week you have school, so our time together is always about homework and stuff. I want to have relaxed vacation time with you, too. That makes sense, right?" Brandon nods. "But I can also understand that only seeing your dad every other weekend makes for a long time between visits. Let's think about other times besides the weekends you spend with me that you might see your dad, so you won't miss him so much. Then we'll talk to him and see if we can't start by at least having you see him more often."

Clearly, the first three reactions break off the communication between parent and child. The last option defuses the outburst, but when we look closely, we can see Nora manages to accomplish several other important tasks:

• Mirror and identify her son's emotion: anger

• Identify its cause: in this case, not being able to see Dad

• Give her child the words to describe his feelings: "upset," "sad"

• Assure her child that someone is listening and someone cares

• Offer possible solutions

• Empower her child by including him in the problem-solving process

• Provide a safe, understanding atmosphere that will make it easier for her child to express his anger readily and appropriately in the future.

Managing anger appropriately is one of the most valuable things we can teach our children, especially after divorce, when a child may have concluded that anger can "cause" people he loves to go away. It's up to you to teach your child that love and anger are not mutually exclusive, that he has a safe place to express his anger appropriately.

Obviously, this does not mean that a child should be allowed to rant, rave, and curse. Once the real issue has been dealt with, you should discuss appropriate ways to express anger. (See the box "Techniques for Dealing with Anger," page 37.) Even in the midst of an outburst, you can let your child know that his mode of expression is not acceptable: "Look, you seem really angry and that's okay. I'd like to talk to you about it. But we have to slow down and be calmer. And you need to use language that I feel comfortable with."

What's a "real" family? Children of divorce often feel that they no longer have a "real" family. This ten-year-old girl not only draws herself crying at the thought of how her family used to be but writes out the message "I feel very sad because I don't have a real family anymore." Although her words and her drawing are revealing, she has chosen to draw herself in profile, which suggests that she is hiding, possibly because she feels she or her family are now "less than" what they were before.

CHILDREN OF DIVORCE FEEL "DIFFERENT"

I grew up with the thought that I had perfect parents and divorce would never happen to me. But when I found out, I felt sad, ashamed, and that it was my fault.
—Boy, thirteen

There was once upon a time a girl who had a happy family
Now it's very sad
And you know who that girl was—that was me.
I was happy, but I never knew this would happen.
It's not fair!
—Girl, twelve

Children seek to belong and do not like feeling that they are different from other kids. Even the teenager who signals rejection of his parents' values by dyeing his hair green is at the same time trying to belong to another group. Because tens of millions of kids have experienced divorce, you might think that a child of divorce really isn't that different from any group of his peers. Yet even if every single child in America were a child of divorce, each would feel different in the sense that he would perceive himself as having changed from who he was before his parents broke up.

Working in the Sandcastles Program, I am always struck by how even children who share a common experience are acutely attuned to the subtle differences between their situation and someone else's. Where most of us would see two children of divorce as having much in common, chances are one would point out that they really aren't the same at all, because her father moved out of state and the other kid's stayed in town, or she moved to a new home and the other child didn't move. These children are telling us that, while they may have all had similar experiences and responses, they are individuals first.

CHILDREN OFTEN EXPRESS EMOTIONS THROUGH THEIR BEHAVIOR

What kind of feelings have you had because of the divorce?
    Sad, torn.

How have you tried to deal with these feelings?
    By pretending nothing's wrong.
    —Boy, twelve

How did you feel when you first found out about the divorce?
    Mad, because I love my dad.

What did you do?

> I did not say nothing. I went in my room and took my awards off the wall.

—Boy, eleven

What kind of feelings have you had because of the divorce?

> I was so angry that I wanted to beat up my dad.

How have you tried to deal with these feelings?

> Once I was practicing karate with my dad for a karate tournament and I gave him a black eye.

—Boy, thirteen

At one time or another, every parent becomes concerned about a child's behavior. Fortunately, we can usually identify a troubling behavior as typical of a phase of development. We and our kids survive the exasperating "terrible twos" because we know the tantrums are "normal" and the phase is temporary. An understanding of what is typical at different ages gives parents the ability to separate the wheat from the chaff, behaviorally, and use that information to respond appropriately. When a two-year-old hurls himself to the floor, kicking and screaming, we consider it normal. If, however, an eight-year-old or a teenager does the same thing, we become justifiably concerned.

Children within the same stage exhibit a wide range of normal responses, behaviors, and attitudes. Still, development is not strictly linear, as all the talk of "stages" and "typical behavior" suggests. The journey from full dependence to independence is not really a straightforward trek up a long flight of stairs. Instead, it's a series of crisscrossing paths, shortcuts, and detours in a multilevel maze, all leading to the center, to the person we each will become. Over the course of childhood, we explore those paths, and we often return to familiar territory before venturing beyond. All the while, we are accomplishing the same tasks, moving toward the same center.

The quest for independence begins at birth and continues through early adulthood. Its lessons are revised every few years and taught again and

THINGS 2 DO

BUS DRIVER

When driving your child to school, pretend you're a bus driver. Monday morning, the bus driver might ask, "How was your weekend? Which parent were you with?"

PURPOSE: It is often less threatening for a younger child to disclose his feelings to a "stranger" (think how many adults confide in the bartender).

again. The toddler insists, "Me do," the ten-year-old explores a new shortcut home from school, the fourteen-year-old takes the forbidden dare, and the seventeen-year-old pledges his life to his first girlfriend. Each is a different route that traverses old paths and new, and each adds to the map we will consult again and again for the rest of our lives.

What parents who divorce find confusing is differentiating typical responses to divorce from behavior that may warrant concern. For example, it is not "normal" for a child to feel consistent, intense sadness. However, for children of divorce, this is a common and often a healthy response. The problem is not that the child feels sadness, but how he expresses it. Virtually every child whose parents divorce feels sad. But how sad is sad? What distinguishes a healthy sadness from a devastating depression? When is a preschooler's longing to be a baby again or a teenager's rebelliousness "normal," and when is it cause for concern?

For parents who divorce, the line between normal, typical behaviors and those that are extreme, abnormal, or cause for concern can blur. No wonder single, divorced parents tend to swing between two extremes: either attributing every problem to "the divorce" or dismissing every problem and chalking it up to their child's current phase. Unfortunately, children's developmental changes and phases do not go on hold while they try to sort out their divorce experience. If anything, they may have to work harder to achieve a healthy sense of self-esteem and trust. So when your twelve-year-old daughter announces she is never eating dinner with the family again, or your four-year-old suddenly begins sucking his thumb, what are they trying to say?

Toward this end, chapters 3 through 7 outline children's basic beliefs and attitudes about family and change, what is considered "normal" within five developmental stages, what constitutes a normal response to divorce in each stage, and how parents can help.

TRULY UNDERSTANDING YOUR CHILD

Without question, a key to a child's healthy development is being understood, loved, and accepted for who he is. If he is more excitable, more sensitive, more curious, more anxious, more mature, or more easygoing than most other children, you should take that into account as you read the advice presented here.

REMEMBER THAT YOUR CHILD LOVES YOU, TOO

"Of course, my child loves me," you may be saying. "I know that." The question is, Does your child *know* that you know that? As parents, we are so concerned with making sure our children know we love them, we often overlook how important it is for them to express their love to us. Yes, children need to feel they are loved. However, it is equally important that they grow up feeling confident in their ability to give love to and inspire love from others, especially their parents.

I don't believe we fully appreciate a child's deep, intrinsic need to express love and have that expression validated. This became especially clear to me while reviewing thousands of Sandcastles Program workbooks. Regardless of the children's ages or what portions of the workbook they had completed, somewhere in its pages most express a need to be reassured that they are loved and a need for the parents to know how much their kids love them. The fact that many of these messages appear after the line *I wish I could tell my parents that...* suggests that these are words they are not comfortable saying. For example, in our Sandcastles Survey (see page 419), 27 percent of eight-to ten-year-olds filled in the sentence *I wish I could tell my parents that...* with "that I love them" (the second most common answer behind "don't divorce/separate," with over 43 percent). For children of divorce, this sentiment has added significance. As their families change so drastically, the reassurance that they are loved and that you value their love is especially crucial.

The next time your child says, "I love you," stop what you're doing, give him your full attention, put yourself at the child's eye level, touch him or hug him, and say, "I love you, too." Listen for the "I love you" he may not speak but expresses in the special drawing, the fistful of dandelions, the surprise dinner he makes especially for you.

I wish I could tell my parents that I love them.

—Girl, ten

I wish I could tell my parents that if someone shot them, I'd get in the way and take the bullet.

—Boy, eight

Dear Dad,

Dad, no matter what happens, I love you and Mom, so please love me back.

—Girl, twelve

Dear Mom,

I want you to know that this divorce is not changing me. I am not worried about the future. All I have to know is that you love me, and I will be okay. I love you, Mom.

—Boy, nine

Dear Mom,

Remember that I will still love you and you'll always be my mom, and I'll always be your daughter.

—Girl, twelve

Dear Dad,

I want you to know that I still love you even though you said you don't have any kids.

—Girl, thirteen

Dear Mom,

I feel sad. I want you to stop crying and everything. I will do anything for you, Mom.

—Girl, eight

A Family Poem

My family gets along well, except they're just apart. It doesn't bother me as long as they love me. Just let me know you care, let me know I'm special, Because it doesn't bother me as long as they love me.

—Girl, twelve

No matter what age your child, you cannot truly gain a full perspective of her thoughts and feelings without temporarily abandoning your personal world and venturing back into hers. There are many windows into a child's thoughts and feelings—her words, expressions, behavior, play, artwork, activities—and if she could, your child would invite you to peer through them all. She wants to be understood; we all do. It is only through letting ourselves experience and feel what our children feel that we truly learn to love and appreciate them for the unique individuals they are.

We parents often joke that our kids seem to be from another planet, and there is a seed of truth in it. As adults, we often assume that we inhabit a "real world," which children first enter as curious bystanders (infants) and gradually grow into full citizenship. From a child's point of view, however, theirs is the "real world." It's the only one they know, and they experience it with the consuming curiosity and emotional intensity unique to childhood. That explains why, as adults, we so often romanticize the happier moments of our pasts. And we should. After all, we may be more independent, have more control, and be all grown-up now, but we've lost something in the bargain. Scary movies will never again be as scary, chocolate as rich, friendships as simple, kisses as sweet as they were "then," in the magical, protected world of a child.

The first step is to realize and accept the many ways your child's world is very different from yours. Next, it's crucial that you be willing to venture into your child's world and to accept her feelings and perceptions as valid and deserving of respect, even when you disagree with them or feel uncomfortable dealing with them. Why is this so important? Simply, your child does not have the capacity or ability to fully enter your world. You, however, can go back, whether that means getting down on the floor to play peekaboo with your baby or spending an evening watching the *Star Wars* trilogy with your teenager. You can also go back in other ways: relearning how to simply listen rather than giving in to the parental impulse to always guide and advise; training yourself to view your child—rather than yourself—as a source of answers.

THINGS 2 DO

"TALK TO ME"

Even when it seems as if every day is about four hours too short, you can still carve out time during normal daily routines to make a real connection with your child. Creatively rephrase the age-old "How was school today?" into something specific: "Were you able to help anyone today?" "Did you get to do anything different today?" "Tell me something funny that happened to you today."

PURPOSE: These little moments keep you in touch with your child. With them, you can open up a trove of useful information about your child's activities, feelings, and thoughts. Driving in the car, loading the dishwasher, running the bath, or walking the dog all present opportunities to "steal back" time with your child.

RESCUING

As loving parents, we often feel compelled to do whatever it takes to relieve a child's emotional pain, solve his problem, or dispel his worries. It feels good and right to always be there, to always shoulder life's burdens for someone less capable than we are. For these reasons, parents often have trouble distinguishing between offering the support, guidance, and love that teach a child how to cope (good parenting) and stepping in to solve the child's problems themselves (rescuing or fixing).

As a means of dealing with problems, rescuing does have a lot going for it: It's quick, relatively painless, and easier than taking the time to listen to and help your child find his own way to a solution. The problem with rescuing is that it short-circuits the process a child must experience and master for himself if he's ever to grow up equal to his future challenges. A child whose parents limit his opportunities to learn these crucial life skills is like a marathon runner whose coaches secretly drive him to the finish line. In the future races that he runs alone, he'll surely stumble. But rescuing also has immediate ramifications, because whenever you rescue, you limit the information and insight your child might otherwise offer.

How is this so? Let's look at a typical parent in the act of rescuing. Thirteen-year-old Avianne told her mother, Edith, "I don't like Marianne [her father's new girlfriend]."

"You don't like her?" Edith replied. "Why not?"

"She's always talking about how she goes this place and that place with Dad," Avianne said.

Edith, who often tried to use "active listening," observed, "And you feel bad."

"Yeah," Avianne whispered, hanging her head.

So far, so good. Edith feels she's got the picture, but instead of considering that there might be more to it, she jumps in to rescue: "Well, that's really insensitive of Marianne, and the next time I call your dad's house, I'll mention to her that she should be a little more considerate of your feelings."

Edith feels she's protecting her daughter; her daughter now knows she's got her mother on her side. Problem solved? Not really. What Edith has really done is offer Avianne her adult view of the problem and said in so many words, "Okay, now I understand the problem from my adult perspective, and this is what the problem is." But is it? Watch what would happen if Edith didn't rescue Avianne.

"And you feel bad," Edith replied, then went further: "You feel bad because you're not with them?"

"No, not really," Avianne said. "I understand that they need their time together. I'm just mad that I never get to go alone with him anywhere like she does."

By not rescuing and cutting short Avianne's expression, Edith discovered that her daughter's problem is not with Marianne but with her father. Remember: Rescuing muddies and distorts the real issues. Once you rescue and "name" the issue, you limit your ability to identify and resolve the whole or real problem and risk causing even more misunderstanding. Just imagine the ramifications of Edith's complaining to Marianne about her "inconsiderate" behavior!

With her fuller understanding of her daughter's pain, Edith could help her identify ways to resolve the problem herself. She might suggest that Avianne speak directly to her father about it, and they might talk about how much time would be enough (perhaps lunch or an afternoon together when a whole weekend isn't feasible). She might invite Avianne to brainstorm (see the activity "Brainstorming," page 48) possible solutions, from the impossible, even humorous ("I guess I could kidnap Dad and take him up in a balloon"), to the practical ("I could offer to go over and help Dad work in his garden on Saturday after lacrosse practice"). Brainstorming also shifts attention from the problem to its resolution.

There is always time to rescue. If your child is in extreme pain or unable to sort out the issues for herself, you should step in and lovingly help. But before you do, be sure that you have:

- listened in such a way that you've encouraged rather than discouraged your child's expression,

- allowed the conversation to run its course until you're certain your child described her feelings,

- refrained from imposing your interpretation of the problem,

- identified the real problem,

- guided your child in problem-solving toward resolution.

HELPING YOUR CHILD TO TRULY UNDERSTAND YOU

Children are usually fully capable of understanding things if they are presented information in a way that is meaningful to them. Too often, we adults conclude that "kids just don't understand," when in fact it is we who don't understand how to talk to and listen to them. In upcoming chapters, I'll offer some specific, age-appropriate scripts for discussing divorce issues with your kids. Here now are some general guidelines.

Before you talk with your child on any important matter regarding your divorce, remember to *plan ahead* and *structure your comments* to

- communicate the point you're trying to make in clear language;
- empathize: let your child know you understand how he feels;
- acknowledge and describe how each change will affect your child;
- anticipate and answer questions you're reasonably sure your child will have;
- invite his further questions and answer them clearly.

This five-step approach is effective no matter what the issue or problem.

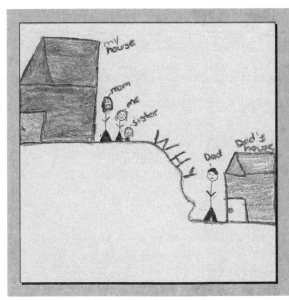

A downhill battle. This twelve-year-old girl wrote: "My family was very happy when my parents were together. It seemed like a dream. Until one day it happened, my parents told me they were getting a divorce. I couldn't understand why. I probably never will, but life will go on."

FIVE STEPS OF COMMUNICATION

Communicate your point in clear language	Empathize with your child	Acknowledge and describe how it will affect your child	Anticipate and answer questions you're reasonably sure your child will have	Invite further questions and answer them clearly
"Your mother and I are separating."	"I know this must come as a surprise to you, and you're probably feeling some strong emotions."	"That means there will be some changes around here. I will be moving out, but I will see you every weekend and a couple of times during the week."	"I will still be your dad, and I will always love you, even though I'm living in a different house. You can always call me, and I'll be here whenever you need me."	"This is probably very confusing to you right now. If you have any questions, I'll try to answer them the best I can."
"I have to go out of town for business, so I'll miss your game."	"I imagine you're pretty disappointed; I know how much this game means to you."	"I know I may be the only dad not there, and that might be sad for you."	"But I'll be back in time for the trophy awards ceremony on Wednesday. I'll call you right after the game, and Andrew's dad promised he would tape it for me."	"Is there anything else we can do to make it a nice experience for you?"
"I'm sorry; we are not buying one-hundred-dollar sneakers."	"I know you had your heart set on them because all of your friends are wearing them."	"You've told me how awkward you feel, being the only one in your group not to have them."	"Perhaps we can think of some way to save for them."	"Do you have any ideas of things you could do to raise part of the money: baby-sit, wash cars, mow lawns?"

THE WORLD, ACCORDING TO CHILDREN

Divorcing
Divorcing is not a good matter. It separates us from mother and father. Why not just be a perfect family where Mom and Dad are loving just as they should be?
 —Girl, eleven

DEAR DIARY

Purchase two blank books or diaries. Together, at the end of the day, you and your child write in the books the best and the worst parts of the day.

PURPOSE: Keeping a daily journal of feelings is a good way to open up discussion.

Journal Journey

Parent and child write in their own separate journals at a specific time every other day. Keeping it short, each writes three things: the best moment of the last two days, the most difficult or saddest moment of the last two days (or since the last time either made a journal entry), and finally how each felt about one of those moments in detail. Share the journals with each other and other family members if everyone is comfortable doing so.

PURPOSE: You and your child can learn how you feel at different times and what specifically causes these feelings. Discussion can lead to discovering ways of increasing the best moments.

Variation: Devote a separate page in the journal to all the bad-, negative-feeling words the child knows: "bad," "hate," "despise," and so on. On another page, list all of the positive words. For two days, each of you can try to use as many words as possible from the positive-feeling page.

PURPOSE: This helps a child learn to focus on the positive feelings she is experiencing. This does not mean we should be sending our children the message that one always has to be positive. This is impossible and unhealthy. But learning to be aware of how often we automatically adopt a negative attitude out of habit or without justification can help kids learn to take control of their general attitude.

LETTERS

Write a loving letter to your child and mail it.

PURPOSE: Children love to get mail. Furthermore, when communication has been difficult between you and your child (especially your teenager), writing a letter can be a useful way to talk to each other. It reduces conflict, as each of you are able to send your messages clearly without interruption, and it gives you the proper time to consider a healthy response.

Of course, parents are obligated to approach matters from their concrete-thinking adult perspective and to judge, advise, and set limits as needed. The problem is that we often get stuck in those gears and fail to recognize those times when discussing matters from a kid's point of view would be better. The story of Robin Hood provides a great example of how children's ideas and values change as they grow.

Imagine that you've just finished telling how Robin Hood stole from the rich and gave to the poor. Your child, a four- to five-year-old, thinks taking from the rich to help the poor is a great idea. She is just developing a moral consciousness and doesn't yet fully comprehend "bad" and "evil." Robin Hood is doing something good; therefore, he is good.

BRAINSTORMING

Help your child learn to think creatively about problems by brainstorming, or rapidly considering numerous potential solutions. Notice I said "potential," not "possible," for the art and fun of brainstorming lies in learning to view problems in a whole new way, even dreaming up solutions that are impractical or impossible.

Start by presenting your child with a problem. Just for fun, begin with something not too emotionally loaded, perhaps with humorous possibilities. You might ask your child to name five or ten ideas, or you and your child (and whoever else joins you) could take turns making suggestions, perhaps building on one another's ideas. Write down all the suggested options and review them. Which are impossible? Which feasible? Which would best accomplish the goal? What would each require?

Problem: Kukie the dog doesn't always get food and fresh water as often as he needs to.

Solutions:

- Teach Kukie to open his own cans of dog food.
- Put Kukie on a diet; he's too fat anyway.
- Teach Kukie to call out for pizza.
- Get Kukie one of those self-feeding dry food gizmos.
- Remember to check Kukie's dishes each time we eat, and feed and water as needed.
- Make a weekly schedule and alternate responsibility for feeding Kukie.

PURPOSE: We want our children to approach problems with the idea that a solution, or resolution, is within their grasp. Learning to think creatively about problems teaches children not to get stuck or overwhelmed and gives them confidence.

By the age of six or seven, that same child will have learned right from wrong and will see moral issues in black-and-white. Even though she is just a year or so older, she will think that Robin Hood is just bad, period, with no excuse for his bad behavior. She will also probably suggest ways that he should be punished. In another year or so, around ages eight through ten, she will understand and begin to consider extenuating circumstances and other variables that place moral issues in the gray areas. She may ask, "Are the poor people starving? Do they need money to feed their babies? Does Robin's stealing hurt the people he steals from?" and so on.

As a preadolescent, she'll want to know even more specifics about Robin's wealth-redistribution campaign: "How is the stealing taking place? Is anyone hurt during the robbery? How rich are these rich people? How much money is being taken from them?" A few years down the line, as a teenager, she'll want to know who Robin Hood is dating, but she'll also consider his actions on a wider scale. She will think about what his actions might mean to the greater society: "What if the rich people move away and take their money in protest and the entire town's economy collapses? Can the poor people get jobs? Why aren't they working? And if it's okay for Robin Hood to steal in order to save a child's life, what else could someone like him do? Murder? What if everyone began stealing?" And so on.

No matter what your child's age at the time of divorce, he will probably reconsider the experience as he grows, seeing it from different angles as time and maturity allow. That's why it is so important to be sure that your child gets the right message from the start.

WAYS PARENTS CAN HELP CHILDREN AT EVERY AGE

1. **Never assume your child knows how much she means to you.** Hug her, touch her as you speak to her, look her straight in the eye. Say, "I love you."

2. **Spend quality time and quantity time.** Kids need both. One of the most important messages you can send your child is "I value you enough to choose to spend time with you as opposed to spending it with other people or doing other things." Accept that there may never be the "perfect" moment, and make the best of the five-, ten-, or fifteen-minute "chances" you get as they come. Don't put your child off throughout the day thinking you're getting other obligations out of the way so you can devote two hours to the ball game or the big dinner out. Children need consistent, continuous contact.

3. **Always speak of the other parent in positive terms.** Remember: Your child's self-image is largely derived from the image he has of each parent.

4. **Mediate your differences with your ex.** Do whatever you can not to fight it out in court. If the two of you have difficulty discussing important issues peacefully, contact your local family court for a referral to mediation. If you end up having a less-than-amicable split, protect your children from it just as you would protect them from any other form of emotional trauma or violence.

5. **Maintain structure.** Children crave structure, routine, and limits. A predictable, structured home makes your child feel safe, secure, and loved.

6. **Invite spirituality into your life.** Read about spirituality, pray together, observe holiday traditions in order to impart a feeling of being special. Spirituality can give change a sense of greater purpose and meaning. It can be a fascinating subject; one that you and your child can find thought-provoking and useful.

7. **Maintain family traditions.** Traditions run the gamut from the nine-course Thanksgiving dinner at Grandma's to your weekly Saturday pizza-and-video family night. Traditions give children a sense of continuity.

8. **Become involved in your child's life.** Show an interest in his day, get to know his friends, find out what's going on at school, whether or not you're the residential parent. Attend school and extracurricular events. Children of divorce often comment on how sad they feel when only one parent attends a school play, even if only one attended before the divorce. If your child is interested, invite him to share in your hobbies, learn more about his, or find something new the two of you can take up together, like cooking, tennis, or collecting comic books.

9. **Find and focus on your child's wonderful qualities.** It's not enough just to love your child; learn to fall in love again, not with the baby he was the first time you laid eyes on him but with the person he is today. Point out his good behavior and qualities, and be specific. Don't simply say, "You're a good person," but "It was a very thoughtful thing you did for your friend. I know running that errand for him took some time out of your weekend, but he really appreciates it," or "You should be proud of this test score. You organized your evenings so you could give the material your full attention and you really mastered it. Congratulations!"

10. **Allow your child to express herself freely.** Listen and focus on her words and feelings without judging, advising, or teaching. Earn her trust by keeping whatever she tells you confidential, if she requests. Never use anything your child shares with you against your child, your ex, or anyone else.

11. **Encourage your child's individuality and social development.** Support your child's participation in activities that enhance his sense of personal accomplishment (learning to play a musical instrument, collecting, hobbies) and those that give him a sense of belonging (sports, group dance, scouting, volunteer work).

12. **Take care of yourself.** Create unstructured "antistress" zones in your day, times to sit quietly, read, take the phone off the hook, just hang out. Learn to relax, take breaks, and find emotional support, from friends, family, and peer support groups, such as Parents Without Partners. If you feel things are getting to be too much, consider therapy.

13. **Wake up every morning and ask yourself,** What can I do for my child today that will make her smile? Then do it.

THE IMPORTANCE OF SCHOOL

All parents would agree that school is important, but for children of divorce, school can and often does mean much more. For some children, school may seem to be the only part of their lives that does not change with divorce. Even for those who are forced to change schools, the familiarity of the routine, the structure, and the opportunities for praise and growth help ease the transition. For children in crisis, school can be a haven.

Even for children who enjoy or excel at school, divorce can have an adverse effect on attitude, performance, and behavior. It's well known that a stable, supportive home environment is crucial to scholastic achievement, and divorce can wreak havoc on that front. On a more personal level, your child's intense feelings of anger, confusion, and sadness can result in daydreaming, difficulty in focusing, lack of motivation, acting out, or emotionally withdrawing from school. Parents must anticipate and be ready to step in when problems arise. Whatever you can do to avoid school problems or deal with them quickly, before your child is labeled a troublemaker or a failure, will be worth the effort. Also remember that teachers today routinely deal with a host of problems outside of education. Most of them will appreciate and welcome your input and involvement. Be sure to let them know you appreciate them as well.

✔ *Stay in touch with your child's teachers.* Arrange to discuss the divorce with your child's teacher, by phone or in person. Note the changes you have seen in your child's behavior. You don't need to reveal everything about your family's personal life, but it will help your child and his teacher if you explain, "I've noticed that since his father left, Marty gets frustrated easily," or "It's been more difficult to get Nina to do her homework since the divorce." Don't assume that no news is good news. Teachers usually don't contact parents about a problem until they've tried to deal with it themselves. For younger children, create a checklist of the areas that concern you (for instance, "follows directions," "participates," "behavior," "listens") and ask the teacher to fill it out and return it daily or weekly. For older children, request a monthly report.

✔ *Seek solutions to school problems at home.* When your child receives a good grade or a positive report from his teacher, be ready to reward him with extra activities, a special movie, or a new book. Conversely, if school performance falls, some restrictions (such as no television on school nights) might be warranted. Before you institute rewards and consequences, however, be sure you have listened to and understood the emotional issues behind your child's school performance. (See "The Art of Discipline," page 28.)

✔ *Deal with acting out and other negative behaviors and attitudes promptly.* Children benefit most when parents step in to head off problems before they get out of hand. Use the tips and activities in this book to help your child understand his thoughts and feelings. Help him to see how thoughts and feelings can affect how he behaves in school, and be sure he understands the concept of displaced feelings (why, for example, he talks back to his teacher when he's really angry at Dad or Mom). Let your child talk to you about his feelings, and listen with an open mind so that he won't be afraid to open up to you with his hurt or anger.

✔ *Maintain the daily routine and structure your child needs to succeed.* Every child needs to have clear, consistent times for homework, dinner, and play. Although they may balk at times, children do find comfort in knowing the limits. Be sure your child has a special, well-lit, quiet, comfortable place to do her schoolwork. Make it your business to be available to help (for example, don't answer the phone for that hour or so).

✔ *Get involved in your child's school activities, even if you are not the residential parent.* Volunteer to chaperon school trips and participate in other activities (making costumes for the school play, gathering supplies for the gardening project, reading a special story, or speaking at career day). Be in the audience for the class play whether or not your ex attends or you two sit together. Allow your child to spend a few hours, preferably a whole night, if possible, with the nonresidential parent during the school week so you both can be involved in his homework.

✔ *Be aware of your child's peer group and any changes in friendships.* How your child's friends think about school is generally how he feels. If you are uncomfortable with some of the friends he is choosing, discuss it, and consider activities that will introduce him to other friends.

THINGS **2** DO

WHAT DO YOU SEE?

Ask your child to view this drawing and ask what he sees. Some people will see a rabbit, others a duck.

PURPOSE: It really is all in how you look at it. The beauty of "reversible drawings" is that both interpretations are equally valid—it is a duck, and it is also a rabbit. Each viewer is right, and neither viewer is wrong. In the same vein, you can discuss with your child how two people—even parents—can have very different feelings about the same situation. Talk to your child about examples from his own life: why a friend may dislike a movie that he loves, why he likes barbecued potato chips and his sister likes green onion, why one person says the wall is blue and the other says it's turquoise. Further explain how we can grow by listening to another person's thoughts and feelings. Discuss how a person who sees only the duck may see something new—something he might have otherwise missed—only when he gives someone who sees a rabbit the chance to point it out.

2

Bodies to Sticks,
Make-Believe to Resolution

Understanding Children's Play and Art

Four-year-old Lourdes sat on the floor with several dolls and stuffed animals. She had laid each on its back and gently covered them all with "blankets"—washcloths. "Goodnight, baby, goodnight," she cooed softly to her favorite, Bina, a dark-haired baby doll her grandmother had given her. Suddenly Lourdes stood Bina up and was screaming "Don't go! Don't go!" to the other dolls. One by one, Lourdes moved each of the other figures away from Bina as she said, "Papa going away," "Mama going away," "Abuela [Spanish for "grandmother"] going away," until only Lourdes and Bina were left. "Don't cry, baby, don't cry," Lourdes kept repeating as she rocked her "baby."

"She's been going through that routine every day for the past two weeks, ever since her father moved out," Lourdes's mother, Carmen, said. Lourdes's father had left the home, but Carmen and her mother were still there. "Once when I picked up Bina and said, 'Look, Lourdes! Baby Bina is happy,' she grabbed the doll back and started crying, 'No, the baby is crying, the baby is crying. Don't cry, baby. Mama not go. Mama not go.' "

Obviously, Lourdes was playing, but as her mother noticed, this was play with a difference. What Lourdes was doing—what all children do on some level all the time—was expressing and dealing with powerful emotions and thoughts through play. It sounds like therapy, and in many ways, it is. Play is a safe haven for growth, a "space" children seek out naturally in times of stress and change.

The more your child expresses her troubling feelings, the more comfortable she becomes. Your understanding and her trust in you will ultimately allow her to "talk out" rather than "act out" her problems. A child who feels safe expressing and talking about feelings will be less likely to withdraw, become depressed, or engage in self-destructive behavior.

Play, as well as art, provides windows on a child's innermost thoughts and feelings, and many of the activities kids engage in every day can be a wellspring of insight for parents who know what to look for. Strictly speaking, play therapy is a technique through which a trained therapist allows a child to "play through" his feelings and issues instead of discussing them as he would in a classic talk therapy session. Art therapy also allows children the opportunity to express themselves nonverbally, but when used in the strictest sense, it also describes a trained therapist's evaluation and interpretation of a child's emotional issues based on his artwork. To be applied therapeutically, both techniques require years of training and represent one of many factors a therapist considers in viewing and working with the whole child.

Before I continue, just a note: In introducing some of the basic concepts of play and art therapy, my goal is not to turn any parent into an amateur therapist or to encourage you to "analyze" your child. In fact, the guidelines for interpretation outlined here are intentionally basic and broad. I have never met nor do I know anything about the children whose artwork is represented here. My comments are based on primary theories and concepts of art and play therapy, my years of using art and play therapy in my professional practice, and my having reviewed more than ten thousand pieces of children's art. While every artwork contains countless analyzable, potentially revealing elements, my intent is not to analyze any of the works but to show readers how to look at their children's work as simply another form of expression, another piece to the puzzle. The most experienced therapists in the field are quick to remind us that play and art offer only glimpses of the whole child. *No single play episode, no one drawing or part of it, ever tells the whole story.* And even experts can disagree on what a given element means. (See the illustration on page 77 for an example of a piece of artwork with two possible meanings.) Your goal is simply to access another way of understanding—*not analyzing*—your child. Remember: Your primary objective is improving communication,

Emotion into art. *This ten-year-old boy's large teeth and open, intense stare suggest anger and surprise.*

and communication must be based on trust. If your child ever feels you have invaded his privacy, betrayed his confidence, or abused his trust, he may shut you out.

You may be asking, "What kind of parent would do such a thing?" The answer all too often is a conscientious, well-meaning parent who, in sharing something her child says, acts out, or draws with others, believes she is doing what's best for her child. Except when you have reason to suspect that your child's play or art suggests he has been or may be a victim of physical, sexual, or emotional abuse, or that someone around him poses a threat to him, what he shares with you should remain strictly between you two. If you have such concerns, consult your pediatrician or a therapist with special training in that area. Consider your child's play and art wondrous cities in a brand-new world. To visit there, you should observe some rules:

• *Do not share your interpretation of your child's play or work with anyone.* Not your ex, not your attorney, not your neighbor, not your mother, not his teacher—no one, with the exception noted above. If the play does elicit emotions that prompt the child to disclose strong feelings toward you, your ex, or other family members, the child should be reassured that it's okay to have these feelings. A parent engaged with the child in his play should be prepared to deal with a range of behaviors and emotions including loss, anger, and vulnerability. In play, your child should feel he has the freedom and safety to express himself. He also needs to know that nothing he says will be shared with others. Only then will he feel secure about inviting the parent into his world and using it as a medium for working through troubling feelings.

• *Never bring up what your child has expressed or said to you during or about his play or artwork in any other context.* Remember, your child may be sharing with you only because she feels that whatever she tells you will be safe. Children instinctively believe that strong emotions, especially when they concern their parents, are dangerous. Don't open a Pandora's box you may never be able to close again. For example, ten-year-old Bethany drew herself near to her mother with her father off in the opposite upper corner of several pictures. Bethany's mother, Dionne, concluded that, even though Bethany always seemed happy to see her father for visitation, she really felt distant from him. And in fact, seeing him only once a week for an overnight visit, Bethany did. Yet instead of finding ways for Bethany to feel closer to her father (such as inviting her to phone him every evening after dinner or spend a weeknight having dinner and doing her homework at his house), Dionne phoned her ex and said, "Bethany feels like she's no longer close to you."

Bethany's father, Jake, took offense and accused Dionne of "turning my daughter against me." Next Friday evening, Bethany shrank back into the car seat as her father angrily demanded, "What do you mean, we aren't close anymore? I spend every weekend with you. I love you. If you don't appreciate it, then I don't know what you want from me." Bethany burst into tears and silently vowed, *I'll never tell anyone how I feel about anything ever again!*

• *View your child—and her work, play, and other behavior—within the larger context of who she is.* While art, play, and behavior offer insight into a child's thoughts and feelings, no single piece of work, play episode, or act should be immediately construed as a cry for help. How children express themselves not only reveals something about them, it also can reflect a great deal about their social and cultural environment, even their access to materials. Four-year-old Sandy's parents became very concerned after noticing that almost everything he'd drawn in the past week was in black. Only after Sandy complained that his older sister kept putting the large box containing hundreds of colored markers, pencils, and crayons on a shelf beyond his reach did they realize what the real problem was: Sandy didn't need a therapist; he needed a step stool.

An oversimplification, perhaps, but the point remains: You can never glean any accurate reading of what a child says, does, or produces without knowing the whole story. Often, a more important barometer of your child's emotional health is his behavior. Sudden changes in behavior, especially toward aggression and meanness, are cause for concern. But should you be alarmed if your child's drawings suddenly assume a dark, violent tone? It depends. If your child regularly views violent cartoons, television programs, and movies, if among his friends rough play is the norm, if your family allows or encourages play involving weapons and violence, then he may just be drawing what he knows. If, on the other hand, your child's media repertoire consists of *Sesame Street, Mr. Rogers' Neighborhood,* and Thomas the Tank Engine videos, and his playmates engage in predominantly cooperative play, then this should be noted.

In artwork, the key is to look for consistent extremes. If over a period of time (say three or four weeks), your child's work is suddenly dominated by angry themes, dark or violent imagery, and the child depicts himself as helpless, pathetic, sad, or depressed, be concerned. Using the techniques outlined here, get involved and try to learn what your child is trying to say. Look for signs of change in the work, too. Sometimes just the act of drawing (and redrawing) a certain theme may give your child the emotional mastery that allows him to move beyond it without any intervention from you.

• *Respect your child's privacy and his ability to work through these issues in his own time, on his own terms.* Just the fact that your child is expressing his feelings is significant, meaningful, and productive, even if no one observes or joins him. As parents, we naturally feel that the sooner we can make the hurt go away, the better. There's no way to bypass the emotional process your child must go through, one from which he will grow. Absolve yourself of any pressure to come to the rescue. By being there for him, proving you deserve his confidence and his trust, and listening when he decides he wants to talk, you will have done everything a parent can and helped immensely in improving his ability to express himself and hasten his journey through this difficult time.

HY PLAY AND ART "WORK"

Children, particularly younger kids, are more articulate and confident while engaged in playing or creating art than they are while talking. This is especially true when the subject is highly emotional, like divorce. Up until approximately the age of eleven, most children's cognitive ability, or understanding, is far more advanced than their ability to express verbally what they know and how they feel. Play and art are often the "show" that leads to the "tell."

No matter what our age, emotions and fears can be hard to discuss. Even we adults sometimes find it easier to express our feelings and discuss our problems as if they belong to someone else. Children do very much the same thing naturally all the time. When they pretend to be someone else, they create a safe space in which they can act out and voice their feelings. If, as Shakespeare wrote, "All the world's a stage," your child's play (and the "work" of doing the activities suggested here and elsewhere) put the script of real life in her hands. Instead of being a mere player in your family drama, she gets to work through her feelings by rewriting the story, directing the other players (including you and your ex), and expressing potentially overwhelming emotions within the safe confines of the "stage"—her imagination. The major difference between the play and reality is that your child can act through feelings, then stop the action wherever she chooses.

THE PLAY'S THE THING: A SUGGESTED SHOPPING LIST

Keep in mind that your child will probably play through issues using toys he already owns. Children are amazingly creative, turning figures and toys into whatever they want them to be. Below is a partial list of the items play therapists find conducive to children's play.

Dolls or action figures (many that can represent different family members)

Stuffed or toy animal figures

Toy nursing bottle; dishes; telephone; dishpan or sink; table, chairs, and other toy furniture; and other items grown-ups use

Dollhouse or dollhouse furniture

Hats, clothes, accessories for playing dress-up

Toy soldiers and army equipment

Toy cars, airplanes, trains

Puppets (at least one "nice," one "aggressive")

Toy gun (or, if you're uncomfortable with your child playing with guns, items that can be fashioned into a gun, such as clay, Legos, Tinker Toys, et cetera)

Soft Nerf-type ball

Legos

Clay or Play-Doh

THINGS **2** DO

PUPPET AND DOLL FAMILY

Part of the fun of any activity is creating the material to be used for the activity. "Making up" a family provides children with one of the most effective ways to express how they feel about family and divorce. Your child could create a puppet family complete with pets on construction paper, then cut out the figures and paste them onto Popsicle sticks. It is best to have your child do all the steps, but if she wants you involved, try to keep to the cutting and gluing instead of the actual drawing of the puppets. If your child seems hesitant, take turns drawing the different parts of the puppets; your child draws the head, you draw the body, your child draws the legs, and so on.

You and your child (and your child playing alone, as well) can play out made-up scenarios. These need not be historically correct or reflect her understanding of what is happening. What you should look for are not the details of the play but the emotions your child expresses. A child may use her mother puppet to express anger at a father puppet when she herself is the angry one, or play out having the family dog puppet leave home, when she's really got her father's leaving on her mind.

Some kids find it helpful to create an animal family, as it is less similar to their own family and, thus, easier to use to express personal feelings. Doll families can be useful in the same kind of play, and they are of course more durable. You might also build a dollhouse in which your child can "stage" his play. In any case, be sure not to pressure your child to create or use any figure (for example, don't ask "Why don't you make a daddy/mommy?"), since his version of this play family is, in itself, a form of expression.

PURPOSE: Puppet or doll play encourages your child's expression and gives her a chance to work out feelings in a safe, imaginary environment that she controls.

THINGS **2** DO

BE A WRITER!

Offer to transcribe a story that your child would like to tell. This can be done by his just talking through a story, or he may wish to draw one or several pictures that he can then "narrate." The story can be about the divorce or anything else. Only your child can dictate what the story or the pictures are about. Your sole job is as faithful scribe, writing out or keyboarding the story exactly as your child tells it.

PURPOSE: This provides you with a glimpse of how your child sees the divorce or another theme in his life. Remember: This is his version, and may not be exactly accurate in detail. The details are not important. Don't offer to change or "improve" the story. If, in your child's "re-creation" of real events, some elements are exaggerated or distorted, don't be alarmed. Your child's exercise of "artistic license" offers you great insight into his perception of these events. By allowing your child to express the events as he sees them in his own words, you effectively make the child feel understood and appreciated. This empowers the child and teaches him to use words and pictures as a medium of expression.

Play is much more than just make-believe; it is literally the work of childhood. Perhaps because we adults think of play as pleasurable activity that is *not* work, we tend to underestimate just how important and productive it is, especially for kids. While play accomplishes different goals at different stages, every form—from a toddler's pushing over a tower of blocks to your twelve-year-old's learning to play chess—presents your child opportunities to explore and to control the world around him and how he responds to it. For most parents, the role of play as a teacher is fairly obvious, but its value as a means of self-expression and self-coping is often overlooked.

When Lourdes comforts her baby doll, she is not only expressing her feelings about her real-life experiences, she is also learning how to deal with them. Like many mental health counselors who use play therapy techniques, I believe that children are normally driven forward, developmentally speaking, toward independence, balance, self-actualization—wholeness. Whether in a therapeutic setting or on the living room floor, play gives children an effective, self-controlled, safe way to face and then master or dismiss the feelings they can neither express verbally nor ignore.

Generally, children will repeat a certain play scenario until they are comfortable with it. How long this may take depends on the intensity of emotions, and you should not be alarmed if your child repeats the same play over weeks, even months. Lourdes played through this scenario daily for two weeks. At first, she seemed very upset and often cried as Bina pleaded with her mommy not to go. Carmen was understandably distressed to see Lourdes so upset, but over the next several days, she noticed that the crying lasted for progressively shorter periods and that sometimes Lourdes actually seemed happier afterward. One day, about three weeks after Lourdes began playing out this scene, Carmen overheard her saying to Bina, "Now baby don't cry. Mommy is not going away. Baby okay." When Carmen picked up Bina and said, "Oh, look, Bina is happy now," Lourdes nodded yes.

Lourdes used play to express her anxiety and fear until she could play the experience comfortably. As she began to master those feelings, she could reassure and comfort her doll with her new realization that her own mother was not leaving. Although she would continue to play out that scene over the next six months—alone, with Carmen, and with her friends—her reactions were much less intense and more matter-of-fact. In her own way, she had faced her fears and, by playing them through repeatedly, had achieved some resolution.

WHY PARENTS SHOULD PLAY, TOO

Entering your child's world of play will do much more than help you understand his feelings. Since play is one of the rare activities in which you are equals, it gives you both freedom to connect in several special ways. In play, for example, your child can make the rules, and you may be the one who is instructed and corrected, for a change. Children recognize that your involvement in their play is something special, and that you are there because you want to be.

Play helps us to understand a child's world. By simply squishing clay in your hands, playing catch with your child, or playing a game of chess, you close off the distraction and stress of the adult world and make yourself a real presence in his. Losing yourself in play lets you reexperience what it was like to be a child and recall the thoughts and emotions that will help you better empathize with your child. Perhaps most important, playing with your child introduces him to the child inside you. An hour of play offers countless opportunities for your child to see you in a new light. For that time, you are neither all-knowing nor perfect. You may not really be in charge, and you may not be better than your child at what you're doing. In other words, this may be the only time when you are, in his eyes, really just like him, really able to understand him. It's no coincidence that these are the occasions on which children are most likely to open their hearts. Children and parents who play together share an intense, almost magical bond of understanding and respect that endures through the normal trials of growing up.

MUSIC STORIES

With your child, listen to a recorded piece of classical music, jazz, New Age, or other instrumental (no-words) music. As the music plays, encourage your child to tell a story about "a family"—not your family—as she "hears" it in the music. Say, "If this music were telling a story, what would it be?" or "If these notes we're hearing were words, what would they be?" Younger children, under the age of six, can be asked to tell a story about an animal family.

Eleven-year-old Sheila "heard" in the music a story of a storm breaking apart a house, scattering its inhabitants. The music served as a springboard and a catalyst for conversation about how fragile a home can be and what makes the home stronger.

Variation: Several family members sit in a circle and take turns playing several minutes of their favorite music. This can be anything they want. As the music plays, whoever chose it moves to it in a way he feels expresses what the music is saying; others in the group follow. After a few minutes, the "leader" talks about what he likes about that piece of music, how it makes him feel, and what feelings its creator or performer is trying to communicate.

PURPOSE: Music is a language, one that often brings out feelings that children have difficulty expressing. Examine the music's tone: Is it angry, sad, or hopeful? What associations does your child make with the music? This activity provides the additional advantage of exposing your child to music and its soothing properties.

CONNECTING

Lie down outside on the grass with the top of your head touching the top of your child's head. Look up at the trees against the sky. Pretend you're floating, and talk to each other about where you would float to if you could float anywhere. What wishes would you make? Ask your child to say the first thing that comes to mind when you mention the following words: "school," "family," "divorce," "love," "marriage."

Variation: Blow bubbles together, and ask your child to tell you where the bubble could take her if she could fit inside.

PURPOSE: It is wonderful to use nature to slow down and connect emotionally with your child. The calm and inspiring atmosphere of the sky and trees can ease conversation and serve as a backdrop for many connecting conversations or activities using imagination and fantasy. Using open-ended questions involving fantasies ("Tell me your dreams") can allow a child incredible expression.

HOW CHILDREN PLAY OUT THE DIVORCE EXPERIENCE

Whatever your child may experience in the divorce process—missing one parent, worrying about her family, feeling lost and confused—will likely find expression through play. The play may be very straightforward; for example, a little boy becomes a superhero who can fix everything (including his broken family) or the little girl draws picture after picture of "a happy family." Loud confrontations between plastic cowboys and Indians, Batman and the Riddler, or a fork and a spoon might not seem to be about you and your ex, but careful observation will help you trace the emotions and questions back to their source. Remember that, while dolls and figures are obvious family replacements, children can fashion families out of virtually anything. More than simply playing out scenes and working with characters, they also play through emotions and concepts. That is why your son's repeatedly tearing apart his elaborately built toy-train layout or your daughter's moving her favorite doll to someplace where she is "alone" might also be viewed as examples of divorce-related play.

OBSERVING AND JOINING YOUR CHILD'S PLAY

The next time Lourdes's mother saw her playing with Bina, she sat down on the floor and simply watched. Again, the same scene was played out. Rather than trying to join or direct the play, Carmen said, "I'm so sad for Bina." The first time, Lourdes ignored her, so Carmen didn't try to join the play again that day. A few days later, Carmen sat down again. This time she asked, "I wonder what Bina is crying about." Lourdes replied, "Because her mama is going away with everybody."

"Yes, I can see how that would make Bina sad."

"Yeah, because her papa went away, then Grandmama, then Mama."

Clearly, Lourdes was worried that she might lose her mother and grandmother, too. Later that day, Carmen broached the subject, taking care to speak in hypothetical ("sometimes"), general terms ("a papa," not "your papa"; "girls," not "you") and to be prepared to stop the instant Lourdes resisted or seemed uninterested. "Sometimes when *a papa* moves out of the house, *girls* can get afraid that *their mamas* might leave too and leave *the girls* alone. That can be scary." Lourdes looked up and nodded.

In a few well-timed, well-worded sentences, Carmen accomplished a lot. She

- helped Lourdes identify her fear of being abandoned,
- gave her the words to express it,
- let her know that she understood how she felt, and
- offered reassurance that her feelings were normal.

She also gave Lourdes the kind of information she'll need to put together the puzzle of her divorce experience.

It's important to note what Carmen *didn't* do: She didn't rescue Lourdes by directly asking, addressing, or reassuring her. By not rescuing Lourdes (see the box "Rescuing," page 44), Carmen not only gave her daughter space to play and express herself, she also gave herself the opportunity to learn what really was troubling Lourdes. Let's play out two possible scenarios and see what Carmen learns through each.

1. **Carmen rescues Lourdes by directly addressing what seem to be her daughter's concerns:**

   "That can be scary, Lourdes. But Abuela and Mommy will never go away."

   "Okay," Lourdes replied softly.

   Here, while Carmen might have felt she did the right thing by reassuring Lourdes about what she believed she was worried about, in fact, she had just disconnected their line of communication. Lourdes is too young, and her mother too important in her eyes, for her to question her mother's version of what the problem is. Carmen simply assumes she knows what Lourdes is thinking, and in jumping to rescue her, she ends up "telling" Lourdes how she must feel. Few children in Lourdes's position have the ability to counter, to say, "That's not what I meant."

2. **Carmen resists the urge to rescue Lourdes and lets the play continue:**

   "That can be scary."

"Yeah," Lourdes replied. "Because, you know what? After Luis's papa went away, his abuela went to heaven."

Now Carmen could see the real issue. She wasn't even aware until then that Lourdes's friend Luis's grandmother had died. By letting Lourdes continue in play, Carmen discovered the real issue. Next, she could reassure Lourdes in the same general, nonspecific language she'd been using in play: "Sometimes papas can go away, and sometimes abuelas can go away. But an abuela doesn't go away just because a papa does."

Remember: Play is a universe with its own laws of "physics." Your child can explore that universe freely and safely only if you refrain from direct, specific questions and statements. Sometime later, when Lourdes is not in play mode, Carmen can reassure her in direct, specific terms: "Lourdes, I want you to know that just because Papa went away, it does not mean that Abuela will go away, too. Abuela loves you very, very much."

While parents can make a valuable contribution to their children's understanding by joining their play, keep in mind that most kids have the ability to work through their issues on their own. Either way, you should observe these guidelines while reminding yourself: Your child's play belongs solely to him. Some play points to remember:

• *Do not interrupt or correct your child's play.* Children involved in play are truly, literally, in their own world—one they create and control from beginning to end. Like Lewis Carroll's Wonderland, a child's play world is a place where the laws of physics, reason, and time are rewritten on whim (and whimsy), where wishes rule, where things are simply because you say so. Saying "No, Timmy, cars don't fly. Make it an airplane," "You can't build a house without windows," or "That bear has already cried; let's make her be happy now" reflects the rules of your world, not his. Such remarks are inhibiting and insulting to your child.

• *Take your place in the "audience" until your child invites you to join him "onstage" or you sense you might be welcome.* Remember, some types of play require the child to play alone. If you do join in the play, follow your child's lead. If he ignores you or requests you go away, withdraw. Most often, as he sees you just want to be part of his world, he will graciously invite you in and even describe what he would like you to do.

• *If you do join the play, don't ask direct questions.* Start slow and keep your comments general. If Carmen asks Lourdes, "Why is Bina crying?" she is demanding an answer, something her daughter may not feel comfortable giving. If, however, Carmen makes an open-ended comment like "Bina seems sad to me," or "I wonder what Bina is sad about," she gives Lourdes a wide range of possible answers, including the valid and acceptable "I don't know." Remember: Statements always offer an out. Questions demand answers your child can't or might not want to give.

• *Keep your comments general.* Avoid the words "you" and "I," and instead use nonthreatening terms your child can easily accept or reject. For example, when Carmen tells Lourdes that "girls can get afraid," she gives her daughter the option of including herself in that group or disowning that emotion for now.

• *Whatever your child says or does, don't start thinking like a psychologist.* In play therapy, even child psychologists stop thinking like psychologists. They watch, listen, and commit to memory the details they will think about later. While the play is happening, they are very much in the moment. Stay focused on your child, on what he says and does. Your rush to interpret may limit your ability to see what's really happening. For example, if Carmen had hastily concluded that Lourdes's doll Bina was crying because her papa left, she would have missed the real issue: her daughter's fear that others would leave her, too. Don't even begin trying to figure out "what it means" until you've left the play.

CHILDREN'S EXPRESSION THROUGH ART

Try looking at a piece of artwork intellectually, without feeling anything, without wondering *What is the artist trying to say?* It's almost impossible, because the need to communicate drives creation, and an equally strong quest to understand what we experience forces us to respond, to try to make sense. If a picture is worth a thousand words, a child's art may be worth many times that, since it expresses concepts and feelings he may not even have words for.

Artwork, like play, is part of a child's everyday life. Unless we are artists, you or I might feel self-conscious about drawing, worried that our house doesn't look like a "real" house, that the proportion and perspective aren't correct, and that the shadows aren't in the right places.

THINGS 2 DO

THE NEW CONCENTRATION

Most parents and kids know the rules to the card-matching game Concentration. If not, here they are: Using a full deck of playing cards, place them all facedown in several rows. For younger children (under ten), you might choose to pick out a few matching cards to lay down (say, all face cards, or all the suits of a few numbers). Each player takes turns turning over any two cards of his choice. Play continues as long as matching cards (two kings, two 4s, etc.) are turned up. When a player fails to make a match, it's someone else's turn. Play continues until all the cards are turned faceup and matched. The twist here is that each suit represents a different emotion; for example, hearts stand for something you like or love, spades are something that makes you feel sad, clubs symbolize something that makes you mad, and diamonds are for wishes. Whenever two number or face cards match, there will be two suits to choose from.

The player who makes a match must make a statement based on the suit of one of the matching cards. For instance:

Heart: "I like going to Dad's/seeing movies/having a new puppy."

Club: "It makes me mad when you and Mommy fight/my friends don't include me/Theresa takes my things without my permission."

After a match and expression, that person takes the match. Each player tries to get the most matches.

PURPOSE: Again, children rarely ever state their deepest feelings directly. In the safety of the game, they may not only feel more comfortable and less self-conscious, they will also hear other people—including their parent—express their own fears, wishes, likes, and dislikes. This aspect can help children to see that they are not alone in or strange for having such feelings. Since each player has two feelings to choose from, you might also note which your child tends to favor.

THINGS 2 DO

THE SANDCASTLE

Encourage your child to imagine a family, perhaps the Royal Bunny Family, and the castle the family lives in. Ask your child to draw or to build (from sand, Legos, Tinker Toys, Play-Doh, or other building materials) the Bunny Family's castle as it appears before and after divorce.

Variation: Ask your child to draw or build her own house and family before and after the divorce.

PURPOSE: Your child will express his view of the divorce through his play family. You may learn a great deal about how your child perceives his world by asking him direct, nonthreatening questions about the family and the home he creates. Some examples: "The little bunny is off alone in the corner. How does he feel?" "That seems like a very big house. I wonder why it's so big." "I see all the little bunnies are outside, but the mommy is still inside. What is she doing? What are they doing?"

Before adolescence, most children find drawing, painting, and coloring totally engaging acts of pleasure and joy. Like the greatest artists, they easily lose themselves in their work as their emotions flow onto the paper in the form of smiling suns, broken hearts, and idealized houses.

READING YOUR CHILD'S ART

Art, like play, is happening all the time, so it provides an ongoing barometer of your child's mood, thoughts, and feelings. Like any other interpretative endeavor, analyzing a child's art is not always easy, *nor is any single piece of work ever to be considered anything more than a very small piece of a much-larger picture.* Again, information is offered below to give you some general guidelines and insights into what your child may be thinking or feeling. Even trained professional art therapists respect the limitations of interpretation; we should as well.

Before you begin reading your child's art, bear in mind a few points:

• *Context is everything.* If, for example, your child draws a dark cloudy scene on a day when he happens to be stuck inside the house because of a storm, it may well mean nothing more than his frustration that day. If, however, similar scenes suddenly begin to figure prominently in his daily work, it's something worth taking note of. (See illustrations on pages 69 and 75 for significant storm imagery.)

• *While every child is an individual, established subjects, symbols, and scenes are common to certain phases of development.* A drawing of a person with indistinct facial features would be typical of a three-year-old. However, the same drawing done by an eight-year-old might be cause for concern. For example, a four-year-old's armless figures are typical and normal; a ten-year-old's warrant further attention. (See the box "How Children Learn to Draw," page 73.)

• *The most important element you bring to reading your child's art is knowing him.* Six-year-old Timmy has loved airplanes since he was three. When he doesn't have a toy airplane, toy cars, boats, and trains are magically transformed so they can fly. He draws airplanes all the time, so

---

STOCKING YOUR ART CABINET

Colored pencils, markers, crayons, colored chalk

White paper, colored construction paper

Paints and brushes, sponges

Modeling clay, Play-Doh

Scissors

Paste, glue

Tape

Stickers

Easel

Interesting materials for collages (photos from magazines; scraps of paper, fabric, or other "pasteable" materials; for children who are over three or for whom these do not present a choking hazard: dry pasta, buttons, sparkles, confetti, glitter; twigs, leaves, seeds, and other natural items)

A fractured family. These two pictures represent a seven-year-old girl's family together and after Mom and Dad stop living together. With its smiling figures, sunshine, puffy clouds, and overgrown flowers, the top picture conveys happiness and contentment. Note, however, that even though Dad is smiling, he has no arms, suggesting that he has limited power. Mom, however, has large, distinctly drawn arms. Perhaps the child feels that her father has no control over the divorce, or that Mom made him move out against his will. Also note that the children's arms are tiny or nonexistent.

The second picture is in marked contrast to the first. Jagged, sinister scrawls of lightning and long, straight raindrops have replaced the soft, round lines of the clouds and flowers. The sun frowns and cries as the parents stand as far apart as possible. Between them lies a murky pool into which the children seem to have disappeared. Interestingly, in the second picture, the mother has no arms, and the father's are small and missing hands. This suggests that the child may be seeing her parents as helpless, unable to provide the happiness and security she seems to associate with her life before the divorce.

they're not significant symbols in his art. His eight-year-old cousin, Bernadette, however, has never cared about airplanes, but ever since she accompanied her father to the airport for his flight to his new home out of state, a small, distant plane has figured in many of her pictures. In her case, this is significant. Major changes in your child's art should also catch your attention. If six-year-old Damon's landscapes used to feature big, sunny skies, cottony clouds, and a smiling sun but now often depict dark storms instead, there is probably an underlying reason.

A smile that's not a smile. Because this six-year-old boy drew his parents after divorce as almost indistinguishable from each other, there's no way to determine which is his mother and which his father, suggesting some problem with gender diffferences. The open mouth and prominent teeth suggest aggression.

WHEN AND HOW TO DISCUSS YOUR CHILD'S ART

These guidelines are similar to those for children's play. As your child hunches over the crayons and paper intently scribbling, he has entered his own world. Respect his space.

• *Do not interrupt.* Even asking "Oh, what are you doing?" can intrude on your child's intense concentration. If you want to join, ask if you may sit down and draw your own picture. Then busy yourself with your own drawing and refrain from looking over his shoulder.

• *Don't intrude to "correct" or "suggest" changes or improvements.* If you say, "The legs should be right on top of the grass, not so far up above the grass line," you're imposing. Perhaps your child was trying to express, consciously or unconsciously, a sense of feeling unstable by not having his feet on the ground. As you look at the children's art throughout this book, you'll notice that, in many instances, the most revealing pieces are not "correct." Feet disappear or float above the ground; people are bigger than houses; figures disappear and dissolve; full-figured bodies evolve into mere sticks. Often, the telling details are in what an art teacher might consider mistakes in drawing, perspective, proportion, and so on. Remember: This is not art class; your child is not your student. For him in this moment, art is an experience in expression, not an exercise in technique.

Thinner. In almost every way, this predivorce family is a happy one. The bodies are full and take up the frame; the parents and the siblings hold hands; the gender differences between the parents are clear. In the first picture, the parents are together on one side, the children together on the other, with no distances between them. After this ten-year-old boy's parents divorce, however, the change is dramatic. These stick figures, although smiling, are less than shadows of their former selves; no one holds hands with anyone else; the gender differences are nil. Also note that the children now stand between the parents, and there is substantial distance between the figures.

The floating child. In a portrait of instability, an eight-year-old child floats above the green grass. The "X" over him suggests he might view himself as a mistake, or as someone being literally taken out of the picture. On the other hand, this "X" could indicate a totally different meaning, a need for perfectionism. Perhaps when he saw his finished work, the child decided the picture of himself wasn't up to par.

• *If your child agrees, offer to join him and take turns suggesting things you can both draw, then compare.* Try drawing the song you hear on the radio, your day, what you think your new house will look like. Ask him what he'd like you to draw. Compare and talk about what you've done.

• *If your child is comfortable talking about his work, keep your questions and your comments general.* Ideally, you want him to describe to you what the drawing means. Do not evaluate it for him in his presence and do not comment or question with an eye to eliciting more information. Instead, consciously ignore the work's emotional content or its message. Comment on specific aspects in a manner that expresses an appreciation for this work as if it were any other:

> "That cloud sure looks fluffy."
>
> "I like the way you drew every little leaf on each tree."
>
> "It's interesting how you got that bright purple color. It looks like you mixed several different colors together. What a great idea."

You can then comment—but not ask directly—about specific elements:

> "I wonder why he's broken/crying/happy."
>
> "Look at how big that is and how small that is."
>
> "Look at how dark that doggy is, and how mean looking."

WHAT TO LOOK FOR IN CHILDREN'S ART

Like any acquired skill, drawing is a reflection of a child's intellectual development. Almost universally, children pass through developmental stages of art in a set order, although they may reach one earlier or later than described here. How a child chooses to express, say, sadness depends on a number of things, including her age, stage of development, artistic skill, and comfort with creating. For example, a six-year-old boy may draw himself with tears streaming down his face, an obvious and direct expression of his feelings. His nine-year-old sister, however, may draw a family portrait in which the figures are grouped by height, their

HOW CHILDREN LEARN TO DRAW

The chart below gives a rough, very general idea of the order in which children develop artistically and the approximate, average ages at which they may reach these milestones. Children demonstrate extremely wide variations in drawing at the same age. In addition, a child who has emotional or developmental problems (such as dyslexia, attention-deficit disorder, language disorder, or fine-motor-skills deficits, to name just a few) may create pictures that are markedly different from those of other children his age. If you are concerned about your child's inability to draw, his seeming lack of interest in drawing, or the fact that his drawing skills strike you as less advanced than his peers', show samples of his work to his teacher and pediatrician.

Age	Child Begins Drawing	Common Divorce-Related Imagery Seen in Sandcastles Workbooks
2 to 3	Scribbles, basic geometric shapes, some attempts to depict world, though most unrecognizable; may begin to draw faces; figures often lack trunks, so legs appear attached to the head	No workbooks before age 6
4 to 5	Recognizable attempts to draw people (often family and self) and objects (houses, trees, sun, clouds); deliberate use of color; imaginative; thinks out how to depict ideas	
6 to 7	Conscious use of symbols and colors to express meaning; things drawn with their true characteristics (eyeglasses, hairstyle, etc.)	1 to 2 houses for before and after divorce; people happy or sad; parents divided; children broken or "evaporating"
8 to 9		child "divided"; "disappearing" father; more dramatic contrast between families before and after divorce; thoughts and dialogue represented in "bubbles"; attempts to tell story
10 to 12	More symbols, greater realistic detail, emergence of personal style; less frequency of houses, trees	Depictions of "parallel lives" between mother's and father's homes; broken hearts; word "divorce," often distorted, cracked, broken; depiction of "how things should be"
13 to 14	Even greater ability to use symbols, color, imagery, shading, etc., but increasing self-consciousness about what work might reveal and how it would be viewed by others	
15 to 17		Children over age 14 rarely draw in Sandcastles workbooks.

clothes color-coordinated or matching, and every detail perfect, in an attempt to impose the sense of order she feels is missing. As children approach adolescence, they become increasingly self-conscious about what they draw and more concerned that what they've created is "right" or acceptable to others. Although teens who participate in the Sandcastles Program are encouraged to draw, relatively few do. Having mastered verbal communication—the skill younger kids lack—teens are most comfortable expressing themselves in this more adult manner. For them, talking is an easier, more effective form of expression than drawing. We can see the influence of growing self-consciousness even among preteens, who often opt not to draw. When they do draw, their work contains substantially fewer of the revealing, unconscious details we see in the six- to eleven-year-olds' work. Increasingly, they tend to focus on what happened (which may explain the large number of cartoon storyboard "retellings" of divorce-related events) as opposed to how they feel about it. This is not to say that an older child's artwork can't be valuable and rich in insight; it can. But younger children—whose creativity is more spontaneous, less thought-out, and less self-conscious—tend to be more emotionally revealing.

LOOKING AT THE BIG PICTURE

As you read through these items, remember that no single element in and of itself "means" anything. When viewed together and considered in the context of your child's unique personality and history, these elements can reveal otherwise unexpressed emotions and thoughts. Sometimes children create drawings that are clearly about the divorce, including:

- Self-portraits that show sad, worried, crying, surprised, confused, panicked, or troubled faces
- Scenes from the divorce: one parent telling the other to leave; parents fighting; one or the other parent alone
- Family and self-portraits before and after the divorce
- The "empathetic world": crying suns, stormy skies, wilted flowers, barren trees, and other images that suggest that a child's emotions *are* his world.

A bolt out of the blue. *A classic before-and-after pair of drawings in which the whole world seems to share in a ten-year-old boy's experience, good and bad. The contrast between the family before and after divorce extends even to the shape of the front door—from soft, inviting roundness with large door-knob to a sharp rectangle.*

Within these drawings and even in those that do not seem to be strictly about divorce, you may find elements that express how a child views himself and those around him. Look carefully at:

• *Size and relative size of figures.* Large figures are stronger, more powerful, more important than smaller figures. While it's only natural that parents would be drawn larger than children, worth noting are instances where one parent is much larger or smaller than the other or where the children or one child is substantially smaller than the other figures.

• *Placement of figures (on the page).* Where a child places himself in relation to other figures (parents, siblings, pets) and the distance between figures denote the relative importance of people and objects. If a house is large and in the foreground, it could mean that the house represents stability for the child. It's interesting to note where the child places himself in relation to other figures. In "Thinner," page 71, for example, the two children are to the right of the mother and father before divorce. After the divorce, they are between the parents. Children whose drawings depict their parents' new love interests or stepparents often place the new parental figure between themselves and one or both biological parents.

• *Vanishing, evaporating, "blob."* The child's transformation from a "real person" before the divorce and her subsequent depersonification after is unambiguous and profound. In the illustrations on page 69 and below, the artists have depicted themselves after divorce as "bodyless," perhaps "self-less." On page 69, the children seem to have dissolved in the lightning and rain; they are represented by a blue puddle between the parents. In the illustration below, the children appear to have fallen between their warring parents like two jagged pieces of a broken plate. We know that these represent the children only because their names, deleted here, were written on the original workbook drawings.

Broken hearts, broken parts. *Size and placement tell us a lot in this eleven-year-old boy's depiction of his family after divorce. It's difficult to see, but the small, amorphous, nonhuman forms at the bottom (between the angry, giant parents) are the boy and his sibling. It is unusual for children to draw themselves as inhuman figures or objects within the context of a family picture. These pieces suggest that the child sees himself and his sibling as incomplete, broken pieces as opposed to a whole person. The parents' words—"I want a divorce!" and "Why?"—reflect not so much what his parents actually said but his own limited understanding of the situation: Why? The placement of the children—between the parents, in the middle of their anger, and beneath the broken heart—suggests they are feeling overwhelmed, "at the bottom of the list," forgotten.*

• *Child divided.* Children show a lot of ingenuity in depicting their sense of divided loyalty: a self-portrait split in two, one with two heads or faces, one in which the child's head seems to be spinning between his parents. The illustration below is typical yet remarkable too for the missing sky over the child, which suggests a sense of unrealness about being between the parents.

A classic child divided. *Soft white clouds and a bright blue but heavily shaded sky are suspended over Mom's and Dad's houses. This preadolescent boy obviously feels torn between his parents. The blank white sky directly above him suggests his only place of peace and calm is somewhere in-between his parents where he feels a part of both of them. The heavy shading could also suggest depression, and the blank space might reflect emptiness and loss resulting from his need to "split" himself between two parents and two homes.*

• *General color and shading.* Dark colors and heavy shading suggest sadness or anxiety, while lighter colors suggest happiness or comfort. Alone these may not be significant (perhaps Dad always wears black, or your daughter has collected only her favorite pastels in the crayon box she used today), but as you can see in several before-and-after drawings, children can use these variations in color and shading deliberately.

LOOKING AT DETAILS

• *Facial expression.* Facial expressions usually speak for themselves. In drawings that depict more than one person, it is interesting to note who is smiling or frowning and who is not. The top illustration on page 75 shows the whole family happy before divorce, then sad and angry afterward in the "after" illustration. (Note the child's clearly downturned mouth, an expression of sadness, and compare that to his mother's and father's straight mouths and furrowed brows, which are more suggestive of anger.)

• *Body.* In children's drawings, the body may represent more than simply the physical body. How it is drawn may reflect the child's perception of the figure's (including his own) whole self. (The drawings in which children seem to "dissolve" are extreme examples of this.) Pay attention to the shape of the body relative to other figures in the drawing. Note that the figures in the illustrations below face off the page, the parents essentially turning away from each other.

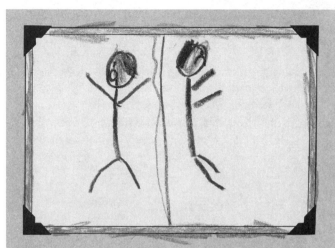

A house divided. *A seven-year-old boy draws his parents divided, angry, and turning away from each other.*

Face-off. *A thirteen-year-old's depiction of anger: figures separated by a line, facing off the page, drawn with sharply jagged features. Also, the arms crossed over the chest suggest anger, and the lack of feet indicate a lack of stability.*

• *Bodies to sticks.* Along with "one house/two house" drawings, bodies that turn to sticks form the most common theme in before-and-after art. Sticks—which may lack faces, hands, feet, and other features—often lack the personal identifying details included in the "before" drawings. The sticks can be read as shadows of the figures' former selves. These drawings clearly show that children see themselves and their families as less than what they were before. (See the illustrations on pages 71 and 79.) When stick figures appear alone, especially in the work of an older child (who, presumably, could draw a fuller figure) or in the context of an apparently thought-out drawing, the sense of alienation and lack of identity are obvious. (See the illustration on page 81.)

Fade to black. *This eight-year-old boy's family is a picture of happiness: everyone smiling, hands outstretched (some touching), the three figures on the left are looking at other family members, while the boy smiles out at the viewer. The figures' identities are clear, and their feet are securely placed on the ground. In the next drawing, divorce has reduced the family—both literally and figuratively—and left the figures floating precariously, their stick arms extended horizontally as if they were negotiating a tightrope.*

• *Hands and arms.* Their presence usually implies a sense of control. When hands and arms are missing in an older child's drawing, it may indicate a loss of control. This is especially likely when one figure has them and another does not or when early figures (ones drawn previously or drawn for the "before" part of a before-and-after series) have them and later, or "after," figures do not. Missing arms or hands may also mean that the figure drawn does not touch or hug others. (See the father and mother in the illustrations on page 69; the father lacks arms in the "before" but has them in the "after," while the mother has arms in the "before" but not in the "after.") Sometimes children will draw figures with their arms up in the air or outstretched, as if they are trying to get someone's attention or have something to say. (See the arguing parents on page 76, and the stick figures in the left illustration on page 78.)

• *Symbolic of relationships.* Two or more figures holding hands indicate emotional links. Note the mother and father holding hands in the illustration on page 71. Several figures holding hands may also identify them as a group. See the illustration below.

A broken chain. *In this ten-year-old's first picture, Mom and her children all appear emotionally linked. In the second, we see that divorce not only removed Dad from the family, it also may have damaged the closeness Mom and the children felt, since they are not holding hands. Also note that all the family members are "floating" in the second drawing.*

• *Feet and legs, stable versus unstable.* Stable feet are drawn to appear flat on the ground; unstable feet usually have toes pointed downward and give the impression that the figure is floating above the ground. Grounded feet suggest stability. Ungrounded feet and floating people indicate instability. It's not unusual for children to draw themselves floating above the other figures in the picture, as shown in the bottom illustration on page 71. Also note how the child has clearly depicted the ground and x-ed himself out.

• *Eyes.* Young children naturally tend to draw eyes that are disproportionately large. Missing or vacant eyes in older children's drawings may indicate emptiness.

• *Other physical features.* After the age of five or so, most children will draw figures with distinguishing sexual characteristics (Mom will have long hair and earrings, Dad will have short hair, and so on). When children are old enough to draw sexual differences and don't—for example, you can't tell which figure is Mom and which is Dad—it may indicate a confusion of gender roles between the parents and perhaps in the child himself. Any graphic, explicit depiction of sexual organs, however, should be cause for concern.

LOOKING AT STYLE

• Jagged lines indicate anger. (See the illustrations on page 69, 78 [right], and below.)

• Faint, "fading" lines indicate uncertainty, low self-esteem.

• Heavy shading indicates anxiety.

Filled with anxiety. *Filling up a page often indicates anxiety and a need to eliminate open space. This nine-year-old boy's drawing of life after divorce is a classic child divided—he's standing literally in the middle of the road—with some interesting twists. In addition to the filled space, this drawing also features jagged lines so densely drawn that it is easy to overlook the two stick figures standing near their houses. It's almost as if the boy's parents have been obscured by the conflict and anxiety of the divorce. It's interesting to note that on the right the parent's property includes flowers and an open (line-free) sky, suggesting that this particular home is more peaceful than the other or that the child has a greater sense of peace with that parent.*

LOOKING FOR CONTRAST

- In before-and-after drawings
- Between parents
- Between parents and children
- Between art done now and art done earlier

THINGS 2 DO

THE DIVORCE GAME

Together with your child, create a board game about divorce. On poster board, mark out a winding path with a start and a finish, then mark spaces that say things like "Parents argue; lose a turn," "Parents show up and sit together at class play; go ahead four spots," and so on. You can also create cards that are drawn when landing on certain spaces.

Samantha wrote on one spot "Dad remarries; lose a turn" and on a different spot "Mom remarries; roll again." Obviously, this indicates that she was more inclined to accept her mother's remarrying than her father's.

PURPOSE: The board game is a fun way to discuss divorce and make it something that can be talked about. It lets your child know you are comfortable with his discussing the divorce issues. You can learn a great deal about your child's views as well.

THINGS 2 DO

SUPERHERO

Ask your child to imagine himself as a superhero. What would be his special powers? Patrick drew himself as a superhero who had a huge remote-control box—"I use it to control everybody."

Further discuss the meanings behind these special powers. What are their limitations? Can they be used for evil as well as good? Look at what your child is trying to accomplish with his newfound powers. Patrick was expressing his need to feel more in control. Ann's superhero could make people fall in love (or stay in love), expressing her wish for her parents to reunite.

PURPOSE: Fantasy helps a child express what might otherwise be too difficult to put into words.

JUST LOOKING AND LISTENING

You need not scrutinize every piece of art, eavesdrop on every moment of play, to get to know your child a little bit better. Whether you look at one or two drawings or use every activity in this book, keep your demeanor calm and relaxed. And when you are playing with your child, really play. Your child will derive more from your just being involved in his world than from anything you can learn by observing him. Have fun!

3

A Life Begins: Understanding Your Infant or Toddler

Newborn to Age Three

The first smile; the first steps; those first precious words—for many parents, this is the most magical time of parenthood. We might live for decades more and never feel quite so intensely the love, the promise, and the possibility we experience the first time we hold a new baby. Poet Carl Sandburg observed, "A baby is God's opinion that the world should go on," and in those first moments, who could argue? When we envision these first few years, we simply cannot picture separation, divorce, or any other tragedy befalling our family.

The single, divorced parent of an infant or toddler has one foot in the wonderland of early childhood, the other in cold reality. Taking care of the littlest ones can be a round-the-clock job, and single parents can feel particularly overwhelmed and isolated. The stress of being solely responsible for a baby or a toddler coupled with the emotional turmoil of divorce makes it easy to lose sight of how precious and wonderful these early years are.

Because the very youngest children do not seem to know what is happening, people often make the mistake of assuming they are impervious to divorce's impact. Many people still believe that a child whose parents divorce before she reaches three or so "is too young to understand what's happening" or "won't remember" or "never really got to know her father, so she won't miss him." We now know that babies are far more aware of their surroundings and changes than was suspected even a decade ago. There is no such thing as a child who "doesn't know what's going on."

This is why divorce and its ensuing changes pose special problems for the littlest ones. You can protect your child by

- understanding the developmental goals of each stage of life,
- anticipating how divorce may interfere,
- watching for signs that your child may be experiencing stress (increased crying, loss of appetite, changes in sleep patterns, and digestive disturbances).

The first two years hold especially important phases of emotional development. Recent research indicates that for each major developmental task, babies have "windows," genetically predetermined periods of optimal learning. With loving care and appropriate stimulation, a baby learns and grows. However, a lack of attention and nurturing at these critical points may hinder a baby's normal development.

How we respond to our child in the first few years may determine his ability to view himself, others, and life in general with an open, positive attitude. This is when a baby first learns to trust or mistrust his environment and begins to fashion some image of himself as a lovable, cherished, and respected individual. That sounds like a pretty tall order for a cooing baby still struggling to get his toes in his mouth, and it is. Only with consistent care and loving attention can a child develop a healthy sense of himself.

How BABIES EXPERIENCE DIVORCE

If he could, a baby might write:

Dear Diary,
Mama is sad, which means I must be sad. Where is Dada? I don't hear his voice, and he doesn't hold me or toss me up in the air anymore. Mama doesn't sing that special song. I don't feel right. I don't like going to bed anymore. I don't want Mama to go or leave me alone.

Long before your baby volunteers that first precious smile or your toddler says her first real sentence, she has been absorbing and responding to virtually everything she perceives, especially your presence and how you comfort and care for her. Lights, colors, shapes, sounds, and textures all compete for her attention, but she loves nothing more than the sound of your voice, the scent of your skin, or the touch of your hand.

Babies come into the world "preprogrammed" to respond to and be emotionally tuned in to those around them. Infants and toddlers are especially sensitive to your cues because of their total dependence on you. Even when you don't think you are actively engaging your baby, he is still observing and reacting to your mood and your attitude. Long before a baby *understands* the words "I love you," he has felt, sensed, and understood your meaning by the way you speak to him, hold his gaze, clasp him to your heart, and softly sing to him. We adults tend to think of our thoughts and emotions as emanating from within ourselves. A baby, however, simply cannot yet conceive of himself as "I," and so, for now, his self-image is a reflection of the feelings, words, and actions of those around him. A baby feels loved because we make him feel loved; he feels secure because we make him feel secure.

Generally, children younger than six months have no emotional boundaries; they cannot determine who "owns" which emotions or to whom or what they are really directed. Always remember that a baby cannot psychologically or physically isolate himself from you and your emotions. It is impossible for your baby to separate your anger, hostility, depression, and nonresponsiveness from how you feel about him. These negative emotions can have a profound and long-lasting effect in two ways. First, they displace the love, warmth, and security he has come to associate with you and is developmentally programmed to depend on. Second, he will respond to them with confusion, anxiety, and fear.

FATHER'S SPECIAL ROLE

We focus on a child's bonding with his mother because the baby cannot help but look to her as the first most significant person in his life. From about thirty weeks' gestation, he has heard every sound his mother made, and within hours of birth, he will show a preference for her voice, her smell, and her presence. For babies, bonding with mother is essential for physical survival and emotional well-being, but recent research suggests strongly that bonding with father is equally important, though for different reasons. Men and women bring to child rearing different styles, attitudes, and experiences. For example, a mother will soothingly rock her toddler; Daddy will gleefully toss him gently into the air. Mother may be more apt to spend time teaching and modeling patience and neatness; roughhousing Daddy teaches body confidence and risk taking.

Children need both types of care, but we are just learning about the important role Dad plays in nurturing self-esteem, acceptance, and confidence. Even if a mother feels her child's father rarely changed a diaper or "just played with him sometimes," she must see him through her child's eyes. A baby lives only in the moment of being held, cuddled, tickled, chased, bathed, sung to, and carried around piggyback. Each moment builds the child's self-esteem and contributes to a positive future relationship with his father.

Research on fatherhood demonstrates a strong correlation between strong, early involvement with one's child and significantly lower rates of child abuse, abandonment, and failure to pay child support. Regardless of how you feel toward your child's father, there are many compelling reasons to encourage and facilitate his ongoing continued involvement in his baby's life.

BABY'S FIRST EMOTIONAL MILESTONE: LEARNING TO TRUST

A baby's first and most important developmental milestone is achieving a sense of trust in her environment. This occurs when she knows that her physical and emotional needs will be met. Children who develop such trust feel comfortable even in unfamiliar situations.

Recent research into the nonverbal communication between babies and parents suggests that babies are naturally engaged in a constant pas de deux with parents and other caregivers. This exchange is crucial for a baby's emotional and physical growth. Without this important input from parents and caregivers, babies risk suffering long-term, even permanent emotional damage. Babies whose caregivers are unresponsive, depressed, or anxious are deprived of the positive interaction they need. Studies have shown that babies who attempt to engage a mother or other caregiver who doesn't respond in an accepting, warm manner will look away and begin to fret. Over time, they stop even trying to provoke a response.

From infancy through toddlerhood, children develop a basic sense of security by being cared for and loved, having an established routine, and living in familiar surroundings amid familiar people. Minute to minute, these children spend far more time in close physical proximity to parents than do older children. Ideally, their every waking moment is spent in the presence of someone who loves and interacts with them. When this occurs, a child has a sense that all is right with her world.

Everything's ducky. *A baby bird looks down from its nest on two loving parents. The caption "I ♡ love both of you!" reflects a sentiment many children wish they could express to their parents.*

How Parents Can Help Babies and Toddlers

• *If possible, be sure your child has frequent and regular contact with your ex-spouse.* This encourages bonding and understanding between parent and child. Parents whose children are very young have to make a special effort to communicate for both practical and emotional reasons. Practically speaking, nine-year-old Randy can tell his father, "I'm not hungry; I already ate at home with Mom," or "I need to take my asthma medicine tonight." Obviously, very young children cannot do this and must depend on their parents to get it right. Shifting between two households almost ensures that something will be overlooked, so talk to your ex. If that's impossible, be sure to write down the important points: "Sally seemed to be tugging on her ear this afternoon. If she gets fussy or starts running a fever, call Dr. Evans right away. His number is . . ." You might also write up a schedule:

> 8:30 breakfast
> 10:00–11:30 morning nap
> 12:00 lunch
> 12:30–2:00 park, outdoor play, or play date
> 2:20–4:00 afternoon nap

and so on.

• *Maintain a calm, positive attitude in the child's presence.* Keep your interactions with your baby relaxed, warm, and happy. This may take some acting on your part, since you're going through a stressful situation yourself, but it will be worth it. If you find you can't manage this, take time for yourself away from your child. Use that time to consider the stresses in your life or talk with a friend. A calmer, happier baby is an easier baby to care for. Regardless of how you may feel about yourself, your baby still loves you and depends on you. With every smile and every hug, you are helping this new little person grow up happy, healthy, and trusting. Make the most of it.

• *Establish and stick to a normal daily routine.* Ideally, that would mean sticking to the routine your baby is familiar with. If that is not possible, then try to keep the changes to a minimum. If you cannot be home to feed and bathe your baby at the appointed hour, be sure whoever does follows essentially the same routine. Make whatever changes you must with special consideration to minimize the chance you may have to change caregivers or schedules again a few weeks later.

• *Protect your baby's "personal environment."* Many babies have a few favorite toys and blankets (child psychologists call these transitional objects; some parents call them lovies). If possible, send these items along with your baby on visitation and be sure they're returned with him. Both parents need to appreciate that these items, however ragtag in appearance, are sacred. Also keep other familiar objects such as mobiles, wall hangings, and things she knows and enjoys in sight. Don't worry if you can't duplicate everything exactly; you're aiming for a similar ambience and comfortableness; not cloning your child's world.

• *Maintain continuity.* Don't overlook your special activities and "rituals." Be sure other caregivers under your direction know and follow these routines. Explain to them the importance of such "little things" as tucking your baby in with treasured toys or playing the musical mobile or tape recorder as she falls asleep. Ensure that caregivers respect your child's wishes, even if they personally don't agree with them. If your child wants his pacifier but the caregiver is "anti-Binky," make sure your child gets the pacifier anyway.

• *Anticipate eating and sleeping problems.* These are common ways that babies show stress. However, do not automatically assume that the stress of separation and change is the only possible cause. *If you notice changes in your baby's normal behavior, consult your pediatrician immediately for evaluation and advice.* While emotional distress may be the source of the trouble, you can never rule out physical causes without a thorough physical examination.

• *Be prepared to pamper and comfort your little one.* Because your child probably will experience some emotional upheaval and resulting changes in sleeping, eating, and general behavior, divorced parents find themselves wondering what to do. How much extra attention, cuddling, and indulging are enough? How much is too much?

Under the age of six months, I believe there is more benefit than harm in going that extra mile. The extra holding, rocking, playing, and comforting only increase your child's sense of trust in his environment and in you. I do not believe you can "train" a five-month-old by allowing him to scream in his crib for an hour in the middle of the night. But with older babies there is another side to be considered. Linda had the best of intentions when she decided to let ten-month-old Colby stay up past ten (so she could spend more time with him), sleep with her in her bed every night (so he could feel more secure), and to make every weekend one long social call (so he could feel loved by her four siblings and his nine cousins). After a couple of weeks of this, Linda and Colby were both exhausted and cranky, and he was having trouble shaking an ear infection.

What children like Colby really need are love and structure. If you want a calm, relaxed baby, make sure he has a consistent, early bedtime and isn't out visiting every single day. If you will not want a two-year-old sleeping with you, make sure your nine-month-old sticks to her bed now. Spend a few minutes in her bed with her and return her to her bed if she shows up in your room (excluding when she is ill). You will let your child know that you are in control of not only her world, but your own.

Routine

Even families who don't make a conscientious effort to stick to a strict schedule do develop a routine. Ideally, babies quickly fall into the rhythm of your daily life, and soon derive security from a basically consistent pattern. Babies as young as six weeks of age already show signs of learning to anticipate future events.

Moving to a new home, having new caregivers, missing a parent who has moved away or returned to the workplace, and adjusting to many subtle changes in the everyday routine can make a baby fretful and anxious. You cannot possibly isolate your baby from change or ensure complete consistency in every detail of her day. While some inconsistency is normal and enhances a child's ability to cope with change, you

A LULLABY FOR BABY

Babies love singing, and you don't have to be a professional songwriter to create wonderful songs your child will love. Sing to your baby; sing the same song at the same time of day—a good-morning song, a bathtime song, a goodnight song that includes the name of each person you like.

PURPOSE: The song establishes stability and helps your baby get ready for the next stage of the day. Singing also calms baby and parent and facilitates eye contact and trust.

MAKE SURE YOU COMMUNICATE TO YOUR BABY OR TODDLER THAT . . .

✔ *He is always safe and loved.* "I'm taking care of you, and I love you. You have many people who love you, too."

✔ *He lives in a world of love.* "Who loves you? Let's see. There's Grandma, Lucy, Uncle Edmund, Cousin Laurie, Cousin Julie, your friend Madison, Joellen's doggy Elmo . . ."

✔ *He will see his other parent (if true).* "You are still going to see Daddy. I want you to spend time with him. He loves you very much."

✔ *Things have changed, but he will be okay.* "I know these changes have been hard for you. I love you very much and I will always be here for you."

can do a lot to smooth your little one's transition and reassure her that, although life has changed, the world is still a warm, loving, and safe place.

Between six and eight months of age, as a baby begins to make a distinction between himself and others, he develops stranger anxiety. Before, he could peaceably be handed from person to person without fuss; suddenly, someone new walks into the room, and the baby starts screaming. If there will be new people in your child's life, be sure he is comfortable with them before you leave. Be aware that your separation from your spouse may make this transition more difficult for your child.

*T*ODDLERS

As any parent knows, toddlers are wonderful and challenging. Never again in your child's life will she reach so many important developmental milestones in such a short time: from crawling to walking, from babbling to talking, from viewing herself as part of you to becoming quite literally a person in her own right.

THE TODDLER'S QUEST: LEARNING AUTONOMY

The toddler is the ultimate explorer. His world expands exponentially with every little step, but his ability to venture forth with curiosity and confidence depends on how well he trusts his environment. Since he was a year old, he's been splashing in the tub; tossing objects over and over again to see how they fall, what sounds they make, and where they land; testing newfound physical skills by climbing and jumping on the couch. These are the sometimes-trying but necessary activities that build confidence, trust, and understanding.

We also build our child's sense of self through how we respond to him. A happy, healthy toddler knows that when he laughs in delight, someone will laugh along with him; that all the boo-boos he accumulates will be acknowledged and kissed away. He learns to trust not only his environment but the love and support of his parents.

As parents, we are aware of the positive impact of these reactions in the moment. What we often don't realize is how our consistent pattern of response, encouragement, and comfort contributes to the joy, courage, and perseverance toddlers call upon as they conquer their world. In addition, that foundation of trust developed earlier is crucial to his ability to make the next leap to a sense of autonomy. Beginning roughly in the second year of life, your child begins to view himself as a separate person. As he seems to begin moving away, more than ever he needs to know you are there for him.

A TODDLER'S SPECIAL NEEDS

While the guidelines above apply to toddlers too, toddlers are not just bigger, older babies. Unlike babies, they have a sense of separation from their parents. They experience anger, though they are unable to understand its cause or ways to manage it, which accounts for the tantrums we associate with the terrible twos. It is not unusual for children of this age to express their anger through biting, hitting, being irritable, and at times withdrawing emotionally even from those they depend on.

When it appears that your child is having emotional problems, don't hesitate to talk to him. Toddlers often understand far more than we assume. Say, "I know this is sad for you not to have Daddy here." Because your youngster isn't yet adept at talking, you may have to do a little more guessing to discover what's really bothering him. This is why play is so important.

If your toddler is verbal, talk to him about what makes him angry and offer alternative behavior. You might say, "When you're angry, you can say 'mad,' 'me mad,' or put on an 'angry hat' [see the box "Angry Jacket and Hat," page 36]. That's okay. It is not okay to hit/bite/punch [whatever the offending behavior]." Help your child express his feelings and validate them. At the same time, be sure to use time-out and appropriate discipline to discourage unacceptable expressions of his feelings, not his expression of feelings in general. (See box on discipline, page 28.)

Vanishing act. Even young children understand that divorce entails both gains and losses. In this nine-year-old boy's "before" picture, he depicts himself as a much younger child; note his sticklike hair, minimally drawn body, and positioning between his parents. In contrast, he appears in the "after" drawing full-bodied, with a head of hair and a big smile. Mom, with whom he's sharing one of three clearly delineated spaces, is smiling too. He is no longer "in the middle," but he does not know where his father is. The fact that he has drawn a space for him, as opposed to simply leaving him out of the picture altogether, draws our attention to the emotional distance between them and the void his absence creates.

THINGS 2 DO

CONNECTING WITH YOUR BABY

Each day brings countless opportunities to make your baby feel loved. Though most of these would seem obvious, in the course of a busy day, we don't always remember to do the little things that babies really enjoy, such as:

Cooing and baby talk
Touching and massaging
Rocking
Singing, dancing, and listening to music
Playing in front of a mirror
Playing in the tub, water play
Making skin-to-skin contact

PURPOSE: Bonding and relaxation result from activities that bring you closer to your baby.

A toddler will understand that one parent is no longer in the home but not understand why. Like a baby, a toddler is also prone to problems with eating and sleeping. Developmentally, however, he has a much greater capacity to worry and so may become very anxious whenever the residential parent is away. Separation anxiety—the fear of not being in constant contact with a parent—first appears anywhere after eight months, often resulting in more crying and clinging behavior. The sudden absence of one parent may prolong this stage or cause a child who has gone through it to regress. And don't even think about toilet teaching a child amid the immediate turmoil of divorce.

SETTING LIMITS

Of course, the mobility and curiosity that make toddlers so amazing also make caring for them nothing short of exhausting. Their sudden outbursts of anger and oppositional behavior can try even the most patient parent, and their limited ability to differentiate what is real from what is not can result in compelling fears and worries. This is the first stage at which discipline is appropriate, and parents must be especially careful to express disapproval for inappropriate or dangerous behavior in a way that does not make the child feel ashamed or discouraged. If your child hits you, for example, an appropriate response is to explain, clearly and calmly, "No, we don't allow hitting," and to give him a one-minute time-out in his room or a specially designated spot.

The routine work of setting limits seems to go on constantly—"If you don't go to the bathroom, you can't go to the park because there's no bathroom there," "If you don't finish your dinner, you can't have ice cream," "If you don't put on your shoes, you can't go outside because it's cold out." Bear in mind that by setting, explaining, and enforcing limits consistently and in a way that teaches your child to reason and consider consequences, you'll also be encouraging your child's self-sufficiency later on.

When everything seems to be spinning out of control, it's not unusual for divorced parents to view their children as one—perhaps the only—area that seems controllable. You may feel that setting more rules or refusing to tolerate behavior like tantrums will prompt your toddler to "shape up." For your sake and your child's, my advice is to forget it. Any sense of control you may derive from suddenly laying down the law will be short-lived and self-defeating. More important, however, young children at this time need consistency, fewer but clearer rules, positive reinforcement, and acceptance, not more conflict.

It is especially important at this time to secure the toddler's environment and make sure it is safe. Screaming "No! No!" every time he approaches the precious glass figurines on the coffee table will only frustrate both of you and create a potential—and totally unnecessary—safety hazard for him. Children this age simply cannot understand why they shouldn't explore electrical sockets with their fingers or leap off the top step. When vigorously and frequently reprimanded for approaching the dangerous or forbidden, children come away feeling that curiosity and exploring are wrong and become anxious about everything. Thoroughly childproofing your home is essential for your child's safety and mental health. It also greatly reduces the time you will spend in the perennial battle of wills. Toddlerhood is the perfect time to train yourself to choose your battles. Parenthood is, among many other things, a constant dance of compromise between how we think things should be and how they really are. There are some stresses we cannot avoid, but if we look carefully at our attitudes and the rules we set, we often find many self-imposed stressors. One of the most common is a rigid adherence to unrealistic expectations and rules.

THINGS 2 DO

BABY LOVE

Give your toddler his own baby doll to feed, kiss, and care for. Talk to him about what babies and children need and what mommies and daddies do for them. Ask him to tell you how he makes the baby feel cared for, what the baby is laughing or crying about, how his baby feels.

PURPOSE: Your child can master any residual fear and anxiety by assuming the role of parent and acting out his concerns. Not every expression is a reflection of his own feelings, but further explore strong statements by mirroring what he says; for example, "Oh, I see, your baby is sad because his daddy missed the party."

Successful and happy single parents are masters at maintaining consistency in enforcing the rules that do matter (such as safety, which should never be compromised), while overlooking or simply dealing with those that do not. For example, when eighteen-month-old Caroline feeds herself, she learns much more than a series of eye-hand-mouth coordination skills. Even as she's fashioned a sticky plastic hat from her dinner, she has also learned to be independent and to have confidence in her ability to meet her own needs.

Most parents would agree that these goals should be given a higher priority than, say, a clean kitchen floor, spotless clothing, or a brief mealtime. However, when we "take over" because we can feed the child quickly and more neatly than she can feed herself, we may be sending her the message that she is incapable and helpless. Parents with unreasonably high standards accomplish little more than setting the stage for needless and futile conflicts. Life will be easier for you and for your child if you get the supersized bib, throw down the giant plastic Splat Mat, and set aside the extra twenty minutes it will take your toddler to maneuver the SpaghettiOs from the bowl to her mouth. View the resulting mess and chaos as a time to encourage and applaud your persistent, courageous little one.

TAKE A BREAK

Single parents may have less time, more pressure, and less support than others. Be creative. Listen to music as a stress buster. Classical music is especially soothing, and some studies suggest it may promote brain development in children. If you work outside the home, try to set aside a ten-minute downtime after coming home and greeting your child but before tackling your house and child-care duties. A special bag of books and toys kept near the crib or playpen to be played with only during this time can keep your child engaged while you savor a cup of tea or just close your eyes for a few minutes.

IF YOU ARE THE NONRESIDENTIAL PARENT

It's easy for nonresidential parents to feel as if they're in "second place." As little ones change and grow so quickly, you may feel that you're missing out on so much that you will never catch up. Relax. Remember that even when parents are married, one parent is usually the primary caregiver, while the other is much less involved in the child's daily routine. The guidelines above apply to both residential and nonresidential parents, but there are a few points parents who spend less time with the child should keep in mind:

• *Maintain your special relationship with the child.* Just living in a different home doesn't mean you can't do the same things you did before—singing special songs, dancing around after dinner, sharing secret nonsense words, and going to special places. Record yourself reading a story or singing so your child can hear your voice when you're not there. Don't think your child is too young to remember.

• *Respect your child's normal schedule and do all that you can to ensure consistency from home to home.* Bedtime, mealtimes, bathtime—these are all parts of your child's day that should be the same wherever she is. Resist the temptation to balk at complying because "it's what my ex wants." Even if you disagree, at this point consistency is precisely what your child wants and needs. She will eat and sleep better, have fewer fits, stay healthier, and make your time together much more enjoyable. In addition, maintain consistency within your home. Don't let her sleep in your bed one night, then spend the next at Aunt Clara's, and the one after at Grandma's. Make special places in your home that are hers alone: bed, play area, high chair or seat at the table, and so on.

• *Try to see your baby or toddler often.* (See chapter 12 on visitation scheduling.) Very young children have a different sense of time than adults. The younger ones derive far more benefit from seeing Daddy part of every weekend and a few hours on a weekday than for one long weekend every two weeks. If possible, arrange to be part of a daily routine as often and consistently as possible—perhaps dropping him off at day care or school—or take him overnight one night each week. When your child is more than a year or so old, phone each night before bedtime, just to say "Goodnight, I love you," or sing a little song. Don't expect your child to stay on the line or talk much to you; and don't be offended if she drops the phone and wanders off. Just because your child is too young to appreciate the finer points of telephone etiquette does not negate the good feelings she experiences when hearing your voice.

• *Make your time with your child easy for both of you.* In addition to maintaining routines, plan your time wisely. Sometimes nonresidential parents are so excited to have the child for the weekend, they try to cram in dozens of visits with friends and relatives. If your family wishes to visit, have them come to you and avoid disrupting your child's routine. This is your special time with your child, so don't make her "share" you with others. Many nonresidential parents exhaust themselves trying to figure out what to do with a child. While pony rides and trips to the zoo often create a big splash, simply playing with blocks on the floor and watering the plants together are exciting to toddlers, too.

FINALLY

It may seem obvious, but I'll say it anyway: Really love your child. If you feel anything other than total, unqualified love for your baby as he stares into your eyes, if you honestly are not moved by the sight of your sleeping angel, talk to someone about it. Too often our own challenging childhoods, relationships with parents, and everyday stress compromise our ability to love and care for our child. Now that he needs you more than ever, take stock of how you're feeling and responding and do whatever you must to make yourself open, available, and loving. If you feel stressed, confide in a trusted friend or loved one. Join a single-parents' support group. If you feel depressed or overwhelmed and find yourself being less responsive or less loving, seek professional counseling immediately.

Raising a baby or a toddler takes patience and a positive outlook, qualities that may be in short supply right now. Remember, consistency, love, and stimulation mean far more to your little one than whether or not the kitchen floor is spotless, all his outfits are neatly pressed, or he goes to the duck pond every day. Even though your marriage didn't have the fairy-tale ending you'd hoped, you hold in your arms the little prince or princess of your dreams. With your love and attention, the baby or toddler you worry about today will thrive and develop into a well-adjusted, happy, and loving child.

Q Dear Gary,
Last month, after six years of marriage, my husband announced that he is leaving me and moving to a city over three hundred miles from here. When I asked about our girls, one and three, he replied that no judge would give him custody or visitation anyway, so he thinks it best to "make a clean break" and disappear from their lives. I disagree, but I'm not sure I want my daughters to be with a father who doesn't seem to really want them. What next?

A It's called abandonment. Fathers who abandon their children may offer what appear to be logical explanations for their behavior, but these usually boil down to excuses. And excuses don't save children from the sadness and rejection they feel knowing they have a father who didn't stick around to know them.

He should maintain contact with his children like any other father who lives far away from his children, with constant phone calls, letters, faxes, e-mail, and visits as often as possible. It is difficult to maintain long-distance relationships, but it's worth the effort to protect your children from growing up thinking their father doesn't love them enough, or worse yet, they are not lovable enough, for him to have a relationship with them. For parents who cannot or will not try to remain in touch with their children, see "The Abandoned Child," page 258.

Q Dear Gary,
Ever since my husband and I separated, our thirty-month-old, Angela, screams when I have to leave for work, even though her nanny of two years is here. My friends and ex think this is just a phase, but I think it's about our separation. How do I know for sure? How can I help her?

A There is no way to know for sure whether Angela is responding to your leaving or the separation from her father. While children do go through stages and experience separation anxiety, the fact that you can link a change in her behavior with your separation suggests there may be a connection. Begin by trying some basic techniques that work for separation in general. Be aware of your body language, facial expression, and tone of voice as you leave. Are you communicating your own feelings of guilt, nervousness, or sadness? Does your behavior communicate that you are feeling overprotective of Angela, overwhelmed by having to go, or ambivalent? Try to adopt body language that says you're calm, reassuring, and firm. Next, try to ritualize your exit and help your child prepare. Ten minutes before you leave, announce cheerfully that "Mommy's putting her shoes on to go bye-bye and will be back soon." Get your child started on a favorite activity—listening to a story on tape, painting or coloring, watching a video—that she can continue doing with the nanny after you go. Verbalize your plans for when you come back: "When Mommy comes back, we'll go out for ice cream," or "When Mommy comes back, we can play on your swing set." Some children have an easier time with the separation if they are the ones doing the leaving. You might try telling your child that you will be leaving soon, have your nanny take the child for a walk, then leave the house before they return. Be sure, however, that you say goodbye before your child goes.

Don't just assume that you have a garden-variety separation problem. Don't overlook the fact that your child probably is missing her father. Even though your daughter is young and her verbal abilities are limited, she probably understands more than you realize. Begin now giving her the words she needs to express her feelings: "I know you're sad when Mommy leaves, and it's different now that Daddy is not here so much. But you know I come back each time, and Daddy will take you out tomorrow [or whenever the next visit or phone call will take place]. I love you and everything will be okay."

Q Dear Gary,
My soon-to-be ex-husband never participated much in parenting. Last Sunday he once again brought our two boys—ages eighteen months and just three—home after a miserable weekend. The boys were crying, and their father was loudly complaining—in front of them, no less—that the little one should be potty trained already and the older one had no table manners. He called them "big babies." Now he's threatening to "straighten them out the old-fashioned way." I'm worried.

A Stay worried. The baby and preschool years are times of spectacular development for a child's self-worth. Unfortunately, some parents can do spectacular damage when they overcriticize and maintain a cold, distant relationship with their children. Your soon-to-be ex may not realize it, but he is planting the seeds for a time when his children will want nothing to do with him. And then, of course, he will blame you for it. The fact that he openly criticizes them repeatedly, they are unhappy, and he views corporal punishment as an effective tool to deal with table manners and toilet learning is quite alarming. His airing his grievance in earshot of the boys is also troubling. Children are incredibly sensitive to criticism. Do all you can to keep your sons out of the "firing range" when you and your ex discuss these issues. Make special private time for a phone conversation with your ex to talk about these problems. (See the box "How to Avoid a Fight," page 213 for tips.)

Discussing the matter with him or a friend or relative that he respects who can properly convey your concern is the wisest option. Or provide him with a book on child development, perhaps. If he is unresponsive to these efforts or this is not possible, seek counseling for your children. Even young children in the hands of a qualified child therapist can convey a great deal and learn to give voice to their emotions. The therapist is an impartial party who can act on the behalf of the children. If she feels the children are in any way being emotionally or physically abused, she can immediately act upon that by reporting such concerns to your state abuse agency for further investigation, as per her obligation. (See "Deciding on Therapy," page 189.) She can also testify in court as to her concerns and what she feels is needed to improve this relationship (supervised visitation, counseling for Dad). In court, a therapist's evaluation carries far more weight than a parent saying, "He did this, she did that."

The therapist should help you understand if there is anything you may be doing that makes the visitation difficult. Often, it is cut-and-dried to a parent; she is right, and he is wrong. But upon closer inspection, it's not uncommon to see how both parents are adding to the problem. Perhaps your ex could join your boys at the playground, in a play group, or other group activity, where he might learn from seeing how other children behave.

Be open to the therapist's ideas but make it very clear from the beginning why your children are in her care. If the therapist is uncomfortable testifying in court under these circumstances, find someone with more experience in the field. You are requesting a nonconfidential evaluation of your children to determine if they are in any emotional or physical danger. The therapist may want to test everyone involved (parents and children), and you can often request that the judge order such testing (although it is expensive). But in addition or even without testing, the therapist can have a few sessions with your children to develop a relationship and find some answers.

Also, Dad should be asked to meet this new therapist. It will give her the opportunity to discuss the matters firsthand with him and also let him know someone other than his ex is watching and taking note of his relationship with his children.

CHAPTER 4

The Age of Wonder: Understanding Your Preschooler

From Ages Three to Five

The preschool years bring rapid intellectual, physical, and emotional growth. Your preschooler's imagination is racing, and he is fascinated by everything around him. He will skip after a butterfly—until he spies an ant. As he crouches down to look at that, he will forget what led him there in the first place. Preschoolers are eternally hopeful, their wishes as real as ground beneath them. Someday he will eat all the chocolate chips he desires, maybe even fly like a bird or catch a star. And why not? He has yet to learn the meaning of "impossible." A preschooler's world is a place where weeds are as beautiful as flowers, empty boxes are more treasured than hundred-dollar bills, and sand, Jell-O, and Duplos are things of wonder.

Your preschooler's "developmental mission" is to become independent. His curiosity, wonder, and sense of adventure fuel his quest to broaden his world. If his babyhood was secure and loving, he knows that it is safe to venture forward because Mom and Dad will always be there to love, comfort, feed, play with, and protect him. For the first time, he has some intellectual understanding of the constants of life—day and night, sun and stars—and a greater ability to look ahead and predict what will happen next. Building on his trust in his world and sense of autonomy, your preschooler is now engaged in developing a clear sense of himself as a separate person and as part of a social group outside his family. He enthusiastically seeks the limits, the boundaries, the places where he might boldly go where no one has gone before.

He is also learning to reason, to exercise self-control, and to name and express his emotions verbally. Preschoolers take great pride in their newfound abilities to tell stories, to think things through, to communicate their thoughts and feelings to others. Language is the preschooler's ticket into the wider world of other people's thoughts and feelings, and what a fascinating place that is. Cooperative play replaces the parallel play of the toddler years. Not only is he learning to master feeding, dressing, and using the toilet alone, he is increasingly inquisitive. His early innate drive to explore is now joined by a seemingly endless desire to understand. Your enthusiastic responses to his seemingly endless questions ("Why?" "What would happen if . . . ?" "How does this work?") offer opportunities to expand his language, thinking, and decision-making skills. They reward him for taking the initiative in understanding his world. Our responses also teach him that what he says, thinks, and feels is important to us.

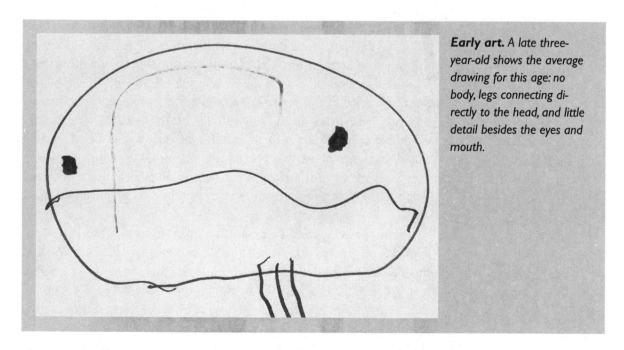

Early art. *A late three-year-old shows the average drawing for this age: no body, legs connecting directly to the head, and little detail besides the eyes and mouth.*

For the first time in their lives, preschoolers begin to show signs of empathy and understanding, although they will remain predominantly

T·H·I·N·G·S 2 D·O

HAND TO HAND

Hold your open hand in front of you facing your child and ask your child to hold his open hand close to yours without touching. Take turns tracing each other's hand movements, mirroring what the other does.

PURPOSE: This fun activity assists parent and child in focusing on each other and becoming more comfortable being physically close to each other.

self-centered until age five or so. Their view of the world expands to include how other people interact. They will remark on how someone treats someone else: Tommy pinches all the other kids, so he's mean; Marissa brought cupcakes to class today, so she's nice. At the same time, they have also grown acutely aware of how other people respond to them.

Your child's world has grown so much larger, yet Mommy and Daddy still reign supreme. To him, you are everything. This is why he measures himself by how you treat him. He knows no other means of testing his self-image, and, as I mentioned previously, his thinking is still largely formed by the emotional "input"—the words, actions, attitudes—of others. He is not capable of thinking, *I'm great and deserving of happiness because my mom loves me, spends time talking to me and playing with me, and hugs me a lot.* However, he feels these emotions very strongly, and he associates Mom's behavior toward him with the positive feelings. Similarly, he will not tell himself, *I am not valuable or lovable because Daddy rarely plays with me and Mommy is too busy for me and I hardly ever get hugs or attention.* Yet he will make an association between the behavior of those closest to him and how he feels about himself. For the rest of his life, he will be inclined to seek out people and situations that reinforce the self-image his parents sketch for him now. This burgeoning awareness increases your preschooler's understanding of other people's behavior and makes him especially sensitive to what you and your ex do, feel, and say in his presence.

How PRESCHOOLERS EXPERIENCE DIVORCE

If a preschooler could write, here's what he might say:

Dear Diary,
G.I. Joe's escaped again today. He's been telling the guards he'd leave. Bo Peep is really sad, because she wanted G.I. Joe to stay. Bo Peep's

MAKE SURE YOUR PRESCHOOLER UNDERSTANDS THAT . . .

✔ *She is not at fault for the divorce.* "It is Mommy and Daddy's fault—not yours—that we cannot live together anymore."

✔ *Nothing she did, thought, felt, or said led to the divorce.* "A divorce happens because of something mommies and daddies do. Nothing you did, thought, felt, or said had anything to do with it. We will always love you."

✔ *She is and will always be safe.* "We will take care of you and keep you safe, even though we are not living all together in one house. Someone will always be here for you," or "I will always take care of you and keep you safe. Grandma, Aunt Jill, and our friend Zach will also be here for you. Someone will always be here for you."

✔ *She will be able and is invited to maintain contact with her other parent (if this is true) and discuss what she would like (a phone call before school, and so on).* "You will be with both of us a lot." (Outline the specifics that you are certain of: visits, phone calls, et cetera.)

✔ *It is not bad or wrong to feel sad or upset.* "It's okay to feel sad or mad and to tell us any way you're feeling, even if you are mad at me or Mommy/Daddy."

✔ *You will always be there for her.* "We will always listen to you and try to help you however we can."

In cases of abandonment, see "The Abandoned Child," page 258.

sheep are sad and scared. They saw Bo Peep crying and asked her why, but she said she wasn't crying. The sheep keep asking when they will see G.I. Joe again, and Bo Peep said she doesn't know. When will the sheep see him and when will it all be okay again? I feel alone.

The preschooler's enthusiasm, determination, and occasional stubbornness can mislead parents into believing that his sense of independence is stronger than it is. In fact, he can be acutely, even painfully, sensitive to criticism, rejection, and punishment. The preschooler's preoccupation with his own needs and wants is a normal part of his development. There is no point in reprimanding your preschooler because he acts as if the world revolves around him and that everything in it belongs to him; in his eyes, it truly does. Your job is to gently teach him about how his actions affect others.

MISPLACED GUILT

One result of this self-centeredness is that children actually believe that they are the force or the cause behind much of what happens in their world. Just as Amy may think that she caused her favorite television program to come on by waving her toy magic wand, she may also believe that Daddy left home because he was angry at her for spilling her milk that morning. Children are more comfortable assuming blame and thinking they caused something to happen than believing that the world is a place where bad things "just happen" without rhyme or reason. Over the long term, however, this misplaced sense of responsibility can create unmanageable, overwhelming guilt, which is detrimental to a child's budding self-image. Parents should be alert to signs their preschooler may be harboring such beliefs; watch out, for example, for sudden behavioral changes; your child may apologize a lot for no good reason, or become a "supergood" kid, doing a lot of nice things, like offering to clean the house. Guilt is a common problem for children this age, because they do see their role as the primary "cause" of the "effect" so literally. Be prepared to repeatedly let your child know that she is not at fault for your breakup.

Because these feelings are so common and your child may not be able to fully express herself verbally, you might reassure her by saying, "You know, some kids feel bad because they think they made their parents split up. I want you to know that you did not make this happen." (See the activity "The Life of Riley," page 236.)

PERMISSION TO LOVE BOTH PARENTS

Like all children, preschoolers need to be sure they have the permission of each parent to love the other. Be aware of the subtle, nonverbal messages you send that could put your child in an emotional bind. Sarah would tell her daughter Cathy that it was okay to phone Daddy after dinner, but then would act sad or aloof after her daughter got off the phone smiling. *When I talk to Daddy, it makes Mommy sad,* Cathy reasoned, though probably unconsciously. Soon Cathy stopped asking to call Daddy and refused to get on the phone when he called.

Like all parents, Sarah needs to send very clear, explicit messages to her child encouraging contact with her other parent: "I want you to talk to Daddy. He loves you so much and wants to spend time with you." The nonresidential parent can reinforce this message by expressing how happy he is to talk to the child: "I love talking to you. I miss you, but I'm so happy when we can talk, even if it's only for a minute. You can call me

HOW TO EXPLAIN THE DIVORCE TO YOUR PRESCHOOLER

What is divorce?

"Divorce is a grown-up thing that mommies and daddies do when they make each other very sad when they are together. The changes that happen can be upsetting for children, but we're always here, and we love you. That will never change."

Why did it happen?

"Mommies and daddies make big mistakes sometimes and hurt each other. We're very sorry that this happened and that it is hurting you. But it is all Mommy and Daddy's fault."

When will the divorce be over?

"Mommy and Daddy will always live in different places but will always love you and care for you."

Will we still be a family?

"Yes. Even though Mommy and Daddy are getting a divorce, you will always be part of us. We both still love you and always will."

anytime, and if I can't talk that minute, I'll be sure to call you back as soon as I can."

To send the right messages, you have to watch not only your words but your tone of voice, your manner, and your body language whenever you speak to your child about your ex-spouse or the divorce. And don't limit your self-monitoring to only those times you're speaking directly to her; beginning around this age, kids pick up and incorporate much of what they overhear in adult conversation. Work to be consistent and positive in your approach to your ex. Even though it might take great self-control to bite your tongue, it's a small sacrifice considering what's at stake for your child and her relationship with your ex.

GENDER IDENTIFICATION

Children this age begin noticing different types and genders of people and developing a sense of their own gender by interacting with both their opposite- and same-sex parent. Divorce can disrupt the crucial interaction children need with each parent, which is why they need as much access as possible to both.

Before this, your preschooler viewed his parents as essentially two of a kind. Now he recognizes and learns from each parent's individual differences, paying special attention to the same-sex parent, from whom he is absorbing what it means to be a boy (or, in her case, a girl). It is not unusual for preschoolers to develop a close attachment to their opposite-sex parent and wish to spend time alone with that parent. When this occurs, the same-sex parent shouldn't take it personally. There will be times when the same children will draw closer to the same-sex parent for the identical reason of sensing and defining what their gender means to them.

Even if your child's other parent had only limited involvement with her before, she still needs to have a consistent, ongoing relationship with that parent now. If your ex-spouse cannot or will not be involved in your preschooler's life, make sure you provide her with opportunities to be around caring people from whom she can learn these important lessons. Grandparents, aunts and uncles, older siblings and cousins, and adult friends can help fill the gap. That said, be careful not to use your child's need for a role model as an excuse to jump into a new romantic relationship (see chapter 15). The rejection your child will feel if you break up will far outweigh the positive benefits of adult companionship.

An early scene. *In depicting himself as considerably smaller than the other figures in his drawing, this four-year-old demonstrates an early ability to show relative physical size. Also note one family member floating upside down in the middle of the page. In older children's art, floating can be an indication of instability, but that's not necessarily the case with a younger child. One challenge of looking at the work of very young children is determining the emotional context of the drawing. This is difficult to do without being present as the child draws and speaking with him about the details of his work as he creates it.*

All in the details. *Although these figures still appear very primitive, they also reveal this young four-year-old's budding appreciation of detail. While the basic figure, like those of younger children, consists of a head connected to legs without a trunk, we now see arms, noses, ears, hair, and some attempt to draw shading into the clothing. Also note that this boy has placed himself in the center, between his parents.*

IMAGINATION AND FEARS

Unlike younger children, preschoolers can and do imagine possible future events. But unlike older children, they don't have the ability to counteract their fears with reason. Because they cannot help but view every event from a "what about me?" perspective, on some level they will interpret a parent's leaving the home as a rejection of themselves. Every major event in the divorce is, in the preschool mind, a springboard from which intense and scary fears take flight:

> *If one parent can leave me,* she reasons, *the other can, too. If they stop loving each other, they might stop loving me. If I have to leave my old house, will I have to leave all my toys, my friends, my pets, too?*

Remember: The preschooler's divorce-related fears are not limited to the divorce but extend through her entire world. Once she understands that Daddy doesn't live with her anymore, you can anticipate her wondering and worrying about everything else: *Will Mommy and Daddy still love me? What about Grandma and Grandpa? Will I still see my favorite baby-sitter, Meredith? Will I get a new doctor? And will he give me bad shots?* Older kids often say, "I am worried that something will happen to me and Mom, and Dad won't be there," and there is reason to believe that younger children also feel this. Change is difficult for everyone, most especially for a little child who is just learning to trust.

DENIAL

Children this age may also apply their newfound powers of imagination to denial. They may tell themselves, "Daddy really is going to come home soon," or—the most common fantasy—"Mommy and Daddy are going to get married again." Older preschoolers may believe, *If I'm really good, Mommy and Daddy will get back together,* while younger ones may keep pretending nothing has changed.

Children this age can hold on to denial tenaciously; it is, after all, a defense against the pain of their loss. When your child says, "When

A BOX WITH A VIEW

Tear or cut out pictures from magazines and make a collage, discussing why each image is important, what it means to your child. Or use these pictures to cover a shoebox that becomes a child's private box used to hold important things.

Variation: Have your child cut out pictures from magazines that represent things he likes and dislikes, then separate each into separate folders, piles, or boxes marked LIKES and DISLIKES.

Variation: Have your child cut out faces that show different types of feelings and make a "feeling-face" collage.

Don't criticize his choice of pictures but rather comment on them in a nonjudgmental tone: "Wow, that lion looks ferocious" or "That family looks so happy."

PURPOSE: These activities give you a glimpse into your child's private world and also help your child to identify, name, and voice his feelings.

Daddy comes home tonight," or "I know that you'll be back together for Easter," listen with your heart. Rather than "correct" him by saying, "Your daddy isn't coming home tonight," or "You should know by now that Mom and I aren't getting back together," show him that you understand. Once again, empathize and generalize: "You know, honey, a lot of kids wish their parents would get back together again, but this is not going to happen with me and your father. It's normal to wish and pretend sometimes that Mommy and Daddy are back together like we used to be. I'm sorry; your dad and I tried very hard to stay together, but we couldn't make it happen."

ANGER

Many children will feel angry at one or both parents but be terrified of expressing their emotions directly. (After all, they may fear their anger caused their parents' breakup.) These children often displace their anger and become aggressive or mean to playmates and others. Or they may begin to hide all of their emotions in order to keep the anger at bay. Parents shouldn't be surprised when that aggression and anger are directed at the "wrong" people, like stepsiblings or a parent's new significant other.

While you must respond to unacceptable behavior by setting limits and enforcing appropriate discipline, keep in mind that it is very likely that it is you or the other parent your child is really angry at. Like any emotion, anger can be overwhelming. Your daughter can blame herself and feel anger toward herself *and* be angry at one or both parents for breaking up or for lacking the strength to stay together despite her "bad" behavior. It's easy to see why many children of divorce feel so angry and so confused. For most parents, this is not easy to face, and you may have to remind yourself that your child is angry not because she doesn't love you or she thinks you're a bad parent. Your child is angry because, in her mind—and perhaps in truth—you "caused" the divorce.

Uncomfortable as it may be, you must be willing to provide a safe place for your child to express directly to you the anger she feels toward you (see also the box "Techniques for Dealing with Anger," page 37). Always remember the following:

- Teach your child the words he needs to express his anger. For younger children, designate a piece of clothing or a hand signal to express the need to talk

- Use noncharged language that is inviting and not accusing

- Speak slowly and deliberately, and encourage your child to do the same

- Mirror and identify your child's emotions

- Identify the cause of your child's feelings

- Empathize with your child

- Include your child in the problem-solving process

- Do not allow unacceptable behavior to pass unchallenged, even if it occurs as the result of anger.

First, this opens the lines of communication and lets her know that you are still very much there for her, that her anger toward you will not push you away. Second, when your child expresses her anger to you, she feels less need to rechannel it toward others. Finally, listening to your child provides a valuable opportunity to discuss what's really happening and the changes your family is experiencing.

REGRESSION

Despite all the outward signs of maturity, a preschooler is still a baby in many ways. It is not uncommon for him to announce that he even wants to be a baby again. Some kids may regress to behaviors such as having toileting accidents, wetting the bed, whining, using a babyish tone of voice, or thumb sucking. An unusual or dramatic change in behavior is a sign of stress. Consult your pediatrician to rule out any underlying physical causes and get advice on how to handle the problem. Remember that even children who are not dealing with the stress of divorce sometimes feel a need to go back to the baby they were before. This "nostalgia" is often expressed in demands for extra cuddles and hugs and flights of clinginess. Regard these demands as healthy expressions, indulge them, and help your child give voice to his feelings:

> "You've been feeling a little sad and lonely because of all the changes around here. I understand, and I have plenty of hugs waiting for you."
>
> "Sometimes we like to feel younger so that our parents will take care of us. Sometimes, I even want my mommy to take care of me. But you don't need to act any differently to get my attention. Let's just talk about how you feel."
>
> "Sometimes when somebody feels all alone, talking to somebody else about their feelings makes that alone feeling go away. I feel better when I talk about my feelings, and I'll bet you will too. I'm here to listen."

In doing so, you teach your child that her feelings matter and that she can count on you to respond to and comfort her. Acknowledge her feelings of dependency. At the same time, doing things that help your preschooler develop a sense of responsibility—such as caring for a pet, helping you cook, or "baby-sitting" a real baby under your close supervision—can help your child recognize how grown-up she can be.

A special note: If your preschooler was recently using the toilet but has regressed to diapers, you may want to give him some time to adjust to the changes before you reintroduce toilet teaching.

HOW PARENTS CAN HELP PRESCHOOLERS

THINGS 2 (OR MORE) TO DO

EXAGGERATION

During this game everyone takes turns exaggerating something that is otherwise difficult for him or her to do. Parents can play, too:

Ten-year-old Tracy was uncomfortable saying "I love you," so she said, "Oh I love you, you wonderful person." Her father, Hal, had difficulty hugging, so he gave a big bear hug.

PURPOSE: We need safe opportunities to test and try out new behaviors that we are uncomfortable with. By exaggerating the behaviors, each person gets a chance to try it out in a fun way.

One advantage preschoolers have over younger children is their budding ability to talk about their feelings and thoughts. While it is less likely your preschooler will be able to fully express her emotions, children this age engage in a lot of fantasy play and often talk to themselves as they do. (See chapter 2.) Tune in as often as you can. As with younger children, your preschooler needs the comfort of your presence and your involvement in his life, but he can also find support in his expanded social environment of siblings, extended family, baby-sitters, teachers, and friends.

• *If possible, be sure your child has frequent and regular contact with your ex-spouse.* Most preschoolers enjoy talking on the telephone, even if for just a minute, so aim for a daily phone conversation with the nonresidential parent, if possible. For example, your ex might call every evening at bedtime and read your child a story over the phone. In addition, the nonresidential parent can send (via fax or e-mail) messages or drawings and make audiocassettes and videocassettes of himself reading a story or speaking to the child. Exactly what you do as a nonresidential parent is not as important as the fact that your child knows that you are thinking of her each and every day.

• *Never criticize your ex in front of your child.* Be sure that your words are consistent with your nonverbal cues. This may take some conscientious self-monitoring on your part, but doing so will help your child's self-esteem, reduce his confusion about the divorce and, as he grows older, his ability to use your negative attitude toward your ex to be manipulative.

• *Maintain a calm, positive attitude in your child's presence.* Ultimately, children depend on and draw from their parents' happiness and strength. This is not to say you can't feel sad or angry at times; that's inevitable. However, children need the security of a calm and generally positive environment. No one can do more to set the desired tone than you can.

• *Establish and stick to a normal daily routine.* Preschoolers often become obsessive about how things are done. Respect your child's personal routines and private rituals, such as tucking her in with a special song or leaving certain stuffed animals in specific places. They comfort and give your child a sense of order and control, something she needs right now. Be sure that other caregivers understand the nature and importance of these routines and request that they accommodate them, too.

• *Protect your preschooler's "personal environment."* Make sure she has her favorite toys and possessions, especially if you are relocating. Send them along with your child on visitation (and send along a tactfully worded checklist if your ex is forgetful) and make sure all items come home again.

• *Maintain consistency.* The preschool years can be trying times, and preschoolers under stress are likely to act out. Typical acting-out behaviors include not listening or responding to direct requests like "Take your shoes to your room," refusing to sleep in his own bed, having fits of screaming and crying, and behaving aggressively toward parents and playmates. These are the first years when a child can really understand discipline and the concepts of rules and appropriate behavior. Learning to master one set of rules and standards is challenging enough for a preschooler; don't burden and confuse her with two. No matter how strongly one of you may feel about subjects such as the proper bedtime, acceptable table manners, and the use of time-outs, your child will be happier, more relaxed, and more willing to follow the rules if they are few, clear, and consistent with each parent, even though parenting styles may differ. [See the box "How to Build a Coparenting Relationship, (Even When You Think You Can't)" page 12, for tips on what to do when you and your ex's styles really clash.]

• *Anticipate problems with eating, sleeping, and acting out.* Your child may also regress to such behaviors as bed-wetting, soiling, thumb-sucking, and increased clinginess. As always, consult your pediatrician to rule out physical causes. Remain lovingly firm about behaviors that are not acceptable, but generous in offering reassurance, support, and understanding.

• *Encourage your child to talk about her feelings.* Use books, toys, and videos or television programs to open the discussion. It's important to remember that your child does not have to speak about the divorce specifically, nor should you try to push a conversation in that direction. If your child is talking about feeling angry, for example, the simple fact that she has named and is expressing that emotion is very helpful.

• *Talk to the other caregivers in your child's life (baby-sitters, teachers, day-care workers) about the divorce and ask how she is responding.* Don't be surprised to learn that your child behaves differently around others than she does at home. She may be unusually whiny and difficult with you at home because she feels secure that you won't leave her but be quiet and compliant at school or with the other parent. Also be on the watch for the sudden onset of new behaviors, like aggression, withdrawal, or a sudden lack of pleasure in activities and people she used to enjoy. Let everyone with whom your preschooler spends time know that you want to be informed of any changes in attitude or behavior and then discuss these changes with your child in a loving, nonthreatening manner.

• *Understand that your preschooler may feel very possessive of you and feel threatened by the sudden appearance of new people in your life.* (I address the issue of parents' dating in chapter 15.) Don't be surprised or angry if your preschooler seems to hate anyone with whom he feels he is sharing you. Try to see it from his point of view. He feels he's already lost one parent, and he's fearful of losing you as well at a time when he needs you more than ever. Reassure him in very clear, concrete terms: "You and I will always have a special relationship that no one can stop. Let's talk about how I can help you feel loved and connected to me."

THE MIRROR GAME

Young children love making faces in the mirror. After bathtime, for example, you and your child might stand before a mirror and take turns making faces: happy, sad, angry, disappointed, and so on. Take this opportunity to talk about what the faces mean and what people or events inspire them.

Variation: One person closes his eyes, then touches the other's face and tries to determine the feelings behind her facial expression.

PURPOSE: Helping younger kids identify their emotions is a first step to their learning to express themselves verbally and use sentences such as "I am feeling angry because…" or "I am happy whenever…" From there, parents can encourage their children by asking, "What would make you have a happy face?" or "What might cause you to have an angry face?" For many children, playing this game allows them to safely vent strong emotions.

LOOK INTO MY EYES

Have a staring contest (staring into each other's eyes, trying not to blink) with your child.

PURPOSE: Eye contact is important when communicating and trying to connect to another person. If your child or you are uncomfortable making eye contact, have a series of staring contests. Let the winner decide what you're having for dinner, which video you're going to watch, or some other fun thing to do.

Q Dear Gary,

Last year my wife and I separated after a rough period in our marriage. Then we were sure we would divorce, but now—after some counseling and careful thought—we've decided to try living together again. Our three kids (three, five, and eight) have been through a lot already. How should we explain my moving back? And what should we do if it doesn't work out this time?

A Make sure it works. See a family therapist, read books, make correcting your past mistakes your first priority. It is difficult enough on children when parents separate. Reunions that don't work add to the stress. Often, couples try again to no avail because they never created any real plan for change. Do your whole family a favor and get help this time.

Be straight with your children:

"Daddy/Mommy and I want to try living together again.

"This time we are going to practice not fighting and being much kinder toward each other. We really want this to work out, but it is totally up to Daddy/Mommy and me. You kids can't do anything to make it work better or worse. Our marriage has nothing to do with how you guys act. So even though we know it's been rough on you, we're going to try again. We don't know if it will work out or not, but we promise you we'll try very hard."

Notice how this message takes the pressure off the kids. They won't feel they've got to walk around on pins and needles for the next month, afraid that their needs or behavior will somehow make it difficult for you and your spouse to get along. Every week or two, hold a family meeting (see the box "Family Meetings," page 400) so the children can express how they are coping and you can talk about the status of the marriage. ("Things are a little better and we are committed to continue trying for a couple of weeks at least." Or "Things are going much better, and we have decided that we will stay together.")

If it doesn't work out, send the same sensitive message you would when you tell children you are separating. However, add to it that it is definitely over and there is no chance either of you will try again. It may sound harsh, but it gives the children the ability to move on to the next stage of coping with divorce rather than being stuck with the fervent but false hope that their parents will reunite yet again.

Q Dear Gary,

My four-year-old boy is having a very hard time with our separation. It's almost impossible for me to go anywhere—even from one room to another—without him running after me, holding me, and often crying. I keep explaining to him that I'm here and I love him and so on, but it's like he doesn't even hear me. Obviously, he's worried about being abandoned. I'm just not sure what to say or do to really get through to him.

A Your son needs to know he has a safe place to express these fears instead of clinging to you out of desperation. Create an animal family with him and at some point have a family member leave the child animal (see chapter 2). This will help him discuss his concerns in the "safe" context of play.

Also talk to him directly about his fears. Do not "rescue." (See the "Rescuing," box page 44.) Hear him out before you rush to comfort him. Sometimes, assuming his fear and then responding with your reassurance ("I'll always be here") don't give him the opportunity to clearly think through how he feels and why or how to express it. You can open up the dialogue by saying something like "When daddies leave a home, sometimes children are afraid that the mommy will leave next and the child will have no one to take care of him. I would probably feel like that if I were you. Is that how you feel sometimes?" Then ask him what the two of you might do together to help him feel less afraid. Promising him you will talk about it every day at the same time (bedtime or breakfast, for instance) can alleviate his worry. Giving him a photo of you or a special small object that can represent your love (a ring, key chain, and so on) will comfort him.

Finally, consider the possibility that he may be acting this way because of other valid concerns. What *does* happen when you're not there? Children around four and five years of age begin to wonder about and fear death. He may be thinking, *What if Mommy is in a car accident and can't pick me up at school?* Calmly explain to him that if for any reason (don't harp on death or illness) you cannot be there, someone he knows—the other parent, a grandparent, relative, neighbor, friend—will always be home with him.

A reward system might come in handy right now, too. Give him rewards for completing tasks like cleaning his room, picking up his toys, watering the plants, or feeding the cat while you are out. This will give him something positive to focus on while you're out of sight.

CHAPTER 5

The Discovery of Self: Understanding Your Six- to Eight-Year-Old

This is an age of self-discovery and transition—from a world dominated by home and parents to one dramatically broadened by school and social interaction with peers. Your six- to eight-year-old is learning to choose his own friends, take pride in his new accomplishments, and become his own person. While a child this age may still experience moments of frustration and anger, he is better able to follow instructions and is very capable of expressing his emotions, fears, and problems verbally. He longs to be independent, and now has the skills, the intelligence, and the opportunities to try. Compared to a child just a year younger, a six-year-old seems the model of self-sufficiency.

In both children's literature and books on child psychology, six is often depicted as a magical age. Up until now, most children learned without being consciously aware that they were learning. Now, for the first time, your six-year-old seeks mastery and accomplishment in school, on the playground, and anyplace else she is among peers. She is also beginning to judge herself in relation to others. ("I am smarter than Grace." "Danny runs faster than I do.")

Starting around now, her peer group takes on greater importance in shaping her self-image. She will learn for the first time the lessons she will carry through life: what it means to be a follower and to be a leader, when to stick up for one's beliefs and when to back down, and what it means to fit in, or not. And, more important, she will confront and negotiate many of these passages with little or no direct input from you or any other adult.

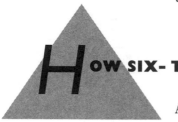

How SIX- TO EIGHT-YEAR-OLDS EXPERIENCE DIVORCE

A child this age might write:

> Dear Diary,
> It's been many days since Daddy left. I'm so sad he's not here to tuck me in. I miss him. Why did he leave? Mommy is sad too. I don't understand why all this happened. I love my mommy and daddy. Why don't they love each other? They always used to fight. I wish I could've been better. I needed so much time-out, and Mommy had to spend so much time helping me with my homework. Daddy was so tired when he was home, but I still would cry unless he came in to tuck me in and say prayers with me. Why'd I do that? It's hard

MAKE SURE YOUR SIX- TO EIGHT-YEAR-OLD UNDERSTANDS THAT . . .

✔ *He is not at fault for the divorce.* "This is our decision, and no one but the two of us is at fault."

✔ *Nothing he did, thought, felt, or said led to the divorce.* "Nothing you did or thought caused this to happen. We tried, but we can't stay together because we hurt each other too much."

✔ *He is and will always be safe.* "We will continue to make sure you are taken care of, as we always have."

✔ *He will be able to maintain contact with his other parent (if this is true).* "You will have plenty of time to see and talk to each of us" or "We are going to try to make sure you visit and talk with Mom/Dad as much as possible." (Outline the details.)

✔ *It's not bad or wrong to feel sad, angry, or upset.* "You probably have many feelings about the divorce. None of them is wrong. It's okay to feel many different things, whether it's sad, mad, relieved, or confused."

✔ *You will always be there for him.* "We are here to help you. Talk to us whenever you want to."

✔ *Many children's parents divorce.* "This happens to a lot of families. We'll have to look for ways to help each other."

✔ *Many kids wish that their parents were together.* "It's okay and normal to wish that your mother/father and I would get back together. But I want you to understand that this won't happen with us because we already tried really hard."

✔ *He will always have both parents and remain in touch with his extended family—grandparents, aunts, uncles, cousins (if this is true).* "You will always be able to talk to and visit your grandparents and everyone else in our family. Divorce doesn't take away your family."

✔ *You understand and appreciate the changes he's going through.* "It can be tough getting used to new things. Your mother/father and I will do all we can to help you."

now. But Mommy and Daddy tell me it'll be better because at least they won't fight anymore. Maybe after they see they stopped fighting, they will get back together again. I'll be better, too.

Children of this age group usually feel intensely sad about their parents' divorce. They begin to worry about feeling different from their peers; it's also the first stage at which they can disguise, hide, and deflect their true feelings. The fact that they are beginning to understand that they are separate from their parents, while at the same time discovering the reality of divorce, separation, and death, can make them sometimes feel especially vulnerable and alone.

PARENTAL IMAGE AS SELF-IMAGE

Despite all their personal accomplishments, children this age base much of their self-image on how they and others perceive their parents. A child desperately needs to see the good in his parents in order to help him define the good in himself. Just as he draws strength from knowing a parent is well thought of, so too he can be hurt by any hint that he or she is not. A child perceives one parent's—or any other person's—criticism of a parent as a criticism of him, too.

This close association and dependence on his parents also account for why children this age rarely admit feeling angry at a parent and instead will often exhibit displaced anger, striking out at a sibling, stepparent, or friend. In the Sandcastles Program groups, for example, we see a very dramatic difference between children this age and those at nine or older. For example, even if seven-year-old Alyssa can recite a list of grievances against, say, her father who abandoned the family, she probably won't express her anger directly toward him, if she mentions it at all. In contrast, her nine-year-old brother, Alex, will be very vocal, specific, and definite in his criticism of his dad.

THE NEED TO FIT IN

In this stage, children are truly social beings, and most of them crave friendships and want to be well liked. While older kids may fear that they won't be accepted because their parents are divorced, younger kids simply see the divorce as something that makes them "different" from their friends. That alone can cause anxiety and pain at this important stage of social growth. Children this age may be prone to blaming every disappointment on the divorce, something parents should listen for and correct whenever possible. The problem for most parents is that a child this age can't or won't simply come out and say, "I feel different from the other kids at school." More typical is a roundabout, indirect expression or gesture.

An incomplete picture. This eight-year-old girl views her family before divorce in a typically happy light: parents are holding hands, everyone is smiling, and she has drawn herself linked to her dog and younger brother. Her "after" drawing shows an inability to redefine her family and life. The one figure she has drawn is awkward and distorted; she literally doesn't know how to complete the picture.

Eight-year-old Dominic's mother was perplexed when he announced on Monday morning that he wasn't going to play in that night's big game. When Denise asked why, he shrugged and replied, "Don't feel like it." Denise wisely deduced that Dominic's dad's calling last night to say he would be out of town on business until Wednesday might have something to do with it.

"You know, Evan's dad is also going to be out of town this week, and Louis's father is working late, too. They won't be there, either, but Evan and Louis will still be playing."

"Yeah, but they have good reasons for not being there. If you guys weren't divorced, Dad would be there, too!"

Denise quickly addressed the real issues. First, she acknowledged Dominic's disappointment: "Dominic, I know you are disappointed that Dad can't be there tonight. It must really hurt." She also helped Dominic see that even though she and his father were divorced, his father also had what Dominic viewed as a "normal" reason to miss the game: "I think you know that even if Dad and I were together, he would still be going out of town for business, and sometimes he would have to miss your games, even though he didn't want to. Adults can't always get their way all the time, either." Denise also reminded Dominic of how much his father was around: "You know your dad really loves to watch you play. He's gone to every game this season." Then she offered Dominic a way to involve his father in the evening's big event: "I'll call Dad's secretary and get the number where he'll be staying. If you'd like to, after the game tonight, you can call him long-distance and tell him how it went."

As unrealistic as Denise's calm, positive attitude might strike you, imagine how wonderful it is for Dominic, and how devastating it would have been if his mother had joined him in blaming the divorce and then criticized his father.

GUILT

Although they are in many ways grown-up, children this age may still believe that they are somehow to blame for the divorce. As paradoxical as it may sound, children are often more comfortable blaming themselves for the divorce, since doing so at least gives a reason to the otherwise inexplicable. Children are more comfortable feeling guilty and in control than they are feeling blameless and at the mercy of random events. In assuming blame, a child also protects the sense of security he derives from

HOW TO EXPLAIN THE DIVORCE TO YOUR SIX- TO EIGHT-YEAR-OLD

What is divorce?

"Divorce is a grown-up thing that mommies and daddies do when they are very sad and cannot make things happier together anymore. It means that we will no longer be married to each other, but we will always be your parents."

Why did it happen?

Some possibilities include:

"We didn't listen to each other enough. You know how sometimes you want to say something so much you don't even hear what the other person is saying? That's how your mother/father and I got to be. We cared more about what we wanted to say and not enough about what the other person was saying."

"We didn't take the time to think *How will he/she feel about this?* before we said or did something that hurt him/her or made him/her angry. That was very unfair."

"We fought too much and didn't learn how to talk to each other about our feelings without being angry and hurting each other."

"We didn't know how to stop arguing and walk away from a fight."

Will we still be a family?

"Yes. Even though Mommy and Daddy are getting a divorce, you will always be part of us. We both still love you and always will. You and Mommy/Daddy, and you and I will always be families. But Mommy and Daddy will not be in a family together, even though we will both belong to you."

What will happen to me?

"You will be able to see both me and your mother/father a lot." (Then spell out custody and visitation arrangements as clearly and in as much detail as you can. See chapter 12.)

believing his parents are infallible and "godlike." He also gives himself reason to believe that he can undo the divorce and "fix" his parents' marriage.

BELIEF THAT THE DIVORCE WILL "END" AND THE PARENTS WILL REUNITE

Six-, seven-, and eight-year-olds aren't the only children of divorce who cling to the fantasy that their parents will one day reunite. Decades after their parents split up, even thirty-five-year-olds may hold the same wish. The difference between them is that younger

A cup of tears. The eight- or nine-year-old boy who drew this seems to identify with his mother (they have the same "saucer" eyes), yet he stands closer to his father. The broken heart between his parents is smiling (like Mom) and crying (like Dad), possibly a sign of mixed emotions. The glass under the heart may represent an abundance of tears.

children don't fully understand divorce, and this, coupled with their faith in you to "make things better," can keep this dream alive. This may be the only way your child can express his desire for the divorce-related conflict and change to end. He may continue to feel this way until and sometimes even after one of you remarries and/or has other children.

EMOTIONAL NEEDS

Your child may often seem so independent and self-sufficient that it's easy to underestimate her continuing emotional needs. Although they may be less likely to ask for it directly, kids this age still need the comfort and reassurance of a warm hug or a special, quiet time spent alone with a parent.

By their nature, younger children are more strongly affected by others' emotions and the general atmosphere, and so the emotional fall-out of parental conflict is often direct and obvious. A four-year-old, for instance, cannot help but cry, whine, or become cranky when parents are tense or arguing. In contrast, children this age can usually distin-

A missing mother. The absence of a mother coupled with sad faces, large "shocked" eyes, and the boy lying on a bed or stretcher may be this eight- to ten-year-old boy's call for help.

JOYFUL BOX

Any large cardboard box will do, though one from a large appliance works best. (You can also take a few large boxes and fasten them together with wide strapping-type tape to make a larger structure.) Have your child decorate the outside with pictures of things that make her feel good. Or create a tent using blankets and chairs. Make a rule that only positive, joyful thoughts, stories, and music can be brought into the box. Get books about children who work through feelings and then feel better. Popular childrens' books series (Sesame Street, Mr. Rogers, and the Berenstein Bears, to name a few) include titles dealing with not only divorce but a range of related emotions (anger, for instance) and events (like moving, changing schools). (See also "Recommended Reading," page 441.) Read them in the box or tent; talk about choosing things that make us feel better when we're sad.

Variation: Make a nest: Let your child take an area of his room—a corner, inside a large closet, under his bed—to create a cozy spot where he can be surrounded by blankets, sheets, stuffed animals, pillows, and other comforting things. Let this be his private spot, where he can be alone and not be encouraged to talk unless he wants to.

PURPOSE: Creating a special "feeling place" enables your child to develop coping and self-comforting skills and get into a life-long habit of searching for positive things to offset the negative. After discussing anger and sadness, the child can think about good things in his joyful box.

guish between conflicts that directly concern them ("Mom is angry because I didn't clean my room") and those that don't ("Mom is angry at Dad"). She can recognize that her parents' argument is between them, but she is not yet mature enough to completely tune it out. The mere fact that they are arguing will make her feel sad and anxious.

HIDDEN SADNESS

Even though most children at this age feel a great deal of sadness about divorce, a surprising number of them will manage to carry on as if nothing bothers them. This may be a result of depression, denial, or a general emotional withdrawal. Even very conscientious parents can misread this "hidden sadness" and assume things are fine. After all, they may reason, little Charlie is busy with school, friends, soccer, and his model trains—he seems fine. The operative word here is "seems," and parents should be on the lookout for signs of withdrawal, depression, and denial, particularly if they find themselves thinking of their child's recent behavior as "too good to be true."

IS YOUR CHILD HIDING SADNESS?

Your child may be keeping his sadness hidden if he:

- doesn't mention the separation or the fact that the other parent is not around,
- seems overly eager to help you,
- often writes notes or makes statements to the effect "I'm here for you" or "I'll *always* love you,"
- seems not to care if parents fight or if one misses a scheduled visitation,
- shows a general lack of emotion,
- is less enthusiastic about people, things, and activities he enjoyed before,
- suddenly shows an attraction to sad movies, books, or news stories.

Gently broach the topic of sadness and explain that it's normal and even healthy to feel sad over the situation. These kinds of statements give children complete permission to express their sadness. Make sure they know you will always help them with any of their feelings.

IDDEN ISSUES

Children this age have the ability to talk about their feelings and thoughts. On the plus side, there's a lot you can do just by listening and talking to your child. On the downside, your child may be surprisingly adept at keeping his true feelings to himself. Seven-year-old Devon may decide it's better not to talk about his sadness, reasoning that the last time he did, Mommy got sad, too. Or eight-year-old Megan might express her feelings very indirectly by talking about some other child's divorce, something that is very common among siblings. One divorced mother who shared a close, communicative relationship with her two children told me in a group setting how, every time she and her eight-year-old daughter discussed the changes in their family, the conversation always focused on her daughter's concerns about her five-year-old brother. To all outward appearances, her daughter was taking the divorce in stride. This mother wisely perceived that her daughter was doing two things: choosing not to talk directly about her own feelings by focusing on her brother and, in some instances, attributing her own thoughts and feelings to her brother.

One set of letters from a Sandcastles workbook illustrates a child's inability to express herself directly. An eight-year-old girl wrote:

> Dear Mom,
> Some kids in the classroom asked and said some of these things about divorce, like "I don't like you guys getting a divorce, but in a way I'm happy about it," "Why do you argue with the other parent on the phone?" These are things I want to tell you.

> Dear Dad,
> Some kids in the classroom asked and said some of these things about divorce, like "I would like to see you more often." These are things I want to tell you in this letter.

A common variation on this theme is the child who becomes fixated on another family's divorce or other tragedy. When eight-year-old Benny wonders at length about what will happen to his classmate Tyler, whose father just died, or his cousin Nicole, whose mother abandoned her family, don't dismiss this as idle chatter or gossip. Listen carefully, calmly mirror what he says, gently ask questions, and then provide the most reassuring, honest answers you can. Odds are that he is really talking about himself in a way that feels safer to him than simply asking you "When you and Daddy break up, what will happen to me?" Remember to remind your child that every family is different, that you will always love him and always be there for him.

Your child is still involved in fantasy play but may be more self-conscious about it and play out any divorce-related issues indirectly. At different times in the months since Benny's dad moved out, his mother has overheard him playing out variations on the same scene: once

Feeling overpowered. *This six-year-old boy may be struggling with his sense of his mother's strong personality; she is centrally placed, larger than the other figures, and is the only one with hands. In the picture of "mommy and daddy not living together anymore," it's clear that it was she who angrily ordered Dad out (note the door). The mother's legs are noteworthy in both drawings; in the first, she has arms but no legs, in the second she has what appear to be four legs but no arms. Taken together, these pictures convey the boy's struggle to determine who is in control and what will happen next.*

Gumby's horse Pokey told him to "get lost," another time the two female Power Rangers took away all the male Rangers' special powers, and when he and his friends play soldiers, Benny often picks out one soldier whom the others kick out of the army. Observant parents can glean a great deal about what their children are thinking and feeling by observing the products of their imagination: the artwork, stories, and essays they write for school or for entertainment (see chapter 2). As they grow, children also reveal a lot in how they respond to movies, books, television programs, news stories, and the lives of famous people they hear about.

How PARENTS CAN HELP SIX- TO EIGHT-YEAR-OLDS

• *If possible, be sure your child has frequent and regular contact with your ex-spouse.* Children in this age range have a good conception of time, and you might keep a special calendar so your child can see what days he will be spending with whom. Encourage your child to have daily phone conversations with the nonresidential parent if possible. In addition, the nonresidential parent can send (via fax or e-mail) messages or drawings and make audiocassettes and videocassettes of himself reading a story or speaking to the child. Exactly what you do is not as important as the fact that your child knows that you are thinking of him each and every day.

• *Never criticize your ex around your child.* Be sure that your words are consistent with your nonverbal cues. Children this age can be surprisingly sophisticated when it comes to understanding the real meaning behind your words. This may take some conscientious self-monitoring on your part, but doing so will help your child's self-esteem, reduce his confusion about the divorce and his ability to use your negative attitude toward your ex to be manipulative.

• *Maintain a calm, positive attitude in your child's presence.* Ultimately, children depend on and draw from their parents' happiness and strength. This is not to say you can't feel sad or angry at times; that's inevitable. However, children need the security of a calm and generally positive environment. No one can do more to set the desired tone than you can.

• *Establish and stick to a normal daily routine.* Kids this age have very intense memories about "how things were" and may cling to particular rituals and routines from before the divorce. Your son may insist that the table still be set the way Daddy preferred it, or your daughter may want her school clothes laid out exactly the way Mommy did. Your child is not trying to be a pill, and once you recognize these requests for what they are—attempts to feel more secure—it will be easier to accommodate them. Respect your child's personal routines and private rituals. They are comforting and give your child a sense of order and control, something he needs right now.

• *Protect your child's personal environment.* Make sure she has her favorite possessions, especially if you are relocating. Kids this age really need private space, particularly if they have younger siblings. Ideally, your child should be able to declare his room off-limits to siblings when he is not around, and he should be able to refuse admittance to outsiders. If that's not possible, keep his special possessions tucked away in a box or a drawer or put up out of reach of siblings and other children.

• *Maintain consistency.* The most you can reasonably hope for is that you and your ex will be consistent within your homes. Obviously, your child will be happier, more relaxed, and more likely to try to follow the rules if they are few, clear, and not widely different from parent to parent. Chances are, however, there will be some differences, and your child's ability to adapt accordingly is part of growing up. If your child has trouble doing this, you might explain, "I know it can be tough learning different rules for different homes. But there is no one right way to run a house or raise a child, and your father/mother and I see some things differently. I'm sure that you'll get used to it eventually, but I know it might take some time. The important thing is that we each want to spend time with you, because we love you."

THINGS 2 DO

TAKE YOUR FEELING PULSE

Ask your child to stop at different times in her day and take her "feeling pulse." Explain that her feeling pulse is the way she feels and responds to different things throughout the day. When she gets home, she can write down her feelings in a journal and discuss the circumstances in which her different feelings occurred. Encourage her to look back over past journal entries and find patterns. After a few days, discuss her entries if she wishes to share them with you.

PURPOSE: Children can begin to control and deal with their feelings more effectively once they can identify them and their cause. This applies to positive emotions as well as negative ones. Additionally, you might be able to help your child notice a pattern; she's sad every day after visiting her other parent because she misses him, for instance. Perhaps then you can help her find a solution to break that pattern. For example, she might phone her dad about an hour after he drops her off and share a special goodnight.

MAGIC CITY

Ask your child to create his own city where he makes all the rules. What would the rules be? Have the child name and design the city.

Kerry's city had no school and no divorce. Dawn's city had forced playtime where parents would have to participate.

PURPOSE: This imagination game allows children to rule their worlds and offers parents insight into what children feel is wrong or should be different. Often in the context of play, children will voice wishes and requests they would never state directly.

• *Anticipate signs of stress.* Symptoms include changes in eating and sleeping patterns, diminished or lost interest in people and activities, and problems with school. Remain lovingly firm about unacceptable behaviors but generous in offering reassurance, support, and understanding. Refrain from making excuses for your child or letting him blame everything on "the divorce."

• *Encourage your child to talk about her feelings.* Use books, toys, and videos or television programs to open the discussion. It's important to remember that your child does not have to speak about the divorce specifically, nor should you try to push a conversation in that direction. If your child is talking about feeling angry, for example, the simple fact that she has named and is expressing that emotion is very helpful.

• *Talk to the other caregivers in your child's life (baby-sitters, teachers, other adults) about the divorce and ask how she is responding.* Don't be surprised to learn that your child behaves differently around others than she does at home. For example, she may be unusually obedient at home but misbehave at school. Also be on the watch for the sudden onset of new behaviors, such as aggression, withdrawal, or a sudden lack of interest in activities and people she used to enjoy. Let everyone with whom your child spends time know that you want to be informed of any changes in attitude or behavior.

• *Understand that your child may feel very possessive of you and feel threatened by the sudden appearance of new people in your life.* Don't be surprised or angry if your child seems to hate anyone with whom he feels he is sharing you. Try to see it from his point of view. He feels he's already lost one parent, and he's terrified of losing you as well. (I address the issue of parents' dating in chapter 15.)

Q Dear Gary,

After a bitter, hurtful separation, our divorce will soon be final. Both my wife and I have explained to our eight-year-old son that divorce is a difficult, unhappy event. Last weekend, he came to my home and asked "Why is Mom planning a big party to celebrate the divorce?" He described the party invitation—a woman shown leaping with joy, a broken chain still attached to her ankle—and wanted to know how "Mom could make such a happy thing out of such a sad thing." What should I say?

A Advise your son to discuss it with his mother, for starters. Parents should be given the opportunity to speak for themselves. Mom should sense her child's pain, apologize, and offer some explanation: "It was my silly way of trying to make a joke out of something that hurt me too much. I'm sorry, and you won't hear about it again."

If Mom is insensitive—"Oh c'mon, I'm finally rid of your father"—your son will learn how pointless it is to discuss these issues with his mother. But at least your child will learn it on his own without any intrusion on your part or damage to your relationship with him.

In your comments to your son, explain how some people use humor as a way of coping with difficult issues and that Mom is obviously not happy about the part of the divorce that separates her from her child (this is your child's main concern). At the same time, however, you should take care not to disregard your son's feelings. It's okay to say, "Sometimes people we love do things that are very hurtful to us. That doesn't mean that they do them on purpose or that they wanted to hurt us. I'm sure your mother didn't mean to hurt your feelings."

Q Dear Gary,

The last time my seven-year-old returned from a weekend at Daddy's he was wearing the same underwear I sent him in and hadn't taken a bath since Saturday morning. My ex said they were just too busy and, besides, "a little dirt never killed anybody." I'm really ticked off about this, and when I see the joy in Bradley's face as he talks about his dad, I get even more angry. Am I making a big deal out of nothing?

A Probably. If your question is whether or not poor hygiene for a weekend poses a health threat, you should talk to your child's pediatrician. Otherwise, the problem with poor hygiene for children usually surrounds social problems caused by friends' and teachers' reactions to a smelly, dirty child. But since this is a weekend thing, it may be a nonissue. Yes, generally children should bathe daily and certainly change their underclothes, but there might be occasions when it just doesn't happen. So for a child to be "bathless" from Saturday morning until Sunday night seems acceptable on rare occasions.

You should pay close attention, however, if Bradley was dropped off at school Monday morning looking disheveled and having a bad odor, or if your son regularly returns home with an unusually strong odor. Problems with personal hygiene can affect his personal sense of self-worth and the way he is perceived by others. In these cases, you are dealing with a more serious issue, one that requires intervention on your part. Discuss with your child how he could prepare his own bath or take along a specific pair of underwear to be put away for Monday morning. If Bradley is not mature enough to be responsible for himself and you feel you must speak to your ex about the matter, follow the guidelines in the box "How to Avoid a Fight" (page 213). Speak to him in a calm, nonthreatening manner, and make it clear that you're bringing this up out of concern for your son's health, safety, social standing, or whatever it may be.

You might begin by saying, "Bradley cherishes every minute he spends with you and is always so happy after you two are together. There's nothing wrong with his skipping the occasional bath, but yesterday he told me that the other kids in school teased him a lot because they said he didn't smell good. Bradley came home from school really sad, and his teacher sent home a note saying this has happened before. For his sake, I'd like us to agree that he will have a bath and a clean change of underwear every day, especially the days he goes to school, no matter which of us he's staying with." If your ex still resists, perhaps Bradley could tell him how painful the experience was for him. If necessary, you can help Bradley by role-playing his telling his father about it. If that still doesn't work, you might have to consider requesting a change in visitation so that Bradley does not spend school nights with his dad or family counseling to try to persuade Bradley's father how important this is. These may strike you as pretty drastic moves, but remember: Bradley's being teased by his friends over something so personal and embarrassing can have serious repercussions in the long run.

Generally, however, I would say that unless you see some real health problem, leave it alone, learn to choose your battles, and remember that the "joy in Bradley's face" is much more important than one night's missed bath.

Q Dear Gary,
I've been seeing a woman for a couple of months. This is not yet a serious thing. Last night we went out for dinner and drinks, returned to my house, and one thing led to another. My eight-year-old daughter (who had been in the care of a sitter and was asleep when I got home) awoke to see my girlfriend and me kissing. She just ran back into her room and slammed the door. To be honest, I was a little relieved, since I didn't know what to say. What now?

A Obviously, you must say something, but give it some careful thought before you talk to your daughter. Be empathetic; she's upset and may be feeling several things at once. Seeing you and your girlfriend kiss may have destroyed her hopes of her parents' reuniting, for instance. Or she may feel jealous that she has to share her father. Acknowledge her feelings—"It seems that you're very upset because I was kissing . . ."—and reassure her that she is the top priority in your life. Talk to her about ways in which she can feel closer to you.

I'm a bit concerned by the casual nature of your relationship with this woman, and your saying "one thing led to another" suggests that you perhaps didn't think about how your behavior might affect your daughter. Consider this incident fair warning of bigger problems that might lie ahead if your child is routinely exposed to your appearing deeply involved (in her eyes) with someone you admit you are not serious about. To a young child, a kiss isn't "just" a kiss, and while you might feel this is something that just happened and means nothing, for that moment your daughter probably believed—and may still believe—you were really "in love." (See also chapter 15.)

6

The Season of Change:
Understanding Your
Nine- to Twelve-Year-Old

Children in this stage often feel they're stuck in an emotional, social, and physiological limbo: No longer dependent young children but not quite teenagers, they begin asserting more of their independence from their parents (going places alone, doing jobs outside the home) while still remaining very dependent on them for emotional support and guidance.

An overwhelming announcement. By using only a small portion of the drawing space, this eleven-year-old boy gives the impression of being overwhelmed by his parents' announcing their divorce. Despite one parent's reassurance that "It's not your fault," he apparently felt he had to hide his sadness. In the workbook, he wrote: "I cried inside my body but not on the outside because I didn't want them to think I was sad."

Your opinion still matters a great deal to them, but those of their peers are beginning to vie for dominance. Not only does your preadolescent long to be accepted by her friends, she also wants to appear to have her emotions and her life under control. Obviously, divorce complicates that picture. For your twelve-year-old daughter, it's a short step from going to the movies with her friends and picturing the day she can drive herself there (in her own car, of course); from thinking a boy is "cute" to daydreaming about her wedding. To your preteen, there is no downside to this growing-up business; she's on her way.

Parents, however, usually see things very differently. We begin to worry about the big issues we've avoided so far: dating, sex, drugs, how much freedom to allow. We feel our sphere of influence shrinking, crowded out by our child's new world, which may include friends we wouldn't have picked and interests we don't understand. Although this can be a precarious time, it is also a golden opportunity for parents to lay the groundwork for the relationship they will share with their child for the rest of their lives. When your twelve-year-old son was six, you could send him to his room; a few years ago a firm "No!" settled the argument (in your favor). But now he might leave the house for a few hours without telling you where he's going. Ideally, parents should work at earning their children's respect, no matter what their age. The fact is that until your child reaches preadolescence, you really don't have to earn his respect. Now, however, you may have to fine-tune your parenting style so that your child's respect for you is honestly earned, not grudgingly given.

The secret here is to respect your child on terms that he understands. Under that smart-mouthed or sullen exterior is a child who's probably as baffled and bewildered by the changes he's experiencing as you are. The parent who listens to her child, who validates his feelings and empathizes with him, builds a shelter he will return to as he grows older and his questions and problems—about religion, ethics, education, and life—get tougher. Think of this shelter as the one private, magical place where your child listens, shares, and one day comes to understand you, too. Make it comfortable and strong, and be sure the door is always open. Children who leave this stage feeling deeply connected to their parents rarely lose touch during the teen years and beyond. However, those who enter their teens feeling they've lost their parents are rarely brought back into the fold.

In September 1997, the preliminary findings of the National Longitudinal Study on Adolescent Health, a survey of over twelve thousand adolescents across the nation, confirmed the importance of the parent-child bond during these crucial years.[1] Adolescents who reported having an emotionally close relationship with their parents were less likely to engage in most risky behaviors (such as smoking cigarettes or marijuana, drinking alcohol). The only factor that did not seem to be affected by family closeness was sexual behavior. Dr. Robert William Blum, one of the study's authors, told *The New York Times,* "What this study showed is that it is emotional availability far more than physical presence that makes the difference. You need to give your kids the message that when they need to talk to you, you're available, even if it's by phone, and that they matter."[2]

A drama in five acts. An eleven-year-old boy, who is in the midst of developing his own ethical code, has used a storyboard to describe his moral dilemma over Mom's relationship with someone other than Dad.

During this period children are also forming an internal code of moral values, largely based on what they learn from you and other adults. Many parents also notice that their children are more opinionated, and some are quite surprised by how strongly their children feel about things, be it a new hairstyle or your divorce. Parents lose touch with their kids most often during this stage simply because the strength of kids' opinions and their seeming lack of concern about their family makes them hard to like all the time.

MAKE SURE YOUR NINE- TO TWELVE-YEAR-OLD UNDERSTANDS THAT . . .

✔ *She is not at fault for the divorce.* Nothing she did, thought, felt, or said contributed to it: "Your mom/dad and I made mistakes and hurt each other. It's totally our own fault that we can't live together anymore. Nothing you said or did has anything to do with this."

✔ *It is okay to wish that parents would get back together, but she cannot cause you and your ex-spouse to reconcile.* "I know it's hard for you, and you would like to see us get back together again. But we've thought this over very carefully, and this is the decision we feel is best for our family. This is a decision between your father/mother and me. Just as no one could make us decide to break up, no one else can bring us back together again."

✔ *She is and always will be safe.* "We will always love you and continue to take care of you as we always have."

✔ *She will be able to maintain contact with her other parent (if this is true).* "You will be able to see and talk to both of us. [Outline the details.] We want to be sensitive to your schedule, too, so we'll be flexible sometimes to accommodate special class trips and sports events and things like that."

✔ *It is not bad or wrong to feel sad or upset, but there are positive ways of expressing these feelings.* "It's normal and okay to feel sad and mad about what's happening. You might be angry at me or Mom/Dad. No matter what you feel, you can always talk to us about it. A lot of times, just talking helps you feel better, and we can help you find healthy ways to express these feelings."

✔ *You will always be there for her.* "We will always be there for you, no matter what."

✔ *Many children's parents divorce, and there are many reasons for divorce.* However, it does not occur because one parent is "good" and the other is "bad": "Both your mother/father and I are at fault, and we accept our responsibility for letting our marriage get to this point. The marriage didn't end simply because one of us was good and the other one was bad. It ended because we both failed to take care of it as we should have."

✔ *She will remain in touch with extended-family members (if this is true).* "You will be able to see and talk to your grandparents, aunts, uncles, cousins, and other relatives, just like you always have."

✔ *Even though you love her very much, the divorce is between you and your ex-spouse.* While you understand that she loves you, you are not asking her to take sides: "We love you very much, and we are sorry that our problems are affecting you like this. However, your father/mother and I both feel that our divorce is between us, and while we will promise to discuss with you those aspects that concern you directly, there are things that will remain between your father/mother and me. We both know you love us, and we don't want you to feel that you have to take sides to prove this."

✔ *While her experience with divorce may be stressful, she can do things for herself to alleviate and deal with that stress, and you will help her do so.* "This whole situation may be very hard for you, but there are things you can do to help yourself. Let's talk about some of the things that can help [activities, hobbies, recreation, sports, relaxation], and I promise I'll make sure that you have a chance to try some of them, if you want to."

How NINE- TO TWELVE-YEAR-OLDS EXPERIENCE DIVORCE

A child this age might write:

> Dear Diary,
> Dad's gone. I can't believe it. Last month I had a big fight with my best friend, and my parents said, "Work it out." Why can't they work it out? I am really mad. They could've given it another try. Dad was being much nicer, bringing home flowers and stuff. Mom says it was too little too late. Well, I'm not even getting married, and if I do, I'll know the person like ten years first. Now we have to spend nights at Dad's, too. It's such a pain. I have a life, and I can't miss all my time with my friends to make an hour drive each way to Dad's house. I didn't make this divorce happen. Why do I have to suffer for it? I really do want to see my dad, though. I hope Mom is okay with it all.

Anger

One major difference between children at this age and younger children is how they react to hurtful, troubling, or frightening situations. Whereas most seven- and eight-year-olds would respond to their parents' divorce with sadness, a nine- to twelve-year-old's reaction is often anger. This is not to say that these children do not feel sad or frightened; they do. However, anger is often the preferred mode of expression because it gives them a sense of control. Besides, anger is more assertive, more "adult," and crying to Mommy or crawling up in Daddy's lap no longer seems like an option. At the other end of the emotional spectrum is what appears to be ambivalence or lack of interest in the divorce and the family. Parents who conclude that their angry children are just being difficult and rebellious or that their seemingly detached children are demonstrating impressive maturity often miss what their child is really feeling. As different as they are, both responses are defensive alternatives to the vulnerability children experience when they are confused, frightened, or unsure what the future holds.

REBELLION

We usually think of the teen years as the Age of Rebellion, but this phase really begins in the preadolescent stage. Instead of communicating their frustrations (which requires more emotional maturity than most possess) or telling their parents that they miss their love (which would be too childish), they act out. Compared to a younger child's scattershot outbursts, often aimed at no one in particular, a preteen's acting out is a marvel of strategic offense; he knows which parental buttons to push. Once again, it's important to remember that even in the happiest, intact homes, most good kids misbehave, talk back, test the rules, and turn the screws. You probably did the same thing, too, to some degree. This really is a normal transition toward full independence and self-sufficiency. It's an inevitable part of growing up, painful as it may be for both of you.

THE BLACK-AND-WHITE WORLD

Preadolescents have a growing understanding of human relationships. Yet because their understanding usually exceeds their emotional capacity for dealing with what they experience, they tend to reduce the complex issues of divorce down to who is good and who is bad. This

THINGS 2 DO

WHAT WE NEED

Parent and child create individual lists of what each would like the other to do in order to show love. It's usually best and easiest for everyone if you agree on a specific number of items, ideally between three and five. Here are Brian's and his mother's lists:

Brian's list

1. More help with homework
2. To be thanked for finishing my chores
3. To do more things with you that don't involve your boyfriend Rod

Mom's list

1. To be greeted when I get home from work
2. To be thanked for preparing meals
3. To spend more "fun time" with you; maybe a movie out every other weekend

PURPOSE: This helps you express what you need from each other. You can learn how your child sees your role in loving him, and your child can learn that a parent has certain needs for love from a child as well.

HOW TO EXPLAIN THE DIVORCE TO YOUR NINE- TO TWELVE-YEAR-OLD

What is divorce?

"Divorce is a legal process that parents go through when they no longer want to be married because they are very sad together and cannot find ways to be happy together anymore. It means that we will no longer be married to each other, but we will always be your parents."

Why did it happen?

Some possibilities include:

"We didn't listen to each other enough. You know how sometimes you want to say something so much you don't even hear what the other person is saying? That's how your mother/father and I got to be. We cared more about what we wanted to say and not enough about what the other person was saying."

"We didn't take the time to think *How will he/she feel about this?* before we said or did something that hurt him/her or made him/her angry. That was very unfair."

"We fought too much and didn't learn how to talk to each other about our feelings without being angry and hurting each other."

"We didn't know how to stop arguing and walk away from a fight."

"We didn't make enough time to be alone together and be romantic. Couples can always find quiet time to be together, no matter how busy they are or how many kids they have. We just didn't do that." (This alleviates your child's fear that he may have been the reason you two didn't have enough time.)

"We were not strong enough for each other, and we let other people and things confuse us about our relationship." (This keeps your child from concluding that interference from others—affairs, in-laws, children—caused the divorce.)

"If other people or things came between us, it was because we let them. Each of us had the responsibility to make sure these outside things didn't affect our relationship, but we failed."

Will we still be a family?

"Yes. Even though your mother/father and I are getting a divorce, you will always be part of us. We both still love you and always will. You and Mom/Dad, and you and I, will always be families. It's just that Mom/Dad and I will not be in a family together, even though we will both belong to you."

What will happen to me?

"You will be able to see both me and your mother/father a lot." (Then spell out custody and visitation arrangements as clearly and in as much detail as you can. See also chapter 12.)

THINGS 2 DO

LAUNDRY LEARNING

Have your child take out or put on an item of clothing he was wearing during a very difficult experience. Discuss where he was when he wore this item and how he felt. How did he get through this time? What coping skills worked for him? Looking back on things, how would he have handled it differently? Do his friends also have difficult times? How do they handle problems? How do they handle conflict?

PURPOSE: This activity helps a child focus on specific techniques for coping with difficult and complex situations. It also teaches a child to use the past as a learning and growing experience.

can be very difficult for a parent, no matter how she has been designated, but obviously harder for the "bad" one. It helps parents to understand that this extreme view is just another component of an emotional self-defense strategy. The tendency to choose sides (see below) and to rally around one parent while rejecting the other is yet another way to secure some control. Your child may demand, "Why couldn't you two just work it out?" or "What's wrong with you?" Again, parents should try not to be put off by their child's attitude and make every effort to see beyond to the real emotions he is expressing.

CHOOSING SIDES BETWEEN PARENTS

Kids this age normally seek approval and companionship of the opposite-sex parent, a normal outgrowth of their increased interest in the opposite sex in general and their need to complete their own gender identification. Divorce complicates the picture and makes it easy for the "rejected" parent to feel that, in favoring the other parent, the child is choosing sides. This may seem especially true when a daughter wants to spend more time with her nonresidential father. Parents can do themselves and their kids a favor by remembering that almost all children go through this phase, whether their parents are divorced or not, and try not to take it personally.

At the same time, you can't overlook the fact that kids this age can and sometimes do take sides. Whether you have been designated the ally or the enemy, you must negotiate this "mined" terrain with care. Remember: It's normal for every relationship to go through rough patches and weak periods. Your child may have a legitimate complaint about Mom, and as her father, you should listen with understanding and acceptance of her feelings. That means you allow your child to express herself, and you try to see through the anger to the real heart of the issue. It does *not* mean egging your child on because it makes you feel better to be considered the "good" parent. Also keep in mind how quickly children can pass through these stages. Perhaps today you're the hero; next year you may be the "bad" one—all because you've gotten engaged, or moved to the next town, or missed a birthday party, or stocked the fridge with Coke instead of Pepsi.

Talk to your child. Let her know that while you can understand why she might want to be angry at one or the other of you, that neither of you is fully responsible for the divorce. You both made mistakes; you both accept some blame. Point out to her that you and your ex are her parents for life, and that her hurtful behavior toward the other probably isn't making any of you feel better, and it's certainly making the "bad" parent feel a lot worse. Say, "I know the divorce hurt you; it's hurt us all. But we're a family, and families who care about each other try not to hurt each other. They discuss their feelings and work them through." This doesn't mean your child has to pretend or spend extra time with the parent. It does mean she has to understand that her anger over the divorce is a general issue to deal with, not a personal issue between her and one parent.

SEEING YOUR DIVORCE AS A PERSONAL REJECTION

Even when your child intellectually understands the reasons for your divorce (that you two couldn't work it out, et cetera), he may still view it as a personal rejection of him. Kids of all ages, especially this age, are prone to think, *If I was a better son, this wouldn't be happening,* or *If they really cared about me, they would work out their differences.* Let your child know that you understand why he feels this way, but be realistic, too. You might say:

> "I know you might think that if your mother/father and I loved you more, we would still be together. I wish it were that easy, because if the whole issue could be decided by how much we love you, we wouldn't be breaking up. We couldn't love you any more than we do. Unfortunately, this divorce is about your mother's/father's and my feelings toward each other, not you. Sometimes even adults find that they change in ways that make it hard for them to go on the way they did before."

DIVORCE DESTABILIZES AN ALREADY-CHANGING WORLD

We talk a lot about the changes a preadolescent goes through, as we see them, from the outside. From your child's point of view, the whole world is changing, too. The physical and emotional changes this period brings are persistent reminders that nothing remains the same. Every child, no matter what age, finds divorce destabilizing. Kids this age, however, end up getting change on top of change, and they are often overwhelmed.

Make sure your child knows that you understand how rapidly and dramatically his life is changing, and that you own responsibility for bringing divorce into his life. Let him know that you've been there, too:

> "I guess you're feeling as if everything around you is changing. I know that's how I felt at your age. It seemed like I was too old to do this and too young to do that. It's a time when you need to feel you can

depend on some things staying the same, and that would include me and your mom/dad staying together. I know that our divorce doesn't help right now, and I'm sorry you have to go through all this extra change and turmoil. Even though it doesn't seem like it to you right now, there are some things that are forever and will never change: I will always love you and I will always be here for you whenever you need to talk."

Aliens among us. A ten-year-old boy offers a fascinating view of how divorce—represented by a descending alien being—envelops his family. In the first picture, it hovers ominously overhead, but in the second ("after parents are divorced"), the "alien" divides into three multicolored jellyfish-like beings that literally take over the family.

GROWING UP TOO FAST

Resist the temptation to include your child in your own problems. Children between nine and twelve typically long to be treated more as adults and less as kids. Their growing emotional maturity makes it too easy for parents to regard them as sources of support. Don't do it! It goes without saying that your child's love is precious and perhaps seems even more so during divorce. Still, she needs to experience childhood as a child. Including her in discussions about your problems or making her your new best friend will force her to grow up too quickly and miss the crucial lessons of this phase.

Be careful not to rationalize her involvement in your personal problems with "But she wants to help me. It makes her feel important." Of course it does; what child doesn't want to be considered more grown-up? Be aware that children who grow up "taking care of" and feeling inappropriately responsible for their parents are at high risk for growing up to become codependent on people with serious emotional or psychological problems and addictions. Codependents often feel unable to love or be loved by anyone whom they cannot "help." It is wonderful and heartwarming to know that your child loves and cares about you. But always remember that you are the parent. Your child needs to feel that you are there for her, not that she has to support you emotionally.

Whenever your child asks you about specific "adult" issues—finance, romance, your conflict with his other parent—try to hear what he is really asking. Unlike an adult asking the same question, your child probably isn't really interested in the hard facts or the lurid details. It's more likely that he's expressing, however obliquely, some fear about issues that concern him, or he is trying to support you emotionally in a way that you should not encourage. Either way, try not to shut him out, and instead use your child's question to open a dialogue.

For example, when eleven-year-old Leah asked, "Hasn't Daddy been paying his child support? Is that why we can't have a vacation this year?" her mother resisted the temptation to reply, "I'm handling the problem fine, and I don't want you to have to be concerned about it." Now, this is not to say that this response is always inappropriate; sometimes it is the right thing to say. It can be, but only after you have listened and identified your child's real concerns.

"You seem very concerned about our money situation," Leah's mother said.

"Yeah. Well, it just seems that we never have enough money, and I've overheard you talking on the phone to the lawyer. I hope this doesn't mean that you and Dad are going to start fighting again."

"Honey, it's true that your father and I are having a disagreement, but I'm handling it, and I don't want you to have to worry about it. Sometimes, we need our lawyers to help settle things. But I promise you that your father and I will not start fighting again. As for the money, we may have to budget a little more, but things will be fine."

ACTING OUT THROUGH PEER RELATIONSHIPS

THINGS 2 DO

LOOK MA, NO HANDS

One person puts her hands behind her back while the other person stands behind her and puts his hands through the person's arms, pretending to be the front person's arms. The person in front starts telling a story while the person behind her uses his hands to express the points of the story. Perform this alone or for an audience of family or friends.

PURPOSE: This is a fun way to get people working together (siblings or stepsiblings) to communicate a single idea. It also shows them the importance of gestures and how they enhance or detract from expression. The exercise also requires the "hands" to listen carefully and empathize with the speaker.

Peer friendships may be a form of expression. An angry child might befriend a child who carries a knife or belongs to a gang. An emotionally withdrawn child might become very close to a quiet, shy child who is seen as the class nerd. A child who feels helpless in her own life may make friends only with other children who need her help or have to be rescued. Remember, your child has always had basically her two parents' personalities from which to draw. Now she will look to friends to find other forms and mixes of personalities with which she can identify.

Your child's friendships can tell you a great deal about his sense of self-worth and possible need to express certain difficult feelings. Try to help your child share these feelings verbally so that he can concentrate his energies on forming healthy relationships with friends rather than using these associations to express what he feels he can't.

In times of emotional difficulty, children may choose friends from the "wrong" crowd. Some adults prefer to take a wait-and-see attitude because they feel such friendships constitute a phase, that getting into some kind of trouble is just part of growing up. I disagree, for several reasons. First, children of divorce may be particularly vulnerable to needing to belong, which may make them more susceptible to peer pressure to engage in drinking, smoking, cutting school, shoplifting, using drugs, having sex, and so on. Second, for all their seeming maturity, preteens still need parental guidance. Third, the world is a dangerous, complex place. Preteens are not too young to get into serious trouble.

If you discover that your child or his friends are engaged in behavior that is inappropriate, illegal, or unacceptable to you, do not hesitate to make your concerns and your disapproval known to your child. Spell out what is wrong with the behavior and why, but do so lovingly. See above for more tips on tackling these hard issues.

HOW PARENTS CAN HELP NINE- TO TWELVE-YEAR-OLDS

• *If possible, be sure your child has frequent and regular contact with your ex-spouse.* At this age, children can conceptualize plans for events months into the future. Make plans for how summer vacation will be spent while there's snow on the ground. It will give your child a firmer sense of what's to come. (One caveat: Allow children to have some input, but reserve the final decision for you and your ex.) Daily phone conversations with the nonresidential parent are recommended, but don't be surprised if your child seems less enthusiastic about this than her younger brother. Remember, children this age are just beginning to move away from their parents and become truly independent. That said, you and your ex-spouse should be sure one or both of you is available to your child whenever she needs you or wants to talk. In addition, the nonresidential parent can fax and send messages. Exactly what you do is not as important as the fact that your child knows that you are thinking of her each and every day.

• *Never criticize your ex in front of your child.* Be sure that your words are consistent with your nonverbal cues. Children this age are masters at deciphering the true meaning behind the raised eyebrow, the rolling eyes, and the smirk. Watch yourself. It helps parents to remember that children this age still define themselves in terms of their parents. When you express anger or disapproval of your ex-spouse, your child comes away feeling that you are rejecting him. This is a particularly sensitive issue for children whose same-sex parent is the object of scorn or ridicule.

• *Maintain a calm, positive attitude in your child's presence.* Ultimately, children depend on and draw from their parents' happiness and strength. This is not to say you can't feel sad or angry at times; that's inevitable. However, children need the security of a calm and generally positive environment. No one can do more to set the desired tone than you can.

• *Establish and stick to a normal daily routine.* Children this age deal better with stress if you can maintain a degree of predictability (homework time, TV time, dinner). Respect your child's personal routines. They are comforting and give your child a sense of order and control, something he needs right now.

• *Encourage your child's personal support network.* At this stage, friends "rule." Children this age really do choose their friends, often using surprisingly "mature" criteria. Chances are, your child's best friend is someone he can talk to and receive emotional support from. In fact, this is the age at which kids often list "my friend" or "my best friend" as the first person they told about their parents' divorce. (In the Sandcastles Survey [see page 419], 35 percent did so; 28 percent told "no one.") You can encourage your child's peer relationships by providing transportation to events and outings, making your home a welcome, safe place for her friends, and letting your child learn from her own mistakes in judging people except when these mistakes could be dangerous.

• *Protect your child's personal environment and her privacy.* Make sure she has her favorite possessions, especially if you are relocating, and allow her to decorate her room as she wishes, within the budget you specify. Kids this age often prefer to spend time alone in their rooms and resent any intrusion into their privacy. There's nothing unusual about a child's locking himself in his room for hours at a time. You should be concerned, however, if there's a sudden, dramatic change in his behavior. If, for example, your eleven-year-old son spent most of the evening between dinner and bedtime alone in his room, doing his homework and logging on the Internet, before the separation and nothing's really changed, I wouldn't worry. On the other hand, if he's given up afternoon basketball games with friends and dinner with the family, his grades have dropped, and he's spending twice as much time on the Internet, you should be concerned. The same would apply if this child suddenly began spending more time after dinner hanging out at friends' homes or talking on the phone.

Love, before and after. In the first picture by a ten-year-old girl, Mom and Dad state their love for their family. Although after divorce Dad and Me are missing hands (possibly suggesting a lack of control), everyone is still smiling, and the girl drew herself close to Dad, the nonresidential parent, perhaps indicating her comfort in maintaining a relationship with Dad.

• *Maintain consistency.* The rules between your homes will probably be different, but ideally you should both reach some general agreement on the big issues: bedtime, curfew, homework, and so on. No matter how strongly one of you may feel about subjects such as the proper bedtime, acceptable table manners, and academic standards, your child will be happier, more relaxed, and more likely to try to follow the rules if they are few, clear, and essentially the same with each parent. Children this age are not as likely to be confused if, say, you forbid playing loud music and your ex-spouse actually enjoys it. If, on the other hand, there are major disagreements over such important matters as school attendance, curfew times, participation in religious observances and family gatherings, you might consider counseling for your child and you and your ex (if feasible). Make it easier for your child to meet your expectations, and your whole family will benefit.

• *Anticipate signs of stress.* These include changes in your child's eating and sleeping patterns, diminished or lost interest in people and activities, and problems at school. Remain lovingly firm about behaviors that are not acceptable, but generous in offering reassurance, support, and understanding. In these children, stress may also manifest in such indirect forms as physical symptoms (headache, stomachache, and so on), eating disorders, a reluctance to attend school, or a sudden transformation into a "perfect" child.

• *Encourage your child to talk about her feelings.* Use books, movies, or television programs to open the discussion. It's important to remember that your child does not have to speak about the divorce specifically, nor should you try to push every conversation in that direction. If your child is talking about feeling angry, for example, the simple fact that she has named and is expressing that emotion is very helpful.

Also be aware that children this age will often talk about their problems indirectly. For example, your son might talk about another boy's family in which divorce or loss has occurred; your daughter might seem unusually interested in discussing a play, movie, television program, or book that deals with strong emotions or a divorce-type situation. It is also common for children to behave as if they are untroubled by the divorce but to express concern about a sibling.

Do not force the child to focus on herself, or even on your family's particular situation. While your child does not seem to be talking about herself, remind yourself that she is, and that whatever guidance, reassurance, or comfort you offer is valu-

DEPRESSION

While no child is too young to be depressed, depression commonly shows up during the preadolescent years. Some mild depression is normal when a child is faced with a crisis like divorce, and some degree of moodiness is typical of the preteen years. However, if your child's behavior suddenly changes, if he seems very down for a long period of time without improvement, or his depression appears to be worsening, you should seek professional counseling. Continued depression can place your child at heightened risk for drug and alcohol abuse, problems with school and at home, and acting out (for example, being promiscuous, hanging out with the wrong crowd, etc.).

You should be concerned if your child

- suddenly seems quieter,
- experiences a dramatic loss or increase in appetite,
- has a change in sleeping patterns; has trouble sleeping or sleeps too much,
- often cries easily,
- spends more time alone than usual,
- withdraws from friends, family, and his social group,
- seems not to feel much about anything,
- loses interest in things and people he formerly enjoyed,
- shows a sudden, intense interest in the depressing or the macabre or adopts romantic notions about depression, alienation, and suicide.

See "The Art of Communicating with Children," page 32.

able even if it doesn't address the "real issue" head-on. Remember that the simple act of listening provides validation and support. Your child may have to repeat these concerns, and you may have these discussions many times before she works it through. This does not mean that she "didn't get it," only that she is moving through the process of understanding.

• *Talk to the other adults in your child's life (teachers, her best friend's parents) about the divorce and ask how she is responding.* Don't be surprised to learn that your child behaves differently around others than she does at home. For example, she may be unusually quiet at home but misbehave at school. Also be on the watch for the sudden onset of new behaviors, like aggression, withdrawal, or a sudden lack of pleasure in activities and people she used to enjoy. Let every adult with whom your child spends time know that you want to be informed of any changes in attitude or behavior.

• *Understand that your child may feel very possessive of you and feel threatened by the sudden appearance of new people in your life.* Don't be surprised or angry if your child seems to hate anyone with whom he feels he is sharing you. He may also feel that you are betraying his other parent or the family, or that by simply being polite to your new friend, he is being disloyal to the other parent. Just beginning to take notice of the opposite sex and contemplating dating himself, he may find the idea of your dating shocking, distasteful, or simply "uncool." While this is a problem more common to teens, parents should not fail to recognize similar responses from this younger group. (I address the issue of parents dating in chapter 15.)

• *Acknowledge your child's newfound strengths.* All too often we tend to focus on the difficulties of these years and lose sight of the important and won-

T·HINGS **2** DO

THE BLOCKADE

Draw a wall on a piece of paper and say, "I feel sad because it seems that there is this wall between us. I love you and want to know how you are feeling inside. How can you help me take it down so we can be closer?"

Twelve-year-old George responded to his mother, "You're mad at me all the time." When she calmly asked him to tell her more, he said, "You always tell me to do this, do that; like shut off the TV, clean my room, get off the phone. All you do is yell and give orders. I can see why Dad left. Dad always said you yell too much, and you didn't love him."

"So you think I yelled a lot at your dad and that I didn't love him? Honey, look, I did love your dad. But sometimes people have trouble showing love, and others have trouble accepting love. And I feel this has happened between us a little. Let's talk about what could help us feel loved and how each of us can show each other."

PURPOSE: For a parent who is having difficulty communicating with her child, it is helpful to show the wall and describe the concept of breaking it down.

derful work our kids are doing themselves to grow up. Acknowledge and support your child whenever he demonstrates maturity (for example, in coming home at the time he promised, completing schoolwork, taking care of household responsibilities). However, be careful not to depend on him to do things that you would not expect were you not divorced (for example, comfort you or listen to you complain about his other parent).

• *Take time to enjoy your child.* Try to find activities you can enjoy together, like biking, gardening, sharing favorite movies, Rollerblading, cooking—anything. Even just hanging out together watching a game or a video is important to kids. Though working around the house together or going out to do errands may not qualify for some as quality time, it should not be overlooked. As far as your child is concerned, the very fact that you have chosen to spend time with her is meaningful. Don't make the mistake of waiting for the "perfect" time or the once-a-year big vacation or event. Be with your child here and now.

Q Dear Gary,
My ex and I have managed to hammer out a friendly divorce. The problem is our twelve-year-old son, who can't seem to forgive his mother for leaving me, even though I was drinking heavily at the time. Whenever we're together, he criticizes his mother and says things to let me know he's on my side. What can I do to set him straight?

A Tell him the truth. It's your job to set him straight and help him understand that spouses have an obligation to meet each other's needs. Explain that you never would have grown or changed if his mother just kept "dealing" with your drinking problem. I hope you have overcome your drinking problem. If not, take care of it immediately. It obviously had something to do with damaging your spousal relationship and, if it continues, it will probably destroy your parent-child relationship as well.

Be sensitive to your son's pain, and discuss the concept of displacement of anger with him. He clearly is finding his own way of expressing anger over the divorce by finding fault with his mother. Keep in mind that he may be choosing sides to feel more in control, more a part of what went on between you and your ex. Open up these topics with your son so he can learn to express his anger in a more appropriate manner. He will be angry at you for your part in the divorce, but at least it will be opened up for discussion, and he won't have to hide his feelings or express them the wrong way. Learning to express his feelings directly and where they belong are important first steps to resolving feelings and moving on.

Q Dear Gary,
My eleven-year-old daughter will do anything to get my ex and me back together. She's been very depressed and recently told both her mother and me that she will kill herself if we can't be "a real family" again. I've read a lot about teen suicide, and I'm scared. My wife thinks our daughter is "too young to be depressed" and is just trying to manipulate us. She refuses to "cater to her" by taking her to a therapist. Who's right here?

A Your daughter. She could very well kill herself if you don't get her help immediately. We are in the midst of a teen (and preteen) suicide epidemic. One study from the mid-1980s found that 32 percent of children thirteen and younger reported having considered suicide at least once in the twelve months prior to the survey. That percentage increases gradually with each year of age, averaging about 40 percent at age eighteen. According to the Teen Suicide Prevention Task Force, the breakup of the family and other life crises (moving, changing schools, losing contact with friends, and so on) can place emotionally vulnerable children at risk for suicide.

Talk of suicide always should be taken seriously, no matter what a child's age, especially when she has shown signs of depression. And don't fall for the dangerous misconception that people who talk about suicide never commit it. In fact, more often than not, people who do commit suicide express their intentions, either by talking about it or showing a dramatic change in behavior.

This may be (with hope, it is) a manipulation on her part. Even if it is, I don't understand how having her see a therapist would be catering to her. (See the box "Deciding on Therapy" on page 189.) Should you reunite with your ex because of your daughter's threat of suicide? No, you should not allow yourself to be manipulated by her. In any case, get her help immediately. Even if she doesn't hurt herself, she is obviously in pain and calling out for help. If your ex refuses, take her yourself.

CHAPTER 7

The Quest for Independence: Understanding Your Thirteen- to Seventeen-Year-Old

Among the few points on which you find nearly universal agreement is this: It's tough being a teenager. Even under the best of circumstances, teens seesaw between dependence and independence, constantly seeking the perfect balance of autonomy and acceptance (from parents, peers, and love interests). They are capable of conceiving their futures and have very strong ideas about what they want and who they want to be. As you and your daughter debate her getting a third hole in her ear or your son comes home with his second traffic ticket, it may be hard to believe that you and your values remain the most important influences in their lives. Yet they are, and when teens rebel, as they so often do, it helps to see their rebellion in terms of their striking out *toward* their own lives rather than striking out *against* you. Although he or she may not care to admit and may not say it, your teenager still needs you.

Current research on adolescents suggests it isn't simply what teenagers do and say that provoke family conflicts in these years but how parents respond to their kids' becoming teens. The transition we commonly refer to as "midlife crisis" often occurs when a first child reaches puberty regardless of how old the parent is. Why is this? When teenagers enter the world of dating and sexuality, parents often experience the loss of the child as a loving, accepting, and dependent individual. Most parents, especially those whose marriages may have cooled or ended, whose careers may have reached a plateau, or whose friends and other family members may be growing old or dying, may feel sad as they contrast their child's life—so full of potential and promise—with their own.

For most parents, the teen years mark the first time since their child's birth that they don't feel needed. Compared to younger children, teenagers seem to want much less of our time, our advice, and our companionship. Instead they seek out and embrace the views of their peers, especially love interests. Since these new attitudes often concern matters of ethics and morals, parents can feel they've been displaced, and in a sense they have, at least temporarily. It is only through experiencing different friendships and love interests that a teenager not only discovers who he is and what he seeks in his relationships with others, but what he will seek in a community, a social group, a spouse.

Typically, teen relationships have their ups and downs, friends and love interests come and go, and occasionally a teen's attraction to a certain individual or group may be cause for concern. It helps to remember that, in exploring different relationships, what your teen is doing is a lot like window-shopping, and chances are that he will try on some other relationships for size before he "buys" anything. I think it's safe to say we've all been there ourselves, and sharing your own experiences (*except* those involving your ex) with your teen can be an effective, nonjudgmental way of expressing your concerns.

> Jodi became concerned when her sixteen-year-old daughter, Heather, began dating Luke, the school "bad boy." After weeks of hearing Heather rhapsodize about his "free soul" and "courage to question authority," Jodi remarked, "You know, back in college I really fell for this guy who just lived for today. To me, he was like James Dean or Jim Morrison, or I guess you would say Trent Reznor. But after a while I saw that the real reason he said he didn't believe in rules was because he didn't want to be obligated to be there for anyone, including me. At times when I really needed him, like when Grandpa had that accident, he was just 'too free' to be bothered. That really hurt me. I've found that sometimes the ideas that make for interesting philosophies and fascinating people don't necessarily make for good relationships."

TEENS STILL NEED PARENTS, THOUGH IN A DIFFERENT WAY

For most involved parents, a teenager's growing independence packs an emotional wallop. Add to this the teenager's newfound, essential realization that parents are people, too, and his quickness to remind us of our flaws and mistakes; it's no wonder that adolescence is a tough time for everyone. In this charged atmosphere parents can become reluctant to broach tough topics like sex, drugs, morals, and ethics, because they aren't sure just what to say. They may be embarrassed to talk about sex, not sure where they stand on ethical issues, or feel uncomfortable taking a stand against something they themselves did in their youth. I believe that we shy away from conversations that will test our moral beliefs because we do not always feel we can really defend them. When your teenager challenges your position—which you know she will—you foresee the discussion deteriorating into a battle of wills and opinions.

Parents can avoid these traps and open meaningful discussions with their teens by first taking the time to carefully consider their positions and why they feel the way they do. As you may recall from your own youth, scare tactics and edicts don't really work and only invite challenge. You need to discover the real reasons why you believe as you do, and prepare your position with care. First, push aside the slogans ("Drugs/sex/drinking is wrong") and clear out your own ambivalence. The fact that you may have experimented with drugs, for example, when you were young does not make you a hypocrite or invalidate your reasons for now believing it's a wrong choice for your child. Don't be afraid to tell your teen the truth: You are now older and wiser, it was a bad decision when you made it twenty years ago, and the world today is a very different place. If you have had bad experiences or know others who have, share them. Kids are often surprised to find out that their parents actually know something about these moral netherworlds they're convinced they discovered.

Teenagers are more likely to rethink their positions if they can see that you have carefully considered your own. Cast your points in terms that teenagers understand, and discuss how these issues can impact their lives adversely in the ways that matter most to them. Although as parents we want our children to feel that we are always going to be there for them, a dose of reality doesn't hurt either. One reason these issues are so charged for parents is that our children will be making their own decisions and possibly inviting consequences we may be powerless to help them with. Teen pregnancy, car accidents, sexually transmitted diseases, permanent neural damage, expulsions, and arrests aren't boo-boos we can kiss away, and it doesn't hurt to let kids know that. Focus on the real consequences of making bad decisions, not the scare stories.

Jodi, like many adults of her generation, knew several people who had wrestled with drug and alcohol addiction. After she learned that some of Heather's friends had gotten drunk at a keg party, she decided it was time for a talk. "Heather, I know getting drunk or high probably looks like a lot of fun, but that behavior is unacceptable to your father and me. It's illegal, and it's very dangerous. But even more important, it could put you or someone else in a terrible situation you would have to live with for the rest of your life. Do you remember my cousin Adam, whom we met last year on vacation?"

"Yeah, the nice guy in the wheelchair?"

"Right, that's Adam. At your age, Adam wanted to be a marine biologist and work with endangered animals. He was starting his first year of college when the car he was riding in hit a guardrail, rolled over, and caught fire."

"Was he driving drunk?"

"No, but his girlfriend was. I'm not just trying to scare you. These are things that can happen to anyone, and I want you to be careful. These problems didn't just crop up yesterday, you know. Your father's college roommate was barred from going to law school because he was arrested with a small amount of marijuana; my best friend from high school had two glasses of wine, forgot to turn on her headlights, and ran over her family's dog coming into the driveway. None of these things had to happen to them, and they don't have to happen to you, either."

How TEENAGERS EXPERIENCE DIVORCE

A diary entry for a teenager might look like this:

Dear Diary,

How could they do this? Dad is such a fool. How could he treat Mom that way? He was never home. Work was always more impor-

MAKE SURE YOUR TEEN UNDERSTANDS THAT . . .

✔ *He is not at fault for the divorce.* "Your mother/father and I made many, many mistakes in our marriage. And although we tried hard, we were unable to make it work. We hurt each other too much. It's no one's fault but our own."

✔ *He will be able to maintain contact with his other parent (if this is true), and his wishes will be taken into consideration in your planning.* "You will be able to see and talk to both of us [detail the plans]. We wanted to discuss with you our time-sharing plan. We think our time with you is very important, but because of your schedule, we want to be flexible and talk to you about the specifics so all of us are comfortable."

✔ *It is not bad or wrong to feel sad or upset, but there are positive ways of expressing these feelings.* "We will always be here for you. You can talk to us about anything. If you feel that your emotions are too strong or you don't know for sure what to do, we can go talk to someone, like a counselor."

✔ *It is okay to wish that your parents were together, but this is not a realistic possibility.* "Most people whose parents divorce wish it didn't have to be that way. Just because your father/mother and I want to divorce doesn't mean that we expect you to like it. However, it's something we all have to live with and we have many options for coping with it. Your father/mother and I getting back together, however, is not one of them."

✔ *Even though you love him very much, the divorce is between you and your ex-spouse.* While you understand that he loves you, you do not want him to take sides or to act disrespectfully toward the other parent: "We know that it's hard to feel as if you don't have any control over this situation, which greatly affects your life. But your mother/father and I are getting a divorce so that we can move on with our lives. Neither of us wants to put you in the middle of our problems by telling you things about the divorce that are private, between your mother/father and me. And I want to be very clear about this: Even if there are times when I seem to be angry or upset with your mother/father, it is not your place to behave disrespectfully toward her/him, and that behavior will not be tolerated by either of us."

✔ *While his experience with divorce may be stressful, he can do things for himself to alleviate and deal with that stress, and you will help him do so.* "Your mother/father and I want to discuss with you the different things you can do to deal with the stress of our divorce [activities, hobbies, therapy, sports, recreation, relaxation, meditation]."

✔ *Just because you are divorced does not mean that your teenager will divorce.* "However your future relationships turn out will be up to you. Just because your father/mother and I divorced doesn't mean that you will divorce."

tant than all of us, Mom used to say. And what's her problem? If he came home for a second, she'd start fighting with him. Now she's surprised he left and moved for a promotion. Why wouldn't anyone who got that kind of treatment? I don't care if I never see him again. I don't need him. But it's not fair to Sophie. She's too young to be going through this. As much as she's a pain, I'm going to have to be a nicer big brother to her—maybe take her out places more often now that I can drive. Someone has to take care of her.

A MAJOR LIFE TRANSITION

Parents' separation or divorce is one of the most difficult life events for a teenager. Studies have shown that only the death of a parent, a sibling, or a close friend is considered more stressful; being arrested, flunking a grade in school, breaking up with a boyfriend or girlfriend, and having a girlfriend get pregnant are all considered less stressful. However, compared to younger children, teenagers have greater resources to help them cope with divorce. Maturity gives teens the advantage of perspective and a greater understanding of human relationships; they generally know, for example, that they are not to blame.

B LAMING PARENTS AS A FORM OF CONTROL

One of our goals as parents is to see our children grow up with a clear sense of right and wrong, a strong moral compass. The adolescent years often become the testing ground for a child's internal moral values, and

Divorce is a demonic theme park. This young teen cynically depicts Divorcing Land as an amusement park or playground (places usually associated with happy childhood memories) where little demons fight it out. By rendering divorce as a delineated physical space, this boy may be trying to contain all of his anger in a single place. Or he may be saying how even happy experiences have been tainted with the sadness of divorce.

THE NEW
AMERICAN BANDSTAND

Although your child's favorite music may sound vastly different from what you grew up with, you may be surprised to discover that the more things change, the more they stay the same. When you have a chance, try to sit quietly and listen to your child's favorite music. If your child is comfortable, try to discuss it with him. Refrain from being critical or hostile. Ask your child what he likes about the music and the lyrics. What do they say? How do they speak to him? What about the singers and musicians? What does he know or like about them, as musicians and as people?

If your child is comfortable talking to you about music, talk about the fact that what makes music compelling is the strength of emotion it conveys. Whether the music is classical, rock, rap, country, soul, New Age, or jazz, all music begins with someone expressing feelings. Chances are, among the musical stars your child admires, at least one and probably several have spoken openly about their divorce experiences. What does he think about that? How are their feelings like and different from his own? Don't preach, but don't be afraid to point out that each person responds to divorce differently.

PURPOSE: This is another way to enter your child's world and to talk about feelings and emotions—his and someone else's, which may be uncomfortable for him to share otherwise. It also provides a good opportunity to point out that while some people may feel they were permanently scarred by their parents' divorce, others do move on and have happy, productive lives.

now more than ever, teens are called on to make crucial decisions about alcohol, drugs, sex, social groups, their academic performance, and their dreams. Through it all, most teens feel simultaneously invincible and vulnerable. They are torn between wanting independence and protection, freedom and guidance. They often fight the powerlessness and confusion by asserting control however they can. Forming and holding to rigid opinions, affixing blame, and exacting some form of punishment upon those they feel have hurt them are some ways that teens try to cope. And, it should be noted, many of these responses serve a healthy purpose.

When a family goes through divorce, however, teenagers can bring these new skills to bear in ways that can be very difficult for everyone. To a greater extent than any other age group, teens are likely not only to choose sides between parents but to actively attempt to exploit the parents' diminished energy and time and even try to run the family. Whereas younger children typically continue to love their parents and view the divorce as the enemy, teens tend to hold their parents accountable for the divorce. Younger children can and do accept that divorce is something that happens despite their parents' best efforts. Teens, however, often feel that their parents didn't try hard enough. A 1992 Gallup poll of children between thirteen and seventeen reported two revealing findings. Three-quarters of these teens felt that it is too easy for parents to divorce, and 71 percent of those whose parents were divorced stated that they believed their parents could have tried harder to save their marriage.[1] For most teens, divorce is not something that "just happened." Their need for control may be expressed in their affixing blame for the divorce on one or both of you.

SHATTERING DREAMS

Because teens are dealing with their emerging sexuality and finding their footing on the carousel of romantic relationships, divorce poses several serious risks. Young adulthood is a time of struggle, but it is also a time of unlimited potential and dreams. At a time when everyone and everything around them seem to be saying that love is magical, perfect, and easy, your divorce is rudely sending them the opposite message. Depending on your circumstances, your teen may learn from divorce that love entails dishonesty, betrayal, pain, humiliation, and misery. This is not to say it's healthy to view love only through rose-colored glasses; it's not. However, most teenagers do not yet know that, nor do they necessarily need to for now. Those lessons will come in their own time, and your teen will learn them for himself. Teens whose parents divorce often lose the luxury of dreaming and hoping about love.

Although they are rapidly separating from you and achieving a greater sense of themselves as independent beings, what you do and how you live stay with your child. While teens will often claim that they don't want to be like their parents in some way, most recognize, deep inside, that they are very much like them and that this similarity transcends heredity or upbringing. Teens often wonder if their parents' divorce predisposes them to bad relationships and worry if they will

Puzzle peace? *A fourteen-year-old girl drew this puzzle of a broken heart. The jagged lines where the heart has been ripped, the jigsaw pieces that extend beyond the heart's boundaries, and the exclamation point following the word "divorce" suggest confusion and the pain of the parents' literally "breaking up." Beyond that, however, lie other possible meanings. After all, the whole point of a puzzle is to be put back together, to be made whole. This teenager may be revealing her hope of reuniting her parents. The puzzle theme may also represent her own puzzlement and confusion over the divorce.*

HOW TO EXPLAIN THE DIVORCE TO YOUR TEEN

What is divorce?

"Divorce is a legal process that parents go through when they no longer want to be married because they cannot be happy together anymore and have hurt each other too much. It means that we will no longer be married to each other, but we will always be your parents."

Why did it happen?

Some possibilities include:

"There are many reasons why. And it's not the specific items we argued about but the whole way we approached things. You may have heard us arguing about [fill in the blank], but those weren't the real problems. Many couples don't see eye to eye. But it's all about the attitude you take toward each other, especially when you disagree. We didn't listen to each other enough. You know how sometimes you want to say something so much you don't even hear what the other person is saying? That's how your mother/father and I got to be. We cared more about what we wanted to say and not enough about what the other person was saying."

"We didn't take the time to think *How will he/she feel about this?* before we said or did something that hurt him/her or made him/her angry. That was very unfair."

"We fought too much and didn't learn how to talk about our feelings without being angry and hurting each other."

"We didn't know how to stop arguing and walk away from a fight."

"We didn't make enough time to be alone together and be romantic. Couples can always find quiet time to be together, no matter how busy they are or how many kids they have. We just didn't do that." (This alleviates your teen's fear that he may have been the reason you two didn't have enough time.)

"We were not strong enough for each other, and we let other people and things confuse us about our relationship." (This keeps your teen from concluding that interference from others—affairs, in-laws, children—caused the divorce.)

"If other people or things came between us, it was because we let them. Each of us had the responsibility to make sure these outside things didn't affect our relationship, but we failed."

Will we still be a family?

"Yes. Even though your mother/father and I are getting a divorce, you will always be part of us. We both still love you and always will. You and Mom/Dad and you and I will always be families. We will not be in a family together, even though we will both belong to you as parents."

What will happen to me?

"You will be able to see both me and your mother/father a lot." (Then spell out custody and visitation arrangements as clearly and in as much detail as you can, stressing that the child will have some input into the plans. See chapter 12.)

THINGS 2 DO

I DREAM ABOUT . . .

With older children, discuss their dreams and aspirations. Also share what your dreams were at their age and what happened to satisfy or discourage them (only if you can do this without blaming your ex).

Additionally, ask your teenager to write a letter to herself about the things she would want to remind herself of in ten years and describing where she wants to be in her life at that time.

PURPOSE: As your child grows it becomes increasingly important for her to begin to seriously consider what is meaningful to her as well as to visualize plans of how to achieve her personal definition of success.

ever be able to have a happy marriage themselves. We all know the adolescent propensity for over-statement and overdramatization, but we must remind ourselves that while the expression may be somewhat exaggerated, the feelings, worries, and fears that inspire them are very real. It's not unusual for teenagers to feel that their parents' divorce marks them as nothing less than doomed.

GROWING UP TOO FAST

Resist the temptation to include your teen in your own problems. He is in many ways more like an adult than a child. A teen's growing emotional maturity and a parent's need to "reconnect" with him make it too easy for a parent to regard him as a source of support. Don't do it. It goes without saying that your teen's love and understanding are precious and perhaps seem even more so now. Still, your teen really is not an adult and certainly not your peer. Including him in discussions about your problems or making him your new best friend will not only force him to grow up too quickly, it will rob him of the crucial lessons of that phase. There is another danger here: It will also empower your child to become your ally in your dislike of your ex. For better or worse, your child's relationship with your ex should be based on how the two of them treat each other.

Only a parent can protect a child from growing up too fast. Be careful not to rationalize her involvement in your personal problems with "But she wants to help me. It makes her feel important." Of course it does; what teen doesn't want to be considered more grown-up? And don't be flattered by your teen's wish to be your "new spouse," emotionally speaking, and the bad feelings he shares with you toward your ex. This kind of behavior is only going to hurt your child in the long run and may very well backfire on you when he switches allegiances.

You should also be aware that teens who grow up "taking care of" and feeling inappropriately responsible for their parents are at high risk for growing up codependent on people with serious emotional or psychological problems and addictions. Codependents are often unable to love or be loved by anyone whom they cannot "help." It is wonderful and heartwarming to know that your teen loves and cares about you. However, always remember that you are the parent. Your teen needs to feel that you are there for him, not that he has to support you emotionally.

WITHDRAWAL AND DEPRESSION

The teenage years can be overwhelming, which is why some teens will just "shut off" during divorce. They might withdraw from you and other family members, friends, and others. They may give up on faking happiness and believe there's no point in even wishing for it. (See the boxes "Is Your Child Hiding Sadness?" page 130, and "Depression," page 154.) We tend to think of teenagers as avoiding and rejecting their parents, and to an extent, they do. However, recent research indicates that parent-child conflicts in the teen years frequently result from a parent's often-unconscious withdrawal from the teenage child—at a time when he needs you most.

The answer lies in understanding how he needs you now and adjusting your parenting style accordingly. Trying to connect with a child who is holed up in his room or whose response to every question is "I dunno" can wear you down and make it too easy to give up. Don't. Keep talking to your child and inviting him to join family activities. Resist the urge to leave him alone. Tell him you know that he's probably hurting because of the divorce, that you will never give up or walk away, that you are there for him. However, he still has responsibilities and obligations to you and your family, and his sadness does not excuse him from them.

How PARENTS CAN HELP TEENS

• *Be sensitive to your teen's true, unspoken feelings.* Recognize that your teen's antagonism toward, criticism of, and withdrawal from you may be his reaction to the overwhelming emotions he feels, not necessarily to you or your ex-spouse personally. Be aware of your own personal feelings about the fact that your child is growing up and away from you. If you feel yourself avoiding your teenager, try to understand why. If necessary, seek counseling to work through your personal issues. Don't reject your teen.

• *Acknowledge and support your teen whenever he demonstrates maturity (for example, in coming home at the time he promised, completing schoolwork, taking care of household chores).* However, be careful not to depend on him to do things that you would not expect were you not divorced (for example, comfort you or listen to you complain about his other parent).

• *If possible, be sure your teen has frequent and regular contact with your ex-spouse.* At this age, teens can conceptualize plans for events months into the future, but chances are, they will prefer to spend time with their peers. Frequent phone conversations with the noncustodial parent are recommended, but don't be surprised if your teen seems less enthusiastic about them than her younger brother. Remember, no matter how painful it may be to you, your teenager must begin to comfortably separate from her parents. While you or your ex-spouse may desire more contact with your teen because of the divorce, bear in mind that it's your teenager's developmental job to move away emotionally. That said, you and your ex-spouse should be sure one or both of you are available to your teen whenever she needs you or wants to talk. Exactly what you do may not be as important as the fact that your teen is secure in the knowledge that you are there for her if she ever needs you.

• *Never criticize your ex in front of your child.* Be sure that your words are consistent with your nonverbal cues. Teens are masters at deciphering the true meaning behind the raised eyebrow, the rolling eyes, and the smirk. They are also quick to note hypocrisy, dishonesty, and other ethical shortcomings. Be aware of these clues. When you express anger or disapproval of your ex-spouse, your teen comes away feeling deeply hurt because you are rejecting his parent, who is still a part of him. This is particularly true when you criticize your teen's same-sex parent.

Remember, too, that in a teen's eyes, your disparaging remarks about your ex are very likely to reflect poorly on you. More than any other age group, teens quickly grow sick and tired of the fighting and see parents who engage in bickering and name-calling as immature or worse. How can you reasonably expect your teen to consider your opinion on, say, dating, premarital sex, or college, if he thinks of you as behaving as a child?

Drowning out an argument. *This thirteen-year-old boy shuts out his parents' fighting by covering his ears, closing his eyes, and, typical of many teens, listening to music. Not content just to escape the fighting, he drowns it out by turning his giant speakers on his parents and happily walking away.*

In addition, since teens have a tendency to take sides and a desire to exert control in the family, remind yourself that such comments will only give your teen more ammunition. It's equally important that your teenager not interpret your sadness or pessimism as the product of the other parent's "wrongdoing." If your teen views you as the pitiful parent, the victim of the divorce, he will have a reason to take sides and will be extremely manipulated by your need to be rescued. This trains a child for codependency, as described earlier (see page 168). No matter what your ex did, you alone are responsible for your emotional state. It's okay to show your sadness to your child but ultimately remember your child depends on you to keep things together.

• *Maintain a calm, positive attitude in your child's presence.* Ultimately, teens draw from their parents' happiness and strength. This is not to say you can't feel sad or angry at times; that's inevitable. However, teens also need the security of a calm and generally positive environment. No one can do more to set the desired tone than you can.

• *Establish and stick to a normal but realistic daily routine.* Teens deal better with stress if you can maintain a degree of predictability in their lives, even though they themselves will usually bend, break, or disregard the household rules. Don't make allowances and exceptions where you would not if you were still married. On the other hand, don't expect him to participate in things he wouldn't have before. So while it may be unreasonable to demand that he go to the zoo with you and his nine-year-old brother, you can and should insist that he go with the family on a two-week vacation. Again, choose your battles.

• *Encourage your teen's social support system.* For most teens, who would rather be seen with anyone *but* their parents, this is hardly a problem. Social acceptance and the ability to forge and maintain close relationships outside the family are extremely important at this age. He can also find valuable support and guidance outside his peer group. Teens long for greater adult influence in their lives, though not necessarily from their parents. You may find that your teen is more comfortable talking to a favorite aunt or uncle, older sibling or cousin, teacher or adviser. Support these relationships.

• *Protect your teen's personal environment and her privacy.* Make sure she has privacy, especially if you are relocating, and allow her to decorate her room as she wishes, within the budget specified. Kids this age often prefer to spend time alone in their rooms and resent any intrusion into their privacy. However, be aware of sudden changes in behavior that might signal problems (see the box "Depression," page 154).

• *Maintain consistency.* Set limits for the most important issues: curfew, grades, participation in family activities, dating, and so on. Don't allow inappropriate behavior, and don't let it be excused by the divorce. Now more than at any other stage, kids will test parents and probably will push the boundaries until both parents resist. Appearances to the contrary, most teens value their relationship with their parents and will back down if they believe their behavior is jeopardizing it. Throughout this book, I've limited my "coparent talk" because, in most cases, it is unrealistic. With teens, however, it's imperative that you two stand together on as many important, big issues as you possibly can.

For the most part, however, kids this age will not be confused if your household rules differ from your ex's. It's all a matter of proportion and priority. You forbid blasting the stereo, and your ex-spouse actually enjoys it; you insist everyone sit down for dinner on weeknights, and your ex runs her kitchen like a twenty-four-hour cafeteria; you don't allow phone calls after ten on school nights, and your ex gives the kids their own line and doesn't care when they talk. Save your fire for the big issues, where you will really need it.

• *Anticipate signs of stress.* These include changes in eating and sleeping patterns, diminished or lost interest in people and activities, and problems with school. Remain lovingly firm about behaviors that are not acceptable, but generous in offering reassurance, support, and understanding. In these teens, stress may also manifest in such indirect forms as physical symptoms (headache, stomachache, and so on), a reluctance to attend school, or a sudden transformation into a "perfect" teen. Watch for signs of depression and take seriously any talk of suicide (see the box "Depression," page 154).

Words and weapons. *A thirteen-year-old boy uses strong, unequivocal imagery and words to express his anger and frustration.*

• *Encourage your teen to talk about her feelings.* However, brace yourself for criticism, questioning, and, perhaps for the first time, your child's expression of disappointment in you. Remember that your teen does not have to speak about the divorce specifically, nor should you try to push every conversation in that direction. If your teen is talking about feeling angry, for example, the simple fact that he has named and is expressing that emotion is very helpful.

Teens will often talk about their problems indirectly. For example, your son might talk about another boy's family that has experienced divorce or loss; your daughter might seem unusually interested in discussing a play, movie, television program, or book that deals with strong emotions or a divorce-type situation. It is also common for teens to behave as if they are untroubled by the divorce but to express concern about a sibling.

Do not force the teen to focus on herself, or even on your family's particular situation. While your teen does not seem to be talking about herself, remind yourself that she is, and that whatever guidance, reassurance, or comfort you offer is valuable even if it doesn't address the "real issue" head-on. Remember that the simple act of listening provides validation and support. Your teen may have to repeat these concerns, and you may have these discussions many times before she works it through. This does not mean that she "didn't get it," only that she is moving through the process of understanding.

• *Talk to the other adults in your teen's life (teachers, best friend's parents) about the divorce and ask how she is responding.* Don't be surprised to learn that your teen behaves differently around others than she does at home. For example, she may be unusually quiet at home but argumentative at school. Also be on the watch for the onset of new behaviors, like aggression, withdrawal, or a sudden lack of pleasure in

THINGS 2 DO

CHARTED WATERS

Divide a paper into four columns, each titled as shown. Ask your child to list one or more difficulties he is experiencing in the left column. Then work through the other columns. If appropriate, parents can share some of their own issues and elicit their children's suggestions on filling in the next three columns.

The situation	How I would like it to be	What I can do to facilitate this	How I can feel better if I can't change it
Less money since Dad moved out	Want to get a car	Get a summer job	Realize that Mom will take me most places I want to go

PURPOSE: This exercise helps kids clarify issues and focus on their problem-solving skills. Additionally, it addresses the reality that some problems have no simple solutions but that attitude and planning can make a big difference.

activities and people she used to enjoy. Let any adult with whom your teen spends time know that you want to be informed of any changes in attitude or behavior.

• *Understand that your teen may feel very possessive of you and feel threatened by the sudden appearance of new people in your life.* Don't be surprised or angry if your teen seems to hate anyone with whom he feels he is sharing you. He may also feel that you are betraying his other parent or the family, or that by simply being polite to your new friend, he is being disloyal to the other parent. Just beginning to take notice of the opposite gender and contemplating dating himself, he may find the idea of your dating shocking, distasteful, or simply "uncool." (I address the issue of parents' dating in chapter 15.)

• *Take time to enjoy your teen.* Try to find activities you can enjoy together, like biking, gardening, sharing favorite movies, Rollerblading, cooking—anything. For many teens, quietly hanging out together watching a game or a movie is an important part of relating to you. Though working around the house together or going out to do errands may not qualify for some as quality time, it should not be overlooked. Don't make the mistake of waiting for the "perfect" time or the once-a-year big vacation or event. Be with your teen here and now.

Q *Dear Gary,*
My sixteen-year-old twin girls have not stopped fighting since my husband and I separated. Neither of us was a saint in this marriage, and the girls know it. Even though we've carefully explained that we were both to blame, they refuse to give up making one of us the villain and the other the victim. Surely they don't really believe that. I suspect something else is going on, but I'm not sure what or how to deal with it.

A It is common for teenagers to choose sides because it makes them a part of the divorce and in control. Blaming Mom, for example, and siding with Dad does serve a purpose: It usually gets parents to react. Dad divulges more than he should as his sixteen-year-old becomes more of a confidante than a daughter. Mom tries to sway her by sharing even more problems in the marriage. Don't fall into this trap.

Your daughters' fighting probably indicates their own attempt to control or master their intense feelings about the divorce. By arguing, they become more comfortable with the parental fights that broke up the marriage. Explain this to them and remind them that your fights damaged your marriage and broke apart your family. However, also tell them that it wasn't fighting that ended the marriage but the mutual lack of sensitivity, healthy communication, and respect that sparked the fighting in the first place. Help your daughters understand your sensitivity to their being out of control and their attempt to join the battle. At the same time, stress that divorce signals the end of the fight, for everyone.

Q *Dear Gary,*
My husband and I have read all the books, spent thousands on family therapy, and tried to present a calm, united front for the sake of our fifteen-year-old son. Despite this, three years after our breakup, our son can't seem to get past his hatred of his father and his stepmother. In his eyes, his father's affair with her ruined our lives. I know there are many factors that go into a marriage and a divorce, but there's no question that my ex's affair, and his future wife's blatant pursuit of him, led to our split-up. How can I stop my son from blaming people who are clearly guilty?

A First, be clear about what your real objective should be: ensuring that your son has a healthy, ongoing relationship with his father. This does not mean that he must forgive him or even feel warmly toward his stepmother. What he does need to do, however, is reach some understanding and resolution about a situation that no one can change. If your son fails to do this, it threatens not only his relationship with his dad but his ability to have healthy, trusting relationships himself.

As his mother, it's important for you to make your son realize that his anger and rage are harmful to him. Start by helping him see the bigger picture. You mention the many factors that contribute to a marriage and divorce; sit down with your son and draw up lists of what these are, then discuss them. (See the boxes "Make Sure Your Teen Understands That . . . ," page 163, and "How to Explain the Divorce to Your Teen," page 167.) Admit your own mistakes in the marriage, and explain that while the affair may have been an important factor, it was not the only one.

Your next step is to help your son work through his anger at his father. You might role-play conversations in which your son can express what he would say to his father. His expressing these feelings directly to his father—in person, on the phone, or in a letter—will help him dispel some of his anger and empower him. However, this will work only if your son does so because he wants to repair the relationship. Ranting and raving in an attempt to push his father away will not make him feel better or alleviate the intense anger and hurt he feels. Ideally, his father has apologized and explained to his son that infidelity is not an acceptable option in marriage. If not, and if your relationship allows, you might gently urge him to do so or discuss the point yourself, but only if you can speak from a place of love for your son, not hatred of your ex.

Finally, your son stands to learn a greater lesson that he will turn to many times in years to come: People make mistakes. You can help your son understand that, even when people make serious mistakes, these people still have value and still can make positive contributions to our lives. Again, you're not asking him to forgive and forget but to accept what's happened and remember the good things his father has to offer him. Through this, both you and he should remember that hurt feelings take time to heal.

CHAPTER 8

The Challenge of Change

Every family, every child, and every divorce is unique. While those of us who have studied divorce can offer insight and guidelines, raising a child isn't like following a recipe. Countless factors—some you know well, others that might surprise you—can come into play. It certainly would be simpler for everyone if we could say, "All chil-

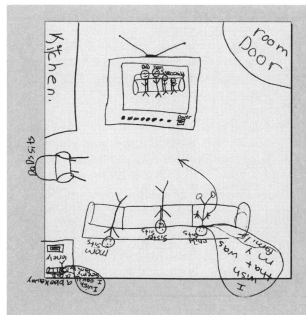

Chasing the fantasy family. *This busy but eloquent drawing expresses one young adolescent's realization of the discrepancy between the ideal, intact family and one divided by divorce. This bird's-eye view shows us Dad, "a block away" and "lonely," saying "I wish I could see my family." In the larger family home, his chair is empty while his family sits on the couch and watches a TV family, also on a couch but complete. Of the perfect, fantasy family, the child expresses a very common sentiment: "I wish that was my family."*

FILL MY SHOES

Take off your shoes and let your child wear them. Now put your feet into the front of his shoes. Each of you talk about what it's like to be the other. What would you do differently; what do you think bothers you now that you are the other person? For example, Mom, wearing Jamal's shoes, says, "Wow, now that I'm Jamal, I am…"

Variation: "I'll be the parent." Announce to your child that she is the parent and you are now her. For example, you could say, "Boy, I feel funny about your getting a divorce. I wonder why this happened." Wait for your child's response. Watch for responses that indicate guilt such as, "I don't know. Maybe you could have done better in school," and use any of the responses to continue the dialogue.

When Jamal put on his mother's shoes, he said, "Wow, I have so much work to do, and I'm so tired. I can barely move. Help me with dinner, and then I'll try to read you a story." Jamal's mother realized she might be showing her child too much of her pressures, and she needed to be more playful. Jamal-as-Mom then said, "I would do one thing differently: Kiss my Jamal more."

When Jamal put his father's shoes on he picked up the newspaper and said, "I have to get on the phone now. I'll be off soon. Watch some TV for a while." His father began to recognize he needed separate times that he could spend uninterrupted with his son.

PURPOSE: Switching roles gives children the chance to express how they perceive their parents in an appropriate and nonthreatening manner. Parents can learn a great deal from such honest expression. Talk to your child afterward about her view. Be careful not to defend yourself but rather understand how your child is feeling and sensing her environment. Also be careful not to insult your child while playing her role. Mimicking her whining will not help in reducing the behavior. Use this role-changing activity to focus on a positive trait you find or want to cultivate in your child.

dren freely express sadness when their parents divorce," "Every child wants to see both parents equally," or "The transition into a stepfamily can be made easier if you follow these three simple steps."

No one can do that, because every family comes to divorce with its own history. For example, fourteen-year-old Angie and her eleven-year-old brother, Chris, had become so upset and depressed over their parents' constant fighting that they welcomed news of their parents' divorce with a sigh of relief. Down the street, sixteen-year-old Dennis and his two younger sisters responded to their parents' breakup with shock and anger. After all, they seemed to be getting along so well all these years. *What happened?*

Parents often seek advice, from relatives, friends, books, television, and professional counselors. Ultimately, however, you are the one who will be answering the questions, wiping the tears, weathering the tantrums, and deciding what to do. As I've said before—and truly believe—no one could possibly know your child as well as you do. But perhaps even more important, no one else can or will be there for your child in these moments the way you can. Sometimes, despite all the "expert" guidance, your kids still can surprise you.

> Marta and Greg have three children and are divorcing after fourteen years of marriage. After reading a few books on children of divorce, Marta was certain that the separation from Greg would make normally shy, three-year-old Stephanie even shier and more withdrawn. Instead, Stephanie became a nonstop ball of energy who chattered to anyone who would listen. Greg worried that moving to a new school would cause ten-year-old Steve, an average student, to fail. Instead Steve has thrown himself into becoming a perfect A student. Neither worried too much about thirteen-year-old Rosalie, who just last year was class president and a star field-hockey player. Yet months after the separation, Rosalie had withdrawn from her usual group of

friends, become interested in vampires and gothic, macabre rock, and began professing her anger at "the world."

Marta and Greg knew to look beyond their children's outward behavior. After Marta spoke with Stephanie's day-care teacher, she learned that while Stephanie appeared to be more outgoing, she was fighting more with her classmates and would often burst into tears. Marta noticed that every time Stephanie had a friend over to play, she would become very possessive of her toys and refuse to share: "It's mine! And this is my house! And you can't take anything unless I say you can!" Marta wondered whether or not Stephanie's possessiveness might be an attempt to exert control over her world, to keep anything else she loved from disappearing, like her parents' marriage had. "It can be sad to lose the way things used to be," Marta offered. Stephanie nodded, clutching her doll. In this brief exchange, Marta had given Stephanie words to express her feelings and let her know that she understood.

Across town, Greg was understandably relieved that school no longer seemed a problem for Steve. Still, he didn't overlook the fact that Steve had begun biting his nails and hadn't made any new friends. His son's apparent lack of joy or pride in his achievements was also troubling. Steve was the kind of kid who would burst through the door grinning whenever he had good news. Now he responded to praise with a shrug or by saying, "It was nothing. We learned that stuff last year." If he didn't care, why was he making the effort? *Maybe he thinks his grades had something to do with our breaking up,* Greg thought. He let his son off the hook by explaining on a couple of occasions that only he and Marta were to blame for the divorce. "Your mother and I made some mistakes in our marriage. It had nothing to do with you or anything you did." Steve smiled and after some further discussion, he hugged his dad. Next report card, he was getting his usual B's and C's, but he had joined the basketball team and made a few new friends.

Marta and Greg refused to be shut out by Rosalie's sullenness. Instead of criticizing the CDs she played, her all-black wardrobe, or her exasperating ambivalence about everything, they just kept talking and letting her know they were there for her. One day when Marta mentioned how as a teenager she had been fascinated by Alice Cooper and Black Sabbath, Rosalie snapped, "It's not the same, Mom. Your parents weren't divorced. You and Dad are. How else could you expect me to feel? Everything just seems so hopeless!"

"But, honey, the divorce has nothing to do with you. You know that. And we love you," Marta replied.

"Yeah, but how can I ever get anything together? If you guys couldn't work out your problems and get it together, what can I do? What's the use anyway?"

"Rosalie, listen to me. It's okay to feel sad. I admit your dad and me getting a divorce has been hard on you. But we're still a family, and things will get better. Maybe not today or tomorrow, but soon. In the meantime, we're both here for you whenever you need us or want to talk, about anything. If you think your dad and I could have done a better job working on our marriage, you may be right. We can talk about that, too, you know."

Happy days are here again. *As this adolescent girl's drawing illustrates, in some families, divorce comes as a welcome relief from unhappiness.*

Marta and Greg had gone into their divorce convinced it was the best option for them. At the same time, however, they held no illusions about how it might affect their children. Whatever their disagreements with each other, both parents agreed that it was crucial they communicate when it came to the children. They also took the time to find out how divorce can affect children and learned not to accept their children's behavior at face value. By keeping their eyes open and considering other, less obvious explanations, Greg and Marta were able to tune in to their children and address their problems sooner rather than later.

You may be thinking, *It can't be that simple,* and you're right. These were not onetime conversations that magically made everything right. Rather, they were just the first steps in a long journey of communication, understanding, and growth. Marta and Greg will probably replay variations on these themes fifty or a hundred times more. Weeks, months, or years later, other questions and problems may arise. But as long as their children are secure in the knowledge that their feelings can be expressed in a healthy way and their questions answered, they stand a good chance of growing up to see the divorce as one difficult episode in, rather than the defining moment of, their lives.

Some divorce-related events, such as telling the kids you're breaking up, are universal and unavoidable. Others, like helping your child

IF YOU EXPERIENCED A DIFFICULT CHILDHOOD OR ARE A CHILD OF DIVORCE

We derive much of our parenting ability from our basic personality. A parent who is naturally positive, comfortable discussing feelings, and physically demonstrative probably experienced a warm, loving childhood. How we were parented directly affects our relationship with our own children as well. If, for example, you never had a close relationship with your mother, you as a mother may find it harder to be close to your daughter. It's important to look at and understand the aspects of our own childhoods that may be working for or against our desire to become better parents.

If you are a child of divorce, you may be especially sensitive to what your own child is experiencing now. On the positive side, you may have greater insight than a parent whose own parents did not divorce. If your child is old enough to know about your childhood experience, he might be more open with you, believing that you do understand what he's going through.

If you have reached some personal resolution with your parents' divorce and grown through it, your experience can be a wonderful asset for your family now. If, however, you still harbor strong emotions, have unresolved issues, or find that certain events trigger old, powerful memories and feelings, this can be problematic for your child. Even though each divorce is unique, the emo-

tions divorce stirs are pretty universal. When your child cries because he misses his father or your ex-spouse accuses you of not spending enough time with your children, you may feel yourself being swept back in time and replaying old emotions. To protect yourself, you may unconsciously avoid your child's sadness, sending him the subtle signals that you don't want to hear about it, or convincing yourself that it's affecting him less than it really is. Another possible effect is that your emotional responses to your ex may be more pronounced. If your ex left the same way your father did, for example, your feelings may be especially intense. You may be more angry than you would otherwise.

If you feel extremely angry at your ex, sad, or withdrawn from your child, take note. Instead of rationalizing why you can't do this or do that for yourself or your child, carefully consider your past. Is your current situation reviving some old struggles and painful feelings? Do you find yourself feeling powerless and helpless, as you did when you were a child? Is seeing your own child struggle with divorce too painful for you? For your child's sake and your own, you must learn to separate your old business from your new business. If you find that it's difficult for you to do that, seek help from a therapist or a peer (single-parent or adult child of divorce) support group.

learn to deal with a new stepparent or a new baby half sibling, may come up ten months or ten years later, or never. In the best of all possible worlds, children and parents would have ample time to adjust to changes and to reconcile themselves with the new facts of their lives. Unfortunately, families in transition rarely have that luxury. So much about the divorce experience seems so far beyond control, it may appear that all you can do is hang on tight and hope for the best.

Parents can do more, and for their children's sake, they should. The few things you really can control are among the most important to your child's healthy adjustment. By simply adopting a positive, forward-thinking attitude toward the divorce and making sure your child feels loved,

T H I N G S 2 D O

CONNECTING CARDS

Using small index cards, index-card-weight sheets, or just plain paper, make a deck of twenty cards. (You can make as many cards as you wish if you think of other messages.) You can also purchase blank flash cards in the children's section of many large bookstores and in teacher-supply stores. Write one of the following messages on a card:

• Ask one question about the other person; this is to be answered honestly. [Note: No questions are permitted regarding personal information about the other parent and the divorce, such as "Did Daddy have an affair?"]

• Find a wishing well or create one using a bowl. Throw in coins and share your wishes aloud. Talk about what will happen if they do come true and what will happen if they don't.

• This card entitles bearer to give three hugs tomorrow.

• Share one goal or fear.

• I appreciate you when _____.

• I would feel more loved by you if you would _____.

• One day soon, I want to _____.

• I feel good when you tell me _____.

• The thing I like most about a friend is _____.

• The thing I am embarrassed about is _____.

• Two things I don't like about myself are _____.

• Two things I love about myself are _____.

• The two most wonderful memories of our family are _____.

• This card entitles bearer to choose his or her favorite game, to be played with other players within the next two days.

• This card entitles bearer to choose his or her favorite music, to be listened to with other players within the next two days.

• Describe your perfect day with each member of your family.

If desired, together fill out the remaining blank cards with other activities or questions that will help the two of you share your thoughts and feelings. Place all the cards in a bowl, bag, jar, or hat. Twice a week, you and your child pick two cards and follow the directions. Do this for four weeks, or as often as you find it useful.

PURPOSE: In times of change or crisis, distance can grow between parent and child. These connecting cards serve as a springboard for intimacy and sharing. Remember to continue this theme of self-disclosure and trust by reviewing the conversations and adding to them in the coming days.

wanted, respected, valued, and understood, you give your whole family a tremendous advantage. For your sake and your child's, don't ever give up. Divorce does not doom a family. Remember that kids do not stand or fall simply because their parents divorce. By listening to, validating, and supporting your child, you make it possible for him to emerge from the experience with self-esteem, confidence, and even a capacity for joy.

Getting better all the time. *As this teen's drawing illustrates simply, parental love and sensitivity during and after divorce can provide the emotional support children need to feel better about their families and themselves.*

We help our children move on not by ignoring their pain but by helping them express it; not by diminishing their problems but by helping them find solutions or, if that's not possible, resolution. Some of the problems divorce presents have no solutions, and our job as parents is to help children cope.

Twelve-year-old Becky had to have two elementary-school graduation parties because her parents could not get along and their respective extended families hated each other. Becky couldn't bear not celebrating with everyone, and her parents were intractable. There simply was no creative solution to this problem. Whenever anyone mentioned the two parties, Becky would just reply, "It's okay, really."

Becky's father, Ed, knew in his heart it wasn't all okay, and one night he said to her, "Look, Becky, you've told me it's all right about these separate parties, and I'll drop it if you honestly tell me it's okay with you. But let's be real. You don't act as if you're happy about it, and if I were in your shoes, I'd be sad and disappointed. It would take all the fun of graduating from me."

Becky started to cry. Ed had tapped into the feelings she felt she could not express. "Yeah, I really don't understand why I have to suffer just because everyone else is acting like a big baby. If you love me and Mom loves me, and all the other relatives love me so much, why can't you just get your act together for a few measly hours one day and behave? Why do I have to suffer? I didn't ask you guys to divorce. I didn't ask everyone else to take sides. This is my party. It shouldn't feel like *West Side Story!*"

Ed nodded and drew a deep breath. After Becky calmed down a little, he said, "Honey, I'm sorry it's this way. I really am. And what I'm about to say in no way excuses or makes up for anyone's behavior. I wish I could give you a perfect day, but I can't. What I can do, though, is help you to have the best day you can. So we can't have one big party. Okay. Let's think about what's going to be great about those two parties."

"Well," Becky said, wiping her eyes, "lots of kids don't get even one party."

"There you go. And what about the cake?"

"You mean the *cakes?*" Becky laughed.

"And Aunt Elena is bringing your new baby cousin, Alison, and Uncle Scott is coming in from out of town."

"Yeah, there's sure a lot to look forward to. I'll still be sad that it won't be one big party, but I won't let that ruin the fun I will have."

"That's my girl. Becky, will you please give me a picture of yourself at the other party? I'd love to see it."

"Sure, Dad. I love you."

Of course, just having this conversation did not magically bring her family back together again. The bitter feelings would still endure; there would still be two graduation parties. But Becky could enjoy her day more just knowing that someone understood her feelings, someone shared her conviction that something was definitely wrong with this picture, that as great as each of her parties might be, the fact that there were two of them really was not okay.

As simple as this exchange might appear, in truth, a lot occurred. Ed was careful to let Becky really express her feelings and deal with the negatives before he attempted to convince her of the positives. Too often, we parents are so determined to eliminate the negative that we trample over our children's feelings as we busily rattle on about the "bright side." Unless your child has expressed and dealt with her negative feelings, there is no bright side, no matter how you present it. And when you continue to harp on it, you send your child the message that her bad or painful feelings are not important to you.

Becky's father was also careful not to defend his or anyone else's behavior or to "set her straight." Saying things like "Well, I would be there if your mother would allow it" would accomplish nothing and simply reemphasize the problem.

Most important, however, Ed allowed Becky to have the chance to understand that life is not always an either-or proposition. We can approach even the happiest of occasions with mixed feelings. It is possible to be sad over the reason why you must have two separate parties and yet be happy to see your friends and your new baby cousin. One emotion doesn't necessarily cancel the other out; one positive aspect does not make up for the negatives. To cope with the myriad complexities of divorce, children need to learn that the glass can be both half empty *and* half full.

Children can be remarkably resilient. I hesitate to even say that, since we too often depend on that supposedly innate resiliency to compensate for the time not spent, the words not said, the emotional or physical absence of one or both parents. It simply cannot. Resiliency, the ability to bounce back from traumatic experience, is the result of a child's having been loved, supported, and cared for, not a substitute for it. Your child's resiliency begins with you. And bear in mind that the communication and coping skills you model and teach her today will be with her forever. In helping your child deal with divorce, you are also giving her the ability to manage whatever else life may bring her way, even years ahead.

From our research at Sandcastles and in numerous other studies, we know that children can have very strong, overwhelming reactions to specific events and circumstances. These reactions can color—for better or worse—how they feel about all that follows. Many adult children of divorce remember vividly decades later the day they heard "the news." Others harbor long-standing feelings of anger and rejection over slights from stepfamily members or a parent's rush into a new romantic relationship. Older and adult children of divorce often retain surprisingly keen and painful memories that focus on what many adults would consider details. One thirty-year-old woman I know still gets teary-eyed when she recalls how her stepfather refused to let her and her brothers hang their Christmas stockings on the mantel of his new home as they had always done at their old home because it would "ruin" the wood. A successful forty-something attorney still experiences a nervous twinge every time the phone rings late at night; it reminds him of the call he answered at age ten, when his father angrily announced he was leaving.

Your ability as a parent to anticipate and respond to these crises can make all the difference. While we can neither control every divorce-related change in our lives nor protect our children from every possible hurt, with foresight and care we can eliminate or at least reduce their impact. Simply considering where you and your child are when you tell her that you are about to remarry or how you announce the fact that the family will be moving to another home makes a big difference in how your child hears and responds to the news.

Responses from kids in the Sandcastles Program show clearly that children do not really expect everything to be "perfect." The fact that they have been touched by divorce has already taught them that we cannot always have things exactly as we want them. What these kids do need to know and will truly appreciate is that their parents made a conscientious effort to cushion the blows, to smooth out the rough spots. Of course, that's easier said than done. What makes divorce so difficult for parents and kids is that it often prompts the responses we don't count on. No wonder even parents who feel that they know their children very well often go through divorce feeling as if they've been swinging at curve balls.

The following chapters address the most common situations changing families encounter. Although they are written so that you can read only what you need right now, I urge you to also read through the chapters that might conceivably apply to you and your children in the future.

DECIDING ON THERAPY

At one time or another, every parent has looked at a child's behavior and wondered, *Is this normal?* For most parents, psychological intervention is a last resort in dealing with a child's negative behavior that

✔ is drastically different, unusual, or uncharacteristic;

✔ is persistent, lasting more than a few weeks;

✔ creates problems for the child or the family that you can no longer tolerate or ignore.

If you have not done so already, take the time to read the preceding age-specific chapter that pertains to your child. Look at not only the chapter concerning his age today but all the developmental periods immediately before and after your separation and divorce. Once you have a clearer idea of the behaviors and feelings typical of children in general and of children of divorce in particular, you can put the behavior in context and decide whether therapy might be warranted. As you consider this decision, remember that turning to therapy does not mean that you are a "bad" parent, that there is something "wrong" with your child, or that you have in some way failed her. As I hope I've made clear throughout this book, divorce can be an incredibly difficult transition. If seeking professional help for your child, yourself, or your family eases this passage, then it is worthwhile, for you will have given your child the gift that divorce sometimes steals: a happier childhood.

How to Choose a Therapist

This is one of the most important decisions you will make regarding your child's therapeutic experience. Needless to say, I don't recommend you just pick a name out of the Yellow Pages. Begin by collecting recommendations from a variety of sources. Your child's pediatrician is probably the best place to start. Others who may be familiar with providers in your area would be your child's teacher, your child's school psychologist, other divorced parents or members of parent support groups, friends whose children are in therapy, and your divorce attorney. Also contact community health organizations and local university medical centers both for referrals and, if necessary, information on agencies that may offer services for a sliding-scale fee.

Most families are limited as to whom they may see by insurance considerations. With the rapid changes occurring in that area, it's impossible to give useful, specific advice. However, before picking a therapist, you should make it your business to find out the following from your insurance company:

✔ What coverage do you provide for psychotherapy?

✔ Are evaluations and testing covered? If so, to what extent? Are sessions covered? If so, to what extent? Find out specifically how many visits or what time period is covered (for example, one policy may cover unlimited visits over a three-month period; another may cover twenty visits per year).

✔ What types of providers do you cover?

✔ In my area, who are the providers you work with? (Get their names and numbers.)

✔ If a referral from a primary-care physician is needed, which physician can make this referral?

Who Can Provide Therapy?

Not only is there a range of professionals from a range of disciplines and backgrounds who provide therapy, but licensing requirements vary, sometimes drastically, from state to state. Outlined here are some of the basic distinctions among types of providers; speak with your child's physician or your local mental health agency to learn more about your state's specific licensing requirements for each.

✔ A *psychiatrist* is an M.D. who specializes in emotional and psychological disorders and mental health. Of the practitioners listed here, only a psychiatrist can evaluate a patient for and prescribe medications. Often a psychiatrist will work closely with a child's therapist but will not meet with the child himself for ongoing therapy.

✔ A *psychologist* usually has a doctorate degree (although this may not be the case in all states) and sees clients for ongoing therapy. If an evaluation and psychological testing are needed, they are usually performed by a psychologist.

✔ A *psychoanalyst* is usually a psychiatrist or psychologist (although some are social workers) who has received training and certification to practice psychoanalysis.

✔ *Social worker, mental health counselor, family therapist,* and *psychotherapist* are all terms applied to people who have completed a graduate degree in the mental health field. This is an area in which requirements vary considerably from state to state. Usually, these practitioners can see private clients and perform the same counseling duties as a psychologist.

✔ *Clergy* may have some formal education in the area of psychotherapy, but states vary widely in whether members of the clergy must have such training and to what degree.

What Are Some Commonly Used Approaches and Methodologies, and How Do They Differ?

✔ *Psychoanalysis* is usually an intensive (two or three or more sessions a week), long-term (continuing for years) method pioneered by psychiatrist Sigmund Freud. The premise behind psychoanalysis is that problems can be better understood and solved by tracing their genesis, usually back to childhood. This method is rarely used for younger children.

✔ *Psychodynamic therapy* is similar to psychoanalysis in that it attempts to trace problems to their roots (usually one's childhood). However, it maintains focus on resolving the present issue as opposed to psychoanalysis's broad exploration of personality. The meetings are usually face-to-face and less frequent than in psychoanalysis.

✔ *Behavioral therapy* is based on the theory that we learn behavior and attitudes and that these can be changed, modified, or replaced with proper focus and practice.

✔ *Cognitive therapy* seeks to solve problems by helping the client change how he views himself and the negative thoughts and behaviors that stem from his self-image.

✔ *Family therapy* brings together two or more family members to deal with their problems in a safe, neutral environment. The focus of family therapy is often the improvement of communication among family members and development of new approaches to solving common, chronic problems. It also attempts to help family members understand why they interact the way they do.

✔ *Group therapy* brings together several clients who have experiences in common. Groups offer "safety in numbers" and support from different people whose similar experiences often give them a unique understanding of one another.

✔ *Eclectic* is a term used by some therapists to describe their multidisciplinary approach. Ask the therapist to explain fully his approach.

What Further Qualifications Should You Look For?

I strongly suggest that you seek someone who has a great deal of experience with the problems of children of divorce. Be aware, however, that there are no standard educational or licensing requirements for specialization. If he states he is *certified* in a specific area, that usually indicates he has had formal training. When a therapist says he specializes in a particular area, it simply means that he concentrates in that area. That said, your therapist should also be able to spot and suggest further evaluation for possible non-divorce-related factors, such as learning disorders, neurological or psychological conditions that may warrant medication, and other factors, that may be contributing to, even causing, your child's problem. Wherever you have a choice, consider the practical issues as well: cost, convenience of location, and so on. When the going gets rough, as it can in therapy, clients and their families can be tempted to rationalize reasons for quitting. If you think you'll resent the two-hour round-trip to the therapist every week, consider finding a qualified person closer. If you know you can't possibly afford one provider's fees, try to negotiate a lower rate or seek out someone equally qualified whose fees are more in line with your budget. In other words: Set yourself and your child up to succeed in therapy.

Which Therapist Will Be Right for Your Child?

Ideally, you should be able to meet with a potential therapist, discuss the problem, and then learn from him how he would approach it. He should explain to you his philosophy and his methods and what that will mean, in practical terms, for you and your child. Don't be afraid to ask questions and express your thoughts on what the goals of the therapy will be. Psychology is a very inexact science; every child is different. Let your therapist know what you seek to accomplish in the long term (improvement of self-esteem, for example) and in the short term (reduction of temper tantrums upon leaving for visitation, for example). After he's worked with your child, ask the therapist to explain to you what areas he will be focusing on and why. This way, you can work together as a team for your child's benefit.

Therapy and the Courts

There may come a time when the professional opinion of a therapist will be sought to determine matters of custody and visitation. Some parents feel it's better to try to kill two birds with one stone, so they choose a therapist who can provide both ongoing therapy for their child and an evaluation and testimony in court, if necessary. Tempting as this might be (for reasons of cost and convenience), I urge you to reconsider. For your child to benefit from therapy, she must trust her therapist implicitly. She must be able to confide in her therapist and feel certain that her trust will never be betrayed. Many parents are surprised to learn that when a therapist is called upon to make an evaluation or to testify in court, the findings are *not* confidential. I feel very strongly about this point; in fact, even when I've been subpoenaed to testify in cases involving my clients, I explain to the judge what I explain to parents before we begin: Testifying damages the child's trust in me, usually sabotages or "undoes" whatever progress has been made, and virtually ensures that one parent—the one the child has expressed the most anger toward, usually—will believe that I'm doing a poor job with the child. Ultimately, the child and her faith in the therapeutic practice are harmed, sometimes irrevocably. Therefore, if your child needs ongoing therapy, find someone who will be there for her, and, if it becomes necessary, get a separate evaluation to comply with the court's desires.

What Else Should You Know About Therapy and Your Child?

Minors have the right of privacy unless they verbalize any desire to commit suicide or homicide or discuss any form of abuse that they are experiencing. Every state has some form of mandatory reporting of abuse. When a child discloses abuse he has experienced or an intention to commit suicide or homicide, state laws demand that the therapist report it to the appropriate authorities. These may include the abuse investigation bureau of that state, a parent, or the person who may be the target

of a violent or homicidal attack. When you discuss your child's progress with her therapist, you should not be given details. Say, for instance, twelve-year-old Sharlene tells me that Dad screams at her a lot and Mom's always out with her boyfriend. All I will—and should—tell Mom and Dad is my impression of what Sharlene has described: Sharlene needs to feel more trusting of her environment. I can then suggest ways this might be accomplished. In addition, your therapist should understand that he is not to release any information about your child to anyone else for any reason without a parent's or legal guardian's express written permission.

What Can You Do to Help Your Child in Therapy?

While your child shares a unique relationship with her therapist, the support of parents is crucial to your child's success in therapy. Therapy works best when parents

✔ bring their child to therapy on time and consistently,

✔ do not discuss the child's therapy with someone else when she is present, or can hear,

✔ respect her right not to talk about therapy,

✔ discuss the concept of therapy in a respectful manner,

✔ maintain communication with the therapist to discuss the ongoing goals and changes that have occurred,

✔ work to support the goals of therapy in the home and at school.

Obviously, you're considering therapy to help create positive changes in your child. Even so, it's not uncommon for parents to sabotage, either deliberately or subconsciously, the therapy process and their child's progress. It sounds paradoxical, but if we look closely and honestly at what therapy is and what it represents, it's easy to see—and watch for—why parents can feel conflicted about it.

Every conscientious parent wants to be everything to his child. Accepting that your child has a problem you cannot solve for him or that he cannot solve alone takes courage and sensitivity. I've heard people say they feel that going to therapy is like "paying to have a best friend," which really misses this crucial fact: Therapy works because the therapist is a stranger with a degree of objectivity about the child and his issues that a parent often cannot provide. The idea that a stranger could have the answers that we don't, that someone we hadn't even heard of weeks before has "beat us out" of our job, can be very hard to accept. Worse, though, it can color a parent's view of therapy and of the changes it brings.

The realization that your child may be sharing extremely private, confidential information about himself, you, your ex, and your family can also be discomforting. Some parents are intensely aware of their feelings, and they may simply refuse to allow their child to enter therapy, no matter how bad the problem. More often, however, a parent will go along with finding the therapist and having the child begin the work, then signal in various ways ambivalence or anxiety about it. The father who rolls his eyes and complains when his schedule is disrupted by having to drive his child to appointments, the mother who casually mentions, "You could have those hundred-dollar sneakers if we didn't have to pay for therapy," the well-meaning but misdirected relative who expresses fears about family secrets being revealed to "a stranger," all send the child messages counterproductive to the therapy process.

Check your behavior and attitudes about your child's therapy and be honest. Even the most well-meaning parents are unaware of how they work against their child's progress. Human beings are, by nature, averse to change, even when it is for the better. Try to be objective about your feelings. It's not unusual for parents to undermine a child's progress in therapy because they understand, even on an unconscious level, that once their child's problem is under control, they will be forced to focus on other issues (like the divorce itself) that they've been ignoring. Your child's problems may have given you an excuse to communicate with your ex more than you would have otherwise or perhaps provided something else to blame your ex for ("After all, if she hadn't left us, Justin wouldn't be having nightmares every night"). As mentioned previously, sometimes a child who is quiet and seems to go along with life is a lot easier to take care of than one who is actually expressing his feelings. Parents of divorce are vulnerable, and a child's demands, questions, accusations—his pain—can be difficult to deal with. Do your best, and if you feel you're coming up short, talk to someone yourself.

Finally, we all mourn our children's growing away from us, and therapy may give your child coping skills he needs, skills that will make him more independent of you. If you are now feeling especially vulnerable or as if you're losing your family as you knew it, this can be a frightening realization.

Finally

Remember: No one knows your child better than you do. Measure your child's progress against realistic expectations and learn to accept the positive changes therapy can inspire. Keep an open mind, and actively seek feedback from teachers and others who know your child well. I recommend that after two to four sessions with your child, you meet alone with the therapist to discuss your child. The therapist should explain to your child the purpose of this meeting and discuss it with him in advance. In this meeting the therapist should explain, without breaching your child's confidence, the issues and how he thinks it's best to proceed. Even though every case is different, your child's therapist should be able to give you some general time frame, subject to change, however. The two of you should agree on long- and short-term goals, and also agree on what will constitute improvement. Five-year-old Elvin's therapist feels he will have made significant progress in overcoming his fear of losing his mother if she can leave for work without his screaming. Elvin's mother, however, does not believe that's "good enough." She wants to be able to leave for three- and four-day business trips. Elvin's mother and his therapist need to reach some basic meeting of the minds on this crucial point, if therapy is to be successful.

Your child's therapist also should offer concrete information on how to support therapy at home. For instance, if your child has been experiencing nightmares, your therapist should be able to give you advice on how to handle these (wake up the child? wake up the child and discuss it? stay with the child in his room? bring the child into your room? and so on). Most important, however, you and the therapist *and* your child and his therapist must have a good rapport. If either of you feels uncomfortable with the therapist, discuss this with her and consider a change. (Make sure, however, that you or your child does not want to discontinue with a therapist because either of you is uncomfortable because the child shared sensitive personal information, for example.) Attempts to work on important, deeply personal problems when the chemistry isn't right are usually doomed. It is not uncommon for people to have a session or two with a couple of different therapists before finding the right match for their child.

9

"Please Stop!"

When Parents Fight

Every day my parents fight,
I go to my room and start to cry.
I hate when my parents fight,
They get me worried day and night.
When I go to school, I get worried,
I just can't concentrate on my work daily.
Sometimes I pray to God:
"Make this family a better one."

—Girl, fourteen

What did your parents argue about?
Everything under the sun.
What did you do when they argued?
I'd go to my room, and me and my brother would hear the raised voices
and be like "Again?"
Do they still argue?
Hell, yeah. The other day they fought about a picture album. Kooky!

—Boy, seventeen

If, to quote the old song, "Love and marriage / Go together like a horse and carriage," then it's not surprising that divorce and fighting go together like thunder and lightning, usually before and, all too often, long after the divorce. Obviously, you cannot turn back the clock or erase your child's memories of hearing or seeing you and your ex argue.

The future, however, is a different story. You can help your child express and deal with his feelings about your fighting and teach your child the difference between good, fair, constructive disagreements and fights that are hurtful or violent. (See the box "Fighting the Good Fight," page 210.) You also have it within your power to curtail the amount of conflict your child is exposed to from here on. We often take for granted that divorce makes people angry, and we practically expect them to argue. After all, they *are* getting a divorce, and people divorce because they can't get along. Why should anyone expect them to do so now? And the legal and emotional aspects of divorce sometimes make adversaries of even the most amicable couples. Yet after providing services for thousands of children of divorce, reading what they write, and studying the pictures they draw, I seriously question if this is really the best we can do, for ourselves or for our children.

WHY CAN'T MORE DIVORCING PARENTS ACHIEVE A "GOOD DIVORCE"?

Ideally, divorcing partners would try to separate the conflict that led to divorce from the divorce itself, especially when children are involved. Unfortunately, human nature being what it is, amicable divorces remain the exception to the rule. That doesn't mean that parents shouldn't try. Even if you manage to eliminate some of the conflict, it's well worth it.

One problem is that we rarely get to see how a positive, low-conflict divorce works. Few parents—especially those who've been through divorce—believe such divorces exist. Granted, it may seem at times that attempting to control or eliminate conflict is a hopeless cause. Besides, the marriage is over. This view overlooks a crucial point, though. Unlike couples without children—who are free to sign the papers, wave goodbye, and live their new, totally separate lives—divorced parents never really say goodbye. They end their marriage only to begin building a new relationship, one that may last several times longer than their marriage.

Sadly, many couples choose divorce to escape circumstances that seem to preclude any kind of resolution or peaceful coexistence. Even divorced parents who sincerely want to get along find that disagreements over parenting, child support, and visitation offer ample opportunity for misunderstanding and conflict. Now that your ex is out of your home and beyond your control, one or both of you may feel less inclined to compromise, maybe even more compelled to have it your way.

These reactions are typical and understandable, but they do have significant consequences for your children, especially if they have already witnessed the two of you fighting before you separated. Out of the countless major studies conducted to measure everything about children of divorce, from academic performance to self-esteem, one truth emerges repeatedly: It is parental conflict—not divorce itself—that places children at risk in virtually every area of their lives. In fact, children from intact families with high conflict fare no better in standardized psychological tests than those whose parents are divorced. Conversely, most children of divorce who witness little conflict between their parents do as well as children from intact homes.

Rescuing Children from "The Middle"

A reluctant trophy. *This young adolescent boy depicts feeling in the middle of parents who fight over him. With each claiming "ownership" ("He's my son," "I born him") and pulling him in opposite directions, the boy is, as he writes, "confuse[d]."*

Throughout this book, I've stressed how important it is for every child to understand that his relationship with each parent is separate from his parents' relationship with each other. Of course, it's not always as neat as we would like. Divorce occurs between two people, but it affects whole families. Even in the best of situations, children may have difficulty emotionally distancing themselves from what their parents feel; among the youngest, it is virtually impossible. The emotions of conflict—annoyance, anger, rage—are intense, frightening, and hard to ignore. If in dealing with your ex, you—an adult—can't stop yourself from making insulting comments, raising your voice, becoming enraged, or getting physical, you are forcing your child to be part of that relationship. Even happy families have their fights, and most adults vividly recall how upsetting, even terrifying, it was to see their parents argue. Depending on her age, your child of divorce may have been living amid conflict for a good portion, perhaps even most, of her life. Whether you've just separated or passed the tenth anniversary of the final decree, it's never too early—and never too late—to reduce or eliminate conflict.

How Children Experience Parental Conflict

Too many parents consciously put their kids in the middle of their fights by asking them to choose sides, report what goes on in the other parent's home, and so on. Obviously, this is wrong. But there are other, more subtle ways that parental conflict keeps kids in the middle. In the Sandcas-

End the fighting. *Virtually all children hate seeing their parents fight, and most fantasize about intervening and stopping it; some actually do. In depicting himself in athletic attire, this boy seems to be describing the exceptional strength and discipline it would take to stop his parents from fighting.*

THE SPLATTER EFFECT

Fill a water gun or spray bottle with water and a few drops of food coloring. Place a pan upright against a wall with paper towels around it. Shoot the gun at the pan, which will cause the colored water to splatter on the paper towels, too. Point out to your child that even though you didn't intend to get coloring on the paper towels, it happened. Then say something along the lines of "Even though Mom/Dad and I were just dealing with each other, you were affected by our disagreements just as these paper towels were splattered, although we weren't aiming at them."

PURPOSE: This sends the message that sometimes when parents fight, the children around them get hurt and involved in some of that anger. It also lets your child know that you take responsibility for the fallout from your anger and you understand that parents do unintentionally hurt children sometimes.

tles workbooks, it's clear that children of all ages regard fighting between parents as *their* number-one divorce-related problem. No matter what age the respondent, the majority of kids write about or draw pictures expressing unhappiness or discomfort with their parents' fighting. Younger kids mention fighting most often when asked to finish the sentences "I am sad when . . ." or "I hate when. . . ."

Older children, when asked what they would do differently from their parents, almost always respond to the effect that they would try to work things out and not fight in front of their kids. When asked what they do when their parents fight, the most common responses involve getting away (going to their room, to a friend's house), finding distraction (listening to music, watching television), or trying to stop the fight (from verbally asking parents to stop or shut up to intervening physically). Younger kids tend to view the fighting, even when it is just verbal, as frightening and threatening. They worry that one of the parents will be physically harmed or emotionally hurt.

Older kids mention these things as well, especially in homes where domestic violence has occurred. Most often, however, they express a weary annoyance over the continued bickering. When asked, "Do your parents still argue?" 32 percent of eleven- to thirteen-year-olds and 37 percent of fourteen- to seventeen-year-olds responded yes. When asked what the fights were about, most offered answers that made them sound more like parents talking about kids: "You name it," "Anything and everything," "Nothing," "Stupid stuff," "Bull," and so on.

In an exercise in which they were asked to write separate letters to Mom and Dad, those that mention continued conflict sometimes take an almost-scolding tone: "Why can't you just stop talking about Dad like that?" "I can't believe you guys are still fighting." "I don't understand why you can't pay the child support on time." A substantial percentage of others simply plead: "You know it hurts me when you say those things about my mom," or "I still love Dad even if you don't. Don't talk about him like that."

DOMESTIC VIOLENCE: A KID'S-EYE VIEW

Dad and Mom would fight
Almost every night.
Maybe if I had the might
I could have stopped the fight
And because of me
They'll never be
A couple again.
> —Boy, thirteen

No matter what their age, children who witness domestic violence often respond with a deep, overwhelming fear for their safety and that of their battered parent (usually the mother) and other siblings. (See the box "Domestic Violence," below.) In several Sandcastles pieces written by children who have witnessed domestic violence, they also express con-

---

DOMESTIC VIOLENCE

My parents always argue. Last time it was like 2:30 in the morning. They were screaming. My brother told me that the last time, my dad took my mom by the neck and shook her up and down. That's why they were having a divorce.

> —Girl, eight

Dear Dad,
I love you with all my heart. But this divorce is going great. Now I don't have to sit in the closet hearing you hit Mommy.

> —Girl, ten

I'm happy now that they are apart,
but how long will it take for love to go apart?
I'm scared sometimes when I'm with my mom

But yet we know we are not torn apart.
I love the things we do and the places we go,
But from all this, my dad won't let go.
Sometimes I felt that my dad would do something bad to us,
But yet I hope he wouldn't dare to kill us.

> —Girl, sixteen

It's impossible to determine exactly how many children live in homes where domestic violence occurs, but estimates place the number anywhere between 3.3 and 10 million children. Between 75 percent and 87 percent of these children have witnessed the violence, of which their mother is usually the victim. Obviously, some of these children will also see their parents divorce.

For children who have witnessed domestic violence, the usual responses to divorce—self-blame, guilt, anger, choosing sides, and feeling different from other children—may be exacerbated. Children often blame themselves for not being able to prevent (by behaving better) or stop the violence between their parents. They may be very angry at the attacking parent and even angrier at the victim for not leaving the situation or protecting herself. It's important to note that domestic violence is not always restricted to spouses. A child in a family with domestic violence is fifteen times more likely to be a victim of neglect, physical abuse, or sexual abuse himself. Studies find that between 53 percent and 70 percent of male batterers also abuse their children. The child who knows his father violently abused his mother is bound to view a range of issues differently from a child who has not. Understandably, perhaps, he may be more likely to choose sides and less willing to participate in visitation or refuse altogether. (See "Supervised Visitation," page 274).

I do not understand why my dad used to abuse my mom.

—Girl, nine

These children need help in understanding what domestic violence is, that they did not cause it and could not have stopped it, and that it is okay to feel sad and to grieve for losses resulting from the violence. It's also important for these children to learn alternative, nonviolent approaches to resolving conflict and ways to preserve their own safety. If this is something you feel you cannot do effectively, seek specialized counseling or help from community organizations or support groups dedicated to families of domestic violence.

Be prepared to answer your child's questions openly and honestly. Be clear in stating that physical or emotional abuse is unacceptable, that no one ever has an excuse to treat someone else that way. This is one area in which it is not only permissible but *essential* that your child understand that the abusing parent was wrong. At the same time, it is also important that you give your child a sense of how the victimized parent might have altered the outcome. The purpose of this message is not to blame the victim; clearly, in the moment of abuse, most victims do not have an out. What you do hope to achieve, however, is imparting to your child the idea that she or anyone else faced with a potentially abusive situation has the right, perhaps even the obligation, to leave it or seek help, even if it means doing something that might be seen as hurting the perpetrator (for instance, calling the police).

Whether or not your child asks about it, you need to discuss the issue of domestic violence if it has occurred in your home. You might say something like this:

"What your father did to me was wrong and illegal. No matter what mistakes anyone makes or how bad a person feels, no one should ever treat someone else in such a manner. No one can 'make' someone else act violently or abusively toward another person. These are choices that a person makes. Pushing, hitting, screaming with rage, throwing things, and threatening to hurt others are unacceptable. People must learn to talk about things that bother them and try to work out their problems peacefully. If someone can't control his anger, he needs to get help immediately. If he can't or won't do that, he's made a choice. Then it's up to the other parent to make sure she and her children are safe. That may mean moving out of the house or even calling the police. These are hard things to do, but our safety always has to come first.

"And no one, myself included, should ever allow herself to be treated that way. A person should leave such a situation as quickly as she can to protect herself and her children and never return unless she is sure she and her family can be absolutely safe."

If your child has witnessed or been a victim of abuse, you should acknowledge that and apologize to your child for not preventing the violence or not removing him from the situation.

If you come from a violent home, have been in other or long-term violent relationships, you should consider counseling for yourself. Each of these factors places you at added risk for entering violent relationships in the future, and the chances that a boyfriend or new spouse who abuses you will also abuse your child are significantly higher than those for biological fathers.

Violence on the home front. *Because it would be too scary and overwhelming to depict domestic violence with human figures, this eleven-year-old boy has chosen cartoonish surrogates. From the exchange between them, it seems that this boy probably heard his mother threaten divorce many times before. Obviously, his father's heard it all and doesn't believe it. The arrow pointing to his darkened nose suggests he might be drunk or possibly high on cocaine.*

cern for their father. One nine-year-old girl, for example, stated that she worried her mother would die because her father hit her or that he would die because someone would hit him. She also wrote, "I don't understand why my dad used to abuse my mom." An eight-year-old boy wrote to his mother:

> Why do you have to call the police whenever Dad does something he's not supposed to?

The same boy wrote to his father:

> Why do you have to do a lot of bad things to Mom, like pull her hair, fight with her, and put bad words on her beeper and pager?

WHAT ONGOING, NONVIOLENT PARENTAL CONFLICT TEACHES KIDS: LESSONS THEY CAN ALL LIVE WITHOUT

Cindy sees a lot of fighting between her parents and, being just six, is convinced that arguing was the cause of the breakup. She will probably grow up trying to avoid conflict at all costs. Her nine-year-old brother, Jared, is pretty sure that there's never any point to trying to resolve an issue, and that the world is divided between winners, like his dad (who just got a new apartment near the beach), and losers, like his mom (who seems to cry a lot now). He's decided he always wants to win, no matter what's at stake. He has lost most of his friends because he insists on always having his way; his teacher complains that he is aggressive, argumentative, and rude. Meanwhile, seventeen-year-old Liselle believes it's normal to be hurt by someone she loves. Every boyfriend she's had since her parents broke up has treated her badly. Last week her new boyfriend slapped her.

If these kids' beliefs persist, they will certainly undermine their self-esteem and ruin their chances for healthy, loving relationships in the future. With their behavior, Cindy, Jared, and Liselle are demonstrating what they believe and what they feel about divorce, relationships with others, and themselves. It's up to their parents to help them see how what they've learned from their parents links to what they feel, what they believe, and how they behave. In talking to these children, their parents should not lecture but listen and gently direct the conversation to unearth the real reasoning behind the behavior. With Cindy, a concerned parent might use an activity like "The Life of Riley" (see page 236) to help her see the difference between healthy and unhealthy arguments and how people make a conscious decision to fight; it doesn't just "happen." Talking to Jared about how we sometimes learn from our mistakes and how no one really "won" the divorce should help him see it differently. His parents might also help him to understand that life is always a gamble, and that no matter how hard we try, it's impossible to win at everything. The most important, rewarding aspects of life—loving and being loved, growing up, raising children—are not contests. His parents might also gently encourage him to consider what he has lost in his never-ending quest to win and to see how sometimes strong emotions cause us to lose sight of what it is that we really want. Liselle needs someone to broach the subject of how she views male-female relationships. A parent might ask, "How do you think men and women should treat each other? Who is responsible for making money? Caring for the children? Should either person be responsible for the other's behavior? Or only for their own?" At Liselle's age, she will probably see that she is not responsible for how her boyfriend treats her, though her parents must make clear that she is responsible for removing herself from the abusive relationship.

We know that children often feel guilty, trapped by the misguided beliefs either that they somehow caused the divorce or they could have prevented it by being "better" kids or intervening. With that in mind, consider what divorced parents usually argue about: the kids. Through the legal process and sometimes for years beyond, child support, custody, and visitation remain potential flash points. Even without problems in those areas, there arise the inevitable differences of two unmarried parents raising children in two separate households with sometimes very different rules, values, and expectations. (See chapter 13.) It's no wonder that children of divorce may feel that they not only caused the divorce but that they are the only reason you two continue fighting.

When problems do arise, look upon them as excellent opportunities to model positive qualities and behaviors. This is particularly important for children of divorce like Cindy, Jared, and Liselle, who often come to inaccurate and unhealthy conclusions about relationships, conflict, and resolution from what they have witnessed.

Parental conflict not only sends kids messages about love, marriage, and relationships, it speaks volumes to them about who they are. To a child's ears, any comment about his parent—positive or negative—is a judgment of him. Any critical barb about your ex goes right to your child's heart. And this is true even if your child is old enough to understand the divorce and even if she also feels hostile toward or rejected by the other parent.

THINGS 2 DO

LIFE LISTS

You and your child each draw up a list of things about your family situation that are confusing to you. These do not have to be only about the divorce. Exchange lists, read them to each other, and discuss.

Examples:

Why does Daddy live with Tina, my stepsister, but not with me?

Why couldn't you and Mommy have worked it out like you tell me to work it out when I fight with my friends?

Why don't we go on vacation or I go to summer camp like all the other kids during the summer?

PURPOSE: This is a pleasant, nonthreatening way for a child to ask a question and create a dialogue about uncomfortable issues.

For these reasons, minimizing your child's exposure to conflict is one of the most important things you can do. Note that I didn't say "reduce conflict"; sometimes that's simply not possible. But you can mitigate the impact by becoming more sensitive to how you talk about your ex and the divorce, how you respond to your ex, and how you handle problems in front of your child.

WHEN YOUR EX PUTS YOUR CHILD IN THE MIDDLE

In the journey through divorce, you resolved early on to take the high road. Whenever your children are in earshot, you are careful to refer to your ex in only positive terms. You've come up with and stuck to neutral, blame-free explanations for why your marriage ended, and you strictly limit venting your displeasure with your ex to late-night phone chats with your sister, when you're sure the kids are asleep. It hasn't been easy, and you've slipped here and there, but overall, you've protected your children from the fallout of your feelings. Congratulations. Last weekend, though, your daughter returned from her mother's house and said, "I know why you and Mommy divorced. It's because you lied to her!" Now what?

Divorce often brings out the worst in people, and, unfortunately, some parents simply do not resist the urge to stir up the pot. They may try to draw their child into their cause by saying negative things about their ex or behave in ways that they know will upset their ex. What should you do when you've managed to stay above the fray and your ex seems to be doing all he or she can to pull you back into the fight?

First, it's important to remember that children are always observant. They notice and don't forget which parent showed up late for visitation, criticized the other, and made life difficult. They also recognize who rose above the mess, made the extra effort, and helped them move on. Believe me, your child does not overlook who slammed the phone down and who answered it cordially, who ignored the other parent at the school play and who said hello, who bad-mouths the other and who behaves maturely.

Second, bear in mind that not everything your ex says or does necessarily demands your response. You might want to think about what's most important to you and what you feel is best for your child. If, for example, the end of your marriage was fraught with angry words and loud arguments, you may wish to spare your child further anguish by letting many of your ex's transgressions go by. When she returns the child late from visitation or, according to your child, criticizes your driving, you might decide she'll never change anyway, and simply address the problems that relate directly to your child (while venting your frustration to another adult). If, on the other hand, you're dealing with a custody battle and your ex is doing her darnedest to poison your child against you, it may be necessary to answer her every charge. Think through your situation. How does your ex's bad behavior affect your child (not you)? How seriously does your child (not you) take your ex's actions and words? How likely is it that your confronting your ex will persuade her to change her ways? Or how likely is it that she'll only step up the attack? What is really at stake?

Third, whenever you repeat to your ex remarks your child attributes to her without your child's permission, you run the risk of breaking your child's confidence and trust. If you have any reason to believe that your ex will confront your child about your confronting her, address the issue with your child only or just leave it alone.

When faced with your ex's bad behavior, you must be sure that your child understands the following:

- You are responding to your child's feelings, not to your ex.
- Sometimes people—even parents—behave in ways that are inappropriate.
- You can be trusted with your child's feelings and confidence; you will not fly off the handle and confront your ex.
- You will help your child find better ways to deal with these painful situations in the future.

> Ten-year-old Janie returned from visiting her father visibly disturbed. For the past three years, she had been living primarily with her mother, Gwen, who worked full-time and had a second part-time job teaching ballroom dancing two nights a week. On those evenings, Gwen's sister baby-sat for Janie and her two younger brothers. Gwen did need the extra money, in part because Janie had a mild learning disability and worked several afternoons a week with a tutor on her homework. But Gwen also welcomed the chance to get out of the house. The divorce had been very difficult for her, and as much as she knew her three kids needed her, Gwen also recognized that she needed a little downtime for herself.

Recently, Janie's father had said, "I think your mother's a bad mother, and I'll tell you why. I know she has to work one job, but two? I'm paying child support, and there she goes wasting it on your tutor, when the whole time she could be home helping you with your homework. As far as I'm concerned, that second job of hers is just an excuse not to be a real mother."

Like most children, Janie would have liked to be with her mother more, and in her father's words, she found a powerful expression of her own anger. Later that night, when Janie angrily repeated to her mother everything her father had said, Gwen had to decide what to do. She could have angrily said, "How dare your father say that? After he's done so many things wrong! If I had a dollar for every time he paid his child support late, he wouldn't need to pay it. That's it! I'm gonna get him on the phone right now. He'll rue the day...." But that would have accomplished nothing, because as difficult as it may be to see, the real issue here was not who said what but how Janie felt.

"It sounds to me that you're uncomfortable with what your father said and angry at me for not being home all the time," Gwen might have said. This feeling response would show Janie that her mother was truly listening to her and help her to further express her own feelings.

"Well, I just think that if you're gone all day from us, why do you have to be gone those two nights, too? Don't you ever want to see me and Keith and Kenny?"

"Honey, of course, I want to see you, but I feel that for right now we do need the extra money, so I can't promise you that will change right away. What we can do, though, is think of some good ways that we can have more time to spend. Do you have any ideas?"

"Mom, could we get up a little early and all have breakfast together?"

"Sure. That's a great idea. And I have one: How about if you get Aunt Ellen to help you guys clean your rooms the nights I'm not home, so we don't have to do that on Saturdays, and we can have fun instead?"

"Okay. But, Mom, how come Daddy says all these bad things about you?"

Gwen took a deep breath. "Janie, I really don't know. How would you feel if I said something bad about Daddy?"

"Sad. Really sad, like I felt before."

"Sure, I'd be sad if I were you. Sometimes you can be angry at someone, but that doesn't make it okay for you to say and do things that will hurt the people around you. Your father is mad at me and may say things that hurt you. We all make mistakes, but we have to try really hard not to make the mistakes that will hurt people, especially the ones we love. I can't control Daddy, so let's find some ways to help you if this situation ever comes up again."

"I guess Dad's really mad. How come you aren't?"

"Janie, I have been very angry about this divorce, but I feel that some things parents should share with children, and some things they should not. Also, different people see things differently. I feel that given the way our marriage was, this divorce was the best decision for all of us. Your father disagrees."

In Janie's case, the real issue was twofold: Dad's ongoing anger against Mom and Janie's feeling rejected by Mom's frequent absence from home. Note that in responding to Janie, Gwen did not take a defensive posture; instead she listened. When you feel compelled to defend yourself, check yourself. Listen to your child and consider that she may be expressing concern over a valid issue. When Gwen took time to think over the situation, she concluded that she was out of the house too often and resolved to ask for a raise at work or to cash in some stock she inherited so she could eliminate one night of teaching a week.

Help your child to understand and deal with anger through activities—"Angry Jacket and Hat" (page 36), "The Splatter Effect" (page 197)—and techniques (see the box "Techniques for Dealing with Anger," page 37).

THERE'S MORE GOOD NEWS

Here's an added dividend, too: Reducing conflict between you and your ex can reduce parent-child conflict. Letting your child in on your disagreements with his other parent is almost as good as saying, "I no longer value your other parent as a person or as a parent." Children of divorce commonly try to assuage their feelings of loss and estrangement by asserting control. Since life severely restricts the ways kids can exert control, they often become manipulative, pitting one parent against the other, for example. A nine-year-old girl wrote in a Sandcastles workbook: "My parents start fighting, then I start crying, then they pay attention to me, and then we become a family again." Here, exposure to her parents' fighting provided this girl with an opportunity to maintain the fantasy that she could bring them together. Her behavior got their undivided attention, stopped their fighting, and let her wrest control of the situation.

You can hardly blame this little girl for resorting to this behavior as often as opportunity allows, but manipulation like this, while understandable, should not be encouraged. Even after they reach adulthood, some children of divorce have a hard time breaking the manipulation habit. The less you do to feed it and the sooner you can break it once it's started, the better for everyone.

HOW TO SPOT—AND STOP—UNHEALTHY MANIPULATION

Most parents know when they are feeling manipulated. The problem is that parents often mistakenly believe they are being manipulated when they are not. By simply asking for what she wants, your child is not necessarily being manipulative. If, for example, your eleven-year-old daughter wants to spend more time with you, asking for it in a healthy way, even when accompanied by a bit of acting out, is not manipulation. To some parents, anything a child does to try to get what he wants is considered manipulation. This is a distorted and potentially dangerous view, since it suggests that children should not try to get what they want and need from their parents. It is a parent's responsibility to provide the love, support, and nurturance a child needs. The fact that a child asks for it does not automatically qualify as manipulation and is never grounds for denying her. Also, a parent who has good reason to change his mind on an issue is not being manipulated. If your daughter can give you a good, reasonable argument as to why she should have a later curfew, for instance, and you agree after careful consideration, you are not being manipulated. Rather, you are teaching your child how to get what she wants in a healthy, mature way.

If your child's demands are unreasonable (and she knows it) or she asks in a manner that's inappropriate (letting you know that she misses you but that getting a new party dress would make her feel better), she may be manipulating you. Strictly speaking, manipulation occurs when someone makes a conscious decision to get something he wants by playing on another's emotions or vulnerability. The ability to do this rarely exists in children under the age of ten or so. While a young child may be able to see the cause-and-effect relationship between, say, his crying and getting Daddy to return him from visitation a day early, he is just repeating a learned behavior that achieves the desired result. He is not thinking, *If I start crying about now, Daddy will feel bad and take me home to Mommy.* Annoying as adults may find it, this type of behavior is not unhealthy manipulation. Nor is that of the nine-year-old girl discussed in the text who learned she could stop her parents' fighting by crying. She had a legitimate need (to stop the fight), and she had stumbled upon a way to do that (crying). In and of itself, this was not an unhealthy response. The danger lies in her learning to use this tactic in her dealings with others and then, for example, crying to her teacher when she gets a poor grade, crying to her friends to get her way, and so on. Her mother could prevent this pattern from developing into manipulation by saying, "I don't want you to have to start crying to get us to stop fighting. Let's think of other ways you can signal me that you're getting uncomfortable."

Older children can and do manipulate, and parents must put some effort into observing behavior and discerning patterns before they make the call:

> Eleven-year-old Jerrie cries at the drop of a hat. Every morning before her mother leaves for work, Jerrie's braids are wrong; her waffle is toasted too brown; the sun isn't shining bright enough—all occasions for wailing and weeping. After she accused her mother, Monica, of "making me sad" because she was refused a second dessert, Monica had had it. She could see that the crying began right after her husband moved out, and, judging from the timing, it was clear that Jerrie felt she needed her mother's attention. While Monica could understand her daughter's emotional needs at that difficult time, she could also see that Jerrie was falling into a bad habit of crying her way to whatever she wanted—even dessert.
>
> "Jerrie, since your dad moved out, I've seen you've gotten frustrated easier and are crying much more. I can understand your sadness, and I'd like to talk about it in a healthy way. But allowing your sadness and sometimes anger to come out if something simple doesn't happen—like me not toasting your waffle perfectly—is an unacceptable way."

From there, Monica and Jerrie talked about how sad Jerrie felt and ways Jerrie could express that feeling without crying over little things. They agreed that each night she would write a list of what she was happy about and another of what she was sad about. Getting the uncomfortable feelings out on paper relieved the pressure of keeping it all inside and helped Jerrie see the positive aspects of her life.

Older children, especially teenagers, can and do manipulate their parents. Again, these children do have real needs, which you should try to meet as best you can. But when you see a pattern developing, you must confront your child and stop encouraging the manipulative behavior:

> Annemarie noticed that her seventeen-year-old son, Bobby, would complain every night at the dinner table about rarely seeing his father for the family meal. By the time dinner was over, Annemarie was feeling so bad for her son that when he asked for the car keys, she gladly handed them over, knowing that small gesture would "make him happy." As she explained, "Bobby seems to really mean it when he talks about how angry he is at his dad, and it really makes me feel bad for him. I'm putty in his hands."

Before we continue, it's important to note here that Bobby probably *is* hurt and angry about his father. The fact that he is using these feelings to manipulate his mother into giving him the car doesn't make them any less valid or his pain any less devastating. Again, the problem is not what he is doing; it is why. Bobby needs to learn that it's okay to express his feelings and okay to seek his mother's understanding and support. What is not acceptable is using her response to him to extract a special favor, especially one he'd probably get if he just asked directly for it.

> Annemarie confronted Bobby in a direct but understanding way: "I've kinda noticed that you share with me about your anger at your dad and then ask me for some privilege. I'm sure you don't realize it [non-threatening], but I feel I'm hurting you by giving in because of your relationship with your father. The next time you want to talk about your father, I'll be happy to do it provided all you want from me is a loving ear, not a special favor. If you ask for privileges, from now on you'll get them sometimes and not others because I don't want you to start confusing your feelings with getting a privilege out of it."

Bobby may be a little taken aback and probably somewhat surprised. But notice that Annemarie isn't threatening to do anything but respond to her son's feelings about his father as she—not Bobby—sees fit.

Remember that your child of divorce will often need a little extra TLC and that there is nothing wrong with his asking it of you, if he feels he needs to. The danger lies in your child's learning to play on people's emotions to get what he wants.

FIGHTING THE GOOD FIGHT

No matter how much people love and care for each other, they are bound to disagree. There's nothing inherently wrong with fighting. The problem usually lies in how we fight. Most of us never learn how to defend our feelings and positions assertively without resorting to words and actions that are hurtful and demeaning to our opponent. All of us need to learn how to fight fair.

For children of divorce, this knowledge is especially important. Whether you and your ex screamed, called each other names, or pushed each other around, or you silently ignored each other and your problems, your child has probably picked up some unhealthy ideas about conflict resolution. Children whose parents divorce are also apt either to view ongoing, unresolved conflict as normal or to believe that any disagreement between people is inherently dangerous and should be avoided at all costs. Obviously, these are not the lessons we want our kids to learn.

Odd as it may sound, your divorce can be something of a conflict-resolution laboratory for your child, in two ways. First, you and your ex can model better communication and compromise now than you did in your marriage. Second, divorce puts your child in situations where fair fighting rules can be practiced and applied. Simply the fact that two parents may have different rules in their respective households is enough to give most children something to fight for (a change in the rules, for instance, or your adopting a rule your ex has that your child prefers). Since a lot of what we argue about isn't necessarily what happened but how it made us feel, teaching your child to express her feelings in a fair, open way gives your child skills she can apply in any conflict with anyone.

The Rules

- Feelings are valid and deserve respect, whether you agree with them or not. If your daughter says she feels hurt by something you did and you think she's simply overreacting, set your own beliefs aside and acknowledge that her hurt is real.

- Name-calling and verbal abuse are never acceptable.

- It's not fair to bring up past mistakes and issues that have already been dealt with. Encourage your child to focus on the issue at hand. Avoid generalizing a single event into a global indictment. ("It's just like last week, when you broke your promise to me.")

- Don't make accusations that can't be backed up (particularly avoid saying things like "You always . . ." or "You never . . ."); these only beg further argument.

- Agree on a signal or code word that can be exchanged (perhaps "time-out" or "take five") if one or both of you

lose your temper, so you can stop the discussion and resume when you've cooled down.

The Good Fight, Step-by-Step

1. *Teach your child to express her feelings in terms of how she feels and why, not with accusations:*

   "I feel sad when you spend more time with your girlfriend than me because I don't get to see you that often."

   Not "I hate your girlfriend. You love her more than you love me," *or* "You never want to spend time with us. That's why I hate your girlfriend."

2. *Remind your child to listen to what the other person says. Repeat back to your child what he said to be sure you have fully understood it:*

   "I understand that you want to spend more time with me and that you feel that I'm not available because of my girlfriend."

   Not "What are you talking about? I'm right here, aren't I?" *or* "How I spend my time with my girlfriend is none of your business."

3. *Show your child how to consider the other person's point of view and feelings:*

   "You only see me on weekends, so I guess that time is very special to you."

   Not "It seems to me that spending the whole weekend together is plenty of time. That's the visitation schedule your mother and I agreed to," *or* "The whole weekend is more time than most kids spend with their dads. We do all the things we want to do, even when my girlfriend's with us. We're together; that's all that matters."

4. *Demonstrate for your child how to calmly explain feelings:*

   "I know you feel differently, but I really don't feel that my girlfriend takes away from the time we spend together. I thought you liked her."

   Not "You're wrong. You have plenty of time with me," *or* "I think you're just being selfish. I have a life, too."

5. *Let your child know you appreciate and respect her for voicing her feelings:*

   "I didn't know that you felt that way, and I'm glad you told me."

   Not "Well, this is a great way to start our weekend—with a fight," *or* "What do you want me to do? Dump her?"

6. *If appropriate, apologize and invite your child to find a solution. Make it clear that it isn't just her problem or your problem but one you can both work on, even if the solution doesn't please everyone:*

"I'm sorry that having my girlfriend here made you feel I didn't want to spend time with you. I will try to see her more during the week, so we can have more time together. However, she is part of my life now, and she will be around sometimes when you are. Let's talk about making certain times, like Friday nights, our special times alone. I can't and I won't make her disappear, but we can find some compromise."

Not "Well, how you feel is your problem. It's wrong, and I disagree with you, but there's nothing I can do about it," *or* "Nothing I can do will ever make you happy, so I'm not even going to bother. Like it or lump it."

Practice

Parents have countless opportunities every day to model conflict resolution. Take a typical situation: Your ten-year-old leaves his dirty clothes on the bedroom floor. Rather than yelling "Get up here and pick up this mess right now!" try saying, "I'm angry when I try to keep the place clean and I find clothes on the floor instead of in the hamper."

Role-play with your child, demonstrate the difference between statements that express feelings and those that accuse the other person. Teach your child the difference between:

"You never let me call Dad!" and "I miss not being able to call Dad."

"You always put Mom down," and "It hurts me when I hear you say bad things about Mom."

"You never care about my feelings. It's always what you want to do," and "I feel left out when you make plans for us but never ask me what I'd like to do. It makes me feel that you don't care."

Acknowledge and reward your child whenever he fights fair. No one likes conflict, and some parents worry that if they let their child know when he makes a fair argument, they will encourage him to fight. The truth is, conflict is a fact of life. Not teaching your child to fight fair won't result in fewer conflicts, just longer, uglier fights, more hurt feelings, and less understanding.

THINGS 2 DO

TRUE COLORS

Have your child draw the colors that she feels represent or express different feelings. Next, draw yourself and have your child draw herself. (Better yet, lie down on a big piece of butcher paper and trace each other.) Use the colors to indicate in which part of the body the feelings first appear. Each of you draws where you feel happy, sad, mad, and so on.

Daughter	Dad
sad = gray in throat	mad = red in jaw
happy = blue in head	love = pink in heart

With a child seven and above, further discuss the concept of how a feeling will cause us to act certain ways. You might say, "I'll do worse on a test if I feel sad that day," "I might win the race if I feel joyful that day," and point out that our emotions can cause us to act differently without even realizing it. Think about some of the ways we act differently depending on our moods.

PURPOSE: It is helpful for children to recognize feelings and how they impact our physical selves. As children get older, they can understand how feelings interact with thinking and affect behavior.

WHEN CONFLICT CANNOT BE AVOIDED

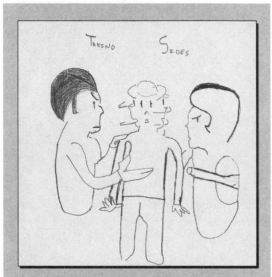

Torn between two loves. *This twelve-year-old boy depicts the confusion and stress of being trapped between fighting parents.*

In a perfect world, your child would still have money for the big school trip even if Dad skipped his child support payment the last three months, Eddie would never see his father slap his mother, and Barbara's parents would be able to converse without shouting and name-calling.

Unfortunately, despite their best efforts, parents cannot always protect their children from these problems. However, how your child responds to incidents such as these and what he learns from them depend on how you explain them to him. Most parents shy away from discussing their conflicts with their children, which is understandable. Again, however, if your child witnesses the fighting, you've already drawn him into an adult world he does not fully understand. To simply turn him loose to wonder what it all means and to start completing his "picture" of the events without all the pieces will do much more harm than good.

Another important point to remember is that whenever we experience conflict, directly or indirectly, the issue is never fully over until it is resolved. Children of divorce often get the impression that disagreeing, arguing, and fighting are in and of themselves bad because they "cause" divorce. Unless they have the opportunity to see both sides of the story (and there are always at least that many) and to understand that there are good and bad ways to fight, children can grow up with a distorted view of human relationships. At one extreme is a child who never stands up for herself or fights for anything, no matter how badly others treat her; at the other, a child who has to beat everyone else before they get a chance to beat her, who is constantly fighting with others, no matter how well others treat her. The challenge is how to explain your conflicts without breaching your and your ex's privacy.

HOW TO AVOID A FIGHT

When it comes to heading off an argument, parents often have more control over the situation (notice I did not say "their exes") than they realize. While it may be impossible to avoid disagreement, there is a lot you can do to move discussions away from out-and-out conflict and closer to peaceful resolution. Regardless of the issue, try to follow these few basic rules:

✔ *Prepare for the conversation.* Don't phone your ex at the office when you know he may be busy or at home when your child is there during visitation. If possible, phone ahead or drop a note asking your ex to set aside time, fifteen or twenty minutes, for a short talk. Think about what you want to say and stick to it. Resolve not to use charged language, hurl accusations, or repeat yourself. If you or your ex might take the conversation off course, make some notes of the points you want to cover to help you stay on task.

✔ *Get what you came for.* All through your preparation and conversation, remember to get what you came for: your ex's participation in solving a problem. While you might feel your ex "owes" you an apology, a promise to never repeat the offending behavior, or a plea for forgiveness, don't feel you've failed if you don't get them. Remember: Your mission is solving the problem.

✔ *Speak with your head, not your heart.* Acknowledge to yourself that there is more to the problem at hand than simply how it affects your child. Yes, the late child support payments do cause hardship for little Jacob *and* make you feel worthless in your ex's eyes all over again. While you cannot deny your personal feelings, make every effort to leave them out of the discussion.

✔ *State the problem, don't criticize.* There's a world of difference between "Jacob's teacher called to say he's not completing his homework" and "You don't bother to review Jacob's homework, and now it's affecting him at school." Avoid using the accusative "you" (say, "We have a problem," instead). Avoid statements using the words "always" and "never," since they beg to be countered. Leave the past out of it; don't feel compelled to throw

in "It's just like it was when you were here. You never cared about his schoolwork then either."

✔ *Be straightforward, diplomatic, and honest; acknowledge your ex's discomfort.* "Neither of us wants to get into this and please just listen and let's not fight. I need the child support payment on time. Can you please do this? Let's put our differences aside and handle this calmly for the kids' sake."

✔ *Include yourself in the problem, even if it's not true.* You may have to swallow hard to do this, and I'm sure there are many reasons why you wouldn't want to do this, but there are even better reasons why you should. First, it positions you and your ex on the same side and makes the problem the enemy, not you or your ex. Second, it defuses any of the back-and-forth that inevitably results when one person claims to be right and the other invariably feels pressed to argue against being wrong. Few people would find anything to object to in a statement like "We really need to be more vigilant about this homework problem. I just wanted to pass it on. You can call his teacher; here's the number."

✔ *Acknowledge that you might not necessarily be right, even if you believe you are.* "I just want to mention something without arguing. I'm concerned that Jason's bedtime at your house is too late, because he always seems to be wiped out, and he often says he doesn't feel good enough to go to school on Mondays. I haven't said a word to him about it, because maybe the late bedtime has nothing to do with it. Maybe just try getting him to bed earlier a couple times and let's see if it makes a difference."

✔ *Compliment your ex's efforts when you can.* Comments like "The boys had a great time on vacation with you" or "Maria is really fond of her new stepmom" send the message that you respect your ex and appreciate his efforts. They also provide some balance to your conversations and keep the lines open by ensuring that not everything you say is negative or critical of your ex.

✔ *Be sensitive to your ex's position.* Prepare not only to talk but to listen.

Admit there has been a disagreement and explain it briefly. Include yourself in the discussion, so that your child can see that it does take two to tango. There's a big difference between "Your rat of a father isn't paying his child support on time" and "Your dad and I are having some disagreements regarding the child support. I'm doing my best to work it out with him." Or between "Your mother is really breaking my chops about letting you guys go alone to the fair" and "Your mother and I are having a disagreement about whether or not you guys are old enough to go to the fair alone. I feel that you are both pretty responsible and that letting you go for just a couple of hours during the day is safe. Your mother thinks that you are too young to be in a large crowd of strangers all alone. We're trying to work out a compromise. I'm going to suggest that your older cousins come along, and I'll give you a cell phone to take so you can beep me if you need to. I think your mom will be okay with that."

KEEPING YOURSELF OUT OF THE MIDDLE

If your child indicates to you that he has a problem with his other parent and asks for your help, proceed with caution. Only offer to intervene if you are well past being angry at your ex and are certain you can listen calmly without being critical. Otherwise, refer your child to his other parent. This is not to say there are not times when it is proper to intervene (for example, when you suspect neglect or abuse). Most times, however, it's a judgment call.

> Seven-year-old Joey loved spending Wednesday nights and weekends with his dad, Mark. Once Mark began dating Carol, however, Joey felt he never had a minute alone with his dad, which made him feel rejected and unloved. Each time he came home from visitation crying and saying he wanted to see Daddy alone, Lydia explained to him that he should talk to his father about it, that Daddy now had a new person in his life, but he still loved him very much. Even though she was personally annoyed at Mark for splitting his visitation time with his new girlfriend (after all, she reasoned, he's got all week for that) and hurt to see Joey so sad, she never voiced or otherwise expressed those feelings to her son.

One day Joey was playing with his Power Ranger figures when Lydia overheard him acting out the role of "Daddy Power Ranger": "I am leaving because you made me mad! I will never come see you again!" Joey intoned in a deep, gruff voice. *That must be it,* Lydia thought. *He's afraid that if he says anything to his dad, he'll never get to see him.* Lydia discussed this with Joey and, with her son's permission, decided to talk to his dad about it. Before Lydia phoned Mark that afternoon, she mentally rehearsed what she wanted to say, always keeping the focus on protecting and improving Joey's relationship with his father.

"What's up?" Mark asked.

"Thanks for calling me back. You know Joey lives for the time he spends with you, and he loves you so much. The last few weeks, though, he's come home very sad because he doesn't feel he has much time alone with you since Carol's been around. Mark, I know this is your life now, and I don't mean to interfere. I've explained to Joey several times that he should discuss this with you, but I'm talking to you because I'm guessing he's afraid that if he mentions anything to you, you'll be angry at him."

"That's ridiculous! Where did he get a crazy idea like that?" Mark asked.

"I don't know, but it's how he feels. Even if you know and I know that would never happen, let's find a way to reassure Joey so he understands. Again, I'm not trying to tell you what to do. I just thought you would like to know how Joey feels, so you can perhaps consider spending more time with him or talk to him about it."

"Well, now that you mention it, I see what you mean. Joey has been a little droopy the last couple of weekends. I thought he was just tired," Mark said.

"Maybe, but he's brought it up so many times. I think you could really clear away some of his fears just by talking to him."

"Okay, Lydia. And thanks."

Lydia avoided all the pitfalls (voicing her own opinion, meddling in Mark's life, criticizing Mark's parenting style) and managed to keep the conversation on topic: Joey. Most important, she gave Mark something he could use to improve *his* relationship with his son. As for how Mark solved the problem with Joey, he could have done it a number of ways: talking to Joey, spending one evening and one day with him alone, giving him more time to get to know Carol better, or just listening to Joey and reassuring him he would never lose his father. If you share a problem like this with your ex, remember that your goal is to help your child, not to force your ex to solve it your way.

It's important for all children, but children of divorce in particular, to learn that people—including their parents—can reach understanding and compromise at least some of the time.

HOW PARENTS CAN HELP: "CONFLICT-PROOFING" YOUR CHILD

When words wound. When Mom and Dad say "bad words to each other" this seven-year-old boy becomes distressed and cries.

• *Keep your business between you and your ex private.* Your child probably knows much more about your relationship and breakup than you realize. This is one area where honesty is not always the best policy. Your divorce is neither a reason nor an excuse for telling your child "everything." A good rule of thumb is: Don't disclose to your child anything about yourself, your ex, or either of your families that you probably would not have told him when you were together. Nothing your ex did (cheated, ran off, abused drugs) or did not do (pay child support, phone the kids now and then) gives you the right to expose his or her sensitive, personal secrets to anyone—especially not your child. Your (or your ex's) being kicked out of college, Grandma's addiction to Valium, and Uncle Ernie's little embezzlement "problem" simply are not things children need or want to know.

One area that is particularly sensitive is parental infidelity. Believe me when I say that kids really do not want to know that Mommy had an affair or Daddy is in love with his accountant. Virtually every child or adult child of divorce I've ever discussed this with has said emphatically

ANSWERING THE TOUGH QUESTIONS

"Did Daddy have an affair?"

"Did Mom ever use drugs?"

What do you say to the tough questions? It's important to remember that tough questions like these have two components. One is the most obvious: your child seeking information. The second is equally important but often overlooked: your child expressing some concern or emotional response to the larger issue. Your basic approach to any tough question should also be "two part," following these guidelines:

✔ *Any question regarding the behavior of the other parent— affairs, indiscretions, failure to show up for visitation—is out of bounds for you to answer.* Begin by saying, "I don't feel comfortable discussing that matter with you. I can't speak for your mother/father, and it's not fair of me to. This is something only she/he can answer, and you should ask your mother/father about it directly."

At the same time, however:

✔ *Always be sure to let your child know that he can discuss with you how the other parent's behavior makes him feel.* Granted, this is where it gets a little tricky. It's crucial that you listen and help your child think through the topic while remaining impartial and keeping your feelings to yourself. You might find it helpful to refer to the boxes throughout this book on how to explain why the divorce occurred, abandonment, and so on.

For example, eleven-year-old Clint asked his mother Ariel, "Did Daddy have an affair?"

"Clint, that's not something I can answer for you. It's not fair to your father that I speak for him. This is something you really should ask him yourself." (If Clint asked his mother directly if she had had an affair, a good re-

sponse would be: "Let's have an understanding that there are certain private questions I'm not going to answer; not yes or no. As you grow, you'll see that it's not helpful for you to know about private issues like that. If I answer that, whether yes or no, then I'm opening a part of my privacy that should remain closed.") In either case, Ariel could continue on to the second part of her answer: "Obviously, this is something you've been wondering about."

"Well, yeah, because Lorenzo on my soccer team, his dad had an affair, then his parents broke up. I started thinking, you know, Dad got engaged to Edie right after he moved out. That seemed pretty fast to me, and Lorenzo said that maybe that's what happened. I'd be crazy if it were true."

"It sounds like you would be very upset about it if you found out it was true," Ariel replied, even though she knew very well her husband had been seeing Edie for some time before he moved out.

"Well, yeah, because that would mean that Dad left us for another woman. How could somebody do that?"

Ariel carefully framed her reply to move the focus from the specific (Clint's father's infidelity) to the general (infidelity, the obligations married people have to each other and their families, how we can behave in ways that hurt those we love, and so on). "Well, Clint, unfortunately affairs do occur more than people would like, and it's usually because someone makes a mistake or doesn't put the time and energy into their marriage. Everyone is different, and everyone has their own reasons for their behavior. I can't speak for anyone else, but I do believe that when mistakes occur, it's important to talk about why they happen. And that's something we can talk about without getting into what your father may or may not have done."

that they wish no one had ever told them of a parent's infidelity. If you now realize you had doubts about your ex from the start, you never really loved her, or you think the marriage was a mistake, keep it to yourself. Don't fall into the rationalization that your child needs to know "the truth" or "the real reason" for your divorce. "We could no longer live together," "We could not make our marriage work," or "We believe we will all be better off this way" will suffice. And they also qualify as "truths" and "real reasons."

• *Discuss and deal with divorce-related child issues privately.* If you disagree with your ex about taking the kids bungee jumping next weekend, or you think the way he dresses your daughter for church is abominable, register your complaint with your ex privately, not in front of your children. If necessary, set aside time to call from work or while the kids are at school or out of the house. If you feel a disagreement brewing between the two of you with a child in earshot, stop the conversation by simply saying, "Let's discuss this later."

• *Don't make your child the messenger.* Communicate with your ex directly—in person or via phone, fax, e-mail, or letter—not through your child.

• *Choose your battles wisely.* Expect and accept that there will be differences—some minor, some major—between your homes. That said, strive for a degree of consistency on the points that really matter. Ideally, parents should agree to basic, age-specific ground rules on safety, health, and school issues, such as wearing seat belts, bedtime, curfew, dating, setting aside time for homework, and so on. As children get older, there's much more latitude when it comes to things like eating and bedtime. For younger children, these really are health issues; for teens, it's probably not even worth mentioning. Sometimes agreeing or compromising on the bigger issues makes it easier for both parents to overlook their disagreements on less significant matters, like hairstyle, eating habits, clothes, and so on.

If you do feel very strongly about a major issue, such as curfew, ask yourself why. Are you really taking into account your child's best interests? Are you suddenly becoming stricter and allowing your child less freedom because you feel your own life is so out of control? Are you trying to win your child's favor by, say, letting your four-year-old have every toy he sees or permitting your thirteen-year-old to stay out after midnight on school nights? Or are you just making sure your ex gets the message that you aren't going to be bossed around? Be honest; these are all feelings divorced parents experience at one time or another. Before you join the battle, be aware that most kids view any wide gap between you and your ex's basic rules as an invitation to be manipulative. Keep in mind first and foremost: What is in the best interest of my child?

• *Consider discussions with your child about your ex's parenting style, skills, and rules essentially off-limits.* If you and your ex cannot reach agreement on something, drop it. Unless your child indicates or you have reason to believe that your ex's behavior is placing your child in jeopardy, consider what goes on in the other household none of your business. If your child comes home from visitation rattling off everything the other parent did that he didn't like or everything he knows you will disagree with, think before you speak. Unless you wish to train your child to be manipulative, don't rise to the bait. You might respond like this: "It sounds as if you're upset about a lot of things that happened. Did you discuss these things with your dad?" Focus on his feelings, his upset over the specific situation, then try to help the child discuss it with Dad or consider creative ways to deal with it and get a better perspective. You might be thinking, *Why should I help my ex?* The short and simple answer is that you're really helping your child, that he will only grow through learning coping skills, and that he will benefit from keeping his father in his life. Also, you would want Dad to do the same on your behalf. Remember that kids go through stages. Next year Dad might be the hero and you'll be the one your kid finds fault with.

• *If you must talk about your ex to friends and family, do so out of earshot of your child.* And always remember that talking on the phone when there's a child in the house should never be considered a private conversation. Children can't help but be interested in what you and others say about the other parent. Politely imploring them to concentrate on TV or the computer or banishing them to their room will probably only pique their curiosity. Simply knowing that you and others are talking about the other parent can be distressing and confusing for your child and should be avoided.

• *When you or your child do talk about the other parent, be neutral and supportive of that relationship.* Every child should be like Joey: free to discuss with you what happened at the other parent's house. If your child is young, you may have occasion to become part of his relationship with your ex; for example, your five-year-old may enlist your help in getting her other parent a birthday gift from her. (If she doesn't ask, offer to do so anyway. Remember that one parental responsibility is teaching good behavior toward everyone, including your ex.) In addition to not verbally criticizing or demeaning the other parent, become aware of the nonverbal messages you may be sending through your tone of voice, gestures, body language, and facial expressions.

You also want to keep this line of communication open so you can help your child if she has serious problems while in the other parent's custody. Remember, if you show no interest in the good things that happen to your child when she's with your ex, she will be even more reluctant to let you know when something arises that she finds difficult or troubling. If your child believes you have declared the subject of her life with Dad or Mom off-limits (whether you've actually said it or not), you have sent the message that an important part of her life (and, by extension, herself) isn't important to you. (See box "Send the Right Message," page 230.)

One of the tough realities of sharing custody is periodically losing control of your child. Often your child is your sole source of information on what goes on when he's out of your care. Of course, you should never "spy" on the other parent, or pump your child for information about your ex's private life. That said, you should still have a good idea of what goes on, where your child goes, whom your child sees, and so on, when she's away from you. Unfortunately, children are always vulnerable to abuse and neglect, not only from their parents but from stepparents, stepfamily members, and other people—strangers to you—that your child may come into contact with. If you suspect abuse or neglect, either by your ex or by others, you must intervene. (See the box "The Hard Facts About Child Abuse," page 375.)

• *Do not compete with your ex.* When you do, everyone—including your child—loses. Accept the fact that, in most cases, your child loves both of you. Resist trying to top your ex by giving your child bigger, better, or more than what her other parent does. And never ask a child to choose or show favoritism with loaded questions or comments like "Isn't this more fun than watching NFL games all weekend?" "Don't you think it's great, not having to do housework?" "I'll bet you missed having a hot breakfast when you were at Mom's."

THE WISHING WELL

Whenever you see a pond or a fountain—even if it's in the middle of the mall—invite your child to pretend that it's a wishing well. You might even put a special bowl outside filled with water to use as a well. As you pitch pennies into the well, take turns making wishes aloud.

PURPOSE: This activity can help a child express wishes that would be hard to express otherwise: "I wish Daddy would move back home with us."

Whether it seems so or not, parental conflict drags kids into the middle and never lets them go. Take a long, honest look at how you relate to your ex. Consider how much conflict your child already endures. Chances are your child will never say to you some of the things written in the Sandcastles workbooks; even those children probably never said them to their own parents. But that doesn't change the fact that these children, and perhaps your own, have strong opinions and feelings about you and your ex's ongoing conflict. These feelings not only reflect on you but shape how your child sees himself. They also can have a profound impact on the type of relationships he will have.

If you chose to divorce to spare your family further fighting, then resolve to honor that intention however you can.

10

The First Day of Divorce

How to Tell Your Child

Thirteen-year-old Larry slammed his bedroom door and kicked his dresser before crumpling to the floor. I can't believe my parents are breaking up! I hate that man! Mom is right; he's not a responsible father. I come home from school and there he is, walking out the door with his suitcase and his stereo. Why didn't he give me enough time to show him that I could do better in school? I'd do my homework more like he asked me. I tried to tell him that when he and Mom were screaming at each other last night after the parent-teacher conference. And I hate that Mrs. Pinder. Teachers can't be trusted. I begged her not to tell them about my bad grade. School sucks. I'm never going to do a single thing for school ever again. But I have to. I have to do better. He's left before, and he'll come back—I know he will. I have to find him and tell him how hurt Mom is. She can't stop crying. I'll call him at work and I'll tell him. He's gotta come back; he's just gotta.

Chloe, ten, sits at her desk, stunned from the news. I can't believe this is happening to me. I knew when they both sat down to talk, something was up. But this? So what if it's not my fault; it still hurts. I don't want Daddy to move out, but he and Mom explained why it's happening. But I'll see him a lot. And he's not moving out just yet. I wonder what my new room at his new place will be like. I still want him here with us. I can't believe it. I know they were having fights, but couldn't they

HOW WERE YOU TOLD ABOUT THE DIVORCE?

My mom told me in the car on the way back from a friend's house that my dad didn't love her anymore. I felt in shock, because my parents don't fight, and if they did, they hid it from me.

—Girl, fourteen

My dad started sleeping in a different room and then he moved out and then my mom told me. I was really sad when I first found out about it.

—Boy, eleven

My mother came home from going out to dinner with my father and was crying and told me. I kind of expected it, but I was also kind of shocked. I just sat and thought to myself, *I was afraid this day was going to happen.*

—Boy, sixteen

My friend told me that if they stopped sleeping in the same room and didn't cook for each other anymore, they were separated. I felt angry that it was my friend and not my parents telling me.

—Girl, seventeen

My mom told my dad, "Do you love me?" My dad said no, and I heard it.

—Girl, twelve

I wasn't told. My dad was crying and packed his things and left.

—Boy, thirteen

My mom told me and I didn't understand. I felt that my heart broke in half. I had a piece and the other piece cannot be found unless they get back together. My feelings have changed since then.

—Girl, ten

fix it? He said he'll call me every day, and I get to go out with him after school two days a week besides the weekend time. Mom says that's all okay with her, too. They promised me they aren't going to fight anymore. I hate it when they fight. This is so sad. I gotta call Evelyn. Her dad moved out too, but she gets to see him all the time.

Larry and Chloe have just heard the same news—their parents are separating—yet their reactions are totally different. Larry's parents made no plans for telling him; he found out when he saw his dad leaving. Now Larry is all over the place emotionally. Without any real information about the situation, he has assumed responsibility for the separation and now seeks control. Believing that his grades (and his teacher telling his parents about them) prompted his father's leaving, he feels he must save his family. Anger, self-hate, guilt, and denial are deflecting Larry's attention from the real issues and focusing his energy on "fixing" problems unrelated to the separation (his grades, his teacher, school) with "solutions" (improving his grades, calling his father) that will never reunite his family.

In contrast, Chloe is very sad and surprised, but because her parents thoughtfully planned how to tell her, she has sidestepped many of Larry's hurdles. She knows it isn't her fault, and she understands that her parents are responsible for the decision. Unlike Larry, she is not anguishing over what she could have, should have, would have done to prevent this. She also has a clear idea of what the near future holds and has confidence in her parents' ability to work out the details. Chloe can see the positive side of the separation (no more fighting), and she is beginning to develop her own coping mechanisms (phoning her friend whose parents are also divorced). Both children have suffered a great emotional trauma; both are somewhat in shock. Yet

Chloe is thinking ahead, free of self-blame and the pressure that's driving Larry in circles of self-recrimination and delusion.

TIME MACHINE

Pretend you have built a time machine and ask your child to be the first human to test it out. Ask him to step inside it (perhaps a closet or a chair to sit on) and go back to a past time, in his own life or a past era he's learning about, and discuss the differences in families. Let him talk to you as he is seeing it from the "other era." Afterward, propel him to the future and have him report how he sees himself and his family then.

Jamie saw herself divorced but remarried to a rich man in her future. She also noted that in the future there were no bosses in families; everyone—children and parents alike—had equal power.

PURPOSE: This is a fun way for a child to consider how her future will be and how she views her past. It gives the child the opportunity to see that there are different kinds of family and consider how she wishes to see her family in the future.

HEARING THE NEWS

Children of divorce look back on hearing "the news" of their parents' separation as the moment their lives changed forever. You have probably anguished over the decision to separate for months or years. Even if you truly believe that this is the best option for your family right now, that may be little comfort when you imagine how your child might respond.

Yes, it is heartbreaking to see your child's face registering shock, sadness, and anger; these are typical, normal, and healthy responses. You can't protect or rescue your child from these feelings. Through your words and actions, though, you can steer your child clear of painful, unnecessary worry and fear. Whether your child leaves this talk feeling secure or anxious, valued or disregarded, guilty or deeply loved by both her parents, depends on how you handle these crucial moments. Don't underestimate your power to set the emotional tone for the future.

Remember: You are more than the bearer of bad news here. You are also—still and always—your child's protector, his comfort, his shelter. While it may be difficult to ignore your own intense personal feelings toward your future ex and the divorce itself, your whole family will benefit enormously if you can focus on the positive results of handling this correctly. What you say, how you say it, even where and when, are all factors to consider carefully. Several major studies on adult children of divorce confirm what we've learned from thousands of children at Sandcastles: This sensitive passage must be navigated with care.

The reluctant witness. *Children should be protected from parental conflict, particularly information about a parent's infidelity. This twelve-year-old girl's bird's-eye view shows her overhearing her father saying to her mother, "I hate you!" "I'm not happy with you. I found someone I love now," and—in reply to Mom's plea, "But the kids and I still love you"—"Well I want a divorce and that's final." "Please don't let them get a divorce," she cries in her room, but when faced with her father loading the car to leave, she merely utters, "Bye."*

BE PREPARED

First, accept that your child will not regard this as just another "big talk." What may have worked for you and your spouse in the past—your style, your tone, the level of discussion you encouraged—may not be appropriate now. For example, parents who believe the less said, the better, usually fail in accomplishing their main goal: sparing the child pain. In keeping their announcement too short, to the point, and discouraging additional discussion, they unintentionally send the message that their child's feelings are not important and that her questions will not be answered. What could be more painful for a child suffering such a loss?

At the other end of the spectrum are parents who feel they owe their kids "the truth, the whole truth, and nothing but the truth." These parents may embellish their announcement with detailed descriptions of the other parent's flaws and transgressions, or they may express their own uncertainty, fear, and anxiety. Often their goal is to make their children feel "included" in the divorce. Rest assured, children need no encouragement in that direction. If anything, they need encouragement and explicit permission to disengage from parental conflicts. Without realizing it, these parents burden their children with overwhelming feelings of guilt, conflicting loyalty, and fear. If your child perceives that you feel helpless, whom will *he* turn to? And if you plant in his mind the idea that his other parent is somehow bad, you are not cultivating a closer relationship with your child, only sowing in him the seeds of low self-esteem and shame.

Finally, there are couples like Larry's parents, who literally say nothing to their children (about 3 percent, according to Sandcastles Survey responses from kids eleven to seventeen). As one seven-year-old relates in the video *Mr. Rogers Talks to Children of Divorce,* "We used to always eat breakfast together, and then one morning at breakfast, my father wasn't there." Mario, an adult child of divorce, recalled, "When my father moved out, I thought no one said anything about why because I had done something so bad that my parents couldn't even talk about it." These children feel unvalued and abandoned, and rightfully so.

BREAKING THE NEWS WITH LOVE

So let's begin with this basic premise: There is a right way to tell your children about divorce and many wrong ways. This discussion deserves and demands all the preparation you put into proposing marriage or announcing a birth, perhaps even more. Children will react with sadness, shock, disbelief, or anger, and they will desperately need to know that you will be there for them, physically and emotionally. Be clear, forthright, and ready to listen to and answer your child's questions lovingly. If you can communicate to your child your own assurance, confidence, and willingness to help her, you not only smooth her way through this difficult time, you set a pattern for future discussion and healing.

Kids know less than we think. *"What is a divorce?" this eleven-year-old girl asks. Adults often overestimate how much children understand about divorce.*

WHAT YOUR CHILD NEEDS TO KNOW

Dear Mom,
I know that you are getting a divorce, but I want to know, where did you and Dad go wrong? I'm okay with it, but I just have to find out. Because all of my feelings are like a book bag. My feelings make it heavier, so I have to let it down while I'm young, before something happens. What happened with you and Dad?
　　—Boy, eleven

Most kids above the age of seven or so will glean from the circumstances—the whole family called together, the somewhat-tense atmosphere—that something big is coming up. For older kids, simply having one or both parents begin a talk with the words "We love you" is enough to put their antennae up. If your children are old enough to know that you two have not been getting along, the news of your divorce may come as no surprise. In this case, your child may respond as if he doesn't care. Believe me, he does.

You will have your child's attention for only about one minute after he understands that this is a serious announcement. In that precious window of time, several crucial messages must be conveyed clearly and succinctly:

- You and your spouse are separating.
- Some changes will be occurring in your family's life.
- The separation has nothing to do with the children; they neither caused it nor can stop it.
- You will both continue to love your children as much as you did before; divorce is between parents, not parents and their children.
- You have discussed and decided with whom the children will live after the separation. (Be particularly certain and sensitive about this, especially if not all siblings will be living with the same parent; see the box "When Siblings Will Be Separated, Too," page 235.)
- Your children will still have a relationship with whichever parent is moving out; outline as specifically as possible how the kids will spend time with that parent, if this is going to happen.

WHAT YOUR CHILD DOES *NOT* NEED TO KNOW

Were you upset at one parent more than the other, and if so, why?
I was more upset at my mom because she cheated on my dad.
    —Girl, thirteen

Yeah, my dad, because I was the first to find out he had an affair.
    —Boy, seventeen

Most parents announce their separation to their kids during a time when their own relationship is fraught with hurt and anger. Your future ex may be the last person you want to see, and it may be difficult for you to imagine that you will ever feel differently. It may help you to know that several long-term studies of divorcing parents have found that, for the majority of divorced couples, hostility and anger do wane over time.

Obviously, no one can predict what your relationship will be like years from now. Remember, though, it is *always* best for kids to be isolated from parental conflict. Use opportunities like this to make even the smallest steps toward that future day when you probably won't feel as angry as you do right now.

SEND THE RIGHT MESSAGE

To paraphrase Dr. Seuss's Horton: Even when we meant what we said and said what we meant, the message rarely gets through 100 percent. That's because, in emotionally charged situations, our words often transcend their literal meaning and betray our true feelings. It is hard to hear a child's pain and often easier for us if we can discourage expression. After you've announced your separation, you need to take special care to respond to your kids' concerns.

Your responses should always indicate the following:

✔ *You have heard what your child said.* Do this by mirroring what he's said: "I understand that you feel sad about Mom's leaving."

✔ *You believe his feelings are valid.* Do this by empathizing: "It must be hard for you to miss her. I'm sure most kids would feel the same way."

✔ *You are open to further discussion.* Do this by assuring him that his feelings are normal—"I'll bet if most kids' moms went away, they would worry about who would take care of them"—or promising your attention: "You know, whenever you want to talk, I'm always here for you, and especially free after dinner."

Following are a few examples of the true, unintentional messages children can get from well-intentioned statements.

If your child says, "I'm really mad at you guys! How could you do this to me," you might respond:

1. *"Well, we tried hard."* A defensive response, this does not acknowledge or address the child's pain and anger. To your child, this is essentially saying "Hey, don't be mad at us! We did the best we could, and it didn't work." (Is this an excuse you would accept from your child?)

2. *"It won't be so bad. You'll get to see Dad every weekend."* This rescuing response ignores her anger and suggests that her feelings aren't such a big deal. To your child, this sounds a lot like "What are you so upset about? It's not like you'll never see your dad again."

3. *"You must be so upset and angry to have this happening."* The only response of these three that tells your child that you have heard her, that you understand her, and that you are open to hearing anything else she has to say.

If your child says, "I don't understand. I thought it was going better," you might say:

1. *"We tried really hard, but it still didn't get better."* A defensive response, it just says, "Sorry, you thought wrong."

2. *"Oh, but this way will be better, because Dad and I won't fight."* A rescuing response, this sends the message "Don't feel bad. After all, who needs a happy family when we can have a great divorce?"

3. *"It must be sad for you, especially when you thought it would all work out."* A response that addresses your child's feelings. "I don't understand" is often kid talk for "I feel sad." This response tells him that you not only understand that he is sad but that his feelings are valid and appropriate.

How to Say It

Cushion the actual announcement with loving words, but don't prolong your child's agony with a lengthy preface, especially if you know he or she senses something is wrong. Be forthright and to the point, taking care to alternate, or "sandwich," the bad news ("we are separating") with the good ("you will see Daddy often"). I often advise parents to use the word "separation" rather than "divorce," for several reasons:

• Technically, this is not a divorce; that will not actually occur for months or years to come.

• "Divorce" can be a frightening word—for younger children, because they really don't know what it means; for older children, because they do. With older kids, you also have to consider what they may know about divorce from the personal experiences of family members and friends. And don't overlook the often-sensationalized treatment celebrity children of divorce get in the media. The divorce of rock star Kurt Cobain's parents was mentioned prominently in accounts of his 1994 suicide by way of "explaining" his various health, drug, and psychological problems.

What divides us. An eleven-year-old girl depicts divorce in a graphic flowchart that traces its effect, from coming between parents, to dividing the family, to trapping the kids in the middle.

• Even if you are certain that you will divorce and that there is no hope of reconciliation, save that information for a later date, so your child can deal with this in stages. By the same token, don't say that there's a chance you will reconcile when there is not. In time, that will only diminish your child's trust in you and hinder his ability to move on.

Be forthcoming, but remember, there's nothing wrong with keeping your focus on the matters at hand. If you don't have the answers, say, "I understand you have lots of questions about what's ahead for us, but Dad and I have discussed only the important issues we have to deal with right now. We'll tell you what the next steps will be as they arise." While there may be much more to say, the news of the separation is more than enough for any child to face and begin coping with.

"WE ARE SEPARATING"

Although it may make you feel like you're rehearsing a dialogue, plan ahead of time who will say what. It's a good idea for both of you to speak equally so that your child comes away feeling that this was a mutual decision and that neither of you is more in charge or more responsible for the divorce than the other. If you must deliver the news alone, bear in mind that much of the following advice still applies. (See also the Q&A on page 246.)

Here is one example that sandwiches the bad news with the good and covers all the points in a gentle, reassuring manner:

MOM: You know your father and I love you very much, and we will both always be here for you whenever you want us or need us. We want to tell you about some important changes that are going to be happening in our family.

DAD: Your mother and I have made some mistakes in our marriage. Mothers and fathers sometimes have problems getting along with each other, and so do we. We have tried very hard to solve them, but so far we have not been able to do that, and we are making each other sad by living together, so we have decided to separate. In about a month from today, I will be moving out of our house. I will move into an apartment about a mile from here. I will still see you

THINGS 2 DO

MAGNETS

Using two magnets that look the same, demonstrate how they have a powerful attraction if facing each other a certain way but cannot be placed together if turned a different way.

PURPOSE: This can serve as a metaphor to show how people—like parents who decide to separate—could have strong feelings that drew them together can also have strong feelings that push them apart.

every weekend and on special days. You will be able to phone me whenever you want. I just won't be living here anymore.

MOM: Your father and I both feel very sorry that even though these problems are between us, they will mean some changes for you guys. We also want you to know very clearly that these changes are not happening because of anything you have done or said. It's our fault only, and we're sorry.

DAD: I will always love you, and your mother will always love you. We are separating because we cannot be happy and are hurting each other by living together.

"THERE WILL BE SOME CHANGES IN OUR LIVES"

Outline briefly but specifically, to the best of your knowledge, exactly what those changes will be. Every child's first questions are:

- "Who's going to take care of me?"
- "What's going to happen to Dad [or whichever parent is leaving]?"
- "Where will he live?"
- "When will I see him again?"
- "Does he still love me?"
- "Will Mom/Dad [the remaining parent] be okay?"
- "Will you still be my parents?" (This is usually asked by children under eleven or so.)

Two homes, one heart. *An eight-year-old boy shows his divorced parents' respective homes as both different and the same. Both parents are drawn approximately the same size and smiling. Both houses have a clock, a picture of the parent, and a window, all in the same relative position. Yet, the boy uses the times on the clocks and the scenes outside the windows (daylight in Mom's window, moonlight in Dad's) to show that the homes are different or perhaps to indicate his visitation schedule.*

Whether your child comes out and asks these questions directly or not, you should assume he is wondering about them, and you should address them now. Don't wait for him to ask; he may never do it. Tailor your remarks to answer these "unasked" questions.

Next, invite your child to share his feelings. He may shrug his shoulders or run from the room screaming. He may say, "I'm really mad at you," or "I don't believe it; I thought things were going better." He may plead "Please don't do this" or snap "Good!" then walk away. Remember, your child will feel much better if he knows that you care and you understand. You don't have to rescue your child from his feelings, and you don't have to defend the events and behaviors that led to your decision. Unfortunately, many times the answers we give our children do exactly that without communicating our understanding and support. Sometimes parents' own feelings of sadness and guilt are so strong they simply cannot bear to see their child's pain and their comments communicate that.

Ideally, you should come to this discussion with a realistic idea of how the visitation schedule will shape up for the foreseeable future. If possible, offer specific details: For example,

WHEN SIBLINGS WILL BE SEPARATED, TOO

Although in most cases, all siblings stay with the same residential parent, there are instances in which it's in the best interest of the children to be divided between the two parents. This must be carefully weighed, because we know that in most families, siblings do provide one another immeasurable emotional support. When is dividing siblings appropriate? Although it's usually best to keep siblings together, there are circumstances under which families decide the children may be separated. For example, a teenage boy who looks to his father as a role model while his younger (under twelve) sister strongly identifies with her mother.

Parents should also be able to outline for the siblings what contact they will have with one another in the foreseeable future and whether these arrangements are temporary or permanent. Make sure the siblings have opportunities to be together and stay in touch, through regularly scheduled, frequent visits and vacations. Do the family and sibling activities throughout this book. Take care that your new family doesn't break down into two cliques—Mom and child versus Dad and child—which can cause feelings of exclusion.

"Daddy will still drop you off at school Monday and Thursday mornings, he will still coach your soccer team, and you will spend every other Saturday and Sunday at his new home. And you can call him on the phone whenever you want to talk to him."

However, never promise your child something you are not certain you can deliver. If you know, for example, that your future ex is planning to move out of town, do not offer vague promises like "You'll see Daddy as much as you want to." You can be sure your child will take your words literally and then feel angry and betrayed by you when they don't pan out.

If there is an area you are not certain about, say so, but couch this information in positive terms and let your child know as much about it as you know if she shows an interest. For example, of the possibility that you may be relocating to a new family home, say, "We will be moving to a new home, but I have not decided exactly where that will be. I do know that we will stay in this town, and I will try to find a place close enough so that you can go to the same school." Or, in the same situation, you may have to say, "We are going to be moving from this house, either to Grandma's or Aunt Brenda's. I know this will be a big change for you. On the bright side, we'll be around your cousins more, and I'm sure we will soon get used to our new home." Days or weeks later, you might say, "Let's talk about what will be difficult about the move and what we can do to make it easier." Don't introduce this in the same conversation in which you break the news, because it shifts the focus from the real issue.

THE LIFE OF RILEY

When something happens, who is responsible? What makes a person responsible? What kinds of things can make a person feel responsible when he really is not? Responsibility is a key issue for children of divorce, and helping them understand how to determine who is responsible can help them alleviate the guilt and blame they often feel for the divorce.

For a child under the age of ten, make a dog out of clay. For older children, just talk about a dog. Tell the story of a dog named Riley (or whatever your child chooses to name it) who lives with and is loved by two different people. You can make these people your child and a sibling, or your child and a friend, or you and your child.

Next, set the scene and act out your parts. "It's time to feed Riley, and I'm sure it's your turn to feed him."

"I know that, but I feel like watching TV instead. You feed him for me. After all, I did it for you last week."

Now have an argument about who should be feeding the dog. When you've reached an impasse or after twenty seconds, stop and ask your child, "Who is at fault here for not feeding Riley? Me, because I refuse to help you out? You, because you don't feel like doing it, even though it's your turn?" Your child might choose himself or you as the guilty party. Ask him why. Then ask, "Is it Riley's fault?" Point out that if Riley were able to feed himself, you two wouldn't have to argue about feeding him. Does that make it Riley's fault? Then explain that even when parents fight about their child, it is *not* the child's fault.

Now change the story a little bit. You and your child take turns letting Riley out. In the past, Riley has chewed up furniture, so everyone knows that whenever Riley doesn't get out, there's a chance that might happen. You've just walked into the living room and found Riley chewing on the new sofa. Say, "It's your fault! You were supposed to let him out."

Have your child argue, "No, it was your fault. It was your turn to let him out!" Play out an argument for twenty seconds.

Stop the play. Ask your child, "Is it Riley's fault we're fighting? Or is it our fault for not working out an agreement to be sure Riley got out in time?"

Don't be surprised if your child replies that Riley is at fault, because he did a bad thing. Carefully explain that animals, like young children, don't always understand the rules. Reiterate that you and the child both knew Riley would chew the furniture and this knowledge gave you the responsibility to prevent that from happening by making sure he got out in time. It is also important to explain that even if Riley knew better, did the two of you have to argue and shout about it? How else could the two of you have resolved it? You could both have calmly discussed it and perhaps agreed to post a schedule.

Then explain that it is the same with parents. They can choose to fight or calmly discuss issues and problems. All children and adults make mistakes, and it is the parents' job to work together to help children, not fight about them.

PURPOSE: Children need to understand that arguments are the fault of the people arguing, not the person or thing they are arguing about. In the case of Riley, each of you had several opportunities to take actions that would have prevented an argument. Discuss how by honoring agreements, not breaking promises, and not shirking responsibility, all of these arguments could have been avoided. Talk about how often people argue because one or both of them believe that the other failed to meet an obligation, and how a lack of communication and understanding can lead to conflict.

Using the example of Riley, point out all the things that you and your child could have done to prevent these arguments: put Riley out in time, kept him out of the living room, trained him not to chew, and so on. This activity is crucial for a child to clearly understand that she is not at fault for her parents' divorce or past or present arguing even if the arguments surround items regarding her.

"PARENTS—NOT CHILDREN—ARE RESPONSIBLE FOR THIS SEPARATION"

At first you blame [yourself] for everything that happened and get all emotional. But later on, you think and say, "No, this isn't my fault. It was my parents' faults."
—Girl, twelve

My mom and dad used to get along. Until I went on a campout. My dad came out of nowhere and started to get a crazy idea. He said, "Why are you out here this late at night?" And then they got a divorce.
—Boy, ten

Your child must know that the reason you are separating—the *only* reason—is that you two have been unable to work out your adult problems. It is crucial for your child to understand that it is impossible for a child to cause parents to separate. Tell him explicitly that nothing he did or said in any way "caused" the divorce or influenced either of you to make this decision. Many children feel at least somewhat responsible for the divorce, so be sure your child hears you say words to the effect of "Separation is something that changes the relationship between a husband and a wife. But you should know that nothing in the world can ever change how a mom or dad feels about each of their children. Your mother and I argued about many things—the house, money, Grandma, you—but those arguments weren't the cause of our breaking up." You want to repeat this message many, many times in the months to come.

Also understand that children may perceive a glaring discrepancy between what you say and what they experience. Yes, divorce is an adult problem between the parents. However, your child probably will have a hard time understanding how a situation that

THINGS 2 DO

NOT-GUILTY SHIRT

Have your child decorate a blank T-shirt, using markers or paints. It could be any scene he wants, with a message like MY PARENTS ARE DIVORCED AND IT'S NOT MY FAULT, or MY PARENTS GOT DIVORCED AND IT'S NOT MY FAULT, AND ALL I GOT WAS THIS LOUSY T-SHIRT.

PURPOSE: Clear, repetitive statements validating the idea that the child is not at fault will increase the likelihood that he will integrate and believe this message.

affects him so profoundly does not in some way "belong" to him. Again, stress that, even though the separation is having a big impact on his life, he played no part in causing it.

WHO SHOULD TELL THE CHILDREN?

You. This might seem obvious, but far too many children—between a fifth and one quarter of kids over eleven in the Sandcastles Survey—learn about their parents' upcoming separation accidentally (by over-hearing private conversations between parents or between parents and others) or from relatives, friends, friends' parents, teachers, and others. It should go without saying that for your child to hear the news from anyone but you—and preferably both of you—is a shocking betrayal of her trust and confidence.

If you do discuss the separation with others before you tell your child, be sure they understand the importance of protecting your confidence. Remember that the more people you tell, the greater the chances that someone will slip up and accidentally deliver the blow when your child is least prepared for it. If possible, make your child among the first to know.

IF YOUR CHILD POPS THE QUESTION . . .

Try as they might, parents are rarely successful in completely shielding their children from the fallout of a failing marriage. Even when they follow all the rules and don't fight in front of their children or criticize each other, children often sense a change in the relationship. No matter how little you think your children know, you should assume that they have picked up on more than you realize. If things are not going well, even if you (and, ideally, your spouse) plan to make the announcement tomorrow, you should be prepared to answer a child who says, "Are you and Daddy going to break up?"

If you are caught off guard, don't avoid the issue. Be honest without making the full disclosure. You might say something like this: "Well, things are not going so well. But I'm not sure of many things. I really want to think things through very carefully before doing anything. As far as you go, everything will be the same, and if things will change, I'll make sure to let you know right away."

Now that you know your child is seriously thinking about it, consider telling her sooner than later, but do not feel you must make the full announcement right then. Don't paraphrase what you planned to say—with your spouse—at a future date, or dismiss your child's question out of hand ("Oh, honey, your father and I are fine, don't worry"); the stakes are too high. For your child, the pain she might derive from a mistaken message about separation ultimately will be harder for her than being unsure for a little while longer. In the meantime, be sure that changes in your mood and behavior, which can be very frightening to your child, are kept in check.

If, despite your best-laid plans, your child springs the question and you blurt out a half-baked answer, seize the first opportunity—and I mean minutes, not days, later—to sit your child down, apologize, and start over again. If you are still missing crucial information (say it's not yet clear who will be moving out or when), be honest: "Your father and I are still discussing whether I will move out, or you and he will find a new place to live, and we'll let you know as soon as we can. Meanwhile, everything will be the same."

THE BEST WAY

Ideally, both parents should be present for the announcement. This gives children their first opportunity to see that even though your marriage is ending, you will still be working together as parents. It also tells them that you are both equally committed to them and can and will separate your relationship as spouses from your relationship as parents. This arrangement also prevents one parent from dominating the floor, as it were, and using this important, sensitive moment to present his or her "case" in a (perhaps unconscious) attempt to manipulate or confuse the child. If you feel it would help your child, you might ask a favorite aunt or grandparent to be present.

THE IMPORTANCE OF SIBLINGS

[When I first found out] I didn't do anything except take my little sisters away from the fighting and arguing. I just worry about my sisters because they are only seven, and I care about them more than anyone. I didn't say anything to my parents about the divorce except don't put my sisters in the middle.

> —Girl, sixteen

What kind of feelings have you had because of the divorce?
    Sad feelings.

How have you tried to deal with these feelings?
    By talking to my brother.

> —Girl, thirteen

Write four things that will not change with divorce.

1. Even if my dad gets married, he's still my dad.
2. My family.
3. My brother won't change.
4. My sister won't change.

> —Girl, eight

Among the many emotions children experience when parents separate and divorce, a sense of being alone and different from other kids is among the most common. Even though it hasn't received much serious study, it's clear that siblings can provide invaluable support to one another in this time. No matter what our age, crisis strengthens personal bonds, and siblings have to look no farther than across the dining room table to see that there is someone else in this world who knows exactly how they feel.

All of this is good, but divorce often creates situations that may be detrimental to sibling relationships in the long run. In high-conflict homes, for example, siblings often form closer bonds as a form of protection from parental conflict. Siblings should support each other, but if you notice that their relationship has suddenly become too good to be true (no fighting at all, for example), take note. It may mean that your children are giving each other too much emotional support to compensate for what they are missing from their parents.

In times of crisis, older children are often pressed into assuming more responsibility for younger siblings. While it is healthy for them to want to do so, remember they too have their own divorce-related issues to deal with. Don't make them grow up too fast. Also respect each child's privacy. We all need our space.

Obviously, it's best if you both come to the discussion with a caring, positive attitude toward both the separation and each other. Often, only one parent really wants the separation, and so the other may remain silent through the meeting or even seem withdrawn, tearful, and possibly fearful. You can be sure that your children will be paying more attention to the silent parent than the one who is speaking. To children, a silent, withdrawn presence telegraphs powerlessness, resignation, lack of control, and hurt. Most children would interpret this parent's demeanor to mean that he or she is being hurt by the parent who wants the divorce. Your child cannot receive this message without automatically rising to that parent's defense by being angry at the "bad" parent and feeling compelled to choose between the two of you.

If you are that saddened parent, be aware of how your expression of that attitude will only hurt your child. It's normal to feel sad and to shed a few tears, but focus on how your child will interpret

THINGS **2** DO

SIBLING STORY TIME

Have an older sibling write or tell a story regarding the divorce for a younger sibling.

PURPOSE: This creates an opportunity for the older sibling to support younger siblings. Also, it helps the older child express herself through helping someone else (often older children won't do it for themselves because they "don't need it"). The younger child is given immediate support and safety to express himself.

WHAT WILL CHANGE?

Ask your child—and every member of your family—to make up a list of four things that will change with the divorce and four things that will not change. At the same time, you make up a list, then compare your lists and discuss them.

Megan's List

4 Things That Will Change

1. Daddy will move away.
2. Daddy will have a new house.
3. Mommy and Daddy will live apart.
4. We won't have a computer.

4 Things That Will Not Change

1. My house
2. My school
3. My mom and sister
4. My dog Ralph

Megan's Mom's List

4 Things That Will Change

1. Daddy will move to a new house.
2. I may have to go to work this summer.
3. We won't have a vacation.
4. Daddy and I will not be married.

4 Things That Will Not Change

1. I will always love you.
2. Our house
3. Your school
4. Your grandparents and other relatives

PURPOSE: A child can feel overwhelmed by the enormous emotional (and often physical) changes divorce brings. Some children may feel that everything is changing even when it is not. This activity helps the child focus on the real changes and the important things that divorce will not change.

your deep sadness. What good will it do for your child to resent and hate the other parent? Resolve to make the announcement with as much calm and neutrality as possible. Right now your child needs love, encouragement, and strength from both of you. Severing her emotional connection to one parent will damage her self-esteem and adversely affect her emotional development, no matter what her age. In addition, it sets her up to rescue you, and to do that she must grow up too quickly, deny and defer dealing with her own emotions, and pretend to be stronger than she really is.

An extremely valuable idea to impart to your children right now is that you are a changing family, with the emphasis on "family." You do this when you gather the kids together and make the announcement to all of them at once. Of course, children of different ages will hear the message differently, and afterward each of them probably will want and need to spend time with each of you alone, at which point you can reconfirm your message in more specific, age-appropriate language. Having your children together now gives them the opportunity to offer and receive emotional support. No child will need to wonder if he or she was given the same information as the others. Children long to belong, and they derive inestimable comfort from feeling that "we are all in this together."

WHEN SHOULD YOU TELL THE CHILDREN?

Once you decide to share your decision, take some time to consider when and where you will do it. Usually when parents reach the point of deciding to separate, they have had time to consider their decision and the possible ramifications. It's not uncommon for parents who have finally reached this point to feel that they just want to get it over with, but consider your child. In our Sandcastles Program workbooks, children over the age of nine frequently describe their reaction to the news as "shock" or "surprise." To get this devastating news a week before a birthday, on the way to school, or minutes before Dad pulls out of the driveway is simply more than any child should have to face.

If at all possible, there should be a period of time between when you make the announcement and when one of you moves out, perhaps a week or two. This gives children time to adjust to the change. By remaining in the home for a while, the parent who will be leaving has numerous opportunities to talk with and spend time with the child, to reiterate and reaffirm future plans, and comfort him. Most important, however, this transition period keeps children from feeling abandoned.

Be sensitive to how your child will probably feel after he hears the news. Ideally, the discussion should occur at home or some other private, familiar place where your child feels comfortable and you will not be interrupted. In our Sandcastles workbooks, we asked kids where they were when their parents told them about the separation. The vast majority were told at home, but too many parents broke the news while driving the car, shopping at the mall, or en route to school.

Plan not only for the announcement itself but for your child's reaction time. Generally, younger kids will want to be with one or both parents; most older kids, particularly teens, we asked at Sandcastles told us that they either went to their bedrooms to be alone or called or visited a close friend for a few hours. Often these kids will seek out one or both parents to continue the discussion later. Give your child as many options as possible. You might schedule the discussion for early on a day when no one has work, school, or appointments—perhaps at the start of a long weekend. Try to avoid such family-oriented occasions as Christmas,

Hanukkah, Thanksgiving, and Rosh Hashanah as well as children's birthdays, graduations, and bar and bat mitzvahs.

WHAT NEXT?

When I knew my parents were divorcing, I was very sad. I went to my bed, started to cry, and got two of their pictures and put them in front of me and started to pray.
—Boy, nine

When clouds weep. *In this nine-year-old girl's before-and-after drawings, a world of happiness changes to a gloomy storm that rages only over Dad. Note the absence of trees in the "after" drawing and how Mom and the child's eyes change, from happy but closed to open yet vacant—or possibly seeing more clearly than before.*

Even if your child clearly hears and understands everything you've said, expect to answer questions for days, weeks, and months to come. You can also expect each child to react in a way uniquely his or her own. What they each need most and what you are best prepared to offer is simply to be there for them, today and tomorrow. In handling this first divorce rite of passage with sensitivity and confidence, you tell your child, "We're in this together."

Q *Dear Gary,*
My husband and I have decided to separate; we have a seven-year-old son and a nine-year-old daughter. It is now late fall, and my husband and I get along well enough that we've agreed to postpone the announcement and his moving out until after the New Year, so as not to spoil the kids' upcoming birthdays and holidays. My problem is my mother-in-law. She says that our living together is "a farce" and that the sooner our kids know what's happening, the better. She also says that once the kids learn "the truth" they'll never trust us again. She feels so strongly about this, she's even threatened to tell them herself. Is she correct? What should I do?

A This is strictly your family matter. How you and your husband choose to handle this is no one else's business. Make it crystal clear to your mother-in-law that this is not her place and she is not to broach the subject with your kids. Explain to her the serious damage she will cause if she takes it upon herself to tell or even imply anything about the separation. Explain to her that while she may believe the children will appreciate her "honesty," this is shocking, devastating news. Remind her of the fate of messengers bearing unwelcome tidings. Her grandchildren may be very angry at and distrustful of her and angry at you and your spouse for not telling them first. Most important, this is an extremely sensitive issue, and they will have questions she cannot or should not answer.

While I don't agree entirely with your mother-in-law, she has raised an important point. No matter how you and your husband have been behaving of late—"dating" in a last-ditch attempt to save the marriage or treating each other as if you don't exist—your children have probably noticed some difference. They also pick up information from friends, some of whose parents have probably divorced. If you are committed to telling them the news at a future date, be aware of the risks. It's not unusual for a child to pop the question. Many a surprised and unprepared parent later regretted blurting out the news. Another possibility is that relations and friends may hint, imply, or directly voice their suspicions about your marriage to your children—another nasty surprise.

Yes, giving the kids one last birthday or holiday with the family together is a worthy goal. The question is, Can you realistically achieve it? If you and your spouse can continue living together in a way that your children will perceive as normal for your family, then it is a kind gesture. If, however, you cannot, or if you feel your children may find out soon through other channels, it might be best to have the talk now so you can control the situation. Here, you might consider your mother-in-law's concerns. Make sure that you're not fooling yourselves into believing that your household is functioning normally.

As for future concerns about your honesty, be honest. "We pretty much decided a few weeks ago but really wanted to make your birthdays and the holidays nice for you. We didn't want to throw this on you if it could wait just a few weeks" is an acceptable answer, and a truthful one. The children may be somewhat uncomfortable with the idea of your "acting" but will appreciate your reasons. If they accuse you of dishonesty, explain, "Your father and I agreed it was best that we be able to answer your questions about the separation, and that took some forethought and planning. We never intended not to tell you about the separation, and we will continue to answer all the questions you have that concern you."

Q *Dear Gary,*
My wife has filed for divorce and told me that she has no plans to ask for custody of our eleven-year-old son, although she does want to see him on weekends and holidays. He has many friends whose parents are divorced, so he probably assumes that he will be living with her. We plan to tell him about the separation together, but I'm nervous about how to explain that he will be living mostly with me, not his mother. I know it will just break his heart.

A There are two possible ways to say that he will be living primarily with you: (1) Any variation on "Mom rejected you" or (2) "We felt this would be best, and I really want you to live with me." It's obvious which message you want to send. It sounds like the mother's decision to allow you to have your child shocks and upsets you the most. Assuming that your son has a good relationship with you, there's no reason it should break his heart at the age of eleven. Besides, he will spend plenty of time with his mother (see chapter 12 for recommended visitation schedules), which you can present to him in a positive light. Don't say, "You'll be living with me and seeing your mother at these times," but "You'll get to spend plenty of time with both of us."

Here's a case where honesty is not the best policy. Never disclose to your son that you consider his mother's decision not to seek custody as frivolous, irresponsible, or something less than motherly. Knowing this will hurt his personal self-esteem and adversely affect his relationship with his mother. Also think of the future: At some point she may wish to have him live primarily with her, or future events (your relocation, illness, disability, death) may require her to assume more or total responsibility for his care. Don't poison the well.

Q *Dear Gary,*
My three teenagers know what a lying, two-timing cheat their father is. Now we've decided to separate. I feel that we need to talk to them together. My husband refuses, saying they already know the story. My questions are: How important is it that he be here when I break the news? What should I say if I have to do it alone? Under these circumstances, wouldn't just telling the kids that we're getting a divorce be enough?

A The whole point of parents' breaking the news together is to provide comfort and reassurance to the children. If either of you is so angry, resistant, or hostile that you cannot reasonably expect to contain yourself for the big talk, it's probably best if one does it alone.

If you do it alone, you should follow the same advice provided above for couples doing it together. The problem is that you can't speak *for* the other parent, and you may end up speaking *about* him instead. Saying something like "You know how impossible it is to deal with your dad. I keep telling him to be more responsible" and so on will help no one, even if it is true.

Focus on the issue at hand and be informative and comforting. For example, when the kids ask, "How often will we see Dad?" you can only reassure them that plans are in the works. "Dad and I have spoken, and he will be living nearby and plans to see you. We just do not know yet exactly when. I'm so sorry. I know that this is hard, and I wish it could be easier. But I am here for you, and you can call your dad and ask him questions, too."

Your children will probably have many questions, especially since they know of his infidelity. When you explain the reasons for the divorce, remember that even if your kids do seem to know it all, they probably don't know everything. And even if they do, you owe it to them to handle this delicate issue in an honest but loving manner, even if it seems to "protect" your spouse. Remember: You are not protecting him but your child's ability to love him. If a child asks, "Is this because of Daddy's girlfriend?" you need not deny it, but it should be placed in the larger context: "Things have not been right between your father and me for a long time. There are many reasons why we are getting a divorce. As for his girlfriend, you'll have to ask him about that. It's a subject I can't discuss now."

Q *Dear Gary,*
My husband abandoned me and our nine-year-old daughter. He told me he has no plans of coming back, no desire to see either of us again, and that I should consider him dead. My daughter adores him, and I know that when I tell her the news, she'll ask me when he's coming back, when she will see him again, and so on. I don't want to give her false hope, but I don't want her heart to be crushed like mine is right now. What do you suggest?

A Therapy. This situation has devastation written all over it. Your daughter has suffered a terrible blow and will need all the love, support, and comfort you can offer. Unfortunately, how she copes with this seems to be falling on your shoulders alone. Usually, I warn parents not to speak negatively about the other parent, because it lowers the child's self-esteem. However, in your case, your child must understand that it is not her fault that her father never calls and visits. If she doesn't, she will believe she did something to drive him away and suffer needless guilt.

You can start with the gentle but painful message that "Daddy has problems and sometimes adults do not always do the right thing." Let her know that neglecting her is unacceptable behavior, but convey this without anger, spite, or saying her father is "bad." If you can't say this calmly and lovingly, it's better not to say it at all.

Do whatever you can to convince your spouse to assume some responsibility for his child (talk to him, his friends, parents, and anyone else who may wield some influence). In the meantime, bring other opposite-sex role models into her life, such as friends, relatives, grandfathers, and so on. Be honest with yourself and be sure you haven't done anything that may have pushed your spouse to give up on having a relationship with his child. If you have any doubts, discuss it with a counselor.

Q *Dear Gary,*
My wife and I will be announcing our separation in the next couple of weeks. I think our eleven-year-old son knows we have not been happy. The problem is explaining why: My wife is in love with another woman. What should we say? How much does he need to know?

A Ultimately, it is your wife's—not your—responsibility to explain her personal choices, but only when the situation calls for more explanation. In announcing your separation, your approach should be restrained; resolve to err on the side of saying too little as opposed to too much. Deal first with the basic divorce issues (see page 142)—living arrangements, visitation, and so on—and keep your explanation of the reason you're divorcing to this: "We have been very sad." (See page 145 on how to word other reasons.) I would caution you strongly to keep the lifestyle issue out of it for now. Just coping with your separation will be overwhelming enough.

An immediate explanation would be warranted, however, if her new relationship is known to friends, neighbors, and family members who might discuss it in front of your son or bring it to his attention. As always with delicate situations such as this, you must weigh the potential emotional damage and pain your child would experience were he to learn of this from someone other than his mother. While it still is not your place to disclose this information to your son, please urge your wife to do so herself if you have reason to believe that he may learn about it from some other source.

CHAPTER

11

The First Goodbye

When a Parent Moves Away

Sitting in a classroom, Larry cannot stop thinking about his parents' breakup: It's been three whole weeks and my dad's only seen me once. We went out for burgers and we talked a little bit. When I asked him why he left and when he was coming back, he just said, "You're too young to understand." I showed him the extra-credit project I did, but he just said I was doing a "great job." When I told Mom what he said, she just smirked and said, "Figures." I guess after the way he's acted, I shouldn't care, but I do. Is he taking his blood pressure medicine? Does he miss me? It's driving me nuts. I mean, what's the point of even trying? He didn't even show me inside his new apartment. It's like I'm being punished for them breaking up. I wonder if it really was my fault.

Later that same afternoon, just a few blocks away, Chloe is packing to go to her father's new place for the weekend. This will be her third overnight stay since he moved out three weeks before. I'd better pack my old jeans, since we're going to finish painting the living room. And a dress, since Sunday will be dinner at Grandma and Grandpa's. They seem so sad about the separation, but at least we talk about it. I have them, and, when Grandma hugged me last time, I felt like she knew she had me, too. It's like my dad's gone, in one way, but he's still with me. Sometimes it feels like the whole world is upside down, but then, like when I talk to Dad on the phone or we make dinner together, it all seems so normal, too. I mean, it's still hard to talk about, but when I ask Mom or Dad a question, they tell me the truth. I know nobody's really happy about this; I know my parents would stay together if they could. But I also know they're both always there for me, even if they're not going to be there together. They still love me.

t is the definitive moment, the clearest, most dramatic sign of divorce: one parent's move away from the family home. We think of "separation" as the severing of ties between a husband and a wife. In reality, however, it also entails a parting between parent and child, usually the father. In a child's personal history of the divorce, this is the pivotal episode, the opening scene of act 2, the realization that the family will never again be the same. (For purposes of simplicity, we'll assume it is the father who has moved out, although the problems described here are common to either situation.)

Dad moves out. *The heavy shading in this seven-year-old girl's "before" picture might indicate anxiety despite the fact that everyone is smiling. This child, like many, defines divorce by noting the biggest, most obvious change: Dad, still smiling, moves to his own apartment.*

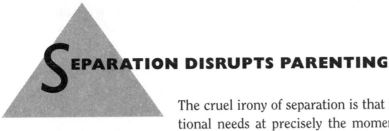

SEPARATION DISRUPTS PARENTING

The cruel irony of separation is that it creates in children greater emotional needs at precisely the moment their parents may be the least equipped to meet them. Except in cases of abuse and neglect, children need both parents more than ever, yet one may be less available emotionally, while the other is less available physically. You and your children will get off to the best start if you and your ex accept the fact that maintaining your child's relationship with both of you requires a sincere, dedicated, and sustained effort on both your parts.

No matter how well meaning and dedicated you and your ex may be, the fact that you're separated usually forces several major changes in parenting style:

• *Residential parents often feel overwhelmed.* At least initially, the added stress of picking up the slack left by the absent parent may be overwhelming. Obviously, there are only so many hours in a day, and those hours now claimed by chores previously shared—cooking, shopping, bill paying, housework, and so on— usually come from the child's "account." Many studies have confirmed that one result of separation is a decrease in the actual time each parent spends parenting.

• *Nonresidential parents can feel cut off from the children.* No longer as intimately involved in their day-to-day lives, parents living apart from their kids may feel left out, rejected, and unneeded. Those feelings create a climate in which misunderstandings can blossom into full-blown conflicts. Regardless of whether or

---

WHEN DAD MOVES AWAY

Dear Dad,
You have given me a lot of help. I miss you tucking me in at night. I always had fun with you. And I will always love you.

   —Girl, nine

Sometimes I dream about having lots of moms and dads. I am afraid that I won't see my dad again.

   —Boy, eight

Dear Dad,
I hope you know that I just love you so much, and I've been meaning to tell you that. Why did you leave from the house? I started to cry, but sometimes I really miss you a lot.

   —Girl, nine

My mom and dad are divorced.
My dad is very sad.
Every time I see him, he starts to cry.

   —Boy, thirteen

Dear Dad,
I would like to ask you if you are going to forget about me when you start a new life. I know that there are going to be a lot of changes, but I won't forget about you.

   —Girl, ten

Write four things that will not change with divorce.

1. I will not stop loving my dad.
2. I will always go on weekends with him.
3. I will always call him to see if he's okay.
4. I will always love my mom a lot too.

   —Girl, nine

not there is a legal obligation to do so, it is the residential parent's responsibility to keep the nonresidential parent involved—by sharing schoolwork, report cards, news of activities, and so on (see chapter 13). When children are old enough, they can do this for themselves.

• *The rules may change.* Even in families where parents share equally in child-care duties, certain responsibilities typically remain Mom's domain (choices of food, clothing, playmates and friends, and so on), and others are typically Dad's (coaching sports teams, dealing with more serious disciplinary matters). In most families, Mom wields the greatest influence over such matters as bedtime, table manners, household chores (cleaning up toys or making one's bed). Many married couples just assume that they agree on these issues when in fact it's more likely that one parent just ceded authority to the other. Or one partner always disagreed on a specific point but, for the sake of harmony, compromised. Now that there are two parental spheres of influence instead of one, conflicts arise as both parents begin making the rules as they see fit. The usual postseparation pattern is that Mom's control over the kids diminishes while Dad's increases.

> Until she and Donald separated, Terry assumed that their son, ten-year-old Jason, didn't eat cold cuts because she and his father had agreed that they're unhealthy. In fact, Donald doesn't see why Jason shouldn't have cold cuts now and then. But when he was married, he never did the shopping or the cooking, and it didn't really matter. However, now that Jason is spending his weekends at Donald's place, he's been eating—and enjoying—a lot of such "forbidden foods" as cold cuts, Vienna sausages, frozen pigs-in-blankets, and even the occasional Slim Jim. Terry accused Donald of not being "a good parent" and "doing this to make me mad." Donald replied, "There's no harm in Jason eating this stuff. Besides, he loves it. So what's the big deal?"

Indeed. Realistically, there is nothing Terry or any other parent can do to guarantee a child will follow the rules of her house when he's in the other parent's care. Jason is in no danger (he's not allergic to any of the ingredients, for example). And while Terry may truly believe that these foods are bad for her son, the fact is that Jason—and his parents—must learn to live with two sometimes-conflicting sets of house rules. What Jason does while in his father's custody is beyond her control. Terry can either wage a doomed battle or seize an opportunity to model compromise, for Jason's sake.

In this and many other divorce-related issues, it really is a matter of choosing your battles—or, as some might say, choosing your compromises. Obviously, there is no room for compromise on issues of health and safety. (For more detailed advice on these situations, see chapter 12.)

By and large, however, most parents do argue about the "little things." When faced with an issue like Terry and Donald's, pause and honestly weigh the benefits of trying to get your way or impose your views against the bad feelings that will be incurred by your fighting. These are often no-win situations. However, when parents compromise or simply agree to disagree, children almost always win.

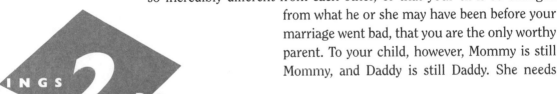

IT'S A HARD TIME FOR PARENTS, TOO

In the midst of your own emotional turmoil, it's not always easy to step back and see your partner in the same way your child does. You may feel that someone who has hurt you (or "ruined" your family, or is hurting you by wanting a divorce, or has committed certain transgressions) does not deserve your child's love. It may seem to you that you and your ex are so incredibly different from each other, or that your ex is so changed from what he or she may have been before your marriage went bad, that you are the only worthy parent. To your child, however, Mommy is still Mommy, and Daddy is still Daddy. She needs

THINGS 2 DO

COLOR MIX AND MATCH

Get paint or markers in the three primary colors: red, yellow, and blue. Let your child pick one color each to represent you, your ex, and herself. Mix together a yellow mom and red child, and you get a beautiful orange. Mix a yellow mom and a blue dad, and you get green. Mix a blue dad with red child, and you have a wonderful purple. Discuss how no color is better than the others, how two people's relationship is unique and different from any other relationship each of the pair has with anyone else.

Talk about how your child and you may make one color,

and you and your ex make another, and how those two different colors indicate that your two relationships are different. Take it further and talk about how the fact that you and your ex make, say, green in no way changes the beautiful purple or orange your child makes with either of you.

PURPOSE: This illustrates that a child can have a unique, beautiful relationship with each parent and that your relationship with his other parent is totally different from yours or your ex's with him.

your love and your ex-partner's love, attention, and support as much as she ever did, and probably even more.

Remember, you and your spouse are the ones who have fallen out of love. Your child probably loves each of you as much as he ever did. I don't think I can emphasize this point strongly enough. Earlier, I stressed how important it is to be sure your child understands that her parents' separation has nothing to do with her. Unfortunately, there's rarely anyone around to give parents the same advice about their children, so here it is: Your child's relationship with your former partner is private and personal and has little to do with you.

A tearful farewell. *This preteen girl captures the profound sadness of saying goodbye.*

How CHILDREN SEE IT: A MIXED BLESSING, AT BEST

Dear Mom,
What I like about the divorce is that we could live in peace without my dad, because we won't have to fight with him anymore. I won't have to lock myself in the room and hear all the bad words my father and you say, so I won't learn no bad words. That's the good thing about the divorce. But what I don't like about it is that I'll miss my dad.
—Girl, nine

We know that two major sources of stress for kids are separation from one or both parents and family conflict. One reason parents often cite for their separation is the fact that they no longer get along. They often view the reduction or cessation of hostility, tension, and fighting as positive. Numerous studies have confirmed that ongoing parental conflict is potentially more damaging to children than separation or divorce. Responses from kids of all ages in the Sandcastles Program underscore this finding as well. When asked to complete the sentence *I hate it when . . . ,* the overwhelming majority responded "my parents fight ['scream,' 'argue,' and so on]." In chapter 9, I addressed more specifically how parental conflict affects children. Here, however, I simply want to make you aware that this step, separation, which we all hope will yield at least one benefit—less fighting and tension at home—comes to most kids as something of a mixed blessing. They may feel that they have traded one source of stress (family conflict) for another (separation from a parent). This is why most kids initially see the separation as a "pure" loss. Where you and your ex may glimpse a silver lining, no matter how distant or dim, the moment one of you leaves, your child's whole horizon is obscured by clouds. When the news comes as a total surprise, there's no bright side anywhere. The departure of one parent symbolizes several major losses for your child.

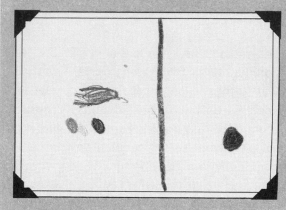

Into a black hole. *A seven-year-old draws himself and his sister as floating above the ground before the divorce. Everyone is smiling with arms, legs, and clear gender differences. After the divorce, however, the family undergoes a dramatic transformation. A black line divides them, but the family members are not even people anymore, just dots.*

THE LOSS OF A PARENT'S DAILY PRESENCE

Write four things that will change after the divorce.

1. I won't see my father as much.
2. My father won't be there for my birthday.
3. My father would be in a different house.
4. My father won't eat with me.
   —Boy, ten

For children, the little things really do mean a lot, and taken together, these little things make up daily life. Adults tend to think in generalities ("He's gone"), but kids are more detail focused and will register and respond to not seeing Dad at the breakfast table, in the backyard pool, on the basketball court, in their room tucking them in. Every little routine, every ritual, every way in which your ex was part of their lives, may spark a renewed sense of sadness and loss.

MAGIC KEYS

Give your child a real key, the "magic key" that unlocks the magic door. Ask what is behind the door. Tell him to pretend that it's anything or anyplace he wants.

PURPOSE: Fantasy is a powerful tool, and using props makes imagining more fun. This can jump-start further communication. You get to stand by and possibly hear what he would love to have ("There's a free candy store when I turn the key"), wishes ("It's our old house, and there's Mommy with all of us together"), or fears ("It's a room with lots of kids whose parents don't want them anymore, and I'm scared"). Make reassuring, nonjudgmental comments ("It can be so scary being a child and feeling like parents don't care") and further discuss the ideas.

DREAM HOUSE

You and your child each build or draw your dream house. What would it look like; how many rooms? Who would be in each room? (Are both Mom and Dad there? Do they have separate rooms?)

PURPOSE: Fantasy helps a child express what might otherwise be too difficult to put into words. Hoping for parents to reunite is a common theme that can be discussed as a result of this activity.

THE LOSS OF THE FAMILY AS HE HAS KNOWN IT

> When I think about my mom and dad not living together, I feel like a part of me is missing.
> —Boy, ten

"Family" used to mean two parents living together with their child in the same house. Now it probably means the child and one parent together most of the time, while the other parent lives someplace else and is less available. For children who must relocate, change schools, or endure other upheavals in their daily lives, the loss will seem even greater.

THE ABANDONED CHILD

Divorce is difficult for children under any circumstances, but children who have been abandoned by a parent face special challenges. A child who is abandoned experiences an often overwhelming sense of rejection. The thought that one of his parents no longer loves him, wants him, or even cares about him is potentially devastating to his sense of self-esteem and his future ability to form healthy, loving relationships with others. While the factors that led to the parent abandoning him may have nothing to do with the child, that child cannot help but take it personally and feel diminished as a result.

Abandonment can take many forms. The most obvious is the parent who simply walks away and refuses to have any further contact with the child. Then there are those absentee parents who send the occasional birthday card or gift, phone once in a blue moon, or drop in to town for a weekend every year or so. A third form of abandonment occurs gradually over time, and usually involves a parent who moves away or remarries and slowly drifts out of the child's life.

Each of these situations presents its own issues, but all have to be approached with care, sensitivity, and tact. The powerful emotions divorce inspires become even more intense in the wake of abandonment, sometimes making it difficult for the remaining parent to discuss the issue in a way that is helpful to the child. As a rule, I recommend counseling for any abandoned child, particularly those whose parent disappears and then resumes sporadic or unpredictable contact. These children in particular must sort out some very mixed messages about the abandoning parent and what his behavior tells them about themselves. (See the activity "Mr. Gray's Bunny," page 288.)

The Other Parent's Role

Before discussing the other parent with your child, it's important to carefully reexamine your attitudes toward the situation and your ex. Without intending to do so, one parent can foster situations that make it difficult for the other parent to remain involved with the child and, consequently, easier to abandon. For example, some residential parents make visitation difficult by not being home when the other parent comes to pick up the child or by using each visitation as an excuse to pick an argument. Others discourage their children from having relationships with their other parent. For example, twelve-year-old Jasmine was angry at her father for having had an affair and for asking her mother for a divorce. Rather than helping Jasmine deal with her feelings in a healthy way, Jasmine's mother, Davida, encouraged her daughter's rage. Together they would criticize and curse Jasmine's father, blaming him for every problem. As a result, Jasmine refused to have visitation with her father and refused to go to therapy, as her father requested, to try to work things out. Rather than explain to Jasmine that her own behavior had been inappropriate and why it was important her daughter maintain a relationship with her father, Davida simply said, "It's Jasmine's decision. I'm not involved." After eight months of being told to get lost by his daughter, Jasmine's father finally did. (See chapter 12 on visitation.)

If you are unsure about your actions, or if your child refuses visitation and you don't know whether or not to accede to her wishes or insist that she go, consult a mental health professional about it immediately. (See "If Your Child Refuses Visitation," page 287.) Also seek counseling for your child if she shows signs of depression or withdrawal, or if you believe she could use some extra help dealing with this difficult issue (see "Deciding on Therapy," page 189).

Unfortunately, for many divorced parents and children, the absent parent simply is not there for the child in any way. Sometimes the other parent, family members, friends, clergy, or mental health professionals can step in and convince the parent, either directly or by speaking with people he trusts, to remain in touch with his child. It's important to remember two things. First, children need to have a relationship with each of their parents, if that is at all possible. Second, in the heat of anger, people often say, do, or decide things that they later regret. In a moment of rage or depression, a father might say, "I never want to see the kids again." Regardless of how you may feel toward the other parent, and except in cases of abuse, you must make it possible for him to change his mind, for the sake of your child.

What to Say to Your Child About Abandonment

Usually, I warn parents not to speak negatively about the other parent. However, when dealing with abandonment, your child's need to be assured of the following facts must take precedence: nothing he said, did, or thought "caused" his abandoning parent to leave; that he is still loved and lovable; and that sometimes even adults make serious mistakes and do the wrong thing. In saying that abandonment is wrong, you are judging—and, to a degree—criticizing the other parent. In this situation, however, facts are facts, and your child's need to emerge from this experience without feeling guilty, rejected, or unlovable far overrides your obligation to polish your ex's image or diminish the severity of the wrong he has committed against your child. This does not mean you can use the issue of abandonment as a springboard to tear the other parent down or to drag your child into your other problems with your ex. Think carefully about how you will handle this. If you feel you need more help, consult a professional.

For children under the age of ten, you might say, "Sometimes grown-ups are so unhappy that they hurt the people around them and do the wrong thing. I know it's very sad for you not to hear from Daddy, and I wish I could do something about it. But sometimes children think it's their fault that a parent leaves them. I want you to know that your father leaving had nothing to do with you. Nothing you said, or thought, or did made him go away. Daddy has problems, and these problems make him forget about how wonderful you are and how much he is missing by not seeing you."

Next, describe how you are different and how you can always be depended on: "But I want you to know that I am always here for you. No matter how sad I could ever be or how angry I may seem sometimes, I will never leave you. We have each other, and we're our own family now, along with all the people who love us and care about us: Grandpa, Aunt Linda, [and so on]."

To an older child, you might say: "I can understand how sad and angry this makes you. And if I were you, I'd probably be thinking what a terrible kid I am that my own mother doesn't want to have anything to do with me.

Please realize that sometimes adults are so swept up in their own problems, they don't think about how others feel. I just want you to know that the problem is your mother, not you. Think about it. You're a normal person. You do great things and also sometimes make mistakes, like your friends. But parents don't leave children because children aren't good enough, or smart enough, or well-behaved enough. Parents leave their children because even though they are adults and should know better, they can still make mistakes and be unable to see that no matter how hurt, angry, or sick they are, the child still needs the parent. I'm always here for you, and nothing could make me sad or angry enough to ever consider being anything but close to you and a part of your life."

From Now On . . .

Most children who have lost a parent benefit from relationships with other adults who can provide role models. Be sure your child is able to spend time with family members, friends, and other adults who can provide her with the experiences she would have shared with the missing parent (fishing or cooking with Uncle Lou, getting facials or building a treehouse with Aunt Ruth).

Like most divorce-related issues, this one isn't going to be "solved" with a single conversation. The most important thing you can do is listen well and often. Discuss the issue with your child as often as he wishes, and be sure to check in on how he's feeling about things. Be open for him to vent his anger, and be on the watch for any signs that your child may be feeling guilty or responsible for the absent parent's behavior. And don't just give answers: "Remember, I told you it's not your fault"—though a valuable message—is still a lecture. Listen with your mind and your heart. And never forget that you have the power—through your love and understanding—to give your child everything he needs to grow up happy and healthy.

THE LOSS OF A SENSE OF CERTAINTY AND CONTROL

Dear Mom,
I have questions for you. What will happen after the divorce? Who will stay in the house? Will we have enough money to pay for the house? Will you be happy after the divorce?
—Girl, nine

This is probably your child's first big loss. Remind yourself that many of his emotions are new and that he is not always certain of how he feels or how to express himself.

COMMON FEARS ABOUT SEPARATION

I am afraid that my mom will die and I will have to stay with Dad.
  —Boy, nine

List three problems you are having or think you might have.

  1. My mom will have trouble taking care of us alone.
  2. Dad will have trouble taking care of us.
     —Girl, nine

When I feel about a divorce, it makes me feel very sad, because I don't like my mom and dad to be divorced, because maybe no one is going to celebrate my birthday.
  —Boy, eight

I am afraid that just my mom alone won't be able to take care of me.
  —Girl, ten

How did you feel when you first found out?
  I felt that I was gonna have foster parents and never see my parents again. I was twelve; that's what I thought.
    —Boy, fourteen

A LOSS OF SECURITY

> Dear Dad,
> I haven't seen you in about two years. It makes me very upset. It's like, if I get really sick and I have to go to the hospital because of an emergency, you won't know anything about what's going on.
> —Girl, eleven

From around the age of four, parents hear questions about "What would happen if [fill in the disaster]?" Now that you are separated and one parent has "gone away," your child's acute feelings of loss will fuel a surprising number of disaster scenarios, all of which are very real to her. Don't be surprised to hear your child ask:

> "If you died, who would come and take care of me?"
>
> "If something happened to you and to Daddy, where would we live?"
>
> "If I got sick at school and you weren't home when the nurse called, would she know to call Daddy?"

You should assume your child has these concerns, whether she's voiced them or not. If possible, speak with your ex and other close relatives and neighbors. Put together a realistic plan of action that you can share with your child. Let your child know that every member of the "team" has the same information and that everyone understands what they are to do, whom they are to call, and so on. Assure her that she will always be safe even if you are not available.

KEEPING YOUR CHILD SAFE

In the turmoil of separation, parents often unknowingly overlook important health and safety considerations. Remember: From the moment one of you moves out of the family home, your child has two homes. In most families, it's Mom who knows who's had all her shots and which pharmacy has the refill order on Marissa's asthma medicine. Plan ahead and see to it that both of you are equally well prepared to meet any emergency your child might face. Always have on hand and distribute the following to all caregivers, including grandparents, relatives, friends, teachers, and child-care workers:

*   A complete list of your child's past illnesses, hospitalizations, and medical procedures and their dates

*   A list of all the vaccinations your child has received and when

*   A list of your child's chronic health problems (for example, asthma) and all known allergies, to food, medication, and other substances

*   The names, addresses, phone numbers, and hospital affiliations of all your children's doctors, dentists, and other health-care professionals

*   A complete listing of all the prescribed medication your child takes as well as the name and phone number of the pharmacy with the prescription on file

Be sure you have the following:

*   Several blank copies of the "Sample Authorization for Emergency Treatment of Minors" form (see page 435)

*   Duplicates of all prescription and nonprescription medicines your child takes (Keep them in both homes, so nothing gets lost in transit between your house and your ex's)

*   Either a copy of or access to a set of your child's fingerprints and a brief, written current description of him, including height and weight

*   A recent photograph of your child

*   Photocopies of both sides of all family health insurance cards

Here comes the moving van. *For this ten-year-old boy, the changes of divorce literally dwarf and overwhelm his formerly happy family.*

THE LOSS OF SHARING LOVE FOR ONE PARENT WITH THE OTHER

List problems you think you might have.

1. When I'm with my mom, I want to be with my dad.
2. When I'm with my dad, I want to be with my mom.
   —Girl, ten

It's common for parents to feel rejected when a child expresses love for the other parent. Sometimes we unconsciously rely emotionally on our children more than we should, and then when they show any affection for the other parent, we feel "betrayed" all over again.

After years of almost-constant fighting, Kevin walked out on his family. A few weeks later, he filed for divorce and angrily informed his wife, Bridget, that he didn't want to see his two daughters, six-year-old Brittany and nine-year-old Colleen, again. Bridget wisely never passed this information on to her daughters. Instead, she explained to them that he was away on business and that, even though they were going to separate, they would see him soon. In the meantime, she made it a point to spend extra time with them and to comfort them however she could.

Bridget prayed that one day soon Kevin would come back into the girls' lives, and about two weeks after he left, he phoned to arrange to take them for a day. As the girls took turns talking to Daddy on the phone, jumping up and down and shrieking with joy, Bridget felt a slow, burning rage consume her. *How dare he!* she thought. *After the hell he's put them through, to think he can just waltz back in here like nothing happened!*

"Mommy! Mommy!" Colleen cried, smiling. "Daddy's taking us to Chuck E. Cheese tomorrow! And then to the movies, and then for ice cream! Isn't that great?"

"Yay!" Brittany exclaimed. "Let's go pick out our clothes!"

As the two girls bounded from the room, Colleen turned to her mother, hoping to see her joy reflected. But with one glance, the little girl's smile faded. Bridget caught herself and offered a wan, "Yes, girls, that's really nice," but she knew she hadn't fooled anyone. Later, reflecting on the moment with a friend, Bridget said, "I know the girls are happy about seeing their dad, but I can't help the way I feel. It's something they'll just have to get used to."

Many divorced parents can relate to Bridget's sense of rejection, but no matter how much your child loves you, she has to love the other parent, too. She also needs your repeated, unqualified emotional permission to do so. In showing her displeasure at her daughters' intense joy, Bridget left them feeling conflicted about loving their father and possibly even forced to choose between her and Kevin. Whenever you fail to support your child's relationship with her other parent, you are sending her the message that she can't have one without losing the other. From their perspective, Bridget's daughters could either live without their father (and make Mommy happy) or enjoy their father (and make Mommy unhappy).

Don't do this to your kids. They have the right to have two parents, and they have the right to fully enjoy each of them. Remind yourself that your child has always had enough love for both of you, and always will as long as you let her. Think back to when you told your child that nothing can cause a parent to lose love for a child. Now turn the tables: Nothing can make a child lose her love for a parent. Don't let your personal emotions toward your ex come between your child and her other parent.

Bridget resolved then and there to clean up her act. Later that night, after the girls were tucked into bed, she imagined Kevin coming to pick up the girls, and she thought through how she would like to see herself respond—and how she would like her daughters to see her. *Even though I don't want him anymore, they need him,* she told herself. It wasn't easy, but when Kevin rang the doorbell the next morning, she smilingly said, "I wonder who's at the door?" Colleen and Brittany bounced out of their chairs and ran for the door.

"Daddy! Daddy!" they squealed. Bridget let herself get lost in the moment and focused on the girls' unbridled joy. *I haven't seen them this happy in weeks,* she told herself, then quickly pushed away the twinge of resentment she felt.

Buttoning the girls' coats, Bridget hugged each warmly and said, "Now, you two girls have a great time! I can't wait to hear all about it when you get home!"

How RESIDENTIAL PARENTS CAN HELP

• *Give your child some idea of where the other parent lives.* If the child is old enough, also be sure she has his work and home telephone numbers, as well as his address. Children often worry about the parent who has moved away. If possible, arrange for the child to visit the parent's new home as soon as possible. If that isn't possible, ask your ex to describe his new home to your children or perhaps give them photographs or a videotape of it. Children need to have a "mental picture" of where the absent parent is and be able to visualize what he does when he's out of sight.

Waiting for the phone to ring. *A ten-year-old girl's heartbreaking depiction of children and a father separated by divorce. To a greater extent than parents often realize, children worry and wonder about the nonresidential parent, usually Dad.*

• *Listen and acknowledge the loss.* Make sure that your child knows—from what you say and how you behave—that it really is okay to miss Daddy and want to be with him. When your child does open up and express his feelings about the separation, put your own feelings aside, if necessary, and focus on your child. You don't have to like his father to be

THINGS 2 DO

HOW MUST HANGMAN FEEL?

Play the game of hangman using a feeling as the word the person is trying to guess. One player thinks of a feeling, then indicates the number of letters in the word by drawing a line, or blank, for each letter. Every time the other player guesses the right letter, it is placed in the space where it belongs in the word until the person wins by guessing or completing the word. However, every time the wrong letter is guessed, another part of the hanging man's body is drawn until the body is complete. Parents can ensure that the child wins by adding more and more body accessories, shoes, glasses, jewelry, and so on, to the hanging figure.

PURPOSE: This well-known game promotes reading and spelling. Used with feeling words, it adds the dimension of discussing feelings.

able to say in all honesty, "I know it must be tough for you to miss Daddy so much," or "I can see that not being able to have Daddy tuck you in every night really makes you sad."

• *Make some firm and realistic plans for your child to keep in touch with the nonresidential parent.* Regularly scheduled visits, phone calls, and shared activities give your child something to look forward to. Not only that, they also give her the chance to regain some predictability and normalcy in her relationship with the other parent. In the interest of making your child feel better, you and your ex may find yourselves blurting out promises along the lines of "You can call Daddy whenever you want," or "You'll get to see Mommy as often as you'd like." If this isn't true, don't do it. For children who are just coming to grips with "losing" a parent, even one postponed, canceled, or deferred opportunity to connect can be devastating.

A scheduled daily call at 7 P.M. every evening, when both households have it on the agenda, is preferable to random calling around the clock. A set time returns the missing parent to the child's daily life. Having a set phone date gives a child something to look forward to and to count on. Knowing when to expect the call gives the parent a chance to be available and to focus all his attention on the child. Regularly scheduled visits—which you might want to institute now, since they likely will be part of life after the divorce is final—are also a good idea. One added benefit is that they give the residential parent a chance to relax and recharge. At the same time, your child should be allowed to contact her parent at unscheduled times, as long as it doesn't greatly interrupt his schedule. Remember, there was spontaneity and flexibility when that parent was home. Use scheduling to ensure and increase contact, not limit it.

• *Give your child unequivocal, clear encouragement to "remember" the other parent.* You may very well want to take down the wedding portrait and feel tempted to cut your ex's face out of all your other photos.

TYPICAL RESPONSES TO PARENTAL SEPARATION

AGE	MAY FEEL	MAY SAY	MAY DO
Under 3	Confused, sad	"Daddy" [or "Mommy," whoever moved out] repeatedly. "Where's Daddy?" "I go with you, Daddy."	Cry, cling to Daddy, regress, have accidents, changes in sleep patterns
3 to 5	Sad, abandoned, guilty	"Why did Daddy go?" "I miss Daddy." "I want to be with Daddy."	Cry, have fits, want to sleep in Mommy's bed, changes in eating and sleeping, withdraw emotionally
6 to 8	Fear, grief, longing for absent parent, sad, mad, hurt, rejected, anxious, guilty	"I wish you two would get together again." "Why can't you two work it out?" "Why can't I see Daddy now?" "I want to see him right now!"	Cry, withdraw from friends, do poorly in school, mope, become overly involved in activities so as to deny negative feelings
9 to 12	Angry, rejected, hurt, overwhelmed, hopeless, out of control, sad, indifferent	"I hate you!" "Why does this have to happen to me?" "What can I do to help you?" "I'm here for you." "I feel like nothing can go right."	Choose sides, become a model child to get you two back together (if he feels guilty), may never discuss the separation in order to appear as if he doesn't care, fight, scream, be nasty
13 to 17	Angry, sad, helpless, indifferent	"You drove him away." "He never deserved you or us." "How can I help you?" "I'm here for you." "I don't care." "Don't put me in the middle." "I don't want to see Dad today."	Choose sides, become a good listener for you, be promiscuous, fight, scream, be nasty, change friends, lose interest in or do poorly in school, never discuss the separation in order to appear as though he doesn't care

People do this, but believe me, they often regret it later. Again, your child is not breaking up with your ex, you are. There is no reason why she should have to remove photographs and other mementos, and you should never suggest or demand so.

• *Make sure your child understands your plans for her in the event of an emergency or other problem.* Without alarming your child, review with her the person or people who will take care of her if you are unavailable (her other parent, Grandma, Aunt Sue, and so on). (See also "Keeping Your Child Safe," page 262.)

• *Accept and work around changes in your respective roles as parents.* And remember that even ex-spouses who achieve a positive, friendly coparenting relationship disagree on some things (as a matter of fact, so do couples who remain happily married). Often the key to coparenting success is accepting that there is your way and his way, not a right way and a wrong way. There is rarely only one right way to parent.

Q *Dear Gary,*
My husband just moved out, and we have decided to divorce. We've had a bad marriage, and the kids (seven, eleven, and thirteen) have gotten an earful of how rotten I thought their dad was. Although he was never particularly involved with the kids before, he really misses them and wants to be involved with them now. The problem is that I have poisoned them against him. I now realize what a mistake that was, and I want to "undo" the damage. Can I? How?

A Seeing and admitting your error is half the battle. Come clean with your kids; tell them how sorry you feel for sharing too much with them and allowing your personal feelings to get in the way of your good parenting and their relationship with their dad.

This is an important point, because it not only explains the situation to them, it also sends the message that parents can make—and admit to—mistakes. It also lets them know that such behavior is not acceptable. These are valuable lessons they can bring to their own children in the future.

Persuade your children to spend as much time with their father as possible. Talk to your ex-husband about gradually beginning to spend time with the children alone. Increase the time and the frequency of visits gradually until everyone is comfortable. (Ideally, this is something that should have been done in the months before the physical separation.) The truth is, your children may have taken sides because you've sent them the message that that is what you want. Now you have to let them know that you want them to love their dad, too. Give your children permission to express their love for their father, and make it clear that this will make you happy, too.

Q *Dear Gary,*
My husband is a workaholic who rarely saw our two preschoolers before they went to bed on weeknights and never spent more than a whole day with either of them. I feel they barely know him. Now, two months after he left, they both seem to be continually cranky, whiny, and demanding. My sister said she thought they missed their daddy, but I can't understand how that's possible. What do you think the problem is?

A You believe that your children "barely know" their father, but the fact is that young children naturally fall in love with their parents. They don't count the hours spent together. For them, each kiss, each hug, each smile they shared with Daddy represented love and acceptance—something all kids need, and something your kids are missing now.

Maybe your children have not expressed this directly or have hidden their real feelings toward their father because they sense it would upset you or because they don't know how to express what's on their minds. Be honest with yourself: How would you feel after caring for almost all their needs to learn that they love their father as much? Jealous? Unappreciated? Betrayed? These are normal reactions, but they should not get in the way of good parenting. It may upset you to hear your children say they love and miss Daddy, but it should also delight you. It would mean you've raised children who can feel love for others, and that's wonderful.

Talk with your children. You might say, "I've noticed you guys have been upset lately. I was thinking, maybe you miss Daddy and want to see him more." Say this lovingly, and I'll bet you'll be surprised by their forthright response. If you believe that your behavior has caused your children to hide their feelings from you, express your concerns more obliquely: "You guys seem upset. Aunt Nancy says maybe you miss your Daddy. You do miss him, don't you?" Your children might feel safer in expressing their responses to Aunt Nancy's concerns rather than yours.

Q *Dear Gary,*
My wife and I are newly separated; we have a nine-year-old boy. When we were together, I laid down the law. Homework had to be done before dinner, I forbade foul language, and doled out the occasional grounding. Now my wife feels sorry for our son because he's a "child of divorce." She's decided to help

him by making everything easy: he doesn't have to do his homework unless he feels like it, he talks like a drunken sailor, and now he's told me that she considers my strictness a form of "child abuse." I feel she's ruining our son, and I've been talking to my attorney about suing for sole physical custody. What do you advise?

A First, you need to acclimate yourself to a new reality: It's called divorce. You no longer have the same control over your son you did before, and, as the residential parent, your ex seems to have more control than before. This calls for new parenting maneuvers and skills. Your child can respect your rules when he's with you, and he should. But all you can do to change his behavior when he's out of your sight is explain to him why, for example, you believe cursing is wrong. Your son is far more likely to be influenced to follow your wishes if you appeal to his reason rather than attack his mother.

Homework and schoolwork are topics you can address with your son's teacher. If your son is no longer completing his assignments, his teacher will welcome and support your efforts to help him. You might also ask the teacher to discuss these matters with your ex, explaining that your relationship makes such a conversation difficult at this time. Perhaps if your ex hears it from your son's teacher, she'll be less inclined to write it off to the divorce and be more motivated to help him improve. Clearly, you care a great deal about your son, and these are important issues. However, your chances of suing successfully for custody are low unless there is confirmation from your son's school that Mom refuses to maintain a home atmosphere conducive to scholastic success.

While it's always difficult when one parent believes the other parent is being remiss in raising their child, remember that a custody battle is rarely a magical solution. In most cases, suing for custody is an emotionally and financially draining process that takes a steep toll on everyone, especially your child. If, after consulting with your son's teachers, you determine that his school performance is clearly at risk or he is failing miserably, suing for custody might be your last resort. But chances are it would be cheaper and definitely healthier for you to provide a tutor to assist your son with his schoolwork every night.

12

Hello, Goodbye

Custody and Visitation

Jonathan glanced across the room at his five-year-old daughter, Jenna, laughing and rolling around on the floor with her puppy, Bosco. He recalled how his heart almost broke three months ago when Jenna said, "Daddy, I don't really live here all the time, so I guess Bosco can't really be my dog."

"Jenna, listen to me: Daddy's house is your house, too. And Bosco is your doggy, even if you two can't be together every day. Understand?" Jenna just nodded and smiled.

A few hours later, Jenna was sitting silently as they drove back to her mother's house. She took just two bites of the ice cream he'd bought to cheer her up. As always, Jonathan didn't know what to say. He'd barely stopped the car in his ex-wife's driveway when Jenna flung open the car door and raced up the walk. Marcie met her at the door, took one look at Jenna's tear-soaked face, and shot Jonathan a look that seemed to say, *What on earth are you doing to this poor child?* Jonathan waved halfheartedly before driving away.

Inside, Marcie knocked on Jenna's bedroom door. "Honey? Hi! Did you have a good time at Daddy's?"

"Go away! Go away!" Jenna cried, her face buried in a pillow.

Marcie leaned against the wall, shaking her head. *If this is what visitation is going to be like, why bother? If Jonathan was doing such a great job, I wouldn't be dealing with this every Sunday night.* Meanwhile, across town, Jonathan was walking Bosco, wondering, *What is it about going home to Marcie that upsets Jenna so? I'll bet it's her mother's new boyfriend, Allen.*

The benefits of a strong, close, consistent relationship with both parents are irrefutable. It's in the best interest of everyone involved to support and encourage that relationship, even though this is not always easy. (Obviously, situations involving abuse are the exception; see "Supervised Visitation," page 274.) For all too many kids, nonresidential parents eventually will come to play a greatly diminished role in their lives. It doesn't have to be this way, and with sensitivity, planning, and common sense, parents can sidestep many common visitation problems.

Fathers usually assume the role of nonresidential parent, and increasingly some are protesting what they consider the "unfairness" of what they view as the seemingly automatic preference given to mothers as residential parents. While in some cases, it might be argued that the father is better suited for that role, it's important for everyone to understand why mothers are usually granted residential custody.

How do judges make this call? Practically speaking, in most families it is usually the mother who quits working outside the home to care for the children; if she works, it is more often she than her spouse who takes off when a child is ill or has a medical or dental appointment. Almost everywhere you find children—at school events, on the playground, at the shopping center, at birthday parties—mothers outnumber fathers overwhelmingly. While it is true that fathers have become more involved with their children than men were in the past, they still lag behind their wives in the amount of time spent caring for their children. There are an increasing number of exceptions, but they remain just that: exceptions.

Judges do, and parents should, base custody decisions on which parent is the "psychological parent." In other words, who has been largely responsible for the general care of the child, both physically and emotionally? The court's intention is to avoid unnecessary change and upheaval in a child's life. So if the child is used to one parent providing most of the care and nurturing, in the interest of continuity and preserving stability, the court will favor that parent. Of course, there's more to nurturing than spending time and physically being there. Sometimes the seemingly less involved parent actually provides the most emotional support. These distinctions are not always apparent to an outsider—

which is all even the best judge can be. All the court usually has to consider is concrete evidence indicating which parent provides most of the child's general care. Even if a father fulfills the role of psychological parent and could argue for residential custody on that basis, if his having the child would result in substantial change (for instance, Dad must work full-time, so a full-time caregiver would have to be hired), the court will probably favor Mom.

While sometimes decisions regarding custody may seem unfair, consider your situation honestly, and remember that the main consideration—ideally, the *only* consideration—is: What is best for my child? Custody battles are emotionally and financially costly, and joining one simply because you want to punish your ex or prove your competence as a parent ultimately harms your child.

CUSTODY

I want to live with my dad because, in my dad's life, I'm number one, and in my mom's life, I'm not.
        —Boy, ten

Full joint physical custody, whereby a child essentially splits her time close to equally between two separate homes (or parents "rotate" out of one home where the child always lives), has been promoted as one pos-

---

THE HARD FACTS ABOUT VISITATION AND CUSTODY

Currently, only 15 percent of divorced fathers have sole custody of their children; 8 percent share full joint physical custody, meaning that the child spends roughly equal time living with each parent. Noncustodial parents tend to be the forgotten players in the drama of divorce. Whenever the media do write them into the story, they're generally cast as the bad guys—the abandoning father, the father who doesn't pay child support, the father who remarries and ignores the children he had before. Unfortunately for children, statistics show too much of this to be true: Fewer than half of divorced fathers see their children more than several times a year, and between 20 percent and 30 percent have not seen their children in the past year. Typically, fathers keep in touch with or spend time with their kids in the months and years immediately following the breakup, but over time, the frequency of contact often diminishes. About one-third of fathers who remarry *never* see their children from previous marriages.[1] Not surprisingly, a father's emotional relationship with his children affects other aspects of their lives. For instance, fathers' compliance with child support orders is highest among those whose visitation routine is regular, frequent, and includes overnight stays. (However, lack of visitation does not relieve a parent of his or her child support obligation.)

SUPERVISED VISITATION

"Supervised visitation" is an arrangement whereby a child and a parent spend time together under the supervision of an individual both parents agree on (a family member, friend, counselor, for example) who is responsible for the child's well-being. Some counties have supervised visitation centers specifically designed as meeting places for children and parents. For parents who cannot behave cordially toward each other, these centers allow one parent to drop off and pick up the child without encountering the ex.

Supervised visitation is usually ordered when a parent or a judge believes another parent is unable to care for a child, likely to harm a child, or likely to say things that will negatively affect the child. A parent who has been abusive to a spouse and/or child in the past, who has threatened to or seems likely to abuse or kidnap the child, who suffers from severe emotional or psychological problems, is or has been a substance abuser, involved in criminal behavior, or in any way poses a threat to the child may be considered a candidate for supervised visitation. In most cases, supervised visitation is considered a temporary situation. Ideally, after three to six months, the parent will either have solved or gotten a handle on his or her problems. The supervised parent usually must also attend separate counseling or group therapy during this time, in an attempt to help him resolve this issue. Often visitation is supervised by a mental health professional, part of whose responsibility is to help the parent improve basic parenting and communication skills with an eye to making the supervision unnecessary. Of course, that is not always possible, and supervised visitation may continue for years. For most parents, however, supervised visitation is a temporary situation, something of a second chance to save a parent-child relationship that might otherwise be lost.

A happy visitation. The lack of hand-holding with Mom while connected to Dad probably indicates this six-year-old girl's private sense of closeness to her father. Interestingly, divorce is depicted as her visitation time with father. Also note the smiling mother watching them depart, suggesting her support for the girl's ongoing relationship with her ex-spouse, support all children need from both parents.

HOW TO EXPLAIN CUSTODY ARRANGEMENTS TO YOUR CHILD

Parents need to explain to children over the age of five what kind of custody arrangement they have reached and what it may mean, since they may hear the terms used by friends or in the media. These terms will probably sound scary and strange to most kids. Offer meaningful examples your child can relate to and be prepared to answer questions. (Because mothers usually are the residential parents, we've written these scripts to reflect that. You would say the same things if Mom were the nonresidential parent.) Become familiar with the terms and definitions of your specific jurisdiction, as these differ from place to place.

"*Shared custody* means that both of us will be making major decisions together for you, just like we always have. So we will discuss which doctor you will go to, which school you will attend, and which summer camp you will go to and try to make the best choice. It also means that both of us will always be a part of your life, like always. We both can come to your school play, graduation, recital—anything that you do or are part of that both of us would usually attend."

"*Residential custody* just means that, for school nights, you'll be sleeping here most of the time. 'Visitation' is the word that means the time you spend with Daddy when he sees you on weekends and Wednesday night for dinner."

"*Sole custody [with visitation]* means that I will be in charge of making all of the big decisions concerning you, like where we will live and which school you'll attend. For school nights, you'll be sleeping here most of the time. 'Visitation' is a word that means the time you spend with your father on weekends and on Wednesday night for dinner."

"*Sole custody [with no visitation]* means that I will be taking care of you and making all of the decisions concerning you, like where we will live and which school you'll be going to. Unfortunately, I cannot promise that you will get to see or spend time with Dad anytime soon. But you and I will be together, and I'll do everything I can to make it all work out."

"*Supervised visitation* means that you will get to visit with and see Daddy. But because Daddy is working out some problems, we've decided that it's best for you to see him at Grandma's/at Dr. Weiss's office/in a special place they made just so kids could be with their parents who have moved away." (If true and appropriate, add that everyone hopes that someday Daddy will be able to spend more time with the child and go more places with him. Obviously, don't say this if there is an abuse situation or if your child is afraid of her father.) (See "Supervised Visitation," page 274.)

sible way to achieve greater balance and provide kids with roughly equal access to both parents. However, for various reasons (from the parent's inability to cooperate sufficiently to simple logistics), joint physical custody arrangements make up the minority (only 8 percent of fathers). Far more typical is joint legal custody (meaning both parents are involved in decisions regarding the child) with one parent, most often the mother, given physical custody and the father visitation rights.

YOUR ROLE IN DETERMINING CUSTODY AND VISITATION

Aside from the basic considerations discussed on page 273, how you and your ex come to a decision about custody and visitation is beyond the scope of this book. Ideally, every settlement regarding custody and visi-

Learning to cope. *This little girl shows how, by offering her their love, support, and permission to love the other parent, her mother and father contributed to her sense of well-being and security: "I'm gonna start being calm, because I know they still love me."*

tation would be designed primarily to provide children with regular, frequent contact with both parents. A carefully crafted arrangement takes into account the child's age and needs, each parent's ability to provide for and care for the child, the family's history, and many other factors. Parents who rely on attorneys and judges to determine what will be best for their family may be disappointed. Remember, they are strangers who will make decisions for your family based on their vast but general experience, not necessarily any specific understanding of your family. Matters of custody and visitation are, first and foremost, about your child and the kind of parenting you want her to grow up with, not just another part of the divorce.

Every family is different, and the schedules in the chart "Suggested Visitation Schedules" (see page 277) are suggested guidelines, not hard-and-fast rules. Visitation is not a one-size-fits-all proposition. This is particularly true of babies and the very young, whose sense of time is very

SUGGESTED VISITATION SCHEDULES

Each parent should be able to take the child on extended vacations without being required to return to make the child available for visitation with the other parent. So, for example, whenever it is noted that the residential parent should have visitation during a nonresidential parent's extended vacation, this should not preclude the nonresidential parent taking the child out of town or for the full vacation time. Similarly, if the residential parent takes the child out of town for an extended vacation, visitation with the nonresidential parent would be suspended during that time. (See also "Supervised Visitation," page 274.)

Age	Time with child each week, basic recommendation	Limited Parenting Skills	Outstanding Parenting Skills	Notes
Birth to 8 months	2 or 3 weekly visits for 2 to 3 hours each	Visits take place under supervision, possibly in primary parent's home, if possible	2 weekly visits for 6 to 8 hours each *and* 1 shorter visit	If the baby nurses exclusively, arrangements may be modified to accommodate nursing.
9 to 12 months	2 or 3 weekly visits for 4 to 8 hours each *and possibly* 1 weekly weekend visit for 10 hours	2 to 4 weekly visits for 3 hours each	2 or 3 weekly visits for 4 to 8 hours each *and* 1 weekly 24-hour overnight weekend visit	Both homes must totally accommodate the little one. Try to duplicate the residential home environment: Use the same brands of pacifier, baby wipes, diapers, detergent, and so on; serve the same foods; have favorite toys on hand.
13 months to 3 years	1 or 2 weekly visits for 6 to 8 hours each *and* 1 weekly 24-hour overnight weekend visit	1 or 2 weekly visits for 4 to 6 hours each *and possibly* 1 weekly 17-hour overnight visit, from 6 P.M. to 11 A.M. *or no overnight visits*	2 weekly 24-hour overnight visits that are not consecutive *and possibly* 1 weekly visit for 6 to 8 hours. *Vacation:* Four 2-day visits per year	Flexibility: Realizing every weekend is being split, the residential parent may take the child to visit grandparents for a 4-day weekend, so the other would "make up" the time over the coming weeks.
4 to 5 years	1 or 2 weekly visits for 6 to 8 hours each *and* 1 weekly 24-hour overnight weekend visit. *Vacation:* Three 2-day visits per year	1 or 2 weekly visits for 4 to 6 hours each *and possibly* 1 weekly 17-hour overnight visit, from 6 P.M. to 11 A.M. *or no overnight visits*	2 weekly 24-hour overnight visits that are not consecutive *and possibly* 1 weekly visit for 6 to 8 hours. *Vacation:* Four 3-day visits per year	Child should be encouraged by both parents to have daily telephone contact with the other parent.

SUGGESTED VISITATION SCHEDULES

Age	Time with child each week, basic recommendation	Limited Parenting Skills	Outstanding Parenting Skills	Notes
6 to 8 years	Every other weekend from Friday after school until Sunday night *and* one other weeknight dinner and homework after school until 7:30 P.M. *Vacation:* 3 consecutive weeks in summer with nonresidential parent (residential parent has visitation) *and* other school vacations split equally between parents	1 weekly 24-hour overnight stay every other weekend *and* 1 weeknight dinner and homework. *Vacation:* Three 2-day summer visits	Every other weekend, from Thursday night until Monday morning (drop off at school) *and* 1 weeknight dinner and homework until 7:30 P.M. *Vacation:* 4 consecutive weeks in summer with nonresidential parent (residential parent has visitation) *and* school vacations split equally between parents	Flexibility: Parents should take into account the child's schedule and commitments. If your daughter plays lacrosse every Wednesday night, but Tuesday is the only weekday night she sees her father, occasionally alternate Wednesdays so he can attend her games
9 to 12 years	Every other weekend from Friday after school until Sunday night *and* one other weeknight dinner and homework after school until 7:30 P.M. *Vacation:* 3 consecutive weeks in summer with nonresidential parent (residential parent has visitation) *and* other school vacations split equally between parents	Every other weekend from 10 A.M. Saturday to 7:30 P.M. Sunday *and* one weeknight visit for dinner and homework. *Vacation:* Three 3-day summer visits	Every other weekend, from Thursday night until Monday morning (drop off at school) *and* one weeknight visit after school until 7:30 P.M. *Vacation:* Half the summer vacation with nonresidential parent (residential parent has visitation) *and* school vacations split equally between parents	See "Notes" for 6 to 8 years, above
13 to 17 years	Every other weekend from Friday after school until Sunday night *and* one other weeknight dinner and homework after school until 7:30 P.M. *Vacation:* 3 consecutive weeks in summer with the nonresidential parent (residential parent has visitation) *and* other school vacations split equally between parents	Every other weekend from 10 A.M. Saturday to 7:30 P.M. Sunday. *Vacation:* Consult with teenager; consider comfort level	Every other weekend, from Thursday night until Monday morning (drop off at school). *Vacation:* Half the summer vacation with the nonresidential parent (residential parent has visitation) *and* school vacations split equally between parents	Teenagers should not make decisions, but they should be consulted. Parents should be flexible, taking into consideration the teen's social commitments, but firm on a few important times (for example, attendance at religious services, volunteer work you do together, certain family meals and outings, etc.)

different from an adult's. For a three-year-old, three eight-hour visits a week plus one twenty-four-hour, overnight visit is preferable to a Friday-night-to-Sunday-night stay. When considering or changing a visitation schedule, you should take into account:

• *The child's age.* Younger children (under age six) benefit from more frequent, shorter visits rather than three full days at Dad's every other week, for example. Two weeks is too long a time for a very young child not to see a parent.

• *Any problems or situations that might compromise your ex's ability to parent safely and successfully.* Throughout, I use the term "limited parenting skills" with the knowledge that everyone has a slightly different idea of what makes a "good" parent. Here I'm referring only to those situations that significantly limit a parent's ability to provide a safe, nurturing experience for a child. (In contrast, a parent who, due to emotional, substance abuse, or other problems, is negligent or abusive should be seeing the child under supervised visitation only.) Here I am talking about a parent who is not very communicative, never spent much time with the child before, or who goes to work and leaves a ten-year-old alone for a half of the only day they spend together each week. Depending on the child's age, certain other behaviors might also indicate a parent who is not able to parent well. For instance, a parent who neglects to keep poisons out of a toddler's reach even after numerous warnings, or a parent who leaves children of any age without appropriate supervision, might be candidates for supervised visitation (see "Supervised Visitation," page 274).

• *Your child's needs.* At some points, your child may go through stages that require a temporary altering of the time-sharing schedule. If a child is especially clingy to Mom and hasn't seen Dad for months, work up to the ideal visitation period gradually. A child who is highly motivated in a certain subject or athletic activity may be better served to spend extra time with the parent who is more sensitive, supportive, or informed in that area. For example, Pam might spend a couple of hours three nights a week at Dad's while she's preparing for the PSATs because she's only average in trigonometry and calculus, and he is a former math major. When Pam's brother Mason landed the title role in the school production of *Hamlet,* his parents agreed that he could skip a couple of weeknight dinners with Dad so Mom, who knows Shakespeare inside out, can coach him with his lines.

HELPING YOUR CHILD DEAL WITH VISITATION

I do not like it when my dad comes to pick me up to go somewhere and fights with my mom.
—Boy, ten

Dear Mom,
Why can't I see Dad more often?
—Girl, nine

Many children view visitation with mixed feelings, because it's a regular, frequent reminder of the divorce. Even a child who is very happy to be spending time with the other parent may at some point question the obligation. Often the way children feel about their parents and the quality of time they spend with them have no bearing on how they react. Un-

The hidden feelings kids don't share. *Many children have conflicted, often-hidden feelings about visitation. This twelve-year-old boy is thinking, I'm going to miss her as he says goodbye to Mom and hello to Dad. All seems well on the surface, yet in his Sandcastles workbook, this boy angrily wrote to his father: "I'm here and you're up there and I think you're a jerk for what you did." It's likely his parents have no idea how he really feels.*

PASSWORD USING FEELINGS

Password can be played with two people or more. A person tries to have his partner guess a one-word answer by using one-word clues. The answer must be a feeling. Each player can think of a feeling as the game proceeds (if playing in a car or while doing some other activity), or you can make cards with one feeling word each: One player chooses a card and gives clues about the word on it.

For example, if the answer is "glad," the clue might be "happy." If the answer is "abandoned," the clue might be "rejected" or "left." The clue words do not have to be feelings; "Vacation" or "movies" could be the clue for "happy."

PURPOSE: This activity helps children group feelings and gain better understanding of their similarities. It can be played at any age, but the answers for older children would represent more complex feelings.

derstandably, parents often assume something is wrong when a child like Jenna "inexplicably" bursts into tears or adamantly refuses to go when the other parent arrives to pick her up. They are baffled by the cone of silence or the cloud of anger that often engulfs a child before she leaves and more often upon her return. Very often children themselves don't really understand why they feel the way they do.

Let's look at it from a child like Jenna's point of view. On one hand, she wants to spend time with her nonresidential parent; on the other, she also longs to be home with her mother. Even before they leave, these children may anticipate their sadness at having to say goodbye again. Unconsciously, a child may be angry at one or both parents for creating the situation in the first place; he may even try to avoid the pain by refusing to visit at all. He may worry about the parent he's not with: *Is he sad? Does he miss me? What is he doing?* When he comes back to you, he may ask himself the same things about the other parent. A child may think that if he seems too happy to see one parent, it will hurt the other. Or he may think that if he downplays his joy over the visit, the other parent won't feel threatened. Some parents, perhaps unknowingly, give their kids the impression that whatever happens at Daddy's house is not to be discussed. Your child might even start finding things he doesn't like about the other parent so he won't feel so torn between you.

HOW INTERESTED SHOULD YOU BE IN WHAT GOES ON "OVER THERE"?

The time your child spends with her other parent is important and precious to her. Most children are eager to share their experiences, but parents can have trouble determining what is appropriate for them to ask about. Where do you draw the line between expressing a healthy interest in your child's life away from you and being inappropriately nosy about what's going on at your ex's? You shouldn't hesitate to ask questions; however, you should be sure that your questions are about your child's experience at Mom's, not about Mom herself. The difference is often in how you phrase the question.

INTERESTED	NOSY
"Did you and your dad go anyplace special?"	"Did anyone else go with you?"
"How was your weekend?"	"Did your mother spend enough time with you?"
"That's a nice outfit Dad bought you. Where did you shop?"	"How much did it cost? Was it on sale?"
"It sounds like you really like your mom's new friend Dirk. Did you have a good time with him?"	"Did Dirk go home that night, or did he stay over?"

OTHER PRACTICAL CONSIDERATIONS

There are also the practical considerations of moving between two households. For example, even young kids who look forward to visitation may worry they will leave behind a treasured toy or their favorite pajamas (sending along a checklist might help), or that Daddy won't read a favorite story the same way Mommy does, and so on. Older children may resent the disruption to their "home" schedule—the sleepover at the neighbor's or the birthday party she'll miss because she's at Dad's. And adolescents may be anxious to live their own lives, with minimal parental contact, period. Nonresidential parents should take into consideration that a residential parent whose time with the child is consumed by extracurricular activities may not have much more time with the child than they do. In the grand scheme of things, these may seem like little things, but they should not be overlooked.

Logistically speaking, there's a lot we can do to eliminate some of these problems. For younger children, you and your ex can keep duplicates of basic necessities, for example. When it comes to making the nonresidential parent's home comfortable, acknowledge your limitations and follow your child's cues. For most families, it is impossible to create equally appointed sleeping quarters in each home. While it's easy enough to make sure a toddler has two sets of pacifiers and two sets of blocks or that favorite family photos decorate both homes, it may not be economically feasible or even desirable to ensure that twelve-year-old David has a computer in each parent's home or sixteen-year-old Stacy has two wall-shaking stereo systems. The truth is, most kids enjoy having two places to call their own. Allow your child to have a say in his room's decor, just as you would if you weren't divorced. And don't feel compelled to keep up with your ex if he or she caters to your child's every whim or goes to great expense.

With older children, you can work some flexibility into your schedules, so that the nonresidential parent knows that part of his day with the child will be spent at the big birthday party or football game. When children enter their early teens, it's appropriate to take their social commitments and extracurricular activities into account. Make sure your older child understands that spending time with each parent remains a priority but that you are willing to be flexible as the need arises. Teens—whose activities and social lives can seem to consume every free moment—may be particularly eager to skip visitation (or being around either parent). While this is a normal aspect of adolescence, it's important to be clear about your teen's family obligations. Even the busiest teenager can and should be required to participate in a few regular family activities (Sunday dinner together, Friday afternoon housecleaning, regular visits to grandparents, baby-sitting younger siblings, and so on) in addition to spending time regularly with each parent.

BE CONSISTENT

"Making Visitation Really Count" (page 285) covers the dos and don'ts of visitation, but one point bears repeating: Make sure your child knows that you take your visitation commitment seriously. It would be easy— but unrealistic—to say "never miss a scheduled visit" or "never change plans." When situations arise that interfere with visitation, be forthright and sensitive in breaking the news to your child. Acknowledge his and your disappointment and allow your child to express his sadness or anger. Explain the circumstances as clearly and in as much detail as you can, and be prepared to offer an alternate plan, like an extra night over at your house next week or your presence at an event you weren't scheduled to attend. As always, anticipate your child's questions and concerns and address them as completely as you can.

Jonathan had just put on his jacket to go pick up Jenna for the weekend. "Come on, Bosco, we're going for a ride!" Bosco wagged his tail in glee as Jonathan snapped on his leash. Then the phone rang. "Hi, Lou," Jonathan said quickly. "Can I call you back? I'm on my way to get Jenna...." A few minutes later Jonathan hung up, devastated. His cousin Lou had called from the hospital where Jonathan's mother had been rushed complaining of chest pain. After taking a few minutes to compose himself, Jonathan phoned his ex, Marcie. "It's bad news," he told her. "My mom's in the emergency room; it might be her heart. I can't take Jenna this weekend, and maybe not next. I just don't know right now. I hope that's okay?"

"Jonathan, I'm so sorry. Sure. Do whatever you have to. Keep me posted, okay?"

"I will. And would it be okay if Bosco spent the weekend there with you and Jenna?"

"You know she would love that. Just bring me some dog food."

"Okay. Can I talk to Jenna?"

"Sure."

"Hi, Daddy! I'm all ready! Don't forget to bring Bosco!"

Jonathan thought his heart would break. "Jenna, honey, listen to me. I just found out that Grandma is very sick, and she needs me to be with her at the hospital this weekend to take care of her. This means that I won't be picking you up today. I'm really going to miss you, and I'm really sorry about this."

"Oh, Daddy," Jenna wailed softly and started to cry.

"Now, Jenna, I'm going to ask my cousin Lou to bring Bosco to visit you this weekend. How's that?"

"Okay!"

"I will call you tonight to say goodnight and read a story. How about *Fox in Socks?* And I will call Mommy later today so she can tell you how Grandma is doing, all right?"

"Uh-huh."

"I love you, sugar, and I will see you as soon as I can."

MAKING VISITATION REALLY COUNT

DOS	DON'TS
For a younger child, keep track of the visitation schedule on a large calendar. Make a paper train, car, heart, smiley face, doll, or other figure and move it into each spot for the next day. Older kids can use a regular calendar. *Children feel much more in control and have an easier time making the transition if they know what to expect.*	Don't miss, show up late, or reschedule visitations except when it absolutely cannot be avoided. Don't show up for an unscheduled visit without making prior arrangements with your ex. *Canceled visitations make a child feel ignored and unloved; these types of "surprises" damage a child's sense of consistency and trust.*
Make visitation meaningful. Arrange your visits with your child so that there is time for everything: talking, listening, cuddling, and those special activities. Whatever you do—whether it's a big trip to the circus or raking leaves—make it quality time by truly being there for your child and enjoying your time together. Include your child in planning the visit, too. *Remember that the point of visitation is not to entertain your child the entire time but to be her parent in all the ways that you were before and maybe even better in some ways.*	Don't ignore your child during the visit or devote all your time and attention to other people and things. (See chapter 15 on significant others and chapter 16 on stepfamilies.) Don't feel compelled to entertain and dazzle your child every minute or ply him with gifts and treats (the "Disney Dad" syndrome). *The ideal goal of visitation is to provide special time to nurture your unique relationship with your child. He wants and deserves your attention.*
Listen to what your child has to say about her life with the other parent. *Remember, your child draws strength and happiness from both parents and needs permission to love both. Another important reason to keep this line of communication open is so that you'll be aware of any problems with the other parent that might develop.*	Don't express through your words or actions that talking about the other parent is taboo or insult the other parent in any way. *Your child wants to share his life with you; for better or worse, your ex is still part of his life.*
Keep whatever business you have with your ex between you and your ex. Respect your ex's right to conduct his life and business—including child rearing—as he sees fit. *Children deserve to have a unique relationship with each parent. They have the right to be protected from their parents' disagreements.*	Don't ask your child to carry messages to your ex for you, ask your child about your ex in a way that invades her privacy, or ask your child to share private information about your ex. *Children already feel that they are in the middle.*
Help ease the transitions to and from visitation by being cordial and polite to your ex. Allow your child some relaxed time at home before and after the visit. If your relationship with your ex allows, you might use this time to share good news of your child's activities and accomplishments. *Children usually need periods of "emotional decompression." Simply playing with or talking to the child before leaving and upon his return can relieve the child's anxiety, build trust in both parents, and generally smooth the transition.*	Don't schedule your time with your child so that you risk returning home with just moments to spare before or after a visit. Don't rush your child out of the house or into a new situation (for example, a party, a movie, sitting down to dinner) immediately upon his return. *Children need cooldown time before and after visits.*

MAKING VISITATION REALLY COUNT

DOS	DON'TS
Use part of your visit to keep your child in touch with grandparents, aunts, uncles, and cousins on your side of the family, as well as close family friends. *Remember that your child's divorce-related losses extend beyond his immediate family.*	Don't make visitation a long series of stops at different relatives' and friends' homes. *Remember that your child wants to be with you. For younger children especially, such visits can be exhausting. If the child is young or there are many people to see, consider inviting a small group over to your house for snacks or lunch.*
Encourage your child to resolve his issues with your ex independently. *It is healthy for your child to learn to respect both of his parents and learn how to work out problems with them.*	Don't interfere with how your ex is raising your child, unless the situation is serious or poses a danger to your child. *Children deserve the opportunity to create a unique relationship with each parent.*
Stand firm on the importance of respecting your visitation arrangements. Make it clear that when it's time to go on visitation or return home, it's time to go. Be sure your older child understands that while she may have some say regarding details of visitation, she cannot decide not to go. *Children do not always understand or appreciate the importance of maintaining a healthy relationship with both parents. These are ways we can help them to keep those relationships healthy and thriving.*	Don't make it possible for your child to undermine the visitation process. Don't leave scheduling in your child's hands. Don't give your child the impression that visitation is optional. *Children of divorce are prone to using manipulation to regain a sense of control. They often view visitation as a manipulatable target, since they can refuse to go, refuse to participate, relay information about one parent to the other, and so on.*
Allow the other parent to take a momentarily resistant child, under the age of five, even if he is kicking and crying. Call the residential parent as soon as the child calms down. *Keep in mind that children under five are prone to loud, dramatic tantrums, and that there may be many reasons for your child's reluctance to go (for example, visitation is new and she's not yet sure she's coming back, a favorite toy was left behind, she is experiencing a period of separation anxiety, the last time Daddy took her she got a shot at the doctor's).*	Don't force a child under the age of five to visit if the resistance is consistent, is escalating, or is out of character for your child. *Knowing your child is important. Keeping in touch with her emotions (through play, drawings, talking, activities) will give you a better sense of when a problem is serious.*
Seek professional help immediately if a child is regularly and intensely resistant about leaving. Choose someone with extensive experience in this area and include the other parent, if necessary. *A therapist can help determine the underlying fears and anxiety that could be leading to such behavior.*	Don't automatically assume that a resistant child is just being manipulative. *Although children may try to manipulate the visitation process, some do have serious problems with the other parent, which should be explored and dealt with as quickly as possible.*

IF YOUR CHILD REFUSES VISITATION

✔ *Do not take your child's reaction personally.* In most cases, your child is reacting to the changes visitation requires, not the prospect of being with one parent or the other.

✔ *Do not automatically blame the other parent.* Unless you have reason to believe that your ex has mistreated your child in some way, do not assume that your child's reluctance to visit is your ex's fault.

✔ *Give your child extra "transition time."* Sometimes when younger children resist visitation, all they need is extra time to emotionally prepare to make the switch. Spend a few extra minutes in your ex's home before putting the child in the car, for example, or phone an hour before the visit and remind the child that you're looking forward to seeing her later.

✔ *If your child is highly resistant, offer to return in an hour to pick her up.* Often this gives a child the extra transition time and the sense of control she needs.

✔ *Encourage your child to discuss her concerns about the visitation.* With an older child, take a walk around the block together and listen to her concerns in a caring, non-judgmental, nondefensive way.

✔ *Enlist grandparents, cousins, and other relatives she will be seeing during the visitation to come along.* Sometimes seeing a favorite cousin shifts the focus to the fun time ahead rather than the coming and going of visitation.

✔ *Do not allow your child to manipulate visitation.* If an older child adamantly, repeatedly refuses to participate, consider counseling. If there are no serious underlying problems, be sure your child understands that visitation is an obligation that must be met. A child who refuses visitation should not be allowed to use that time for other pleasurable activities (for example, spending the weekend at a friend's house).

See also the chart "Making Visitation Really Count" (page 285) for other tips.

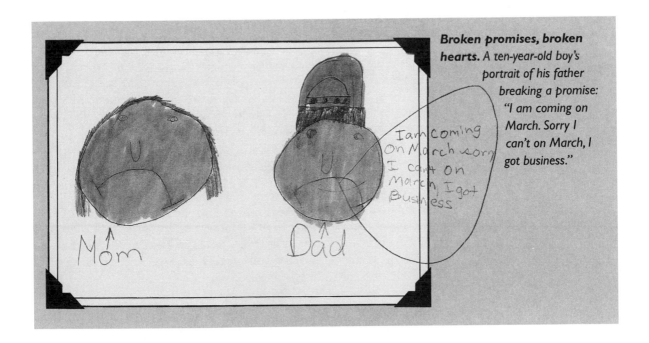

Broken promises, broken hearts. *A ten-year-old boy's portrait of his father breaking a promise: "I am coming on March. Sorry I can't on March, I got business."*

MR. GRAY'S BUNNY

This activity is designed to help children in cases where one parent has abandoned the family or has infrequent or inconsistent contact with the child.

Create a man (if it is the father who is absentee) out of craft materials, or just have your child draw him; call him Mr. Gray. Discuss his pretend strengths and weaknesses. Mr. Gray has a pet bunny rabbit that he loves (have your child name the rabbit; or it can be a snake or any animal your child particularly likes). He takes care of it, feeds it every day, gives it water, and even lets it out for walks and cuddles it.

But then Mr. Gray has to go away on a trip, and he forgets to leave enough food for his bunny. Who did the wrong thing? Does Mr. Gray not love the bunny anymore? Or could he just have made a big mistake? When he remembers the lack of food, instead of coming right back to feed the bunny, he calls Mrs. Gray to care for the bunny. Do you think the bunny still misses Mr. Gray, even though Mrs. Gray is taking great care of her?

Now you can develop the story to match what is going on in your child's personal life. If your child's father pops in from time to time, make the story work that way. Mr. Gray then decides he has to stay away (for his new job, if applicable) and will visit every so often. But he will never say when. How does the bunny feel? Do you think she misses Mr. Gray? I wonder if it is hard for her to see Mr. Gray when she knows he will leave and she will not see him for a long time. Would the bunny feel better if she knows exactly when she can expect Mr. Gray to come into town to visit? Use the story to find out how this is affecting your child and ways to cope.

Also use the story to discuss responsibility. Sometimes the bunny feels lonely, and she thinks, *Maybe if I were fluffier* *and cuter, Mr. Gray would spend more time with me and call more often.* Discuss who is at fault: Is Mr. Gray a bad man, or is he mixed up and not taking care of those around him? Why does he do that? Mr. Gray is exactly that—he's gray; far from black-and-white, neither all bad nor all good.

Take the story further and discuss how Mr. Gray bought a new bunny that lives with him (for stepsibling issues, when a father remarries and has a stepchild living with him). How does the first bunny feel? What would make the first bunny feel better? This helps the child problem-solve and consider what can and cannot be remedied.

PURPOSE: When one parent abandons or greatly limits contact with the child, it causes the youngster great pain. Often the child feels personally responsible for the rejection. It is difficult to explain to a child why a parent will not continue contact with him. This must also be done carefully so as not to harm the child's own self-worth, for if the child is told his father or mother is bad and evil, the child will consider that some of that evil must be within himself because he comes from that parent. This activity helps broach the subject in a gentle way. It also helps the child to see he is not the reason for his parent's action.

The last part of this exercise helps a child give voice and express the "weirdness" of his father's living with strange children while he sees his own child more infrequently. It further works to alleviate the child's personal sense of failure in being unable to "win" his parent's love back from the new children in his parent's life. Finally, it helps the child realize what he can and cannot solve and opens up the door to discussing better attitudes for those problems that cannot be solved immediately.

TRADITIONS, HOLIDAYS, AND VACATIONS

For most of us, the best childhood memories center on special family times like vacations and holidays. Listening for the jingle of sleigh bells on the roof, holding the candle to light the menorah by yourself the first time—these are the treasured memories that remind us what "family" means. Even sharing those times that don't quite make it as Kodak moments—the interminable August drive to Aunt Millie's farm, that war against the elements Dad referred to euphemistically as a "camping trip," Grandma's paper-dry Thanksgiving turkey—strengthen the family bond. It almost doesn't matter where you were or what you did, you were there with Mom and Dad, a family, together.

Where does your child of divorce fit into this picture today? For too many, holidays will be marked by emergency court hearings to determine who goes where when and homes fraught with tension and anger as children are packed up to travel to the other parent's home. Most of all, there is sadness as parents consider their children's supposedly "special times" and find them coming up short on happiness.

There are ways you can ensure your child's vacations and holidays are remembered for what they were instead of what they were not. You don't have to give up the important things you did together as a family. If every birthday was occasion for a day at the amusement park or a special new outfit, there's no reason why that should change. Now that you're divorced, you may not be available to take your child to the park until the day before or after his birthday, and that new outfit may not be as expensive as the ones before. This doesn't mean, however, that you should give up. Nothing in life is perfect.

On the other hand, you shouldn't go to extremes trying to keep things exactly as they were before. Your child knows things are not the same, and making too much effort to convince yourself or him otherwise is dishonest and pointless. Telling your child that spending a holiday with you alone or you and your new spouse will be "just like," "as good as," or "better than" the times he spent with you and his other parent will only invite comparison and disappointment.

Follow your child's lead: Invite her to talk about how she feels. Don't be insulted if she tells you that she misses the other parent, feels that certain occasions aren't "as good" as they were before, or says she feels especially sad at those times. Resist the temptation to make it all better; you can't. Instead empathize with her:

> "I know it must be very hard for you not to be with both me and Mom on New Year's Eve. Those were wonderful times, and I'm sorry our divorce is making you miss them. But we are still a family, and we're together. We can celebrate that, even if it's in a different way. You and I can throw confetti when the ball drops, and then you can phone Mom and say 'Happy New Year.' "

THERE'S MORE THAN A "DAY" IN "HOLIDAY"

In most instances, there's much more to a holiday than just the "day" or "days" it claims on the calendar. We all have intense, sometimes highly emotional, associations with holidays and celebrations, and tradition often figures prominently in our ideas of what we "must" or "should" do during these times. Parents who get caught up in the "one way" or "one time" things should be done set up themselves and their children for disappointment. With the exception of religious observances and holidays, most occasions are full of unmined possibilities for celebration. Be flexible and creative.

✔ *Remember, most holidays aren't just days but little seasons unto themselves.* For most kids, Christmas starts the first day Santa starts taking orders at the local mall and doesn't end until the tree comes down. Passover starts with the household preparations days beforehand; it culminates, rather than begins and ends, with the traditional meals and observances. These little seasons are filled with passing moments you can make into memories.

✔ *Recognize and celebrate the different facets of the holiday.* Many holidays have both religious or traditional and secular aspects. You and your ex might consider dividing holidays along these lines as well. For example, Mom will take Suzanne to church on Good Friday, and Dad will take her to the Easter-egg hunt; that year Dad will accompany Suzanne to midnight mass on Christmas Eve, then she will open presents at Mom's. Thanksgiving might be divided between the traditional Thursday feast at your home, then a few hours that Friday with your ex volunteering at the local soup kitchen.

✔ *Think in terms of what holidays mean to you and your child today, and don't be afraid to make your own occasions to celebrate.* For families who have suffered losses, holidays become, quite understandably, occasion to mourn rather than rejoice. But need it always be so? Every year Marilyn dreaded Father's Day, a painful reminder of her ex's having abandoned the family. A few weeks before the big Sunday, her seven-year-old son Doug said, "Mom, I was thinking. Since you do lots of things a dad would do, like play ball with me, and since I do lots of things a dad would do, too, like feed the pets, why don't we give ourselves a special treat for Father's Day?" They went out to dinner to celebrate the family they are rather than mourn the family they are not.

✔ *Children pick up their ideas about holidays from their parents and family, so be sure to send the right message.* Rather than compile a laundry list of what's "wrong" and "missing" in your family celebrations, be sure your child gets this message: "Being with you is what makes this day—or any day—reason to celebrate. I love you."

FAMILY TRADITIONS

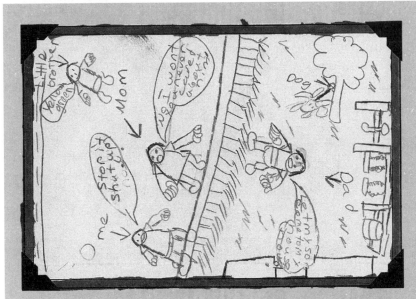

The custody battle everyone loses. When parents fight over visitation, they threaten a child's ability to maintain a relationship with the nonresidential parent. This ten-year-old boy's drawing indicates that he believes the grass is greener on the other side of the "fence," at Dad's. His lush lawn, full tree, swing set, and dog are in stark contrast to Mom's barren yard. (Also note the little brother shown sitting dangerously near the road.)

The traditions that bond and define families don't come just once a year. Every family has its own traditions—Sunday-morning brunch, pizza and Monday-night football on TV, special outings to celebrate good report cards. While you may have to adapt some of these (for instance, taping the Monday-night game and watching it with your child when he's with you on Tuesday), you shouldn't summarily abandon all of them just because you're divorced. Since you now have two different households, it might be a good time to create some new traditions that are not related to the "big" holidays. Giving your child the chance to experience new "minor" family traditions will probably make him more willing to consider and accept other changes.

Holidays

We all know that holidays can be stressful under even the best of circumstances. Between being bombarded with unrealistic images of family togetherness and our personal longing for such happiness, we often judge ourselves and our current and former loved ones too harshly. Yes, these should be times of joy, but the truth is that there may be moments when you or your child don't feel so joyful. Give your child and yourself permission to mourn what was, but temper that with reason to embrace what is today.

KEEPING THE "HAPPY" IN "HAPPY BIRTHDAY"

Families and holidays being what they are, we are not always in the position to do exactly what we want to do, to celebrate exactly as we would like. Between dividing holidays and missing one parent or other family members, children of divorce know well the art—and the pain—of compromise. At the risk of seeming to contradict myself on the subject of giving kids authority over parents, I believe the one day in your child's calendar of special days for which his vote should count the most is his birthday. After all, it is his birthday, and it may well be the only festive occasion on which he can celebrate as he wishes, when he wishes, and with whom he wishes. Given that this is *your child's day,* one for which he can invent any tradition he wants, you should put your fears of manipulation on hold. This is the one day your child is within his rights to ask for whatever he desires. To what degree you can accommodate him is another matter, but don't automatically assume that just because your child doesn't want to see your new boyfriend at his party, he's "manipulating." However, if your child doesn't want you present at his party, empathetically discuss the matter. Your child is obviously trying to convey a serious message, and you should do all you can to discover the source of his anger.

Of course, a child's birthday is a special day, but don't overlook the other ways you can share it. Most children end up having a multiday celebration, with a little party at school, a cake at home on the special day, and a get-together for friends on the nearest weekend day. If you cannot attend one, consider going to another or planning a special night out with dinner and a movie a few days before or after. With a little imagination, flex-

ibility, and creativity, both parents can share this joyous day. Besides, I've never known a child to refuse a gift or a treat just because it wasn't exactly his birthday.

What if your child wants something that just isn't possible—like both his parents together at the same party? Or he wants to include both sides of extended family, and they would be uncomfortable together? Remember, there is no one "best" way. There is no research into whether children of divorce benefit from having two separate, modest get-togethers or one big party. The rules are yours to make. Everything depends on your family.

If your child requests his two parents together at his party, consider it and discuss it with your ex. Perhaps being together at an intimate family gathering would be too stressful. But what if the celebration involves thirty of your son's screaming classmates at the local roller rink, amusement park, or *Pizza Planet?* Are there any factors that would make it more comfortable for the two of you? Maybe excluding new love interests from the festivities? Promising to both attend for the last hour's "cake" activities? Starting out by both attending for a brief time with the option to stay longer if it goes well?

Remember, this is your child's day. You have before you a lifetime of very special occasions for which your presence and behavior toward your ex will be foremost in your child's mind. Perhaps today you cannot bear to be in the same room, but promise to revisit the issue every year. Your feelings probably will change with time. Never say "never."

Some holidays are obvious: Mother's Day and Mom's birthday with Mom; Father's Day and Dad's birthday with Dad. The child's birthday can be split between parents, or if you are friendly, you might have one party with everyone together. Here, take your cues from your child.

Most parents alternate holidays so that each parent has the opportunity to experience the whole occasion with the child. (For example, this year the kids spend Thanksgiving with Dad, Christmas with Mom, and Easter with Dad. Next year they'll spend Thanksgiving and Easter with Mom, Christmas with Dad.) Another option is dividing the holiday time between the two parents. For example, the child could spend Christmas Eve with one parent, and then Christmas Day with the other. Multiday celebrations, such as Hanukkah and Kwanza, also can be divided evenly. In many families, the division of holidays must accommodate other, often-inflexible factors: distance between the parents' respective homes, parental work conflicts (for instance, Mom has the Labor Day shift in the ER), financial considerations, and family situations. Clearly, both parents should be prepared to change plans in certain urgent situations. If, for instance, Jenna's mother had long planned to take Jenna for a ski vacation over Christmas, but doctors are reasonably certain that this may be Jonathan's mother's last Christmas, a change is certainly warranted. Or, say, Jenna's mother remarries, and a new baby arrives in the middle of the summer vacation she was to have spent with her dad. Considering how left out she might feel and how important it is for her to bond with her new sibling, her parents should discuss cutting her summer vacation with Dad short and making it up over the remaining three-day weekends or with a weeknight spent at his house. Parents who refuse to be reasonably flexible should look into their own hearts and consider the potential pain they are causing their children.

However you decide to divide the holiday time, plan it far in advance, and clearly describe the schedule to your child, so she has time to mentally prepare for the transfers from one home to the other.

When your child anticipates or recalls time spent with the other parent, be positive and encouraging. If you are the parent who will be alone for the holiday, don't make your child feel guilty or sorry for you. Let your child know that you will miss him greatly but that you have arranged a pleasant time for yourself and will be okay. This way your child can enjoy the holiday without worrying about your sacrifice or loneliness.

SUMMER VACATION

Dear Dad,

You have been a better dad than you were before the divorce. The thing that bothers me is that you want to try to get us the whole summer. I wish you would let us stay with our mom, and you could visit us two or three times a week.

—Boy, twelve

Especially for the nonresidential parent, extended vacation time is a great opportunity to bond with a child. Summer vacations are an especially good time for kids to fall into a parent's daily life and get to know him on a different level. This is great if you know you'll be around enough to make this time meaningful for you and your child. The problem is that nonresidential parents, often fathers, assume that a child's just being in the parent's home constitutes quality time. It doesn't. Other parents view summer as "get-to-know-your-stepmother/father/siblings" time. It's really not.

Remember: The main point of any visitation is to spend time with the parent and other family members the child feels comfortable with. The unfortunate truth is that many nonresidential parents' schedules do not allow for large blocks of free time. Taking a child over the age of six for a few weeks at a time in the summer is a great idea, *if* the parent will be reasonably available. If Dad gets Suzy for a month of summer vacation, but she ends up spending most of every weekday with his housekeeper, his new wife, or in a day camp with kids she's never met before, the experience may prove an unhappy one. Similarly, forcing a child to spend a long stretch of time with new stepfamily members, living under their rules in their house, creates too much pressure on everyone. (See chapter 16.)

A more realistic plan would be to have the child spend the parent's vacation with him, but remain with the residential parent as before. Summer is a good time to increase visitation if possible; for example, Dad could pick up Susan from day camp three afternoons a week, and they could have dinner together one extra night. Whenever a child is with the nonresidential parent for more than a week, the residential parent should be allowed visitation following the usual schedule.

Parents who live a long distance from each other usually adjust their visitation and holiday schedules so there are fewer but longer visits with the nonresidential parent. So, for example, where two parents living in the same town might split the summer vacation fifty-fifty, it stands to reason that a nonresidential father living a thousand miles away would have the child most of the summer, while Mom has her for the state holidays, winter breaks, and three-day weekends they would have otherwise split equally. Another possibility for long-distance visitation is having the nonresidential parent come to the child. If the parents' relationship allows, the nonresidential parent might take a short trip with the child, take the child to visit with extended family on that side, or stay in the child's home and allow the residential parent to go away for a short vacation or away on business.

HOW TO HELP YOUR CHILD DEAL WITH CUSTODY AND VISITATION DISPUTES

Dear Mom,
I've learned that you and Dad are fighting over me because you love me so much.
—Girl, ten

YOU BE THE JUDGE

Ask your child to assume the role of a judge and decide a fictitious divorce case. Pay close attention to her hidden concerns while she discusses the case. If your child is amenable, she might act out the trial using dolls, stuffed animals, or action figures.

PURPOSE: Children, especially those under the age of eight, often learn to cope with their fears by acting them out in play, often many, many times. Letting your child be the judge gives her the power she could not have during the real divorce and lets her make the decisions she would have

made if she could. Ask her to tell you what the parents should do. In her interactions with the other "characters," you may hear a lot about how she views not only the divorce but you and your ex-spouse. Don't be surprised or shocked to hear her attribute to you or your ex-spouse things you never said or did, or talk about things that never happened. Children literally "fill in the blanks"; because court is so foreign to them, they're more apt to create things or adopt attitudes they've heard from friends or seen on television. They may also be repeating misinformation received from (or misunderstood from) the other parent.

Dear Mom,
Thank you for letting me in on all the conversations that had to do
with my living situations.
　　—Girl, eleven

A custody or visitation dispute that ends up in court provides the ultimate test in parenting. Whatever issue brings you to court, no matter
who's right or who's wrong, it is never a happy occasion. Parents arrive
in court as adversaries, determined to prove their points, often at the expense of discrediting the other parent. Usually, at least one parent
makes the horrible mistake of sharing the news with the child: "Your

Judge and jury. This ten-year-old boy
draws his family after parents are divorced as a lone figure sitting before a
judge.

REASONS TO CONSIDER CHANGING CUSTODY OR VISITATION ARRANGEMENTS

- A parent refuses to allow visitation.
- A parent actively attempts to alienate a child from the other parent, either physically or emotionally (consult with a psychologist to determine this).
- A parent wants to move the child far from the other parent (although in some circumstances this may be legal and acceptable; consult with a psychologist or an attorney).
- A parent or anyone who has access to the child while under that parent's supervision is emotionally, physically, or sexually abusing the child.
- A parent abandons a child and then participates in visitation inconsistently.

mom's taking me to court again." "Your dad's suing me again." That leads to the other parent's feeling compelled to justify his or her position to the child, which usually cannot be accomplished without at least mentioning what the ex has done wrong. By the time it's all over, the child ends up hearing more than the judge ever will, certainly more than he needs to know, and probably a lot more than he can handle emotionally.

This is not to say there are not sound, valid reasons for going to court. There certainly are. But most of the issues that end up being settled in court could have and should have been handled elsewhere, through attorneys, mediation, or by you and your ex setting aside your feelings and simply dealing with the problem. If you must go to court, ask yourself if the time, money, heartbreak, and stress will really be worth it. If the answer is yes, proceed, but with caution.

Explain to your child calmly and clearly what is going on. Remember how detrimental parental conflict can be, and be sure your child knows he's not in the middle. You might say, "Sometimes parents disagree and need to go to an impartial third party to help them straighten things out. We are arguing about things that have to do with you, but we are not arguing *over* you. The fact that we are having this disagreement is our fault, not yours."

Realize that once the discussion is open, your child will also speak with your ex and possibly get conflicting information:

"Your father and I have had some disagreements about money. Unfortunately, we have not been able to work things out, so I have asked a judge to tell us what is fair. Your dad may tell you about it, and if he explains it differently and you want to talk to me about it some more, please do. It doesn't have to be a big deal. But you know how Dad and I used to argue. I don't want that. I just want to solve this problem and move on. I hope you don't have to hear much more about it."

If the issue is one that directly affects the child, you should explain your position without criticizing the other parent. A good example is one parent's decision to relocate a substantial distance away. In this situation, it's important to get some idea of how your child feels about this. A parent who presents his case in an emotional manner might pressure a child to give an answer that she knows will please him. It's very important that you remain calm and not carry on about how sad you'll be or how hurt you'll feel if you don't get your way. A statement that would cover all the points of such a dispute in a neutral manner is:

> "Your mom wants to move out of town with you to live with your grandparents. I think that's nice, but I would see much less of you, and I'm just not okay with that. I can't move now because of my job, so I asked Mom if you could live with me for a while. Mom and I both want you to live with us now, and we can't figure out a way to work this out. So I asked a judge to decide for us what will be the best for you."

FINALLY

When custody and visitation don't work, everyone suffers, especially your child. For children, every visit is potentially fraught with reminders of why there has to be visitation at all. Here more than anyplace else, you really have to set aside your feelings toward your ex and work to ensure that your child has the best childhood possible—complete with two involved though no longer married parents.

Q Dear Gary,
Last Saturday night, while my twelve-year-old son and fourteen-year-old daughter were visiting my ex-wife, a family friend ran into my children coming out of a movie theater at ten at night, then running to catch a city bus home. I am shocked! They and their mother know they have no business out alone at that time of night. Whom should I approach with this first: my ex or my kids?

A Your ex, assuming you have a decent relationship with her. Approach her only if you feel you can discuss it in a respectful manner without getting into a fight. Justified or not, anger is not a good starting point for constructive conversation. Make sure you cool down first and then approach her calmly, explaining your very valid concerns about your children's well-being.

I suggest dealing with your ex first as a way to avoid yet-another disagreement or potential battle involving your children. Furthermore, any parent would prefer being approached first about any concern regarding her parenting skills before that criticism is shared with her children. Most would see it as common courtesy.

If you do need to discuss it with your children, do it gently. Don't say, "I don't care if your mother lets you go; I forbid it." After divorce, parents must respect each other's ability to parent and make proper decisions for their children. Only if a child is being placed in danger does any parent (or person, for that matter) have the complete right to step in. Discuss it gently with your children, respecting their opinions. Explain to them your concerns and fears, but show a willingness to consider creative solutions. For a twelve- and fourteen-year-old to be at the movies at ten on a Saturday night does not sound outrageous. Taking a city bus home, however, depending on where you live, could be seen as inappropriate. Discuss other forms of transportation, going with a group of friends on the bus or having a carpool to bring everyone home.

Going to the movies on Saturday night is the norm for young teenagers in many places. That doesn't mean it's right, but it does mean that you have to appreciate the social group your children are living in and respect the fact that, as a divorced parent, you cannot be totally in charge of parenting your children. Work this out with warmth and respect for your ex and children. There will be many issues like this one along the way. Develop a healthy pattern of communication now. If you don't, your opinion will mean less to your ex and your children in the future.

Q *Dear Gary,*
My husband and I have been divorced three years now, and we essentially co-parent, with our children—ages ten, twelve, and thirteen—alternating weeks in our respective homes. While my ex and the kids seem to have fallen into the groove, I can't help but feel extremely sad every time they leave. Apparently, I don't hide it too well, because my kids even talk about how bad they feel leaving me all alone. I need to get a grip on this. Please help.

A Just the fact that you have written tells me that you realize your children should not have to worry about you as much as they do. It's up to you to send your children the message that they are not hurting you by "leaving you alone."

Perhaps invite a friend over before they go, to make the transition easier for you. As soon as your children leave, go out with your friend. Knowing that you will be having a good time while they're gone will relieve your children of having to worry about you. More than anything, keeping yourself busy will help. Go out with friends, do volunteer work, take up a hobby or two, enroll in a class, or tackle that big project around the house you've been planning.

When you do speak to your children, choose a time that's ideal for you. If you feel especially sad around dinnertime, for example, call them before or after. If you've planned something exciting or interesting to do that day, try to call them afterward, so you can talk about what you did and how much you enjoyed it.

Q *Dear Gary,*
As a divorced dad, I live for Friday afternoons when I pick up my kids for the weekend visitation. My five-year-old and ten-year-old daughters literally jump into my car smiling. The problem is my eight-year-old son. He screams, cries, and once even threw his duffel bag into the pool, thinking then he'd "have to" stay home with his mother. If all three acted like he did, I'd guess my ex had poisoned him against me, but judging from my other two, that's obviously not the case. My ex, who really needs the downtime on weekends, is at her wit's end. A couple times she's let him stay with her, just to quiet him down. Needless to say, this isn't a habit we want to encourage. We've tried everything: punishments, rewards, threats, bribes—nothing works. Any ideas?

A There are many possible reasons for your son's reluctance. It's your job as a parent to consider the possibilities and then listen to your son. Only he can tell you for certain.

You say that your ex-wife really needs the "downtime." What messages might your son be getting from hearing the visitations discussed in those terms? How he views his relationship with his mother and his relationship with you is worth exploring. You may see your three children as a unit, a group with the same wants and needs. But each child is an individual. A middle child—a boy in the middle of two girls—may simply feel he needs more private time alone with his mother or his father. When you speak in terms of your son's mother needing time away from him, he may be interpreting that to mean that she will not welcome him back when he returns. On the other hand, your son's reluctance could amount to something as uncomplicated as not wanting to sleep in the den at your place.

Talk to your son in a quiet, nonconfrontational manner. Begin by saying, "Look, Robert, *obviously* something's wrong here. Let us help you with this." Talk to him about why it's hard for him to leave his mother's home. Gently ask specific questions, such as "When does the feeling you want to stay home start? What kind of feeling is it? What makes it go away?" and so on. Finally, if you cannot find the answer yourself, consult a therapist about the problem. Visitation is too important.

CHAPTER 13

One Heart, Two Homes

Parenting the Child of Divorce

Sherry tore open the envelope; from the return address, she knew what she'd find: another note from Mrs. Anderson, her thirteen-year-old son Max's homeroom teacher. *Another D! What is going on with him? I've grounded him, taken away his privileges, yelled at him. Why doesn't he listen to me the way he listens to his father?*

"Hi, Mom," eight-year-old Amy called from the back door.

"Hi, Amy. Where's Max?"

"He rode his skateboard to the store."

"He what?"

Amy slapped her hand over her mouth and muttered, "Oops! He's gonna kill me."

"He is not going to kill you, because I'm probably going to kill him first." Sherry shuddered at hearing herself talk like that. "I didn't mean that, but he is in trouble. Now you go wash for dinner."

"Okay." Hearing the front door open, Amy sang out, "Somebody's in trouble! Somebody's in trouble!"

Max's skateboard clattered against the tile floor, and he lurched toward the staircase shouting, "You little rat fink!"

"Max, you watch your mouth, young man! Apologize to your sister right now!"

"Okay. I'm sorry—," Max began contritely, "that you're my sister!"

"Max!" Sherry stamped her foot in frustration. "What on earth has gotten into you? You know you're not allowed to go anywhere without permission, much less the 7-Eleven. And you've gotten another D in social studies. What's going on with you?"

"I dunno," he answered softly, avoiding his mother's eyes. "Did you show it to Dad? Is he mad too?"

"I'm not mad at you, Max, but I'm concerned. I faxed your last two report cards over to your father's office," Sherry began before she remembered her ex, Martin, hadn't said anything. In fact, he hadn't even acknowledged receiving them. "I'm sure he feels the same way I do," she added. *This is the kind of thing Martin always handled so well. Three years after the divorce, and I still can't get the hang of the "bad cop" role.*

"Well, if it bothered him so much, why doesn't he say something to me or punish me like you do? It can't be that bad."

Sherry ignored Max's smirk. "Go to your room. You can come back down when I call you." She felt her throat tighten and tears welling in her eyes. *I can't let him see me cry.* "Now!"

Sherry is one of nearly seven million single, divorced parents today.[1] Although the number of fathers receiving primary custody of their children has increased, single, divorced residential fathers remain a minority, and full joint physical custody—where the child splits his time between parents—still involves a minority of children of divorce.

FINDING A NEW PARENTING STYLE

No matter what you may feel about your ex as a parent, his or her absence has created a void. To a greater extent than most of us realize, our child's other parent has a significant influence on how we parent. Married parents tend to complement each other and pick up their partner's slack. If, for example, your ex-husband loved playing on the floor with the kids and that wasn't your thing, you may not be their first choice for play. Or if your strong suit was discipline, your ex may have let you handle that while she became the one your kids turned to with their problems and their confidences. Most of us develop parenting styles we are the most comfortable with, and generally we delegate to our partner those aspects of child rearing we feel least adept at.

Children always need a full range of parental involvement, whether they are living with one parent at a time or two. Single parenthood inevitably demands that we adapt our parenting style to compensate for what our ex brought to the mix. If you are experiencing a bitter breakup, you may find it especially hard to admit how valuable your ex's parenting contribution really was. If you feel tapped out and stressed by single parenthood, you may regard any change in parenting style as just one more thing you have to do. Try to look at it from your child's point of view.

Once upon a time, under one roof, he probably found someone to talk to, someone to play with, someone to cuddle with, someone to set limits for him, and someone to make him laugh. The presence of two people who between them provided "parenting" defined the home, and he needed them both. He still does, even though his "new home" consists of only one parent at a time.

RESIDENTIAL (OR CUSTODIAL) PARENTS

Single, divorced parents who provide most of their kids' care give the hugs, pack the lunches, enforce the rules, dry the tears, and track down those lost shoes. Most are acutely conscious of having to be two-parents-in-one and do their best to give their children a safe, loving environment, to "make up for" the divorce. This is why it is so deeply painful when a child who has problems with

SHUFFLING THE DECK

Help your child make his own deck of cards using index cards or blank flash cards. The activity will include drawing pictures in the center of the cards, leaving room in the four corners for numbers and hearts, stars, sad faces, or angry faces. Explain:

- Cards with stars will have pictures of things the child wishes for.

- Cards with hearts will have pictures of things she loves.

- Cards with angry faces will include the things that make her angry.

- Cards with sad faces will be for things that make her sad.

Use the cards as a regular deck to play card games, and these symbols for the four suits.

PURPOSE: Having guidelines can help children to be more expressive. Notice whether or not your child draws one category differently or hesitates to complete that set. The child who can't think of a single thing to draw for angry faces obviously has difficulty accepting her anger. Some children simply may not think of more than a few things that make them sad. The deck can be completed over time and thus used as a tool for expression when future feelings arise.

HELP YOURSELF, HELP YOUR CHILD

Two major sources of stress are major life changes and situations over which you have little personal control but that make great demands of you and your time. Divorce and single parenting easily meet both criteria; in fact, after the death of a spouse, divorce is the second most stressful life event. Almost all single, divorced parents are at risk for stress. Chronic or severe stress can cause fatigue, insomnia, headaches, loss of appetite, overeating, muscle tension, and indigestion. Unmanaged, these symptoms can develop into more serious health problems, including heart disease, high blood pressure, and serious depression. At the very least, stress makes getting through the day more difficult and less enjoyable.

It's impossible to eliminate stress from our daily lives; even happy, positive events, such as a promotion at work, cause stress. What we can and should do is reduce as much stress as we can. Studies prove that we each have a different tolerance for stress and that life events in and of themselves do not "cause" stress; stress results from how we respond to these events, how we think about them, and how we view ourselves. People who expect perfection, who obsess about the past or the future, who seek unusual approval from others, and who do not express or release anger in healthy ways are more prone to stress. Those who are flexible and accept imperfection, who live in the present, who focus on their positive attributes, who express themselves clearly and listen to others, and who don't let anger and tension build up experience less stress. To a greater degree than most of us realize, it really is up to us to protect ourselves and our families from the fallout of unmanaged stress.

Stress doesn't just go away. It's up to you to make a conscious decision to reduce and deal with the stress you cannot avoid. Find what works for you—whether it's a strictly scheduled program of rigorous physical exercise, fifteen minutes of meditation, or an hour-long bubble bath—and make time for it.

Taking Time for Yourself

You may well be thinking, *Time for myself? What's that?* If you're like most parents, taking time to be alone, to relax, to pamper yourself, is a distant memory, if even that. Try to give yourself a special time each day, even if it's only the fifteen minutes you spend alone in the shower or the quiet time driving to pick up the kids from school. Exercise is great for reducing stress and increasing physical stamina. It also prompts the brain to produce endorphins, chemicals that elevate your mood. Don't overlook opportunities to slow down and reflect, or think of nothing at all. Even if it means just having that last quiet cup of tea alone before you wake up the kids, reading for enjoyment, taking a hot bath, or phoning a close friend to chat, claim some time and space for yourself. You not only need it, you deserve it. And so do your kids.

the divorce lashes out in anger or withdraws. Many parents, who already admit feeling guilty for not being able to provide their children with a "perfect" two-parent home, wonder if they're doing anything right. It's not unusual to feel that there's not enough time, not enough attention, not enough of you to go around. And it's not just your imagination. Single mothers spend less time with their children than married mothers. The stress of juggling child care, housework, and outside employment is real, and with fewer resources and less backup, single parents often feel they're stretched to the breaking point.

Of course, none of this is news to parents today, but for divorced parents, and especially those with primary custody, there's more on the line than baking those extra cookies or making time for a backyard game of catch. For children to grow after divorce, they need love, time with parents, sensitivity, limits, support, structure, and understanding. Too often, the key provider is the residential parent. In an ideal world, all divorced parents would separate their problems with their ex from their relationship with their children, and every responsible parent would cooperate fully with coparenting. I have observed that while coparenting is a laudable goal, the fact is that parents divorce because they don't get along, and they often don't get along because they have strong, sometimes irreconcilable, differences. To expect two people who could not cooperate peacefully before divorce to comfortably do so soon afterward is, I believe, unrealistic.

Far too many divorced residential parents are the "only" parent. (See page 273.)

NONRESIDENTIAL (OR NONCUSTODIAL) PARENTS

Nonresidential parents commonly feel that no one, including their ex-spouse, supports their continued involvement in their children's lives. In most instances, mothers are favored in custody decisions, especially when young children are involved. Mothers have primary custody in 72 percent of all divorces. For fathers, intense and direct involvement in day-to-day child care is still fairly rare. Even in intact families with both parents employed full-time outside the home, the average father of young children devotes only 33 percent to 40 percent as much time to child care as the mother.[2] One irony of divorce is that many fathers report that they actually spend more time with their kids since they divorced than they did before.

It takes time and energy to remain actively involved in the daily goings-on of another household. Even nonresidential parents who see their children frequently may feel that they are not as close as they were before or that their children are closer to the other parent than to them. We know that divorced parents often forge civil, even friendly, relationships several years after they have divorced. Before that point lies a "danger period," when poor communication with the ex and decreased contact with the children leaves the nonresidential parent vulnerable to feeling left out, unneeded, or unwanted. Relatively minor disagreements over the children, continued legal conflicts, and the emotional trauma of being divorced may make it seem easier to walk away. Both parents must ensure that this does not happen to their child.

NONRESIDENTIAL FATHERHOOD: PROTECTING THE BOND

Pushing Dad out of the picture. *Drawing her family with Dad out of the frame, this eight-year-old girl may be illustrating a separation from him that is physical, emotional, or both. Through drawing Dad with clothes and hair similar to Mom's, this child is likely illustrating her confusion of gender roles and identification.*

This Friday afternoon, like every other, Martin caught himself glancing at the clock as his employees rambled about strategy, client loads, billable hours, and upcoming court dates. *My staff sure knows how to talk,* he mused, absentmindedly patting his vest pocket. *The Bulls tickets are there, all right, just as I promised.*

The minute he was free, Martin grabbed his briefcase, told his secretary to say he'd gone for the day, and jumped into his car. Martin prided himself on being involved in Amy's and Max's lives. When he and Sherry broke up, he vowed that his kids would never be "missing" a father. Just last year, after reading some books and articles on the subject, he decided that full joint physical custody would be the best arrangement. He even put a down payment on a bigger condo closer to his office but within their school district, so the kids could live with him every other week, or three days a week. It was only after much soul-searching, that Martin admitted that his demanding schedule, along with the kids' ages, their attachment to their neighborhood, and other factors, would make it hard on everyone.

Still, Martin vowed that all their memories of him would be happy. That meant a trip to the toy store and at least one big outing every weekend, plus a really great vacation each summer. Last year, it was Key West; this year, the Grand Canyon.

As Martin stood waiting for someone to answer the door, he overheard Max shouting, "But, Mom, I can't do any better! Mrs. Anderson says I'm being lazy, but I'm not!"

"Max, we've talked about this many times. You know spending half an hour on your homework with the TV on isn't enough. I've told you time and time again, and I think Mrs. Anderson is right," Sherry replied.

Why doesn't she just get off the kid's case? Martin wondered. *He's got it tough enough growing up without me here.*

Sherry opened the door and whispered, "Thank goodness you're here. Max is having trouble in school again, and I think he'd listen if you spoke to him."

"What do you mean, trouble in school?" Martin asked. Just then Amy and Max bounded into the foyer, loaded down with backpacks.

"Hi, Dad!"

"Hey, Pop!"

"Hasn't he told you?" Sherry asked, glaring at her son. "He's gotten three D's this semester. Remember, when I called last month? We talked about him not paying attention?"

"Oh, yeah, right." Martin felt like he was the one in trouble. "From what I heard standing outside here just now, maybe you're nagging him too much about it. Give him a break."

Max nudged Amy and grinned.

"A break? This isn't the first time I've talked to him about it— it's the thirtieth! Don't you ever ask him what he does during the week? I fax you his report cards. I understand you can't attend meetings at school, and I can live with that. But I need you to pay more attention to what's going on here. Maybe if we told Max there'd be no more basketball games or camping trips until his grades improved—"

"No more games?" Max whined. "You can't do that."

Martin rose to Max's defense, and his own. "That's my time with the kids to spend however I see fit." Sherry glared. "But I will talk to him. Promise," Martin whispered.

As always, though, the weekend flew by, and while driving the kids home, Martin began mentally preparing his defense: The right moment hadn't arrived, he'd try to talk to Max next weekend, he really did care, but what could he do? After hugging the kids goodbye, he drove away sadly. *I'm not really sure just what the problem is, or what this Mrs. Anderson said. I don't even know which classes he failed. What kind of a dad am I turning into?*

Like many single, divorced parents, Sherry could use some parental backup from her ex. Martin, like many parents whose home is not their children's primary residence, cherishes his relationship with them. His belief that extravagant outings, toys, gifts, and other treats will "make up for" the divorce not only qualifies him as a Disney Dad, it also reveals how important—and fragile—he feels his connection to his kids really is. As he told his best friend over lunch the next day, "I just feel so cut off from the kids now. When Amy mentions her new best friend or a teacher, I realize I don't even know who these people are. And Max. What can I do? I can talk to him about his homework, but I'm not there every night to check his work. Why even get into it with him?"

Contrary to what most parents believe, kids usually do not want "what makes them happy" as much as they want both parents fully involved in their lives. As one fourteen-year-old boy wrote in his Sandcastles workbook, in a letter to his father: "Why don't you show me true love instead of just buying me stuff?"

Across town, Jeffrey is serving sloppy joes, and his daughters, Emily, thirteen, and Louisa, seven, are excitedly filling him in on their day. A software designer who works at home, Jeffrey sees his daughters every other Thursday through Sunday.

"Then, Dad, guess what Ted did in bio?" Emily asked. "I'll give you two hints: It involved a frog, and it was really gross!"

Jeffrey laughed. "Let's see, knowing Ted and how much he hates it when you tease him about being in love with Vanessa, I'd say it had something to do with her, too."

"Yep! But I'll spare you the details."

"Thank you. Louisa, what do we have to get ready for tomorrow's Brownie meeting? Didn't that note you brought home mention some art supplies? You know, you really have to learn to be responsible about these things. How many times have I told you—"

"Yeah, Dad, I know," Louisa replied, a little disheartened.

"And, Emily, please, honey, listen to me: The small fork is for salad. Remember, we set places so the first utensils we use are outside—"

"And we move in toward the plate with each course," Emily finished with a trace of sarcasm.

"And that napkin—on your lap, please."

"Sure, Dad."

Jeffrey winces inside when the smile fades from Emily's face or Louisa stares down at her plate. Finishing the meal in silence, Jeffrey wonders, *Why do they take this so hard?*

TEN MEDITATIONS TO BANISH SINGLE-PARENT GUILT

1. At one time or another, all children have problems, not just children of divorce.

2. Nothing I can say or do will change the fact that my spouse and I are divorced. Although I can love and support my child, I can't "make it up" to him.

3. It's okay to say no.

4. It's okay to take shortcuts.

5. The better job I do taking care of myself, the better parent I'll be to my child.

6. By ending our conflict through divorce, my ex and I have spared our child the pain of witnessing our fights.

7. There are many happy, healthy, successful adults who are children of divorce.

8. I will use my divorce to teach my child valuable lessons about the importance of respect, honor, love, and trust in a relationship. I will also teach my child that every relationship needs work and attention to flourish, including the one she and I share.

9. The fate of my marriage is no reflection on my ability to be a loving, nurturing, and effective parent.

10. My family can and will grow through this divorce as it would any other challenge or hardship.

Jeffrey doesn't realize that despite his easy rapport with his daughters, they have begun to feel like he's always on them about something. Entering her teens, Emily resents his well-meaning but incessant picking, and Louisa is starting to wonder if Daddy would love her more if she were perfect.

Like Martin, Jeffrey is a model divorced father: caring, involved, and committed. But instead of overindulging his daughters, he overdisciplines them. Aware that Gena is much more casual about things like etiquette, he spends his time with the girls trying to compensate for what he believes they don't get from their mother. Trying to cram seven days' worth of guidance, advice, table manners, and discipline into a day or two makes for tiring, stressful visits. In Jeffrey's family, it's beginning to drive a wedge between him and his daughters.

Both these fathers believe that they really are doing what's best. Single parents need to develop a well-rounded, balanced parenting style. Neither Martin nor Jeffrey has done that, and now they wonder what's going wrong. Slowly, each is beginning to feel a little cut off or shut out. As their children grow older and stake their claims for independence, as all kids must, these fathers risk losing touch and becoming "secondary parents."

One reason nonresidential parents feel this way is that even when they see their children several days a week, they are a step removed from the relaxed, unplanned time residential parents take for granted. Most parents are so intent on making every minute count, there's just not enough time left to simply be, to hang out, to drift through a Saturday afternoon without a plan. It's the relaxed conversation about nothing, the shared joke, even a few hours sitting together in front of the tube, that encourage a different kind of bonding and the sense of truly knowing each other.

THINGS 2 DO

PRIVATE FAMILY ALBUM

Give your child a camera (younger children can use a disposable or an inexpensive children's camera) and film. Encourage her to take pictures of the things she loves: people, pets, dolls, toys, special places. She might also want to include pictures of your family before the divorce. Don't be surprised if she asks for a special picture of you and your spouse on a happy occasion, such as your wedding. Nothing should be forbidden or discouraged. After the new film is developed and the other pictures are collected, help her put together a special photo album. You can buy a photo album for this purpose or make one from a three-ring binder; educationally oriented toy stores carry kits so your child can make her own.

PURPOSE: Photographs never change, and pictures of special people, places, and objects help give children a sense of comfort, security, and permanence. This is particularly crucial if you have relocated, and your child has had to change homes or schools. Children can also take their photo albums along with them when they visit their other parent.

Variation: Have your child take pictures of your family or anything else he wants to put in his own album. After developing the film, set aside time to look at the pictures together, making only nonjudgmental responses. Allow the child to tell you why he chose to take these particular photos. Purchase a wallet or other holder for your child that he can fill with family pictures.

PURPOSE: A child's photographs of important things express to a parent who and what the child views as significant in his life. Having an album or a wallet allows your child to feel like his family and all of its parts are with him always, an important feeling at a time in life when his family is drastically changing.

Variation: Have your child take pictures of important things in her life for an album. After developing the film, ask your child to redraw some of the pictures as she would like to see them.

Cheryl redrew the photograph of her mom to include her dad holding her mom's hand; Joseph redrew his house much larger than in the photograph, with a separate room for himself; Shannon redrew a picture of herself with different color hair, taller, and "prettier." (Her dad realized he never tells her how beautiful she is.)

PURPOSE: Redrawing pictures can help a child express the changes she would like to see as well as consider ways of creating those changes.

Variation: Have younger children take pictures of faces expressing different feelings, then place the face representing his feeling for that day on the refrigerator.

PURPOSE: This helps a child develop a unique and personal understanding for feelings and a form of expressing how she feels at different times.

TAILOR YOUR STYLE TO FIT YOUR NEW LIFE

When faced with a major change or disruption in our lives, we often try to compensate, to "make up" for what we feel we and our children have lost. One way parents try to do this is to become "superparents." Now that work keeps Mommy from being home in the afternoons, and Daddy isn't there to toss around the football after dinner, Mom feels like a failure if she doesn't bake—from scratch—and decorate the 3-D Barbie dream-house birthday cake. Because of his inability to afford or procure the best tickets for Disney on Ice or the local pro sports team's biggest game, Dad feels he's less of a father than he was before.

Every parent has felt that irresistible tug to do, buy, or promise whatever we think it will take to make it all better, to make the hurt go away. Yes, we will admit to ourselves, staying up until 3 A.M. working on that cake, busting the budget to get those tickets, *are* irrational. We know we don't have the time, or the patience, or the money to do it easily, yet we accept the trade-off and the sacrifice because we love our kids. Isn't it worth it? Sometimes the answer is no.

I've said a lot about the importance of consistency, but it's unrealistic and self-defeating to overlook those aspects of life that do and must change. Single residential parents, especially those who also work or have other responsibilities, probably don't have an "extra" three hours to spend creating an elaborate cake. Most divorced families do not have a lot of extra money to spend on lavish vacations or expensive tickets. Parents who refuse to admit and adapt to such new constraints set themselves and their children up for added stress. If she's like most of us, Mom will not wake up tomorrow on four hours' sleep feeling her best. And Dad will probably put in some overtime to cover that vacation, time he might have spent with the kids or doing something else he enjoys. You may feel that you have made the sacrifice, but the person who ultimately gets shortchanged—of your time, your attention, your presence, your patience—is your child.

We all know the scene: Billy yanks off the big blue bow, tears off the wrapping, plays with the overpriced, hard-to-find Super Colossal Whatever for five minutes, then spends the next four hours entranced by playing with the box. Not to make anyone feel belittled, but the fact is, as parents, sometimes we *are* the box. And sometimes that is all our children really want. Your time and your emotional availability are most important to your child. The Disney World trip can be a wonderful experience, but an hour with you at the local duck pond can bring the same delighted smiles. Of course, kids need and want to feel special. But does your child feel special at Disney World because he's one of millions of visitors or because you're there with him? Giving to our children of our time and ourselves makes being a parent a wondrous, enlightening experience. It may not feel "natural" (and we may not have done much of it when we were married), but now is the time to look objectively at our emotional and financial resources and plan how we can spend them wisely.

POST OFFICE

Have your child write herself a letter (or dictate it to you if she's too young) detailing how she is coping with the divorce and what is bothering her. Ask her to write about anything that she hopes will change in the near future and how she hopes to be doing four weeks from now. Put it away in a "mailbox"—a shoebox, a drawer, or a file—for four weeks, and look at it again at that time. You can offer to share and discuss the letter, especially if the child is young. Talk about what changes, if any, have occurred in how she feels now. An older child will probably notice these changes on her own. Still, let her know you will discuss it with her, if she would like, but it's not necessary.

PURPOSE: This allows a child and parent to focus on the fact that things change over time, and so does the way we look at them. Chances are your child will feel essentially the same way about some things (such as sad that you two have divorced), but her feelings will change in tone and intensity over time. This exercise also helps her see that we can feel very intensely about something, or have feelings that are frightening and overwhelming, but that they become less intense as time passes. The realization that no feeling lasts forever can help your child to face and deal with other difficult feelings in the future.

RETHINKING TIME

We speak of saving it, borrowing it, and making it, yet most parents feel that time is controlling them, not the other way around. While we cannot create time, we can do a great deal to make the most of the time we do have. For single residential parents, time spent at home is usually allocated to three separate and demanding responsibilities: caring for our children, caring for the home, and caring for ourselves.

Try Scheduling

Many of us naturally balk at the idea of schedules and routines. After all, we may have run the household pretty well without them before, so why change now? In fact, some people find that having a simple routine for, say, doing the laundry, deciding what's for dinner, or keeping the house neat simply eliminates having to think about it. The hassles of making up a shopping list, determining what ingredients are in the pantry, and deciding what you're going to cook are virtually eliminated when you spend twenty minutes a week planning the dinner menus. An even simpler approach is to have "food nights": Monday is chicken, Tuesday is pasta, Wednesday is fish, and so on. If your children are old enough, getting them involved in preparing the meals is an excellent learning experience and a good way to spend some quality time together.

Another way busy parents can achieve greater control of their time is to keep a "family calendar" posted prominently on which they designate a time or a day for, say, doing the laundry, running errands, returning phone calls. Sherry won't go to the local shopping center unless she has a reason to visit at least three stores. Jeffrey purchases a dozen children's birthday cards and small gifts at a time instead of making a trip every time his child attends a party. And Martin, tired of being interrupted by his kids while he talked on the phone, decided he won't answer his calls between dinnertime and their bedtime. The kids are happy to have Daddy to themselves, and his friends appreciate getting his full attention when they do speak.

Abandon Perfection

Set priorities, even if you have to change some. The quest for perfection is a leading cause of stress. Perhaps when two adults were home to run the house, every room was reasonably neat, every toy shelved, and every dish dried. Maybe now that you're the only parent at home, every room can't be perfect. Compromise: Common living areas must be picked up every night before bed, for instance.

WE NEED RULES

Explain to your child how we need rules in order to survive and how they allow us to thrive. Take out a checkerboard (or chess pieces, tic-tac-toe, any game at all will do) and tell your child you are going to play this game in a new way: with no rules. Be positive and enthusiastic. After a minute, she will realize that the game isn't any fun without rules and guidelines.

PURPOSE: Children say they don't like rules, but this demonstration shows them that you create rules for your home in order to allow everyone to be happy.

And Speaking of Compromise . . .

When your spouse handled all the cooking, it didn't bother you that Simone demanded her chicken be grilled while Davy preferred fried. Now you just don't have time to run a restaurant for every meal. Compromise is another valuable skill kids can learn from the changes of divorce. This week the chicken will be grilled; next week it will be fried.

Give Your Child the Gift of Responsibility

Often parents do more for their children than they really have to. We look at the rumply bedcovers or the supposedly clean but sticky plates and decide it's just "easier" to do the job ourselves. Children develop a sense of responsibility only by being made responsible. Perhaps when you stayed at home and didn't have to work, it was okay that your seven-year-old didn't make his own bed or your fifteen-year-old daughter refused to do her own laundry. Look again; these may be chores your children should have been doing anyway.

There's nothing wrong with explaining to your child that he or she is now old enough to assume certain responsibilities or that your time is limited, but try to keep the divorce out of it. After all, your children would be doing chores around the house if you were still married. Rather than paint for your child a dreary picture of all the things you now can't do or the new chores he has to take on, stress the positive results you'll all be working to achieve: more time to spend having fun, for one. You might also make up a checklist for each child and give out an allowance at the end of the week, when all the chores are complete. You can encourage a positive attitude and strengthen team spirit with a special reward—for example, a night out at the movies if the children keep the common living areas neat or put their own laundry away without being asked repeatedly.

WAYS CHILDREN CAN HELP AROUND THE HOUSE*

DUTY	2	3	4	5	6	7	8	9	10	11	12	13	14	15	16
Putting away toys and objects	☺	☺	☺	☺	☺	☺	☺	☺	☺	☺	☺	☺	☺	☺	☺
Helping to fold laundry		☺	☺	☺	☺	☺	☺	☺	☺	☺	☺	☺	☺	☺	☺
Putting away own laundry				☺	☺	☺	☺	☺	☺	☺	☺	☺	☺	☺	☺
Doing own laundry								☺	☺	☺	☺	☺	☺	☺	☺
Dusting				☺	☺	☺	☺	☺	☺	☺	☺	☺	☺	☺	☺
Sweeping and vacuuming					☺	☺	☺	☺	☺	☺	☺	☺	☺	☺	☺
Washing dishes							☺	☺	☺	☺	☺	☺	☺	☺	☺
Drying, putting away dishes								☺	☺	☺	☺	☺	☺	☺	☺
Making own lunch, preparing own snacks							☺	☺	☺	☺	☺	☺	☺	☺	☺
Cooking family meal (once a week)												☺	☺	☺	☺
Regular food shopping															☺
												(or when old enough to drive legally)			
Setting table					☺	☺	☺	☺	☺	☺	☺	☺	☺	☺	☺
Clearing table					☺	☺	☺	☺	☺	☺	☺	☺	☺	☺	☺
Feeding family pet				☺	☺	☺	☺	☺	☺	☺	☺	☺	☺	☺	☺
Walking dog, cleaning cat box								☺	☺	☺	☺	☺	☺	☺	☺
Major housecleaning (bathroom, kitchen, etc.)											☺	☺	☺	☺	☺

*Younger children may require supervision. Children should receive appropriate praise and encouragement for their efforts.

Becoming a New Kind of Parent

Two of the biggest issues, and areas where parents do tend to split responsibilities, are discipline and emotional understanding. Typically, these roles split down gender lines, with Mom as the one the kids run to when they have a problem and Dad the one who lays down and enforces the law. Parents often feel they most need to change their parenting style of discipline and emotional support, and it's not easy. The kids probably ran to Mom because she is naturally a good listener, and they may have obeyed Dad more readily because they knew he sticks to his guns. Chances are these two people didn't consciously plan to assume the roles; they assumed the roles that naturally fit them. Unfortunately, many divorced parents never adapt or broaden their parenting repertoire, and their children often suffer.

If you feel there are aspects of parenting you could improve, do so. Talk to a therapist, take a course, read books, join a parent support group, or talk to a friend you consider a good parent. Accept the possibility that, even after doing all that, you still may not be the greatest listener in the world, your disciplinary resolve may falter now and then, and your play skills may be nil. The truth is, you *cannot* be two parents, and you will probably never completely integrate the positives of your ex's parenting style. Remind yourself that your child knows you two well enough that she probably won't expect you to either.

What your child expects and deserves is that you make the effort. You may discipline differently (restrict access to the phone instead of a full grounding, for instance), and you may not do it as well. What matters is that you do it. If your daughter comes home needing a shoulder to cry on, she shouldn't have to wait until this weekend when she sees her closest confidant, Daddy. If your son needs extra help building that Star Trek model, don't feel you can't do it just because you have to read the instructions four times and your wife used to do it with her eyes closed. Don't be put off or discouraged by the fact that you might not be as good a listener as Mommy or as tough a disciplinarian as Dad. Remind yourself that when you were together, you had the option of choosing which parental responsibilities you shouldered. Now you don't. Sometimes simply not avoiding an issue and giving your child your full attention and your best effort count for a lot.

RESPECTING THE OTHER PARENT

The blame game crushes kids. A twelve-year-old boy expresses the immeasurable pain he suffers when he looks to his mother for warmth and sympathy only to be crushed by her hostility toward his father.

There are exceptions, but most children of divorce tend to feel "in the middle." The Sandcastles "Letter to Mom/Letter to Dad" exercise has produced some interesting results about kids' feelings of divided loyalty:

Dear Mom,
I really wish to see my dad at least once a week. I really need him sometimes because sometimes I really need him. I got you, but I wish I could have a whole big family like I used to have when I was little. So please talk to him nicely.

Dear Dad,
I wish you were nicer to my mom and not scream at her in the phone 'cause that really hurt me.

Dear Dad,
I would like to let you know that I am very sorry of what had to happen between you and Mom. And I want you to know that I love you

and I'm sorry, if you ever have to think that I love my mom more than I love you 'cuz I love you both the same.
—Girl, twelve

Clearly, these kids already feel as if they're walking an emotional tightrope.

Often without realizing it, one parent may indicate to a child that the other parent isn't a good parent or that there's something wrong with the time they spend together. You may feel justified in making com-

---

SEND THE RIGHT MESSAGE

Parents often ask, "How much should I ask my child about the time he spends with my ex?" As one father put it, "On one hand, I'm afraid if I don't ask enough questions, it will look like I don't care. On the other, I don't want to seem like I'm prying. Also, I don't exactly agree with some of the little things my ex does, and I worry that my child can tell I'm criticizing her no matter what I say."

The answer is simple: Pretend your child just came home from a weekend at Grandma and Grandpa's or dinner at Aunt Carrie's. Be interested and supportive. It sounds easy, but the problem lies in how we so often telegraph our real feelings through what we say and don't say and how we act. The transition period after a child arrives from spending time with the other parent is a classic example. Below are three very common types of responses—which all seem innocuous enough—and the damaging messages they send.

Max and Amy return from Martin's, and Sherry meets them at the front door. After quick hellos, Sherry says, "I missed you this weekend. Run upstairs now and get into your bathing suits. Your cousins are coming over for a swim and a barbecue. Hurry. They'll be here in twenty minutes."

The unspoken message: I don't really want to know about the time you spent with your father. You're there because you have to be, and I don't even care to acknowledge it.

The better message: "Hi! Your cousins are coming over in a few hours [note the extended time to cooldown], so do whatever you want until then. I'd love to hear about your weekend, but if you feel like hanging out in your room, you know that's okay, too."

Gena asks Emily and Louisa about their week at Jeffrey's. When Louisa tells her about the great new baby-sitter who watched them Saturday night, Gena explodes. "He left you with a sitter all night? You guys just watched videos all night? How old was that girl anyway? What did your dad think he was doing?"

The unspoken message: Maybe Dad got out and enjoyed himself for a few hours [as all parents should], but let me point out the realities of his limited parenting skills and his poor judgment.

The better message: "It sounds like you had a very nice time with the new sitter. It was nice of your dad to find someone you enjoy being with so much."

Over dinner on Wednesday, Max begins telling Martin about the great three days he, Amy, and Sherry spent at the lake with Ivan, whom Sherry's been dating seriously for more than a year. "Oh, really?" Martin responds. "What lake was that? Did you guys rent a cabin or stay in one of those little motels? Did Ivan buy your mom anything special there? How about you guys? Did Ivan have his own room?"

The unspoken message: I am obsessed with your other parent, and I'm still upset that we broke up. I want you to tell me everything, even though you will be violating your other parent's privacy, and it's really none of my business.

The better message: "It sounds like fun, and this Ivan sounds like he's pretty nice to you, and you guys enjoy being together."

See also the box "How Interested Should You Be in What Goes On 'Over There'?" page 281.

ments to your child like "You went to another movie this weekend? Didn't you do that last weekend, too?" "You'd think that seeing you once a week, she'd at least cook you a real meal," or "It would be nice if your dad attended an occasional school function." Some, like Sherry, criticize the other parent directly in front of their children.

Of course, most parents would never dream of telling a child they were hurt because she seemed happy to go to Daddy's or that they felt they were competing for her love. Yet in many families, children do pick up these messages. Earlier, I discussed how to become aware of how we communicate nonverbally. Here I'm talking about the way we talk about visitation, the other parent, and the child's time with the other parent. We reveal more than we realize just in asking, "So how was your visit? What did you do?"

Remember that divorce changes the way children see things. Perhaps when you were still together, your daughter didn't notice much when you joked about her mother's cooking, or when her mother mentioned how much she disliked your interest in pro football. Now that you're apart, even seemingly innocuous comments carry much more weight. How you behave toward each other when you are together also has a new meaning for your child. Expressions of animosity or hostility toward the other parent make children feel more conflicted, more torn apart. (For more on this problem, see chapter 9.)

MAKING THE OTHER PARENT COUNT

Dear Mom,
I feel really bad that you and Dad aren't getting along so well. I just want things to get better between you two and to work things out, and I really love you both a lot. I want you both to live together again, because I feel torn between you two and I only want to have you two next to me all the time when I need you.
—Boy, twelve

A lot of divorced parents wish it weren't so, but now that you two are apart, seeing you together on special occasions takes on a whole new meaning for your child.

Anna's twelve-year-old daughter, Olivia, was thrilled to land the lead in her ballet school's production of *Swan Lake*. She seemed to be walking on clouds until one Saturday, a week before the recital, when her father broke the news that he wouldn't be able to attend. For the next week, Olivia seemed unusually quiet, even sad. The day before the recital, Anna and Olivia were eating dinner when the girl half whispered, "I don't think I want to be in the ballet anyway. Besides, who's going to see me?"

"What's the matter, honey?" Anna asked.

"I just don't want to dance tomorrow night if Daddy can't be there."

Olivia never seemed to mind that her father missed her ballet recitals or school plays when he lived here, Anna thought. "But, sweetie, he hardly ever came to your recitals before," she pointed out. "And, besides, I'll be there—"

When Olivia threw down her fork, ran to her room, and slammed the door, Anna didn't know what to say.

What Anna overlooked, and what Olivia was unable to express, is that children have moments when they need to see both parents together, when they feel their loss more deeply. Even if they understand that you are divorced and that you will never be together as you were before, they may long for the comfort of being together with you both again, even if it's only for an hour or so. We reassure them that they still have two parents, that we will both be there for them, but it's important to remember that in certain circumstances—like this one, when Olivia anticipates seeing her friends together with both of their parents—children are bound to feel more sensitive—more a child of divorce—than in others.

And let's look ahead. In addition to birthdays and holidays, there will be communions, bar and bat mitzvahs, sweet sixteens, graduations, engagement parties, weddings, and, someday, the arrival of your own grandchildren. Remind yourself that these will not be "your" moments or your ex's, but your child's. Unfortunately, many divorced parents do not even consider attaining a brief, temporary state of peaceful coexistence until they have to. Usually, it's a college graduation, a wedding, or a new grandchild—all once-in-a-lifetime occasions with great meaning to the child—that forces the issue. Adult children of divorce often harbor painful, even bitter, memories of worrying whether or not they could expect both parents to even participate. If they do agree to be together,

A brewing storm. *A ten-year-old girl shows how divorce transforms the relationships in her family, placing her in the middle, literally divided between her parents. Notice clouds over both parents in the lower picture and the sun peeking through on the mother's side.*

their child then anguished over where to seat them, what ceremonial roles each should play, and how they each might behave.

Starting today, vow that your personal behavior in such situations will be your responsibility, not your child's and not your ex's either. If your relationship with your ex permits, start practicing now. How? By being cordial, participating with your ex in your child's birthday parties and other brief "public" gatherings, the three of you going out for a special birthday dinner, and attending your child's plays, sporting events, and parent-teacher meetings.

Understanding this responsibility and anticipating your child's re-action if one of her parents isn't up to the challenge can ease the stress and the pain. For example, the next time a similar situation arises, Anna might forgo mentioning that Daddy was never there before and say, "I know you think it would be great if Daddy could be there too, and he really wishes that he could. But sometimes things don't always work out the way we like. So I have an idea: I'll videotape your performance and get a copy made, so you can watch it with Daddy the next time you see him." If you feel comfortable doing it, you might plan a lunch out together with the three of you to celebrate your child's accomplishment, or both parents can resolve to make a special effort to attend the next event, even if you don't sit together. Whatever you do, let your child know you understand how much it means to her, even if she cannot express it for herself. Also show her that you

THINGS 2 DO

IT'S ALL HOW YOU LOOK AT IT

To illustrate the idea that how we feel affects how we see things, try this. When you serve a meal, bring out small portions: half a glass of a beverage, half a plate of food. Ask your child what she sees (you probably won't have to even ask, since you'll get her opinion as soon as the plates touch the table). Then serve your child her full portion. When she's full and ready to leave the table, ask her to stay, and bring out more food. Again, fill only half the plate or half of the glass, then suggest to your child that she eat this, too. As she groans and accuses you of torturing her, say, "This is the same amount of food I gave you before, and you complained it wasn't enough." Her response will be that, before, she was starving. Discuss with your child how our mood, our needs, or our wants in one moment can change how we may see the very same thing. Whether we see the glass as half empty or half full all depends on how thirsty we are.

Ask your child to apply the same reasoning to other situations. If it's snowing outside and 60 degrees inside, it would feel warm. If, on the other hand, it was 102 degrees outside, that same 60 degrees would feel quite cool. If you were literally dying of thirst, a glass of unsweetened lemon juice would hit the spot. If you had a fridge full of drinks to choose from, though, that sour juice wouldn't be your first choice. And so on.

Finally, talk about parent-child relationships in this context. If we feel loved by a parent and see him often, then that day when we don't spend time with him we might not mind (seeing the glass half full); if we feel rejected by a parent (or haven't seen him a lot lately), we may feel upset when we can only spend dinnertime and not the whole night with the parent (seeing the glass half empty).

Miguel learned to appreciate the time he does spend with his dad, who lives out of town, instead of lamenting about how limited their time together is. This new attitude helped him create ways to keep in touch, focusing on how he could spend much more time with his dad (letters, phone calls, e-mail) instead of feeling overwhelmed and distraught, and, as a result, avoiding communication.

PURPOSE: Children need coping skills and the ability to understand feelings and why they feel certain ways. Helping them get into the habit of seeing both sides of a situation can help them develop a sense of perspective, an ability to see the bigger picture.

will include the other parent as much as you can, by sharing photos, videos, programs, and other mementos.

In families where both parents cannot participate in important events, make an effort to acknowledge and celebrate your child's accomplishment separately. For example, in lieu of attending the recital, Olivia's father might send her a special card the day before, call her that day or after the show, send her flowers, take her out for a special treat, or keep a photograph of her in costume, framed and prominently displayed in his home. Remember, you don't always have to be there physically to be there emotionally. But the reason for not being there shouldn't be "because I can't stand to be in the same room with my ex." Instead think, *What's in my child's best interest?*

You may think you are too busy or too overwhelmed to share information about your child's school, friends, interests, and activities with your ex. But think about the kind of information you would be exchanging if you were still together. Then you did it because it was the best thing for your child. It still is. Make the effort, even if you communicate via letter or fax. Keep a large envelope where you collect artwork, school papers, organization newsletters, report cards, invitations to parties scheduled for visitation times, pictures, and anything else that will keep your ex up-to-date. This is important for residential parents and nonresidential parents alike. If a child began feeling feverish and listless, Dad should share that information with Mom.

FINALLY

Do you wish that your parents would stay together?
Yes. I mean, who wouldn't?
　　—Boy, fourteen

Ideally, children should have both parents in their lives. Providing an environment in which your child's relationship with the other parent can thrive will not only improve your child's life but your own. Just because you are a single parent doesn't mean that your child has only one parent. Even after divorce, your child can still have the very best that both of her parents have to offer.

Q Dear Gary,
My husband and I divorced a year ago; we have two children, nine and eleven. As part of the settlement I'm staying in our home, while my ex lives in an okay apartment across town. My father-in-law has taken to telling my kids that their father's living in a "rat hole" because I insisted on "living like a queen." The kids have made a few remarks along those lines, which I've let pass, but enough is enough. How can I set them straight without putting down Grandpa? How much do they really need to know about our financial situation?

A First, speak to your father-in-law and explain why you take issue with his comments. Explain to him that the divorce settlement is something your husband agreed to, and you are staying in the family home because it is the best option for your children. Try to make him see how, by speaking of you negatively to your children, he is only hurting them and making them feel angry at you and him.

Second, talk to your children. Explain to them that when parents separate, the whole family must maintain two homes on the same income. Whether your ex is living in a "rat hole" or not is probably subject to debate. When adult children divorce, their parents may have a hard time not taking sides and focusing on what their respective children have lost as a result. You can tell your children that Grandpa is upset about the divorce and hurt to see his son living in a place that is not as nice as your home. However, also make clear that it is not your children's fault that their father lives where he does or that you as a family have to make sacrifices you didn't before. Let your children know that this is the result of your and your ex's decision to divorce, you accept full responsibility for it, and—perhaps most important—as a family, you will get through it.

Q Dear Gary,
Our four-year-old son, Josh, has become a real handful for his nursery-school class. He fights, tears up other children's projects, and defies his teachers at every turn. My wife and I have been apart now for about a year. How can we determine how much of this is just typical acting out and how much of it is directly related to our divorce? Any tips?

A While it's important to be aware of divorce-related changes, parents should be careful to sort which behaviors seem to correlate to the changes in your family and which may be just part of growing up. Obviously, Josh is expressing anger and seeking negative attention, so you need to play detective. When did the behavior start? Can you trace it back to any particular changes (for example, the separation, a move to a new home, the appearance of a parent's new love interest, the arrival of a new caregiver, and so on). Also realize, however, that children can react to a major life-changing event, like a parent moving out, long after it has occurred.

Begin by talking to him, using nonspecific, nonthreatening language: "Josh, I know a lot of kids get mad when . . ." Listen carefully to him, all the while keeping in mind that as he grows, your separation may take on new meanings for him. Josh may suddenly feel more fearful of being abandoned (something common at his age). Remember, children will revisit their experience many times as they grow older and respond it to anew. So while Josh may have been too young when you first separated to feel threatened, he is now responding to the situation with the normal fears typical of his age. Before, the concept of abandonment was simply beyond his understanding. Now, however, he can imagine—and fear—being abandoned, and so he is experiencing a new response to an "old" situation. Brace yourself: You'll be playing with variations on this theme for years to come.

On the other hand, he may be sad about something very specific you have overlooked, such as the fact that he no longer accompanies Daddy to get the morning paper on school days. Try to discover these connections and talk to your son about them.

In the meantime, Josh needs to understand that there are limits to behavior and that he is expressing his anger in a manner that is inappropriate and will not be tolerated. Do what you can to make it easier for Josh to learn new behaviors. Schedule bedtime, activities, and mealtimes, since fatigue, lack of physical activity, boredom, and hunger can easily trigger or exacerbate his frustration and anger.

Use natural consequences (in this case, no play dates after school, "because we can't have children to our house if you fight"). Ask Josh, "When you're angry, what else can you do?" Help him problem-solve. Encourage him to draw about it, tell his teacher, punch a chunk of clay. Teach him the actual words that give shape and expression to his feelings. Children who have the power of words are often less compelled to act out their feelings. Role-play situations your son may find himself in (for example, having to wait on line for a snack) and help him act out acceptable behaviors. Give Josh rewards (colorful stickers, his favorite dessert, and so on) for noticeable improvements, no matter how minor.

Finally, sit in and observe his preschool class. Look for situations that might make it more difficult for Josh to control his unacceptable behavior. Is his classroom a warm, loving, structured, and orderly environment? Is everyone on staff capable and professional? Is the student-teacher ratio appropriate? Is the supervision adequate? Do the teachers appear to be tuned in to the children? Are their interactions with them conducive to good behavior?

Discuss with your son's teacher your insights into his problem and what techniques you have had success with at home. Ask the teachers to help by keeping you posted on his behavior in school and rewarding his progress in improving.

Q *Dear Gary,*
Due to my ex's work schedule, he can see the kids only on weekends. I love my three kids, ages eight, eleven, and fourteen, more than anything; don't get me wrong. But between their care, and playing homework cop, chauffeur, and cheerleader, I've begun to feel more like a slave. Meanwhile, my ex considers his time with them "too precious" to "waste" working with them on school projects or taking them shopping for clothes. He works hard making sure every weekend's a whirlwind of outings, presents, and treats. I never was happy with it, but I bit my tongue. Lately, though, disputes over anything from taking out the trash to studying are met with a remark about my being "meaner" than Dad. Last week, my fourteen-year-old informed me she'd rather live with him. I'm furious, resentful, and heartbroken.

A A family meeting is in order here. Explain to your children that you are "off duty." Be clear: It hurts your feelings and makes you angry to spend so much time doing for them only to have them react with anger when you ask them to meet their own responsibilities. Let them know you are a family, and the more everyone helps out, the more time there will be for fun. Then clearly reiterate what you expect from each of them.

The deeper question is, What is happening in your home? If you feel "furious, resentful, and heartbroken," something isn't working. Children who sense that the possibility of their leaving home will be threatening to you can be manipulative, pure and simple. What you must discover is how your children have come to feel that it's okay to behave as they do and be manipulative. Explore your self-esteem with a counselor or a good friend. Perhaps you are unknowingly sending them the message that you don't demand or deserve their respect by, for instance, catering to them at the expense of your own health or always changing your plans to accommodate theirs, no matter what. While you may resent all the mundane responsibilities you've assumed, be honest with yourself. Do you have a hard time letting go of your duties? If, for instance, another parent offers to drive the kids to soccer practice, do you automatically refuse? Does being the chauffeur make you feel needed? Are you substituting feeling needed with feeling loved? If so, find other ways to show your love, both for your children and for yourself.

Finally, consider that while your children may be wrong in their behavior, they may not be far off the mark in assessing the home situation. Perhaps you need to infuse more joy and optimism into your relationship with your kids. One way to start is to give yourself fewer things to feel resentful about. Use natural consequences: Dirty laundry stuffed under the bed will not be washed; homework your children neglect to do will not get done; a table not cleared after dinner will not be set with food tomorrow night (at least not by you).

Next, renegotiate your "coparenting contract" with your ex, even if it means making yourself unavailable to work on Junior's class project. Your ex, with prompting from your son, will probably step in to help rather than see his child suffer. A word of caution, however: One parent's perception of the other's failing to help a child with homework can become fodder for future custody or visitation battles. If you believe that your child is ready to shoulder more responsibility or you feel that your constantly helping him is doing more harm than good, discuss how you intend to handle this with his teacher before you put your new plan into action. Explain to the teacher that you will be taking less responsibility for your child's homework (although be sure you add that you will remain involved in all aspects of his schooling). Ask that she make a written note of your conversation and enter it into your son's file. Better yet, always follow up with a letter to the teacher outlining what you have discussed and how you both agreed to this course. Close your letter by saying, "If this misrepresents your understanding of our conversation, please notify me immediately."

Remember, we all learn to be responsible by being responsible.

14

Our New Life

Dealing with Divorce-Related Change

So this is it, fifteen-year-old Carly thought as her mother pulled into a numbered parking spot inside the condo complex.

"What do you think, honey?" Jan asked as they got out of the car. "See, there's our apartment. And we have a little yard in the back."

"It looks nice, Mom," Carly replied, all the while thinking, *It looks so small from out here. And everybody's scrunched so close together....* Jan opened the door, and Carly peered past the little hallway, through the eat-in kitchen to a larger room with an old couch pushed against a wall. "There's the living room, and down that hall are three bedrooms and the bathroom. Your room is the first on the right."

"*The* bathroom? Mom, you've got to be kidding! Three kids and *one* bathroom?"

Jan was taken aback. "Yes, the bathroom. Honey, it's a very nice little place. Not as big as we're used to—"

"Yeah, no joke," Carly quipped as she strolled down the hall, flipping on light switches. "And this is my room? Mom, it's green! I hate green! I can't live here!" Jan felt her smile melting. *Is this my daughter? This ungrateful little snot?* She took a deep breath, then called, "Now, Carly, wait just a minute. This was the biggest place I could find within the school's boundaries. You know we can't keep the old house."

"Yeah, I know," Carly said softly. "It's just, I don't know. That was my room my whole life. I thought I was always going to live in our house; like for my sweet sixteen, I'd have a party in the backyard and come down those stairs and stuff. I know it's stupid. I just can't believe we're moving."

"I can't either, honey, but listen. How about if we measure the windows and see if we can still use those lilac curtains from your old room? Look, we'll repaint. That'll be fun."

"I guess."

"Sweetie, if I could do anything to keep our house, I would, believe me. But it's just not possible. I know this must be difficult for you; I'm sad we're moving, too. But we'll all be fine. This is our home now, and it's up to us to make it feel like home. So, are you going to help me paint or not?"

Carly brightened. "I'll do it on one condition: You let me sponge paint the walls blue with white clouds. Jenny did it in her room, and it's awesome."

"Fine, honey. After all, this is your home now," Jan replied, all the while thinking, *How am I ever going to fit everything in here? It* is small!

Divided lives. *When asked to write* four *things that will change with divorce,* this preteen girl included: *"I'll have to divide my toys and clothes; I'll have practically two different lives."*

For the overwhelming majority of families and children, divorce is but a single link in a long, winding chain of adjustments and losses. Parents should not overlook the stress inherent in such changes as moving, coping with diminished financial resources, and returning to work. Few families emerge from divorce economically unscathed. The basic arithmetic of divorce—two households to support instead of one—

almost ensures that only a small minority can hope to maintain the lifestyle they knew before. For most families, divorce means a different standard of living and all that entails:

- Moving to a smaller home or an apartment, to a less desirable area, or in with friends or relatives; in some cases, all three

- Changing schools, due to the move itself or because private or religious school tuition is no longer affordable

- Coping with household changes when a previously nonworking parent returns to work (finding and dealing with child care, decreased parental supervision)

What these changes mean depends on the family. For one family, it may mean turning to public aid and living with relatives; for a middle-class family, it may mean Mom's going back to work and no summer camp for the next few years. Whatever economically dictated adjustments your family makes—whether major or minor—you can be sure your child will notice. These are each major, important transitions in their own right, which I'll address later in this chapter. What they all have in common is that they often result from or reflect the financial fallout of divorce. How you present these new facts of life to your kids will have a significant effect on how well they deal with them.

CHILDHOOD ECONOMICS

Dear Dad,
I want my money. When am I getting my money?
—Boy, thirteen

For better or worse, we live in a consumer-oriented, status-conscious culture that leaves its mark on our kids from a very early age. They seem more attuned at ever-younger ages to the subtle social significance of the neighborhood they live in, the kind of car the family drives, and the brand of their clothing. I admit being surprised and even shocked by some of the things kids say about money. Depending on their background, children as young as five or six demonstrate an acute perception of economic and social status. Some studies even suggest a

THINGS 2 DO

correlation between an adolescent's self-esteem and his perception of his social status.

IF I HAD A MILLION DOLLARS

Pretend that each of you just received a million dollars, then ask:

"What would you do for yourself?"
"What would you do for someone else?"
"What would you do for [name other family members, close friends, even pets]?"
"What else could you do with the money?"

PURPOSE: Like many of us, children old enough to understand the concept of having a million dollars may view it as a dream of unlimited possibility and power. Unlike other wishing games described throughout the book, the million-dollar game introduces an element of power and the possibility of doing something nice for other people. Having to decide how to spend the money gives children a chance to make a number of decisions, and their reasoning behind each choice often offers parents an interesting view of a child's values and concerns. Parents should be aware that younger children will often wish for others what they themselves would like to have.

Money wars. *Kids often witness their parents' arguments about child support.*

For most kids, divorce means having less than what they had before, ranging from small impulse purchases, like toys, to the promise of fully funded college tuition. This is true even when child support is paid regularly and both parents work. When a parent fails to provide sufficient support, it usually has a direct effect on kids, and they often understand that, sometimes too well for their own good. I'm sure parents would be surprised, if not flabbergasted, by how

THE HARD FACTS ABOUT CHILD SUPPORT

According to the United States Census Bureau, the household income for a divorced mother and her children falls an average of 30 percent the first year.[1] Contrary to popular belief, not all mothers and children receive financial support after divorce. Only 77 percent of divorced fathers are even ordered to pay child support, and divorced mothers are awarded spousal support, or alimony, in only 12 percent of all divorces, often necessitating their return to the work-force.[2] This forces millions of families—even middle-class families—onto welfare and other forms of public assistance. For children, divorce is the leading cause of poverty. These economic changes often dictate major life changes. For example, one study found that within one year of divorce or separation, almost half of custodial parents and their kids were living with friends or relatives.[3]

much kids do understand about the intertwining effects of divorce and family finances. One six-year-old told me, "When I grow up, get married and divorced, I will always pay my child support on time." Clearly, there are a number of things wrong with this picture.

From the three-year-old whining in the shopping cart for the latest Technicolored marshmallow cereal to the sixteen-year-old who will just die if seen in anything but those hundred-dollar sneakers, kids absorb the message that getting and having can make them happy. As they grow older, the picture is further complicated by peer pressure to conform and belong, to do and to have what "everybody else" does. It helps to remember that, even if your family had all the money it needed when you and your ex were together, these problems would still arise. Then you might have said no for any number of reasons: Your budget couldn't bear it; the item was unnecessary or too expensive; you want your child to learn to resist fads or peer pressure. These are all reasons you would have given your child then, with a clear conscience.

Today, however, you're probably saying no because money just doesn't stretch as far. Whatever the reason, it boils down to the divorce, so when you see your kids doing with less or without, it can't help but rekindle feelings of guilt about what they're going through and, possibly, anger at your ex-partner. Child support issues in particular often spark ongoing resentment and criticism of both parents. "He's late again" and "She spends it on herself, not the children" are all-too-familiar—and, for children, painful—refrains.

Dealing with the financial aspects of divorce can be tough, and parents who do not meet their responsibilities are hardly sympathetic characters. Parents caught up in divorce-related financial straits can

find it very difficult, if not impossible, to shield their children from their anger and bitterness, especially if it is justified. Besides, a child old enough to understand that Daddy pays child support is

SELF-WORTH SCALE

Reproduce the following scale, and let your child indicate where he belongs by circling the hyphen (-) in the position that best describes him. He can also show how he views you and your ex-spouse.

SAD - - - - - HAPPY
MEAN - - - - - KIND
SERIOUS - - - - - FUN
BAD - - - - - GOOD

Other word pairs:

cold-loving, not sweet–sweet, peaceful-angry, okay-great, boring-adventurous, disloyal-loyal, not artistic–artistic, dishonest-honest, beautiful/handsome–ugly, not studious–studious.

Then ask your child to choose three items that describe her and draw herself depicting one of those evaluations:

Helen chose "kind" and drew herself helping an old lady across the street. Ian drew himself as "ugly" and then drew his dad and mom as ugly.

Respect your child's choices and don't defend her or yourself: "You're not ugly," "You're much smarter than that," "I did very well in school." These are her feelings and evaluations. Help her continue to identify and understand why she feels that way. "You feel you're not a pretty/smart person. That must be hard for you. It must affect many areas of your life."

PURPOSE: This activity will give you and your child a good sense of how she views herself and her parents. Please do not use this direct information about your ex-spouse against him if your child chooses a negative rating. Remember, she is trusting you and needs someone to trust. Be that someone.

sure to make the connection between a few skipped payments and the fact that there are no new school clothes or your family's moving in with Grandma. Unlike past marital infidelity, for example, these are parts of the divorce that probably can't be kept "secret." In view of these factors, it can be difficult not to criticize and blame the other parent. Still, it is extremely important that you don't. Remember the old adage "The apple doesn't fall far from the tree"? For kids it has a profound though different meaning. To be told that a parent is lazy or rotten or doesn't care about him damages a child's sense of personal history and self-esteem. Even if these statements are true, and your child is old enough to reach the same conclusion himself, hearing it said by someone else—especially you—is psychic poison.

DON'T GIVE YOUR CHILD PERMISSION TO MANIPULATE

Divorce is when your parents say goodbye. You might be sad, but just think of the bright side: When you're mad at Mom or Dad, you can go to the other parent's house. You'll get more money from both. More presents, etc. That's why divorce isn't that bad.
—Teenage boy

Sometimes it's in everyone's best interest to candy-coat the truth or at least present it to the child in a nonjudgmental, diplomatic way she can understand. Instead of saying, "You don't have new shoes for school because your lousy father doesn't pay his child support on time," swallow hard, take a deep breath, and say, "Your dad and I are having some financial problems right now, and we're working on them. For now, though, we might need to hold off on some purchases for a little while or watch our spending. But I want you to know that we are making some sacrifices now so that we can be sure to have the most important things."

You might be thinking, as many parents do, *Well, if he isn't making the payments on time or at all, and that's why I can't give her the shoes, why shouldn't she know the truth?* Telling your child the truth in this instance will do no good and will certainly damage her sense of self and her opinion of your ex—and, possibly, of you as well.

As long as Elisa had been married to Gerald, he had always underreported his true income. When the court determined his child support payments based on his reported income, she already knew their three children were being cheated. She and Gerald agreed that she would live in the large family home until the kids graduated from high school, but after a few months, she could see that it was impossible to maintain the same lifestyle she and the children had before. They never really wanted for anything, but many of the extras they took for granted—like summer camp, extravagant gifts, elaborate parties—were now out of the question. Elisa was beginning to feel pressured to return to work—something she didn't really want to do—and feeling increasingly angry at Gerald because, in her words, "This was all his fault." One afternoon, after her fourteen-year-old son started complaining again about not being able to attend soccer camp with his friends, she snapped. "Craig, I do the best I can, but your father is late and misses payments all the time. What really makes me mad is that he has a lot more money than you think. To give you an idea of how selfish he is, I can tell you that what he takes in cash out of his gas station every week is about the cost of your camp. Maybe you should ask him why he can't fork over the money."

"What?" Craig stammered, on the verge of tears. "And he says that he loves me—that's a laugh! I guess he doesn't really care at all. Maybe I *should* tell him what you said and see what he says then!"

As Elisa saw Craig's face redden and chin tremble, she realized she'd made a terrible mistake. Gerald had been late a few times recently, but he'd never actually missed a payment. "Well, wait a minute, honey," Elisa replied. "I didn't mean for you to say anything to your dad. I just wanted you to understand why things are the way they are. Look, don't say anything. I'll talk to your dad."

"Okay, Mom," Craig said quietly, all the while thinking, *Dad's not listening to you. If he really loves me, and he knows I know he has more money, he'll give it to me.*

That Friday night Craig repeated what his mother had told him as his father listened quietly, fuming. Yes, he did take cash out of the business, but due to some leakage from an underground gas tank, he'd just been hit with a fifty-thousand-dollar fine from the Environmental Protection Agency. Between that and the cost of lawyers, he was on the verge of losing the business altogether. "Craig, I admit it isn't right for me to make my payments late, as I've done a couple of times. I probably should have told your mother what's been happening in the business."

"But she said you've been missing payments, and that's why I can't go to soccer camp," Craig said.

Gerald felt his back stiffen. "All right, let me show you something." He took a large envelope out of his desk drawer and spread dozens of canceled checks across the table. "See your mother's signature there on back? And the dates? I've never missed any payments, and if I was late, it was by three or four days. And," he added, lying, "there's never been an 'extra' penny."

"So Mom's a liar?" *Man, how could she do this to me?*

"No, Craig. I just think your mother is upset about having to go back to work and angry at me. I don't think she really meant it. But with what's happening to my business now, I'm not so sure you'd be able to go to soccer camp even if your mom and I were still married. I know you're unhappy about the divorce and sad about the things you and your sisters can't always have anymore. I'm very sorry about that. But believe me when I say I am doing the best that I can."

That Sunday night, Craig stormed into the house, and choking back tears said to Elisa, "You lied to me! Dad's not hiding anything. You always want to make us hate him and love you more. Now I feel like I don't trust either one of you!"

Who knows where this will end? One thing's for certain: Nothing Elisa or Gerald told their son changed the fact that he won't be attending soccer camp this year, and much of what each of them revealed to Craig has only made him feel hurt, angry, and betrayed. Even in the best of circumstances, it will probably be quite a while before he ever opens up to or really listens to either of them again.

If your child's other parent has serious character flaws, rest assured she will discover them in her own time. Ask yourself what she may gain by learning this sooner or from you. The fact is that sometimes the truth hurts too much. No matter how you might explain it, your child may wonder if her life has changed because one or both of you no longer loves her, or loves her less than you did "before"—when she still had her own bedroom, saw her old friends every day at school, and always had nice shoes. Older kids may feel that having suffered through the divorce, they're even more entitled to have the things they want. One seventeen-year-old girl, writing in her Sandcastles workbook, informed both her parents she had received a full scholarship to college:

> Dear Mom,
> I would like a late- to early-model car—bright yellow Mazda Miata, to be precise. I think I deserve this car because I have already earned a full tuition, all expenses paid scholarship. P.S., Mom, I love you lots.

> Dear Dad,
> I would like a late- to early-model Mazda Miata. I feel I deserve this gift because you haven't given me anything else lately.

Hard as it is to accept, we cannot rescue our children from disappointment and pain. We cannot accompany them to their new school and make friends for them; we cannot replace what they believe they have lost, whether it's the newest Barbie doll you cannot afford or the down payment on a used car. Learning to deal with loss and disappointment is part of growing up, and it is hard work.

HOW PARENTS CAN HELP CHILDREN COPE WITH ECONOMIC CHANGES

• *Prepare your child for change.* If the family must move or a parent must go to work, talk to your child about what will probably happen. Don't make promises you are not absolutely positive you can keep; for example, don't tell your children they will be going to the same school until you've found a new home in your school district. If you are not sure about something, say so while describing how you are trying to deal with it.

• *Remind your child of what won't change.* Most parents would think to say, "I will always love you and be here for you," and that certainly helps. But think about your child's other sources of support: grandparents and extended family, friends, organizations he belongs to, school, your religious community, sports teams, and so on. The realization that not everything is changing, that some parts of her life are immune to the effects of divorce, can be very comforting.

• *Make your family's adjustment a team effort.* Even if the team is just you and your child, let him in on decisions and find ways to work together. Children of divorce are prone to seeing change as something that someone else causes, something that happens to them. Give your child every opportunity to exert some control, within reason. Jan realized letting Carly sponge paint her room gave her daughter something to feel good about and also gave her a "pride of ownership." If your child is old enough, you might consider taking him to visit two prospective pediatricians, dentists, or music teachers to see which he likes better. As you organize your new home, let your kids have some say about which drawer will be the flatware drawer, which closet will hold the toys, what flowers to plant, and how to arrange their rooms.

• *In difficult times, focus on dealing with the problem at hand, not the past.* At one time or another, we're all guilty of playing "connect the

THINGS 2 DO

HOW I LOVE MY FAMILY

You and your child each list personal attributes and positive things about your family. Then create a list of how your child adds to the positive traits of the family. Compare lists.

PURPOSE: This helps a child see her own uniqueness and specialness as well as her family's attributes. It also helps her see how she is an important part of making her family special.

dots." After Carly's emotional outburst, Jan found her thoughts running from *The apartment is small* to *If only I'd never met him twenty years ago, I wouldn't be in this situation*. While it may be true, this kind of thinking is counterproductive. Even more damaging is voicing such sentiments to your child. Talking too much about the past—the one thing no one can ever change—may exacerbate your child's feelings of hopelessness and powerlessness.

• *Remember that attitudes and emotions are contagious*. No one's perfect, and there may be times when you feel overwhelmed by changes. That said, however, strive to model the kind of behavior and attitude you want to encourage in your child, even if you sometimes feel you're faking it. Later that night, Jan called her sister and listed everything about the new apartment she hated, something she wisely chose not to share with her children. By the time she got off the phone, however, she felt she'd gotten much of her frustration and disappointment off her chest. Even more important, her sister had pointed out many benefits of their new location, like proximity to family and the city, the kids not needing to change schools, and the new skating rink nearby. Jan added these to her list of "positives" she'd share with the kids.

MOVING

Write four things that will change with divorce.

1. We will be living in a new house.
2. I will be living with different people.
3. I'm not sure who I will be living with.
4. My life will be different.

　　　　　　　　　—Boy, ten

MAKING A NEW HOUSE A HOME

A friend of mine, whose family moved more than twenty-five times before she finished high school, recalls, "Whenever we got to a new house, my sister and I would rummage through the packing boxes looking for those few special things we had to see right away: a particular doll, the night-light made of seashells, a framed photograph of our grandfather. It could never begin to be home until we saw those things in their new proper places."

Other ways to make your new place a home:

- Have it clean before your child moves in.

- Put up shades and curtains before you move in, if possible.

- Make a special box of the items your children must have immediately and take it with you (don't leave it with the movers).

- Make an adventure out of your first few days' "roughing it."

- Let younger kids keep a couple of the really big moving boxes and cut out windows and doors, so they can have their own "new homes" (see the activity "Joyful Box," page 130).

- Let children make decisions about which shelf in the linen closet will hold the towels, and who gets which side of the closet if they're sharing a room.

- As much as possible, try to make furniture arranging a family decision; it can be fun.

- If your children are young or feeling a little insecure, have plenty of night-lights plugged in.

- Treat yourselves to a special celebratory dinner in your new place, even if it's only pizza.

- Help kids create their own change-of-address cards for friends.

- Even if you're not totally settled in, consider an informal housewarming for close friends and family shortly after you move in.

In our increasingly mobile society, it's easy to underestimate the impact of relocation on a child. Whether your family moves across the street or around the world, the simple fact that you are leaving behind the physical manifestation of "home" makes it a potentially difficult transition for everyone. Many times a move involves not only changing homes but schools as well (I'll address school-related issues in the next section). In either case, it's important to help your child begin to feel as at-home as possible from day one.

You may feel that the benefits of moving outweigh the drawbacks, or you may be resigned to moving because you have no choice. Whatever your feelings, remember that no matter what your child's age, moving to a new home is a very big deal. Infants may experience disruptions in their sleeping and eating patterns, and toddlers and preschoolers may cry to "go home" or become uncharacteristically clingy or fussy. For young children, provide constant reassurance and comfort with frequent hugs, calm family meals, a steady routine, and lots of love.

For older children, say age five and up, you can do a lot to help them make the transition. You can begin by introducing the idea a few weeks ahead of time, talking about it, and answering your child's questions. Remember that you cannot overemphasize the aspects of home that will not change: your love for one another, your daily routine, certain important possessions. If possible, you might opt to put together a younger child's bedroom first, even if that means just making sure he sleeps with a favorite stuffed animal or wrapped in a familiar comforter. Older children benefit from having a chance to visit the new place a couple of times before moving day, finding where it is on a map, exploring the new neighborhood, and having some say in decorating their rooms.

Statistically, most families move to smaller or less expensive houses or apartments. Many are forced to stay with relatives or friends for a period of time, which can be difficult for even the closest of families. If your child is old enough to understand these changes, you can expect some disappointment, complaining, even rebelling. Being forced to share a bedroom with a sibling for the first time or having to abide by the rules of the house in which you are a long-term guest can be stressful. Be understanding, but make it clear that nothing you or your child may do can change the situation right away. For many children, being among extended family members is a definite plus. The sense of family is reinforced, they receive extra support and love, and the residential parent gets some much-needed help.

THE FAMILY FLOWER GARDEN

A garden is a wonderful family project and an evolving metaphor for life, growth, and change. Create a garden with your child. Your "garden" can be a window box, a few large pots on the stoop, or a row of plants on a sunny window sill. Start small and keep it simple. To ensure success, follow the basics of soil preparation, location, and plant selection and care. If you don't have a green thumb, talk to people at the local garden center. They can give you lots of advice.

Flowers are either annuals (which last only one growing season and can be grown from seeds or purchased as small plants), perennials (which come back year after year and are usually purchased as small plants), and bulbs (most of which are planted in the fall for spring-to-summer bloom). The growing cycle of each type teaches its own lesson: Annuals exemplify the spirit of carpe diem; perennials, perseverance and change; bulbs, the rewards of patience (and in some cases perseverance, since some return each year). If you can, select flowers from each group.

You can choose plants for their appearance, their ease of care, or simply because they're your or your child's favorites. You can also plant with a purpose (flowers for cutting, flowers to attract butterflies, flowers for their scent) or meaning. Since humankind has been cultivating plants, they've been invested with significance and meaning. The Victorians elevated this to a fine art, even attributing specific meaning to different colors of the same flower. In the "language of flowers," roses and lilacs say "love"; violets, "faithfulness"; gladiolus, "strength"; and zinnias, "thoughts of absent friends." In their names alone, common flowers like forget-me-nots, sunflowers, butterfly weed, and money plant conjure wonderful images.

Visit a local public garden or garden center. Ordering from catalogs (which are full of information) is also fun. Through catalogs, you can find some unusual plants, such as pink daffodils, black tulips, and white sunflowers.

- Easy-to-grow annuals: alyssum, wax begonia, coleus, impatiens, sunflower, petunia, marigold, zinnia, four-o'clock, ageratum, calendula, moonflower, fuchsia, cleome, cosmos, morning glory, coreopsis, lantana, lobelia, nasturtium, annual geranium (pelargonium), salvia, dusty miller, torenia, garden verbena

- Easy-to-grow perennials: butterfly weed, money plant (honesty), pansy, yarrow, Chinese lantern plant, aster, astilbe, daylily, campanula (bellflower), iris, hosta, dianthus (pinks), carnation, bleeding heart, perennial geranium, baby's breath, coralbells, lavender, monarda, peony, rudbeckia, lamb's ears, veronica, violet

- Easy-to-grow bulbs: daffodil, narcissus, crocus, tulip, hyacinth, scilla, fritillaria, allium (some varieties of fritillaria and allium grow over three feet tall), and Asiatic, Chinese, and Oriental lilies

- Flowers that attract butterflies: alyssum, marigold, four-o'clock, nasturtium, lantana, monarda, butterfly weed, coreopsis, daylily

- Flowers that attract hummingbirds: fuschia, nasturtium, salvia, monarda, daylily, coralbells, petunia, lily

- Flowers for bouquets: almost all large bulbs, especially tulip and daffodil, Oriental and Asian lilies (not daylilies), bearded and Dutch iris, monarda, zinnia, sunflower, marigold, carnation, rudbeckia, peony

In addition to planting and caring for the garden, keep a journal together noting what you planted where and when. Photograph the garden from year to year, make up special bouquets from it, dry flowers for potpourri, or press them to commemorate a special day.

PURPOSE: Creating life and tending to growth are wonderful experiences for children and their parents as well as a metaphor for our personal lives. Gardening is a bonding experience that children enjoy. Further, discussing a flower's needs helps a child express his own needs.

Acknowledge your child's loss and grief over leaving a very special place behind while at the same time pointing out the advantages of your new home. Acquaint your kids with local points of interest: parks, playgrounds, zoos, amusement parks, museums, theaters, mountains, lakes, rivers, and so on. At the same time, don't overlook the things about your new home that your child may find equally attractive. One adult child of divorce recalls, "Things about a new place that our parents probably never gave a second thought—like having a frosted-glass window, an ironing board that folded out of the wall, an orange tree in the backyard, sliding glass doors, a big driveway to play in, or living on the second floor—were exciting to us in ways few adults could ever imagine."

TALKING TO YOUR CHILD ABOUT MAKING FRIENDS

This is a time when your child may truly need your help. Before you offer any help or advice, try to really put yourself in your child's place. Unless you moved or changed schools during your childhood, you have no idea the potential depth of his isolation and loneliness. For most kids, the friends they have are more or less a "given," people they grew up with, go to school with, and, in most cases, people who have known them much of their lives. Now every initial encounter is a "cold call," fraught with possible rejection. It's not easy to make new friends. (Think back to how you saw new kids treated when you were in school.)

✔ *Be positive but realistic.* Saying things like "Don't worry, honey, once they get to know you, everyone will love you as much as I do" or "It's easy to make new friends" is just setting your child up for disappointment. Statements like "It takes time, but you'll slowly find friends" give your child realistic support.

✔ *Encourage your child to join clubs and organizations with others who share her interests.*

✔ *Listen carefully when your child criticizes other kids.* It's not unusual for kids to become angry with and highly critical of themselves and others when friendship doesn't blossom. "Everyone at my new school is an idiot; they don't even know who Hanson is," "Every-

one here is so rude," and "I don't care if I never make friends with any of those jerks" are the kind of sweeping generalizations that indicate something else is going on. Depending on how persistent your child is and how easily he makes new friends, he may become discouraged. Speak to him about the real problem: his disappointment and hurt feelings.

✔ *Share your own "new kid" experiences.* If you moved as a child, talk about that or any other similar experience: moving away to college, or your first job. You can even discuss how you feel now with this move. Be vulnerable and open; admit what hurts. But emphasize the positive aspects of your life now and be reassuring. Let your child know that it takes time to adjust to change and that you're adjusting, too. Gently encourage your child to keep trying. Remind him that even he and the best friend he had in the old neighborhood started off slowly and argued sometimes, although they were really close.

✔ *Make it easy for your child to entertain friends.* Allow her to invite friends to your home or on outings, even if only to a local park or a movie.

✔ *Encourage your child to stay in touch with his old friends.* Never dismiss the importance of those relationships or suggest they can be replaced.

Even if your child is not changing schools with this move and can remain in touch with her friends, encourage her to get acquainted with children in your new neighborhood. This is often a lot harder than parents realize, and even ordinarily outgoing kids may have a difficult time making their way into established neighborhood cliques. Let's be honest: None of us ever enjoys being "the new kid in town" or the new anything anywhere. While it's important to impart a positive attitude, don't inadvertently raise hopes for things that may never happen. After all, just because your son was class treasurer, star linebacker, or the chess champ at his old school doesn't mean he will be here. Depending on your new neighborhood, his new friends may not be exactly like his old friends. And do not ever tell a child that his new friends will be "just as good" as the ones he's leaving behind. Each friendship is unique, and friends are not interchangeable. Remarks like this send your child the message that his old friends don't really matter and show disrespect for his feelings.

You can make it easier for your child by establishing yourself in the new community. Parents who take the lead in meeting new people and helping their kids introduce themselves—for example, by joining a group picnic or inviting another family over for cake—clear the trail for their kids. Besides, you will want to know something about the families of your children's friends anyway. Consider joining social and religious organizations as well as those devoted to single or divorced parents, such as Parents Without Partners.

CHANGING SCHOOLS

If your move keeps you within the same school boundaries, chances are your child will be able to maintain his current friendships and social activities. However, kids who find themselves suddenly attending a new school usually lose their social network, too. Depending on your child's age and the distance between your old and new homes, maintaining friendships may not be easy. Older kids can write letters, talk on the phone, and exchange e-mail. If you live close enough, they may even be able to share a weekend or have a sleepover. Generally, however, the greater the distance and the younger the children, the greater chance they will lose touch. This is one of many reasons why changing schools is so difficult for kids. If you never had that experience yourself, think back to your first day at a new job. When your child starts a new school, he's starting several "new jobs" at once: social and academic.

SOCIAL ADJUSTMENTS

Regardless of how your child felt about her old school, she had a definite, unique place there. She may have been the best reader, teacher's favorite helper, or the kid to watch on the basketball or tetherball court. Even the class clown, the chronically tardy, and the athletically challenged have their own identities in the "school universe." Coming to a new school means much more than getting used to a new teacher's style, new classroom rules, or making friends out of twenty or thirty total strangers. Granted, any one of these can be difficult. The hardest task of all, and the one she probably will have to solve on her own, is finding her new place in this different system.

You can help by being sympathetic and open to her concerns. Be careful not to dismiss the importance of what matters to her, like belonging to certain cliques and clubs or having a date for the prom. Keep in mind that your child derived a sense of security and confidence from knowing where she fit in before. Until she regains her footing, issues that may strike you as minor (such as not being asked to join a team or not being invited to a birthday party) may be very painful to her.

Do not overlook your divorce as a factor in your child's social adjustment. Chances are that in her old school, among her old friends, she didn't really have to explain or talk about the divorce. Now, however, kids will probably ask why she has only one parent at home or why her family moved. An unwillingness to talk about the divorce or fear of how other kids may think of her because of it may result in even more shyness and sensitivity. It may also cause your child to lie—the other parent is out of town, even dead—in an effort to present a more positive and acceptable image.

Finally, a word about cliques. Regardless of how well your child adjusts to the move and the new school, don't lose sight of the fact that he probably longs to be accepted by his peers. The unfortunate truth about being a new kid is that not all other children will welcome you with open arms. If your child is under nine or ten, ask his teacher about other kids in his class she thinks he would get along with, then arrange play dates or outings for them. An older child will probably resent your meddling, although you can try to plan events and outings—for example, to the local water park or science museum—that he would feel comfortable inviting another friend to join. For reasons of personality or personal history, the type of group your child may be used to or would prefer associating with may not be available or open to him. Among adolescents in particular, the most welcoming cliques can be those of kids with problems. There's very little snobbery among kids who cut class, drink, or use drugs.

Parents should take notice if their child's new friends seem very different in manner and attitude than her old ones. Discuss your concerns with your child, but don't jump to conclusions. Perhaps your child's new friends dress in a style that's sloppier than her old friends' because that's the local trend. Or invite the new friends over to your home and really get to know them. If you're still worried, talk to your child. Be specific about what bothers you and how you think it's affecting your child. Say, "I know you want to make new friends, but it bothers me that you ask to go to the mall every single day after school. You know I don't think that's an appropriate place to hang out." Or "I know you're a responsible kid, but I cannot allow you and your friends to spend their entire time visiting you holed up in your room with the door shut. We entertain guests in the family room." Avoid saying things like "I don't like the looks of your new friends," or "What the heck is going on in your room anyway?"

Try to guide your child's choices through reason. If that fails and you find you have real cause for concern, lay down the law, outlining your reasons:

> "Carly, I know you like hanging out with Claudia, but last week while I was shopping, I saw her at the mall when she should have been in school. She was also drinking a beer. You know that is unacceptable behavior. Sometimes having friends who do things we know they shouldn't makes it easy to do the wrong thing. I'm afraid that's what might happen if you stay with Claudia. I'm confident you can find friends whose values and behavior are more suitable." Then allow her to express her feelings and thoughts.

ACADEMIC ADJUSTMENTS

No matter what grade your child is in, he may find himself further ahead or behind in his new school. Children who find themselves academically ahead are prone to boredom; those who are behind may get frustrated and discouraged. Listen to your child, look at his homework and his books, and determine where he is in relation to his current class. If he's relearning something, ask his teacher to provide extra or alternate assignments to challenge him until the rest of the class catches up to him. If his new math class is just finishing fractions and his old one had just started before you moved, let his teacher know, so she can provide extra help.

A PARENT'S RETURN TO WORK

Once upon a time there was a family that had a beautiful house and only the dad worked. For two weeks the little girl heard her parents arguing, and one day they told her that they were going to get divorced. She and her siblings were going to live with her mother, and her mother had to get a job, but she said everything was going to be okay.
—Girl, ten

It is rare for a man to alter his career plans or quit work because he's married or has children. This is why whenever divorce prompts a formerly unemployed parent to return to the workplace, it's usually the mother. Obviously, this is a big change for everyone, but how it will affect your child depends on a number of factors, including his age and your support system. Needless to say, parents who work outside the home tend to have less time and less energy to expend on parenting. At the same time, the very circumstances that force these changes often make kids feel more deserving and demanding of your extra time and attention. For many single parents, working outside the home is a source of guilt, which is often followed by resentment over having to do so much, followed by guilt for feeling overwhelmed and resentful. (In chap-

TEN COMMANDMENTS FOR A HAPPY FAMILY

Using poster board or any paper, create a personal Ten Commandments for a Happy Family (possibly, five suggestions from you and five from the children). The commandments might include such things as smiling in the morning, putting toys and clothes in their places, saying "please" and "thank you," getting ready for school on time, having story time with a parent, or listening when others are speaking.

For young children, have some sort of daily reinforcement. This might be a magnet, star, or check placed next to the name of a child who complied with most of the commandments that day. For the ambitious, you might create a flag or kite with your child's name and have it "fly high" above the commandment chart when he is cooperative.

PURPOSE: This system spells out your expectations and encourages compliance. The list has input from the children, so they have a stake in seeing that the family is functional and happy. This activity also serves to give kids a sense that they are redefining and helping to create their new family system. While psychological issues and problems do play a major role in family life, the simple courtesies of a smile, good-morning greetings, good manners, and responsibility are the cornerstones of living successfully with others. Having your child understand and work toward this goal can indeed improve the odds for happiness.

ter 13, I offered some general advice for making the most of the time you do have to spend with your kids.)

ARRANGING CHILD CARE

Choosing between child care in your home and in a day-care center is an important decision. Each option has its pros and cons, for both parent and child. General child-care books and parenting magazines routinely include information on how to interview and work with caregivers, so here I will limit my remarks to the issues that pertain particularly to divorced families. Presuming that both parents must work, you should consider

- dependability and continuity of care,
- safety,
- your child's personality and stage of development.

Children of divorce, especially the younger ones, really need continuity and daily routines. Whether that is best provided by a caregiver in your home or by group day care depends largely on the employee turnover in each situation. For continuity, a single caregiver who remains for an extended period is preferable to a day-care center where the employee turnover may be high. Hiring a nanny to work in the home, however, is no guarantee of continuity. And some well-run, established day-care centers and all in-home day-care providers offer consistency in terms of who cares for your child. Whomever you hire, be sure to inquire about her future plans, how long she intends to work in this field. If your child is going to day care, find out who will be caring for her—an employee or a co-owner—and what the turnover rate is.

If you decide to hire someone to care for your child in your home, think about your contingency plans if, say, your caregiver falls ill or is called away on a family emergency. Few working parents can afford to lose a week or more because they lack child care. A parent with a very demanding job and no nearby relatives or friends to care for the child in a pinch may opt for day care for dependability. Create a contingency plan if your child is ill and cannot go to day care. Will you take off from work or have Grandma come and stay with your child?

If you do hire someone to care for your children in your home, consider hiring through an agency and check references carefully. If possible, talk to former employers in person, ideally in their homes. When you consider qualifications, think practically. In most instances, hiring a single caregiver to work in your home is more expensive than day care.

You should also consider your decision from the point of view of your child's social development. Before the age of fifteen to eighteen months, children have less need to socialize with other children. After that, however, interacting with other children offers opportunities for intellectual and emotional growth, something good day care offers. If you do decide to have your child's caregiver drive her to play dates, playgrounds, and other activities, make the arrangements and oversee the schedule.

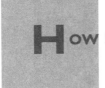

HOW PARENTS CAN HELP WHEN THEY GO BACK TO WORK

• *Talk to your child about the fact that you will be going to work and explain in age-appropriate terms what that will mean.* Bear in mind that your child will probably feel somewhat anxious about it, so keep your focus on the positive (the nice baby-sitter who will be watching him; you will phone home a few times a day) and reconsider how your child may view what you consider negatives (more fast food for dinner, less time to clean the house—few kids would complain). Whatever you do, be sure your child understands that wherever he is, whomever he's with, he will be safe, that you are only a phone call away, and that in an emergency, you will be there.

Stress the positive aspects of both work in general and your working in particular—from a brighter financial situation the whole family will benefit from to your personal feeling of pride and accomplishment. Explain the work you'll be doing and how important it is. Let your children know that lots of mothers work, and talk about some working mothers your children know.

• *Suggest changes that will make your life easier* and *empower your children.* Offer an allowance for help around the house, such as making lunches, washing vegetables for dinner, and putting all the laundry in the hamper. Even the youngest kids can usually do something. (See the chart "Ways Children Can Help Around the House," page 317.)

• *If at all possible, take your child to where you will be working, so he has a "picture" of where you are and what you are doing.* Ask him if it's okay if you hang some of his artwork in your new workplace and tell him that you'll have a copy of your favorite picture, perhaps of the two of you together, on your desk.

• *Let your child know you are thinking of him, but don't harp on how sad you are and how much you miss him.* Loving notes tucked into backpacks and lunch boxes or a special phone call to ask how school was or just say hi can mean a lot.

• *Take the time to really listen to your child when you are home.* Keep the lines of communication open, so you will know what's happening at school, with the baby-sitter, and with your child's friends.

FINISH THE SENTENCE

This sentence-completion game literally goes anywhere—you can play it in the car, at the playground, over lunch, right before turning out the light at night. Basically, a parent starts a sentence, and the child completes it. Then the child starts a sentence that the parent completes. Some sentence beginnings include:

"I feel really happy when I…"
"A wish I have is to…"
"When I grow up, I will never…"

PURPOSE: Children will often say things in the context of a "game" that they wouldn't say otherwise. The game also gives you a chance to let your children know that you have similar feelings about things.

• *Set a time when you will phone home from work to say hi.* Your child should have your number in case of emergency. However, if your child calls you several times and finds you unavailable or is cut short because you have to run to a meeting or take another call, he may feel hurt and rejected. In these cases, it's best to suggest a set time and limit calls.

• *Set aside time each day to devote exclusively to your child.* Turn off the TV; don't answer the phone; resist the temptation to fold laundry while you're overseeing homework unless you must or you have set aside other quiet time. Even if you reserve only fifteen minutes a day, you will be sending your child a very positive, esteem-building message: He deserves your full attention. You may feel that even fifteen minutes is more than you can spare, but if you don't set it aside voluntarily, your child probably will claim that time—and probably even more—by being whiny, uncooperative, demanding, or just plain difficult. View this not as time spent or wasted, but time invested—in your child's self-esteem and your sanity.

• *Even in your worst moments, do not blame the fact that you now work on your ex.* Parents must return to work for all kinds of reasons; divorce is only one. Chances are that any child over six or so has already made the association herself. Talking about your having to work as if it were some kind of punishment sends kids the wrong message. It will only give your child another reason to be angry about the divorce or angry at the parent she believes caused it. While your returning to work certainly has an effect on your child, it is not her problem but yours, one you must work through for yourself. Elisa recognized that her negativity toward the prospect of returning to work would affect her children, so before she even began job hunting, she spoke with a counselor. Once she was able to stop blaming Gerald for the fact she had to work, she was better able to communicate a positive attitude to her children.

This is not to say that your child won't be upset at not having you around as much as she did before. She probably will, and you should address those issues in a positive, forthright manner.

RELIGION

Religious differences pose perhaps the greatest challenge to the divorced coparenting system. Although religion usually teaches sensitivity, kindness, and forgiveness, disagreements about their child's religious training can force parents into intense, seemingly unresolvable conflict.

Few of us come to our religious belief through the same logical processes we rely on to make most of our other decisions. Whether one makes religion a major part of daily life or turns to faith only in times of crisis, everyone regards his personal beliefs as his own. Only we truly understand why we believe as we do, and only we can determine what is best for ourselves. That said, as parents we all reserve the right to provide our children with the religious training and exposure we feel is best (usually what we believe ourselves). When couples marry, even if they are of the same faith, one or both often make some compromise in how they practice their faith. Even two people of the same faith may not agree on what role religion will play in their lives. (For instance, will they attend services every week or only on special holidays?) Couples from different faiths may opt to follow one or neither. And some couples feel it's best for each to pursue an individual faith, believing even marriage cannot be reason to compromise what they see as their religious obligations.

As I've said many times throughout this book, divorce often heightens the differences between parents. For many people, the emotional turmoil of divorce serves as a catalyst for change in their religious views. Those who were ambivalent about their faith may suddenly become more involved; others may reject what they believed in the past for a different faith or a new system of belief. If you have experienced a dramatic change in your religious views, consider why. If you are in the midst of reexamining your own spirituality, consider maintaining the traditions your child is familiar with until you are certain that what you've chosen is right for you and your child. Children of divorce need more consistency and less change.

Even if both parents are genuine in their respective beliefs, a child can feel confused. She may see the two people she loves most in the world teaching her different lessons and perhaps criticizing each other (explicitly or implicitly) in the process. It's fascinating to me how all established faiths teach us to understand others, and yet parents often teach children to be insensitive to the beliefs of others in the name of religion. If you and your ex disagree about religion, accept that you probably won't change your ex's mind, and focus instead on finding a comfortable middle ground. Begin by first taking a warm approach to the other parent's beliefs. You might say to your child, "I know it is confusing to you to hear all about the religion I want you to follow and then go to your father's/mother's and hear something totally different. I feel my religious beliefs are healthy for me and for you as well because [then outline the reasons]. But I can understand that others, including your father/mother, see things differently and may have their reasons for following other religious principles and teachings."

If you attempt to shove religion down your child's throat, you will send a negative message about your faith. There is no more surefire way of turning a child against religion in general than turning what should be a beautiful, life-enriching experience into a punishment. Here the spirit you teach your child is as important as the letter of the religious text you ascribe to. In a loving, caring atmosphere, one in which your child sees firsthand the joy and internal peace you derive from your faith, a child will be motivated to experience such faith for himself. After you have lovingly planted the seeds of faith, your child's spirituality can grow.

Be aware that children often pay a lot more attention to what we do than to what we say. To suddenly object to your ex's taking your child to weekly services when you were totally ambivalent about her doing so before the divorce, or to suddenly start paying lip service to beliefs that you never put into practice, will only confuse your child. Whatever your or your ex's faith, think before you criticize or provoke a fight over it. Parents who care about their children's spirituality do best not to cheapen religion by making it just one more ball put into play in the game of divorce.

Interestingly, religious differences can prompt parents to think about what they believe and why in ways they might never have had to before. Encourage your child's questions, difficult as they may be. Present your views openly, and graciously acknowledge differences as well as everyone's—including your ex's—right to believe as he sees fit. When your child has a question you cannot answer, seek the answers together. Teaching and practicing religion this way will enhance your child's appreciation of your faith and bring her closer to you.

FINALLY

> Dear Mom,
> It hurts to see you two going your separate ways. But I think it was for the best. Now things are going much better. The house feels peaceful.
> —Teenager

No matter what changes your family will face, it's important to acknowledge them as challenges while at the same time letting your child know you have confidence in his ability to meet them. New situations can be difficult for everyone, but they are also rich in opportunities for personal growth and family bonding.

Q *Dear Gary,*
We recently moved, and my girls, eight and thirteen, must begin attending a new school. The eight-year-old appears to be doing well: She's joined Brownies, made friends, and is doing well academically. My thirteen-year-old is another story. She seems moody and depressed, and she hates her new school. The kids are all "snobs"; the teachers are all "idiots." She was never that outgoing to begin with, so I've tried to gently push her to join some clubs, go out for some teams. When I do, she just glares at me. All she wants to do is hole up in her room and e-mail or phone her old friends. Maybe if I forbid that, she'll be forced to "join the party" here. Any advice?

A As every parent knows, no two children are alike. While you may feel proud of your younger daughter for taking the initiative and adjusting so well to your move, don't compare and don't criticize your thirteen-year-old for what she will not, perhaps cannot, do. Clearly, she needs the support of her old network. Children's friendships are extremely important; I know an adult child of divorce who for twenty-nine years has continued to correspond with a friend she made when she was twelve. Don't dissuade her. Support your child for who she is. If she was always the type to have a few close friends as opposed to joining groups, if she was always more introspective than "bubbly," she is not going to change, nor should you encourage her to.

Teenagers are often receptive to exploring the reasons behind their feelings. Unlike younger kids, they feel more comfortable talking about their feelings and derive some pride in being able to deal with their problems in a more "adult" manner. When teenagers seem resistant to talking about what troubles them, it usually isn't because they don't want to talk but because they feel that they are not being understood. Empathize with her. Tell her you understand how much it hurts to feel that you have no power, to have to move to a new school, to be forced into a new situation. Also let her know that you understand that her friends are very special to her and that they cannot be replaced. Allow her to grieve for what she has lost.

You may be surprised to learn that thirteen-year-olds do understand defense mechanisms—the things we say and do to protect ourselves from sad or intense feelings. You might say, "I know how hard it is to leave old friends behind, and how it might seem that you can prevent feeling that pain again by not making new ones. Maybe this reminds you of how you felt when your dad and I separated." Talk to her about displaced anger without minimizing the intensity of her feelings: "Sometimes when we get angry about something we cannot change, we direct that anger at something else. This is normal, and I understand why you're doing it. I've done it myself. Remember the time I had that flat tire, and I kicked the car door? Let's talk about some ways that you might express that anger that won't make school so painful for you."

Most important, spend extra time alone with your daughter. Let her know that you love and accept her as she is, that she doesn't have to change to "fit in," that you respect her feelings, and that she can always turn to you.

CHAPTER 15

"There's Someone I Want You to Meet"

Your New Significant Other

Fifteen-year-old Rachel burst into the house, ran into the family room, dialed her best friend, Danielle, and practically screamed: "Todd asked me out! It was on the way home—wait: I think I hear the door. I've got to go, my mom's home from work and I have to tell her that, yes, we *will* need a prom dress. Bye!" Rachel ran down the hall and was just turning to go into the kitchen when she stopped. Mom was already on the phone.

"Well, I met the most wonderful man today," Iris said, cradling her cell phone against her ear as she filled the pasta pot with water. "We just met at work during a meeting and had coffee. His name is Maurice. He's so nice—and good-looking, too. Yeah, you're right; maybe it is about time."

Rachel turned and ran to her room, cursing her mother.

Twelve-year-old Jeremy came home from soccer practice, dying to tell his dad about his big game. But his smile faded when he saw "her" car parked in the driveway. In the kitchen he found the two of them just putting on their jackets, obviously on their way out. *Probably to another one of her art-gallery things, I suppose. Mom could never get him to go anywhere she wanted to go. Now he's wrapped around her finger.* The room was filled with the familiar yet weird sound of his father laughing merrily at another of Yvonne's witticisms. Pushing past the two of them, Jeremy opened the fridge.

"What's up, Jer?" Simon asked.

Jeremy glared hard at a milk carton. He felt his disappointment in his father rising and overwhelming him. He was too old to cry and too young to say what he really felt. *He never, never laughed at Mom's jokes like that. Or smiled at her like that. Or looked so happy just being around her. This lady is all over my house, unbelievable. How will Mom ever come back to us now, with this blond bimbo practically living here?* Jeremy grabbed a bottle and took a big gulp of Coke, turned around, shot his father a scowl, then ran back outside. *I can't stand him! Or her!*

No matter how difficult their marriage or its breakup, most divorced parents believe remarriage or a serious long-term relationship awaits. We tend to focus on divorce and remarriage, so we sometimes overlook the chasm in between: those months or years we spend back on the field, playing the dating game. What even the most conscientious parents don't immediately realize is that this field of dreams can easily become a minefield if potential concerns and problems—especially your child's feelings—are not anticipated and dealt with in a fair and forthright manner.

The push to move on, to find someone new, can be hard to resist. Friends and family may be urging you to "get out there" and prove to yourself (and your ex) that you're still desirable and lovable. Being only human, you may be anxious to meet someone new and grab another chance at happiness. We all deserve that. Some truly feel that a new, affirming, loving relationship will provide more than comfort and affection. For them, the nightmare of divorce won't really end until they are "safe" again as part of a new couple. Given the pain that divorced people often endure, it's sometimes awfully hard to argue against that. And then a shrinking minority of experts offer single parents a pat, guilt-easing "Don't worry. Whatever makes you happy will make your child happy, too." It sounds great, but don't believe it for a minute.

Regardless of where you are in the divorce, how old your child is, or the suitability of your significant other, your being in a new relationship has real meaning for your child. No matter what your child's age, she may view your new interest as a "replacement" for her other parent, the coup de grâce to her fantasy of your reconciliation, the end of a possible "happily ever after." If you have a teen, he will see your dating as an encroachment into a brand-new world he believes belongs to him alone. These are complicated issues, and there are others, as I outline below. But at the very least, the presence of a significant other in your life, no matter how casual or serious your intent, means that your child must now "share" you with someone from outside the family. For kids still recovering from the trauma of divorce, this may be more than they are willing or able to do.

A billion miles away. A nine-year-old boy illustrates the immense emotional distance between his parents.

THE HEALING TIME

You and your child need many things—communication, understanding, and patience—to help you understand and live with the changes divorce has wrought. Most of all, however, both of you need time: time to adjust, time to learn, time to heal. Children need their parents like never before, and parents need to be there to guide them and protect them from additional stress and upheaval. The issues that arise in the early postseparation period are often the most difficult and have the potential to be the most devastating if not recognized and addressed quickly. Refraining from serious dating or relationships in the first year after separation gives children and parents the *minimum* adjustment time. If your breakup is extremely troubling to your child, you might consider waiting even longer.

Let me just say I know that there are many parents and even some experts in the field who will take issue with this. After all, we each have a right to be happy. I agree. However, the strength of your future relationship, marriage, or step- or blended family is being built right now, even if you haven't met anyone. That's because whatever form your future family takes, it can never be stronger than its individual "parts." Creating a new family is complex and difficult, no matter how much you love your new mate. Your chances of success and happiness will be greatly enhanced if you take the time now to ensure that your child is secure in his relationship with you. Once parents understand the full range of

DRAW THAT FEELING

This is a game that can be played by two people. You can also play it with two or more pairs of players, each pair forming a team that plays against the others. One player thinks up a situation (a walk in the park, eating ice cream, riding a bike), writes down what he was thinking and the feeling it evokes so that no one else sees it. Then he draws a picture that depicts the situation he has written down. You can agree to a time limit for completing the drawing—say, one minute, for instance. Once his team has guessed the situation correctly, it has three chances to guess the feeling it evokes.

PURPOSE: Having the child create the answers facilitates his expression of feelings and specifically the situations that prompt those feelings. It might be as simple as drawing a football game to show happiness, or it could be as intense as drawing Dad not showing up for visitation to express anger.

CHARADES

In this game of charades, you and your child take turns acting out and guessing feelings. Create clue cards that state different feelings. (For older children, you can use more sophisticated feeling words, such as "rejected," "ecstatic.") One of you selects a card at random, then acts out a scenario that brings about the feeling stated on the card, while the other guesses what the feeling is. Charades can also be played in teams.

For example, for "happy," your child or team might act out going to camp, parents being nice to each other, getting a puppy.

PURPOSE: The game will help parents notice how their children feel about certain issues as they make choices to act out these feeling scenarios. Furthermore, it will help children learn to identify feelings and how situations directly affect feelings. Finally, expressing ideas without words is a great example of the power of nonverbal communication, which you can discuss with your child.

repercussions a new intimate relationship can have on children, they can proceed at a pace that's comfortable for everyone. Equally important, they will be forming the parent-child "keystone" subsequent relationships and marriages rise around or collapse under.

CONSIDER WHY YOU ARE DATING NOW

Keep a nonchalant attitude regarding meeting someone new so that your child sees that it would be nice for you if you fell in love, but it is not required to maintain your happiness.

Be aware of your own internal push to find someone new. Are you (or your family) pressuring yourself to meet someone immediately? Consider how important it is for you to remarry soon and why. Unfortunately, second marriages have a higher divorce rate than first marriages, for two reasons.

First, people often repeat patterns and remarry someone with a personality similar to that of their first mate. They often remarry a person who may look different—taller, more hair, less fat—but inside share a common personality with the ex because they are unconsciously attracted to the same person. Sometimes the new relationship works better because we have learned from our old mistakes, even though we still have the same problems. In relationships, history definitely repeats itself.

Second, remarriage is fraught with immediate pressures not usually found in a first marriage, not the least of which is the children. When each partner brings children to the relationship, there's tremendous pressure for everyone to "blend." Suddenly your new marriage isn't about one relationship between two people, but potentially dozens of relationships among several people, not all of whom will be as verbal or mature as you and your new mate. For example, if each of you brings just one child to the marriage, it means that each "new family" member will have to develop or maintain relationships with three other people, and that counts only the immediate family, not extended family or new in-laws. People in second marriages often feel that not only is the honeymoon over, it never even started.

Quick remarriages complicate the issues of a blended family. Children have scarcely had the time to adjust to the most significant changes in their lives when they are suddenly thrust into a new family, having never experienced closure on the old family. The divorce never afforded the opportunity to create a new individual relationship with parents because parents have already found a new focus in life, their new partner. Divorce forces children to redefine their entire lives, the very basis of their existence: family. It is quite complicated enough without the rushed introduction of a new stepfamily.

How CHILDREN SEE THEIR PARENTS' DATING

YOUR DATING SHATTERS THE DREAM OF RECONCILIATION

Dear Mom,
I just want you and Dad to come back together, but I know that is not going to happen because you have a boyfriend.
　　—Girl, eight

Even in children mature enough to understand that their parents will not reconcile, the hope of reconciliation usually lingers. Whether your child's hope blazes or flickers, your dating threatens to blow it out. Again, the vision of a future reconciliation haunts many children of divorce for years, even decades. As long as you remain uncommitted to anyone else, your child can always imagine turning the page to find a happy ending. Instead, you have slammed shut the book on this particular dream.

You never imagined it would sound so mean, did you? Unfortunately, that's pretty much how kids see it. After all, they may reason, you could choose not to date anyone. Your child may be angry at you for dating and, depending on her age, may express this to you directly. However, given how threatened children can feel by the arrival of someone new in a parent's life, this anger is often and understandably directed at your new love. Like Jeremy, kids often think, *If it weren't for her* . . .

If you suspect your child feels this way, be patient and understanding. Help your child understand that it is normal to wish parents would get back together, and it's okay to be angry, hurt, and disappointed when you realize that is not going to happen. At the same time, be sure your child understands that you and your ex separated or divorced because you had problems that prevented you from staying together, and that the new person has nothing to do with that (although in cases of infidelity, see page 378). Whatever you say, accept your responsibility for the marriage ending, for making the decision to separate or divorce, for not giving it another chance. Make sure your child also understands that this decision was made by both of his parents, that it was made before the new person arrived (if true), and that his rejecting the new person will not change your relationship with your ex. Finally, establish clear, consistent rules regarding etiquette and what is acceptable. Being responsive and sympathetic to your child's feelings does not mean allowing him to be rude to a guest, even if that guest is your new boyfriend whom he professes to hate.

YOUR CHILD MUST NOW SHARE YOU

> I'm sad when my dad pays more attention to his girlfriend.
> —Girl, ten

Perhaps the most common issue of a new love interest is the real time and energy it takes away from the parent-child relationship. One of the best ways to help your child feel comfortable with your significant other is for your child to see that this person respects your parent-child relationship. Whether you're dating or not, your child needs to spend quality, private time with you. If you are sharing time with both your child and your love interest, be sure that there is also ample private time. Don't assume that just being with you is the same as being with you alone.

KIDS FEAR THAT THEY "AREN'T ENOUGH" TO MAKE YOU HAPPY

> I don't understand [why] after my mom gets a divorce, she wants to get a new boyfriend.
> Boy, nine

> Dear Dad,
> Why are you having girlfriends when you have us?
> —Boy, ten

Unfortunately, this is the hurtful message that many children receive when parents date. A child may feel that she is not important enough or special enough to make her parent feel complete, that there is someone else out there "better" and more interesting than she is. When a parent avidly and conspicuously seeks companionship, his children often feel rejected, "not good enough," and devalued. Even if they understand that a parent's love for a child and his romantic love for another adult are two totally noninterchangeable relationships, it can still be difficult for your child not to feel she's been pushed aside or forced to share you.

T H I N G S **2** D O

WOULD YOU LOVE ME IF . . .

Ask your child, *Would you love me if*

I had a scary face?
I got angry at you a lot?
I forgot to tuck you in and say goodnight?

Then create more examples with your child.

PURPOSE: As your child answers yes to the above examples, you can explain how parents and children always love each other. "Just as you can always love me no matter what, I will always love you no matter what happens or what you do." Often, children are fearful that their parents may stop loving them after divorce as the parents stopped loving each other. Clarifying that you will always love your child, no matter what, is important and especially effective when it is proven to her through her own unconditional love for you as her parent.

KIDS FEAR FUTURE REJECTION

Unlike a child from a maritally intact home, your child has already experienced loss. While some children seem to automatically reject every new person in a parent's life, others seem to attach themselves to even the most casual dates. Perhaps they're happy to see Mommy or Daddy happy, or they enjoy the attention most conscientious dates offer them, or they're just outgoing and friendly. While you may be dating with nothing serious in mind, your child probably does not understand that. To many kids, a friend of a parent is a friend of theirs. If any of your dates has paid special attention to your child—anything from simply being friendly and playing with her a few minutes to giving gifts and taking her on special outings—that person is, in your child's eyes, a friend. There is nothing inherently wrong about this, but remember your child's perspective and the potential pain if she meets and becomes attached to someone only to lose the friendship when you two say goodbye.

None of this can be avoided once your child gets to know someone. What can be avoided—and should be whenever possible—is the "serial rejection" children experience when they're introduced to every person you date even once. A serious friendship between your significant other and your child should be allowed only after the two of you have agreed to a long-term commitment. While I can't offer you guidelines on what constitutes a serious relationship, I believe it's in the best interest of your children not to have them meet anyone until you feel confident that the relationship is going somewhere. That means meeting your date outside the house in the beginning. This may sound old-fashioned and call for more sacrifice than some parents are willing to make. In the long run, however, everyone will benefit. It is no longer about you and what will make you happy. It is about you and your children and what will make all of you happy and comfortable.

DATING PARENTS AND THEIR TEENS: CRASHING THE PARTY

Dear Mom,
I'm feeling strange seeing you with a new boyfriend.

Dear Dad,
I hate it when I see you with your girlfriend.
—Girl, thirteen

Rachel is beginning to date and expects the exciting fanfare that comes with dating. Choosing the right dress, waiting for him to call, falling in love, even breaking up are all brand-new to her and exhilarating. She believes, and rightfully so, that her dating process deserves the attention of her family. Unfortunately, Iris's return to the dating game has rudely interrupted her daughter's moment in the spotlight.

Deep down, many teens believe there is something "weird" about parents' dating, and in a way, there is. It's unusual for parent and child to be on the same footing, in the same phase, doing the same things for the same reasons. One reason we can so readily turn our attention to what our child is going through is that we're not going through the exact thing ourselves at the same time. A child derives a sense of security and confidence knowing that her parents have already grown up—and through—the things that she faces today.

Possible Competition Between Parent and Child

Same-gender children may often feel competitive with the parent. And in order to feel young and attractive, or masculine, virile, and desirable, parents might unwittingly flirt with a child's boyfriend or girlfriend or seek to be the focus of a party or gathering. Be aware of this mistake and exercise self-restraint in your conversations with your teen's dates. Remember: Your teen can find his own buddies and rivals; he needs you to be his parent.

WHEN YOU INVOLVE YOUR KIDS IN YOUR DATING LIFE

Parents often mistakenly assume that their child should share in the excitement of their dating. When your child is a teenager, it's easy to fall into the buddy role with him, soliciting his opinion on what you should wear, where you should go to eat, what movie you should see, and so on. Usually, however, there's more to it than that. Teenagers often get involved in a parent's dating life so that they can have some say in choosing your new love or their new stepparent.

Parents sometimes misinterpret their child's interest and enthusiasm as the go-ahead to date freely and act teenagerish themselves. The truth is, children like to see their parents happy. If your weight lifting or cleaning the garage made you this happy, they would be all for that, too. While your teen may be comfortable with your dating and have a positive attitude toward your possible remarriage, she probably does not want to see you being "swept away" by the one who will bring happiness back into your life.

It took Iris three days to finally get at what was wrong. Sitting on the back porch, Rachel blurted out, "You know, last week, I had great news about Todd, but then you met Mr. Wonderful."

"I guess I kind of stole your thunder, huh?" Iris replied. "You're right: You had exciting news, and it deserved my full attention. I got a little carried away. I remember when I started dating. Every phone call, every new dress—my folks got such a kick out of seeing me so excited. I would be so nervous about everything, but just knowing they cared made me feel so much more confident. You deserve that from me now. I really am excited for you. Wow—Todd. You've been talking about him for months."

Significant others are part of the family. *For this child, grandparents and Mom's boyfriend make up the family, and Dad's girlfriend is also a significant figure in her life.*

PREPARING YOUR CHILD AND YOURSELF

Dear Dad,
I felt bad when you had a girlfriend and you never told me. Also the day I slept over and she slept over, but I didn't know, but I found out by looking under the door, and I saw her shoes.
—Girl, twelve

THE BAKING GAME

The tactile stimulation of working with dough provides a therapeutic outlet for many adults and kids, and the added bonus of a house filled with the comforting aroma of cookies baking makes this a multipurpose (and delicious) way to connect with your kids. Here is a simple dough recipe and variations on the baking activity.

Cookie Dough That Will Make Shapes

3 large eggs
1 cup (2 sticks) margarine
½ teaspoon vanilla extract
4 cups flour
2 cups confectioners' (powdered) sugar
3 teaspoons baking powder

Preheat the oven to 350° F.

Grease two or three cookie sheets; set aside.

In a large bowl, beat the eggs, then add the margarine and vanilla. Mix until thoroughly creamed. In another bowl, sift together the flour, confectioners' sugar, and baking powder. Add to the egg-margarine mixture, and mix until thoroughly blended. Turn the dough out onto a floured surface and roll to ¼-inch thickness. Cut into desired shapes, then place on the cookie sheets.

Bake 10 to 12 minutes, or until lightly browned. Makes approximately two dozen large cookies or 3-inch-tall cookie letters.

FEELING FACES

Make the unbaked cookies into faces, using raisins, chocolate chips, or any other garnish to form eyes, noses, and mouths. (On baked cookies, you and your child can use the decorative colored frostings in tubes.) Make faces that express a range of emotions—happy, sad, anxious, worried, surprised—and talk about what might have caused the cookies to have these feelings.

PURPOSE: Not all kids are comfortable talking about their feelings. However, they are often very eager to offer their interpretations of others' feelings. Listen closely to your child's explanation of why the cookie feels the way it does.

A HEART A DAY

Make cookies, cutting the dough into hearts. Decorate the baked cookies with frosting letters spelling out MOM on some and DAD on others. Let the child take one of each of the cookies with him in his lunch every day as a reminder of both parents' love with him. This is especially useful for very young children.

PURPOSE: This serves as an enjoyable memento of his parents' love for him.

A COOKIE FAMILY

Shape the dough into letters or cut the dough using letter-shaped cookie cutters. For young children, you might use figure cookie cutters of different sizes. Spell out (or cut forms to symbolize) MOM, DAD, and the child's name. Allow the child to position the dough on the baking sheet however she wishes.

PURPOSE: Applying some of the same principles we used in discussing children's art (see chapter 2), you can learn a lot about how your child views the relationships among you by how she positions the cookies. For example, Mom and Dad side by side may indicate a wish that you reunite, while Mom beside the child with Dad stuck in the far corner tells you how she sees her relationships with each of you.

FEELING WORDS

Bake cookies in the shape of feeling words (or the first letter of the word): "love," "anger," "sad," "happy." Then as each of you eat that word, try on, or act out, that feeling. Discuss the word and describe the physical and emotional aspects of the word.

Suzy and her father tried to feel what love does to us when we feel it alone and focus on it. Suzy noted how her head actually felt lighter as her breathing slowed, and she felt she had to smile. Anger made her fists tight, teeth clenched, and she could feel her whole body stiffen.

PURPOSE: It's important that children learn not only to identify and to express feelings but to understand how they make them think and feel—physically and emotionally. An activity such as this provides a safe place for your child to experience emotions.

Long before you start dating, you should open up the topic for discussion. While it may be some time before you meet someone that you will introduce your child to, he should know that you are dating and why. As Rachel's mother explained after her daughter asked, "And why do you have to date right now? Are things so bad around here?"

> "You mean you think I'm dating because I need something other than you to be happy? Listen, if I never met a man I liked again in my life, I would die a happy woman just because I have the love I share with you and your sister. It's just that as an adult I'm still looking for added opportunities to find someone I can talk to who has been through many similar things. You know how you look for friends whom you can talk to about things you think nobody else understands? It's the same for adults."

Many children have no idea that a parent is even dating until they are introduced to the significant other. If you and your new partner make it blatantly obvious that you already are in love, your child may worry that saying anything negative about it will hurt you. Older kids may keep their feelings to themselves, for fear they won't appear "mature enough" to deal with the new relationship. Help your child understand why you are dating so that he doesn't feel personally rejected.

YOU CAN'T HURRY LOVE

Dear Mom,
I have no problem with you having a boyfriend. I just don't want him to be like his way or no way. I want us to share opinions with him.
     —Girl, eight

As a result of going through the divorce with you, your child may feel closer to you now than ever. Look at it from her point of view: You and your ex decided to end your family as she had always known it, and you enlisted her help in building a new one. She may have had to move from her old house, change schools and friends, learn to live without both of you under one roof, and cope with the stress of change. You've told her repeatedly that you are still a family, that you are each special to one another, that nothing will ever disrupt her life like that again. Don't be surprised, then, if she starts thinking, *If my family is so special and our relationship is so special, why is a total stranger being invited to join our club? Wait a minute!*

Where, when, and how you introduce your new friend deserves careful consideration. Once you're sure that it's time for them to meet, choose a time when your child won't be tired or distracted (the end of a long school day, for instance) and a place that is pleasant and "neutral." Your home may not necessarily be the best place to make the introduction. For young children, a brief—thirty- to forty-five-minute—meeting at a park, ice-cream parlor, or playground is appropriate. If your child is over the age of nine, you might ask her where she would like to meet your new friend and suggest a quiet place, like a museum or a casual restaurant. Keep the meeting brief, not longer than an hour and a half, and relaxed. Avoid important events, like recitals, family gatherings, and any occasion that may be special to your child (a family birthday, the day he leaves for or returns from sleep-away camp, a major holiday when he may miss your ex especially).

Even after your child gets to know your friend, continue being sensitive to your child's feelings. Remember that when you bring a guest into the family home, every member of the family becomes a host with the implicit understanding that all will be on good behavior. That's fine on occasion, but having your date drop by every day after work or for dinner several times a week places an incredible strain on kids, no matter what their age. To minimize your child's feeling that he's sharing you or that your date is monopolizing your attention, try to keep your "distraction" low-key and discreet. Save your long telephone conversations for after your child has gone to bed, for example, and don't enlist your child in that long trek to the mall for the perfect birthday gift for the special him or her in your life.

Even the most subtle pressure on your child to like your date or join in the fun may make him feel like a traitor to his other parent and is bound to meet resistance. Don't repeatedly ask your child how much he likes your new friend or try to "sell" your date to your child by rattling off his or her good qualities. Believe me, until your child decides on his own how he feels about your new friend, you may be jeopardizing the good relationship they might have had were it allowed to develop naturally.

Even when your child is comfortable with your date, set clear limits on his or her involvement with your child. Regardless of your relationship, your significant other is not, in your child's eyes or anyone

WHAT TO SAY ABOUT THAT SPECIAL SOMEONE

CHILD'S AGE	CONVERSATION ABOUT YOUR DATING	SUGGESTED INTRODUCTION
Infant, toddler	"I'm going to see a new friend. I will be back soon."	"This is a good friend of mine. I wanted you to meet each other."
3 to 5	"I'm going to see a friend. I'll be gone for about three hours at the most. I will call you in one hour to make sure everything is okay."	"This is the man/woman I was telling you about."
6 to 8	"I'm going out to see this man/woman. We just met at work and he/she invited me out for dinner. We're going to talk for a few hours, and then I'll be home. I like having friends who have had similar experiences and have interests similar to mine, just as your friends are similar to you. I know some kids get a little upset when a parent starts to date because they are still hoping their parents will get back together. What do you think? Even while I go out with people, we're still going to have our private time together."	*Before the meeting:* "I really like this man/woman, but I have a long way to go to see if there's any future. But it's time to at least let you get to know him/her a little. We'll talk later about what you think."
9 to 12	"What do you think about my starting to date? You know, it's been a while since your dad/mom and I separated. It's normal to want to find friends whom you can talk to who have had similar experiences. Adults are no different than kids in that regard. I know some kids get a little upset when a parent starts to date because they are still hoping their parents will get back together. What do you think? Even while I go out with people, we're still going to have our private time together."	*Before the meeting:* "I like this man/woman, but we have a long way to go before we decide to make a commitment to each other. It's time for you to get to know him/her, and we'll talk later about what you think."
13 to 17	"I'd like to start dating. I know it can be a little weird to have your own mother/father dating at the same time you are, but let's keep talking about it, because I want to be there for you and talk about your dating without mixing in my present experiences."	*Before the meeting:* "I want you to meet the man/woman I've been dating. We've dated awhile now, and it's time for you to get to know him/her a bit and see what you think. I want this to be comfortable for you. And I want you to be open to this even though we've discussed how it may be a little hard for you."

else's, a parental figure or an extension of you. The rules you have for what you say and do around your children do not automatically extend to your date. You need to explain to him or her that certain subjects—namely, your ex, your child's problems with the ex or you—should always be off-limits. And behavior that you may feel is natural and normal for you to engage in around your child—for instance, walking around in a bathrobe or good-naturedly teasing one another—is not necessarily appropriate for your date.

Your date should respect your child's privacy as any other adult would. I strongly recommend that significant others not bathe children or help with using the toilet. While it's fine for your significant other to play with your children and perhaps help them with their homework, they shouldn't do anything that will make it appear that they are taking your place. Unless it cannot be avoided, a significant other should not regularly drop your toddler off at preschool or accompany a child to the doctor or dentist.

WHEN YOUR CHILD DOESN'T LIKE THE NEW FRIEND

> Dear Mom,
> Do you know when you go out with your boyfriend and you stay out for a long time and you don't call? Well, I don't like it when you do that. I am happy that your boyfriend does not come to our house anymore, because he thinks he knows what is happening and me and [my sister] don't like that.
> —Girl, ten

> I feel like putting a bomb through the woman's throat that's going out with my dad. I could but I won't because when she blows up, it may hurt my dad. So maybe I'll just egg her apartment.
> —Boy, eleven

Kids can find a million reasons not to like or approve of your new love. This is not unusual, but it should not blind you to the fact that your child's objections may be valid. The unfortunate truth is that not all adults are sensitive to children or respect how they wish to be treated.

Sometimes this comes out in something as seemingly minor as your new friend conferring a nickname on your child that she hates. At the worst extreme, it may result in physical or sexual abuse. Anytime you sense your child is uncomfortable around someone, make it a point to find out why. Don't jump to the conclusion that your child just has a bad attitude or is critical of your friend because she wants to see you and your ex back together.

This is what Simon thought about Jeremy. He'd seen the hurt expression on Yvonne's face enough times to know he had to do something. Not only was he hurt for Yvonne, but he was embarrassed by his son's rudeness. One afternoon while they were washing Simon's '65 Mustang convertible, Simon broached the subject. "Jeremy, it seems that you don't care too much for Yvonne."

Jeremy dropped a wet rag into a pail and stared down at the white suds. "I dunno. I guess I don't."

Well, this is going nowhere fast, Simon thought. "I've been thinking about it, and Yvonne has been spending more time here at the house. I was wondering if maybe you and I shouldn't plan a little extra time to do things together, alone."

Jeremy looked up and smiled. "Sure, Dad."

"Jeremy, I want you to understand that I care a great deal for Yvonne."

"I know, Dad, but it just seems like she's here all the time, and you're always doin' stuff with her. Every time I come home I never know if she's gonna be here or not or if I'll get to talk to you alone or what. And it seems like everything she wants to do, you want to do. Whatever she thinks is funny, you think is funny. It's weird. You weren't like that with Mom."

"In the beginning of our relationship, it was very much like that. But as I've told you before, your mother and I didn't pay enough attention to our relationship, and we let things come between us. I've learned an important lesson from our divorce, and I'm really trying to be sure the same thing doesn't happen with Yvonne. But maybe I'm trying too hard, and it's making you uncomfortable."

"Dad, to be honest, you do sometimes act a little goofy, too."

"I hear you. How about if I let you know when Yvonne will be here, so we can be sure to have time alone, too?"

"That sounds great. I know she's not a bad person, Dad. It's just all so weird for me."

"That's okay. I would probably feel the same way if I were in your shoes. This is your home, too. But, Jeremy, let's promise each other we'll always try to talk."

Remember, your home is your child's home, too, and just as you would expect him to respect any guest, so every guest should behave respectfully toward him. This means your guest should not

- tease your child;
- correct or discipline him, except when there's a clear and immediate danger;
- call your child nicknames she doesn't like;
- pry, interfere, or offer unsolicited advice about anything (even if it is "well meaning");
- enter her room or other private space;
- join in an activity or conversation without being specifically invited by you or the child;
- touch or interact with your child in any way the child finds uncomfortable, no matter how "innocent" it seems, including roughhousing, "play" punches, tickling, and so on;
- mention to the child anything you have discussed with him or her about the child ("Oh, so your mother told me you really think you look ugly in those braces." "Your dad sure is worried about your grades.");
- attempt to coerce your child into doing anything he does not want to do.

Demonstrating your willingness to listen to, consider, and respond to your child's concerns—even if you ultimately do not agree—sends your child the message that nothing and no one can come between the two of you.

When a child feels resistant to your new relationship, is hostile or unwilling to be open to someone new, try to elicit his specific concerns. Ask questions that will enable him to better describe why he is uncomfortable with this person. You may determine that the child's concern is chiefly about his discomfort with change and the loss of his parent's attention. It may become necessary to set limits with the child and quietly insist on good manners toward your new significant other.

OTHER FACTORS TO CONSIDER

Most of us want the people who like us to like our children, and vice versa, especially if we are considering a serious long-term relationship. While falling in love can be wonderful no matter what your age or cir-

THE HARD FACTS ABOUT CHILD ABUSE

Every child is at risk for physical and sexual abuse. While it's appropriate to teach our children about "stranger danger," it's important to recognize that most child abuse is perpetrated by someone the child knows—a parent, relative, stepparent or significant other, or family friend. Family disruption, such as divorce, is a major risk factor for child abuse. A 1981 study found that children living in a household headed by a single mother were nearly two and a half times more likely to suffer child abuse than children in the general population as a whole. Other studies have noted a similar pattern for sexual abuse.

There are several possible reasons for this: less direct parental supervision of the child and the child's increased, sometimes very close, exposure to new people (friends, relatives, coworkers, and other associates of a new romantic partner or spouse, as well as people your child is exposed to through step- and half siblings and other step-relations). According to David Popenoe, author of *Life Without Father:*

"Despite the fact that immediate family members have the most access to children, fewer than half of the sexual abuse perpetrators, it turns out, are actually family members and close relatives. And strangers make up only 10 percent to 30 percent of the cases. The remainder are acquaintances, including mothers' boyfriends, neighbors, teachers, coaches, religious leaders, and peers."[1]

Several studies have indicated that stepfathers and mother's boyfriends are more likely than biological fathers to physically or sexually abuse children, and when they do, the abuse is more likely to be considered serious. This may be because they have no biological or emotional bond to the child, but one study suggests that their lack of understanding of normal child behavior may also be a factor. The child's "disobedience" was the most common reason abusers offered for their violent response. The same study found that mothers' boyfriends were the perpetrators in 64 percent of nonsexual child abuse cases not involving biological parents (the group responsible for most abuse). This is significant considering how relatively little time most boyfriends spend taking care of children. These trends continue in stepfamilies as well. One study determined that a daughter is seven times more likely to be abused by her stepfather than her biological father. Another, done in Canada in the early 1990s, found that, statistically, a child living within a parent-stepparent household is forty times more likely to be abused than a child living with his biological parents.[2]

All parents should be familiar with the signs of physical or sexual abuse. Don't automatically assume that someone you know and may even love could never do such a thing. A person's love and affection do not always protect your children from abusive, violent, or criminal behavior. Listen to and believe your child. Also remember that children often have a hard time disclosing abuse out of fear of the abuser. Where a significant other or spouse may be involved, these fears are complicated by the realization that revealing the abuse might cause the person to go away and make the parent unhappy. Let your child know that he or she is all that matters to you now, that he or she has no blame for the abuse, and that you will do everything in your power to make sure it doesn't happen again.

If you have any reason to suspect that your child may have been victimized, it's crucial that your child be seen by a doctor and evaluated by a therapist with experience in this area. The incident should also be reported to the police.

cumstances, the fact that you have a child does change things. Now it's not enough for your beloved to love you. You must consider how he regards your child as well, and that is not always easy to determine.

During courtship, we all try to put our best foot forward. When parents have children, that often means being extra nice to the kids. Unfortunately, love can be blind in this area, with devastating results, ranging from a new marriage that never gels to child abuse at the hands of the new partner (see box "The Hard Facts About Child Abuse," page 375). It's your responsibility to evaluate your new partner in terms of the relationship you share with him and in terms of his relationship with your child. To that end, be on the watch for the following behavior:

- "Courting" your child by being overly solicitous, giving money or gifts, offering to take him places
- Insisting on being included as part of the family, forcing himself into family occasions and assuming a parental role
- Criticizing or finding fault with your child about anything, especially if you have not shared a concern or asked for advice
- Criticizing your parenting skills, especially if he is not a parent himself
- Insisting that your child refer to him in a way that is uncomfortable for you or your child ("my new daddy," "Uncle" or "Aunt So-and-So," et cetera)
- Showing an unwillingness to accommodate a child's schedule, interests, and limitations (for example, complaining that your child's school calendar makes winter vacations difficult, showing no interest in your child's accomplishments or interests, criticizing a three-year-old's table manners or a teenager's desire to be with friends)
- Describing a poor relationship with his children or stepchildren from a previous marriage or relationship.

Heeding the RED FLAGS

Parents often turn a blind eye to inappropriate behavior because they don't think of their new friend as a stranger. Yet if they knew of a true stranger behaving toward their child in the same manner, they would be alarmed. So you should be, no matter how well you think you know someone.

A few months after Rachel's mother began dating Maurice, the sales manager in her office, their relationship began to get serious. Rachel, however, hasn't liked him from the start and continues to be silent to the point of rudeness whenever he is around. The last time he was at the house, Rachel barely acknowledged his presence.

Enough of this is enough, Iris thought. "Just what is your problem with Maurice, young lady?" she asked in a moment of exasperation.

"He looks at me weird, Mom," Rachel answered softly.

Somewhat taken aback, Iris asked, "Weird how?"

"I don't know, it just seems like he's been sort of staring when I turn around, and then he suddenly looks away. And he's always hugging me."

"Oh, he's just being nice. You know, Maurice comes from a very affectionate family—they're always hugging and kissing."

"Well, I don't like it. None of your friends or even my uncles ever hugged me like that. I can't describe why it bothers me so much; it just does."

Iris was about to say, "I've never been this close to another man," but stopped herself. She began to repeat what Rachel had told her. "So you're a little creeped out by how he stares at you and seems to hug you in a way that makes you feel uncomfortable." Rachel nodded. "Okay, honey. I'll make sure Maurice doesn't hug you again."

The next time Maurice visited, Iris made it a point to be on the lookout for the behavior Rachel described.

"That's a really cute little skirt you're wearing, Rachel," he said, smiling. "I bet the boys really like to see you in that."

When Iris caught his eye, he looked down and suddenly changed the subject. Later that night, when she told him that Rachel would prefer that he didn't hug her, Maurice became very defensive.

"Iris, what's the big whoop here? It's a little friendly hug. What's her problem?"

This is not the man I thought I knew, Iris thought. "Maurice, it's not Rachel's 'problem'; it's mine. And as her mother, I want to be very clear about this. I am not asking you; I'm telling you: Rachel does not want to be hugged, and I expect you to respect that. If you can't or won't, we shouldn't be seeing each other."

When your child is fearful of, or has genuine misgivings about, the character of the man or woman you are dating, as Rachel did, you may do well to consider the child's perspective and think clearly about the relationship, even putting things on hold to give yourself some distance from it. If you feel your judgment is clouded or that you need another opinion, discussing this triangle with an objective third party may be helpful. Certainly, you will want to move slowly in the relationship when you feel your child has valid concerns regarding your new love interest.

WHEN YOUR CURRENT RELATIONSHIP INVOLVES INFIDELITY IN YOUR MARRIAGE

> Mainly, my dad left my family because . . . he got two women: someone to have fun with and someone to pay the bills. We weren't the ones to have fun with.
> —Girl, thirteen

It is so easy to blame the significant other for destroying the possible reunification of the family. This is why I strongly suggest that, if you did have an infidelity and are going to be continuing that relationship, you wait at least a few months before involving your significant other in your kids' lives or even allowing yourselves to be seen together in public. For your children's sake, there are many reasons to cool it for a while. First, the situation is difficult enough for your children; it is horrible if they feel the whole world knows their parent had an affair. Remember that kids can be cruel, and news travels fast, even into your child's school. Furthermore, it's unreasonable to expect a child to respect or be kind toward the person he believes destroyed his family. The truth is, the person you had the affair with was not the one to destroy the marriage. It is the greater fault of the parents who allowed the marital relationship to deteriorate and the one parent who decided to have an affair instead of properly dealing with the marital issues. But your child loves his parents too much to see life this way when there is a convenient target around. Wait some time after the divorce before you begin to publicly date this person in order to help your children cope with a very complicated situation. That done, any future relationship can begin on a positive note.

Two happy families. *Showing both parents happy with new partners, this girl is moving toward resolution.*

What has worked best so far (in helping you deal with your feelings about the divorce)?
My father's relationship with his girlfriend.
　　—Girl, thirteen

Dear Dad,
Your new fiancée is wonderful. She's very dear to me. I can't wait for us to all move in together.
　　—Girl, fourteen

As fraught with peril as your reentry into dating might appear, it also holds the hope of happiness, perhaps even the creation of a new family. Beyond *"The Brady Bunch* Theme," songwriters haven't paid too much attention to the divorced single parent's quest for love and happiness, which is a shame. Maybe you can't indulge a wild, whirlwind courtship or fall foolishly head over heels the way you could before. But that doesn't mean your new love can't be exciting, wonderful, and affirming. With care and luck, you may one day look back on your divorce as the first step toward the relationship you always wanted and finally achieved.

Q Dear Gary,

My ex-husband and I divorced two years ago. In that time, he's quit his accounting job to teach at a university, lost twenty pounds, taken up yoga, and become quite a sharp dresser. Honestly, I am happy for him, but our girls—fourteen and eleven—think he's fallen under his girlfriend's "spell." They criticize him constantly and refer to him as "a pod person" and "a victim of brainwashing." I've tried to explain to them that people change. When I point out that I've returned to school, starting working again, and have a few new hobbies myself, they say, "That's different; you're still Mom. Dad's just doing what she wants him to do." Help.

A There is something personal going on here that you are missing: Your daughters feel rejected. There's a new love in Daddy's life, and this love has made him—at least in their eyes—a better person. Your daughters couldn't make that change in him, and thus, they are now seeing themselves as second fiddle to their father's girlfriend; that hurts. From their point of view, it is the girlfriend's fault because she has done what they as his children could not. That is why your changes are okay: You did them on your own or perhaps along with your daughters' good wishes and inspiration. Had you done it all because of a new man in your life, you too might be accused of the same crime.

Your situation is especially hurtful to your children because they are girls and look to their dad for a special bond. Their love for him is uniquely theirs and never to be shared. Unfortunately, divorce rewrote the script, and not only has he shared it, but—as they see it—he has developed it uniquely and exclusively with someone else.

Get to the bottom line with your daughters. Don't let them avoid the real issue with answers like "Just because" and "I dunno." Ask them if they wish that they had been the ones to be able to make the changes in Daddy. Wouldn't it have been great if they were given the same opportunity to bring joy to Daddy's life? Do they think that now the only person who truly brings him joy is his new girlfriend? How does that make them feel? What is Daddy doing that shows them they aren't the real joy in his life anymore? Is he really spending less time with them? Or do they get the sense, when they are with him, that he wants the time to be over soon?

Perhaps he never spends any time alone with his girls, and the new girlfriend is interfering in their relationship with him. Help your children see these issues, and then decide who can fix this problem—them, their dad, or all of them?

They may come to realize that Dad still spends private time with them and loves them dearly. Maybe he needs to say this more often. Or maybe Dad is missing the boat and oblivious of his daughters' feelings and their need to resolve this problem. Once your children have a better understanding about the issue, they are ready to talk to Dad and work toward resolution.

Q *Dear Gary,*
My four kids—boys nine and eleven; girls six and thirteen—are always rude to my girlfriend. No matter where we go, no matter what we do, no matter how nice Sandra is to them (and, believe me, she bends over backward), they treat her like dirt. Interestingly, when it's just the two younger kids and us, things go well. This leads me to believe that the older two are instigating the rudeness and the two little ones following their lead. Sandra and I have been together two years now and would have announced our engagement months ago were it not for this situation. I feel we need to get this under control before we move ahead, but I can't ask Sandra to wait forever, or to put up with much more of this. I need a real plan of action.

A It's easy to understand why this situation is so upsetting to you and your fiancée, but before you rush to discuss this matter with your children, take a step back and consider the big picture. There are three key issues to deal with: your children's feeling threatened by Sandra's presence in your life, your children's dislike of her, and your children's unacceptable behavior toward her. Your first step is talk with your two older children alone. Explain to them (following the basic guidelines on page 384) that your relationship with Sandra is real, important to you, and that their behavior will not affect that relationship. You can greatly diminish the manipulation potential here by being very clear: Nothing they do will cause you to end this relationship.

Next, empathize with them; let them know that you understand why they might be worried about having to share you with someone else, how Sandra's presence precludes the possibility of you and your ex reuniting, and how it must be strange for them to see you with someone else. They are old enough to understand that your loving someone in addition to them will not take anything away from them or change your feelings toward them.

Listen to what they have to say. Be prepared to hear some criticism of Sandra or your behavior around her. Hard as it might be, bite your tongue and refrain from jumping to defend yourself or your fiancée. You say in your letter that she "bends over backward" to be nice to your kids, but bear in mind that they may be seeing her actions differently. Talk to them about how they might feel if they had a boyfriend or girlfriend whom you treated rudely. Have them consider how it would feel to become distanced from someone you love simply because you weren't crazy about someone they cared for.

Finally, address the issue of their unacceptable behavior. Let your children know that while you understand their feelings (which they may not yet be able to control or change), you will not tolerate their behavior, which they can control. Defuse another manipulation opportunity by explaining to them how impressionable their younger siblings are, and tell them how differently they act toward Sandra when the older two aren't around. You might say, "We are a family, and we need to get along. I'm not saying that you have to love Sandra or treat her as your mother. At the same time, however, you must behave in a civil, polite manner toward her." Once you've said your piece, don't push it. Step-relationships develop over time, at their own pace.

16

More Than "Another Chance"

The Stepfamily

Dear Mom,
I feel a little bit scared that you will get a boyfriend and live in my house, and I don't want to have a stepdad.

Dear Dad,
I love you, Dad, very much. I don't want to have a stepmother.

—Girl, eight

Today most people who have experienced divorce—parents and children alike—eventually become part of a new family through remarriage, typically within five years of divorce.[1] Whether becoming part of a new family is a distant dream, a fervent hope, or a new reality, it's hard to escape the prevailing notions of "stephood." From *Snow White* and *Cinderella* to hit horror movies like *The Stepfather,* popular culture effectively poisons the well for stepparents. At the other end of the spectrum, step- and blended families are swamped by the unrealistic ideals of such popular TV sitcom families as *The Brady Bunch,* where everyone got along even better than blood siblings. Before divorce overtook a parent's death as the leading cause of single parenthood, a stepparent essentially did replace a deceased parent, and most stepfamilies were formed out of economic (stepfathers supported widows and their children) or social (stepmothers cared for widowers and their children) necessity.

Parents now remarry because they are in love and because they truly do believe that their children will be better off and happier in their

ANNOUNCING YOUR REMARRIAGE TO YOUR CHILDREN

✔ *Plan your announcement carefully.* Set up a specific place and meet when there will be plenty of time to talk and no one is tired, hungry, or pressed to do something else. Think carefully about what you will say.

✔ *Arrange to tell your child before you tell your ex to prevent your ex from making the announcement.* This may take some fancy logistical footwork, but you want to be sure that your child hears it from you first (not your ex or anyone else), that your ex hears it shortly after your child does, and that your ex doesn't hear it from your child. The simplest plan is to tell the child in person, then tell your ex before your child returns to her. (See page 405 for advice about explaining your new spouse's parental role to your ex.)

✔ *Unless it's impossible, make the announcement in person.* If you cannot make the announcement in person and must do it by phone, take care to arrange a good time to talk.

✔ *Deliver the news yourself.* You should be alone with your child, without the future stepparent.

✔ *Don't make it a surprise.* Ideally, your child should have a period of time to get to know your future spouse, his future stepparent. The possibility of remarriage, the child's feelings about your relationship and your future spouse, and what the future might hold for your family are all topics you should have addressed, ideally more than once, before now.

✔ *Avoid expressing great enthusiasm and using "happy" adjectives.* Saying "I have wonderful news" sends the message that any doubts or concerns your child may express will only rain on your parade. Remember that your child is not here to help you feel good about your decision. No matter how happy you are, the point of this conversation is not to talk about how you feel but to find out how your child might.

✔ *Be straightforward, brief, and honest.* You might say simply, "I have important news. Gloria and I are going to get married. We're planning to have a wedding in the spring, about six months from now."

✔ *Clearly and directly ask for your child's thoughts.* "I want you to feel free to tell me whatever you want about this. I'm listening. What do you think about my marrying Gloria?" This comment carefully avoids any assumptions you might have if you're unsure how your child feels. If you get no response, empathize: "Many kids have mixed emotions. They might be happy for their parent, and sad because their parents aren't getting back together. They might feel they're losing some of their parent's love and attention."

✔ *Only after you've gotten a sense of your child's feelings should you offer more detail.* You alone can determine whether knowing more will give your child a greater sense of control and belonging or if it will simply overwhelm her. Talk first about what will not change: "I'll always love you, and although I might go out here and there with Gloria alone, as I have in the past year, or spend more time with her, we'll still have our private time together, just you and me, and we'll go out together with Gloria and her son, Nick, lots of other times." If your child seems comfortable with that, you might bring up living arrangements and other general points: "Gloria and Nick will be moving in with us. We will talk about living together: what our rules will be and so on. Gloria will also be bringing her dog, which you've asked me about before."

✔ *Find out from your child what is important to him.* A great question to ask is, What would make this most comfortable for you?

new family. A stepparent can bring very real benefits to a new family: practical and emotional support for the biological parent and the children, increased family income, more adult involvement with children.[2] Most stepfamilies have all the ingredients for a happy new family, but no one's yet discovered the perfect recipe that works for everyone. This leaves most stepfamilies to struggle figuring out how much discipline the stepparent should mete out, what the children should call the stepparent, where to draw the lines of compromise. At the same time, the parent and stepparent are helping each member find his or her place in the new family while establishing a new marital relationship. It's a tall order, and success requires the time, patience, and understanding of everyone involved, including your ex-spouse.

TELEPHONE

While sitting at the dinner table, play telephone. One person whispers a difficult word or phrase into the next person's ear, and each person tries to repeat it to the next person in a whisper. Usually when the last person to hear the message says it aloud, it's a totally different word or phrase than the one first used.

PURPOSE: This promotes family togetherness and illustrates how easily we may misunderstand things that are not communicated clearly and directly.

GETTING TO KNOW YOU

On index cards or blank flash cards, write topics such as

Favorite food, color, hobby, sport, number, superhero, movie, actor, poem, museum, play, singer, musician, painter, writer, car, song, city, book, drink, TV show, place to go; "my best quality"; three wishes; best friend; dislikes; happiest time; saddest time; "my most difficult trait"; "if I were an animal, I would be…"

The list is literally endless.

A leader chooses five cards and reads them aloud. Each person in the group then responds. After every person has responded to all five cards, take turns going around the group and give each person thirty seconds to recall what the person sitting next to him said.

PURPOSE: This activity helps stepfamily members get to know one another in a fun way. You can also learn a great deal about your child and stepchildren from their responses.

INTRODUCING STEPSIBLINGS

It should go without saying that, unless it's absolutely impossible, stepsiblings, especially those who will be sharing a home, should meet before you marry. The good news about kids is that they're kids. They can usually get along without much interference from us.

Avoid the temptation to give your child's future stepsibling a big buildup. Of course, you want your child to like the other child, but forcing the issue is self-defeating. Ultimately, your child and your new mate's child will have to find their own relationship. Don't push.

Plan the introduction to occur at home, perhaps to be followed by an age-appropriate outing (playground for little ones, movie or sports event for older children). Keep it brief and informal, and be mindful of choosing settings that don't force children to interact if they're not comfortable. Making a vacation weekend of the first meeting or introducing the children at a dinner out probably calls for more intimacy and more conversation than the children want to handle. Better to start off with a good experience, no matter how brief, for everyone. From that point, it's up to the children to find their relationship and up to you to give them the time and space to do that.

To a greater degree than in biological families, the happiness of stepfamilies often rests on the happiness of children. And that happiness depends on the unique and exclusive relationship between parent and child. The major source of conflict in many stepfamilies is not the new family structure but continuing conflict between the new couple's ex-spouses. Unfortunately, that conflict often revolves around the children. Granted, the transition to a new family is difficult for everyone, but especially so for children, and for many of the reasons that make divorce hard: the lack of control over the new circumstances that shape their lives, the uncertainty about what the future holds, the loss of what they had before.

THE GOOD NEWS ABOUT STEPFAMILIES

While a stepparent can never replace a biological parent (even a stepparent who is "more of a parent" than his biological counterpart still may not be seen by his stepchild as his true parent), a child and stepparent can develop a loving, warm, affectionate relationship if the con-

THE HARD FACTS ABOUT STEPFAMILIES

Currently one in every three Americans belongs to some form of stepfamily (which includes the blended families formed by two divorced parents and their respective children), as a stepparent, stepchild, or other step relationship.[4] Ten million children currently live in stepfamilies.[5] Twenty-five percent of all children under eighteen will live in a stepfamily home at some time,[6] and by the century's end, half of all Americans will be part of a stepfamily at some point in their lives. Twenty-one percent of all married couples with dependent children contain at least one stepparent.[7] In 14 percent of stepfamilies, children live with their biological dad and stepmother; in the remaining 86 percent, they live with their biological mom and stepfather.[8]

Statistically, second and subsequent marriages are more likely to end in divorce; and the presence of stepchildren can add to marital stress. However, it's important to keep the big picture in perspective. Second marriages that do survive tend to be more stable than first marriages. Stepfamilies who make it through the initial transition period, which is about two years, are usually more stable than first-marriage families at the five-year point.[9]

(Children who live in step- and blended families are also at increased risk for physical and sexual abuse. See box "The Hard Facts About Child Abuse," page 375.)

ditions are right. Stepparent and child should be free to find their own special relationship without the burden of unrealistic expectations or a "timetable," and they should be supported, especially by both biological parents. Everyone should understand that even when a child and stepparent achieve the closest relationship they can, it may not resemble a parent-child bond (especially if the child is older when you remarry) as much as that between a child and a favorite relative, a mentor, even a trusted older friend. These relationships can be very special and important, and should not be considered less meaningful simply because they don't adhere strictly to the "parent" mold.

Healthy, loving stepfamilies are made, not born. Research indicates that a stepfamily, rather than being something less than a "normal" biologically parented family, may in some ways actually be better. Contrary to popular misconception, stepfamilies per se are not bad for children. In one of the largest, long-range studies of stepfamilies, Dr. Mavis Hetherington found that 80 percent of children of divorce living in stepfamilies have no behavioral problems. Statistically, they do nearly as well as children whose parents never divorce (only 10 percent of these children are considered to have behavioral problems).[3]

Experts who have studied stepfamilies extensively point to their many positive aspects. If divorce teaches children that marriages sometimes don't work, seeing a parent happy and fulfilled with a new partner shows them that there are second chances, that you can create with someone the kind of relationship you want and deserve. In stepparents and stepfamily members, children have opportunities to learn about flexibility and tolerance, about creating family relationships for which the script isn't yet written. While this lack of set role models and rules is often cited by stepfamilies as a source of stress, it can also provide a great opportunity to create the family that works for you, that plays to each member's strength and true feelings.

THE "PARENTING" IN "STEPPARENTING"

"Come on, Henry! We have to hurry," ten-year-old Rebecca admonished her younger brother with big-sister exasperation. "Diane will be home soon!"

"All right," eight-year-old Henry replied, walking cautiously, his arms filled with place mats, cloth napkins, and flatware.

"Daddy, where are my flowers?"

"Here Becca," Ron called from the kitchen, where he was just finishing making dinner. "You made such a pretty arrangement. I can't believe all these flowers came from the field behind the school. Oh wait—I hear Diane's car. Ready?"

Rebecca and Henry stood by the table, their hands behind their backs, almost bursting with anticipation. This was their first long weekend with their father and Diane since their marriage, and the first time they'd visited their new home. Rebecca's glance swept the living room and the family room. *No toys,* she thought, then remembered following behind Diane last night as she gathered all the crayons, books, dolls, and other toys she said "cluttered" the house and tossed them in a plastic laundry basket. "I know your father allowed this mess back in his house, but I've spent a lot of time and energy decorating this place, and we all have to be a little neater."

"Okay," Rebecca had replied quietly, her face reddening. The day before that, Diane had remarked on how Henry never hung up his bath towel the "right way" and then asked Rebecca, "Where did you two learn how to answer a phone? We always say, 'Baker residence,' not 'Hi.' That's just not correct." *But that's how my mom hangs our bath towels and how we answer our phone,* Rebecca thought.

The front door opened, and Diane headed straight for the kitchen. Ron barely said hello before she tossed her briefcase on the counter. "You would *not* believe the day I had today—"

"Hi, Diane!" Rebecca and Henry called out as they scampered into the kitchen.

"Oh, hi, kids." After flashing a quick smile, she turned back to Ron. "Sally called in sick, again. So I said, 'Sally, the next time you call in sick, there'd better be a good reason.' You need help setting the table, hon?"

"No. As a matter of fact, go in and see for yourself. I think you'll be surprised," Ron replied, winking at Rebecca.

"So, she says, 'I've been here for five years—.' " Diane stopped, glanced at the table, and shook her head. "Ron, do you think these place mats go with these napkins? And these flowers are sweet, but if you wanted to make a nice presentation, you could've bought some real flowers down the street. Anyway, I'll fix the table up."

Rebecca glared silently at her father. "Sweetie, I'm so sorry," he whispered. "Diane didn't mean it." He placed his hand gently on her shoulder, but all Rebecca felt were the hot tears rolling down her cheek. She turned and ran to her room.

Suddenly realizing her mistake, Diane looked angrily at Ron. "Please tell me the kids didn't do this." He nodded and sighed. "How could you set me up like this? What's your problem?"

"What's yours?" Ron snapped. He drew a deep breath, then whispered, "Diane, you didn't say two words to the kids. And those flowers—Rebecca picked and arranged them herself. It's kind of obvious the kids did this."

"You should have told me. I'm not a mind reader, Ron. I've never had kids before. I don't always pick up the cues, okay?"

"You sure don't, Diane." Ron quickly wiped his hands on a dish towel before tossing it in the sink. "When it comes to my kids, you don't seem to get anything."

Whether or not they're parents, most adults hold fairly strong opinions about child rearing. If your new spouse has children, time and experience have probably tempered some of his views, making him flexible and open to compromise. If your spouse has no children, you cannot expect her to instantly absorb the knowledge, tricks, and parenting skills you've spent years acquiring (and, to be honest, are probably still working on). It is up to you to give your new spouse every possible advantage when it comes to dealing with your child.

ANTICIPATE AND ADDRESS PARENTING ISSUES BEFORE THEY ARISE

At least in the beginning, children may resent a stepparent's attempt to play the parent, and stepparents may feel insulted when they're not invited to become full partners in parenting. As soon as you know you're going to be sharing your life with your new spouse, put parenting on the agenda. Make it a point to find out his views and feelings, how he sees himself as a stepparent, and what parenting skills he has and which he may need to develop. Talk to your partner about how you handle certain issues (like discipline, praise) and why. Address these issues clearly, taking care to explain to your new spouse that you already have a parenting partner, your ex.

Make it easier for you both by acknowledging that every parent's style is a little bit different. Ideally, you will have gotten to know your new partner and his child well enough before marriage to have a good idea of their relationship. As your new partner gets to know your child, listen carefully to what he says about your relationship with your child. Consider each other's approaches and try to find one that you and your child will be comfortable with. This isn't always as easy as it sounds, and you may have to carefully choose where you will agree and where you may agree to disagree. Keep in mind that you both don't have to ascribe to exactly the same rules and that there may be situations where two stepsiblings may have slightly different rules even under the same roof (for instance, different curfews for a twelve-year-old as opposed to a seventeen-year-old, different homework schedules for an honor student as opposed to a child who's in danger of failing).

The key, as always, is communication between you and your new spouse *and* communication with your respective children. Keep an open mind whenever your spouse raises a point about your child. Remember that parenting is an evolving art, not a science. The rules that worked last year or last week may not work now, and it is your right and your responsibility to parent as you see fit today. Of course, don't be surprised to hear your child say, "Before her, you were much nicer. We never had to put away our own laundry," or "You're just making us eat dinner as a family because that's what he wants." Be aware of when you might be changing the rules to appease your new spouse, but also be honest: Maybe your kids should have been responsible for their clothes and eating dinner together before, too. If you feel that's the case, don't hesitate to gently but firmly explain this to your child. You might say, "I know it seems like we're all eating together because that's what Ned wants. But the truth is, I think it's good for us as a family to have a special time set aside to be together without being interrupted. I look forward to being with you, and while I know you don't like it now, I still expect you home for dinner unless we make other plans."

Most of all, talk to your spouse about your child, your relationship with her, the joys and the challenges, and how important protecting that relationship is to you. Parents often skirt this issue because they don't want to hurt the new spouse or make him feel left out. In fact, however, your relationship with your child is special and exclusive to the extent that on some level, it *does* exclude everyone else, including your child's siblings and his other biological parent. This is no reflection on anyone else, simply a fact. A stepparent who understands and respects your parent-child relationship and your ongoing parent-parent relationship with your ex can sidestep many future misunderstandings. Children who enjoy strong, open relationships with their biological parent are less likely to feel threatened by a stepparent or stepsiblings and less likely to act out.

IF YOU ARE A STEPPARENT, MAKE SURE YOUR STEPCHILD UNDERSTANDS THAT . . .

✔ *You do not want or intend to replace his other parent.* "I know I'm not your mom/dad, and I promise that I will never try to take her/his place."

✔ *You would like his input on how he will address you.* "I don't expect you to call me Mom/Dad, and if you want to call me by my first name, that's fine. I'll go along with whatever makes you most comfortable."

✔ *You respect his other parent.* "I've met your mom/dad, and she/he seems like a great person. You're lucky to have such wonderful parents."

✔ *You recognize that your new relationship with this child may be difficult for him.* "I want you to know, I can understand how awkward this is."

✔ *You respect his relationship with his parent.* "I want you and your mom/dad to spend time alone together, without me intruding. I remember how important it was for me as a kid to have my mom or dad all to myself sometimes."

✔ *You are willing to give the relationship time.* "These kinds of relationships are new to everybody in the family, and I know it may take us some time before we're totally comfortable together. There's no rush. Let's take our time and find out what works best for us."

Let your new spouse get to know your child. Often parents try so hard to ensure their new spouse will fall in love with their child that they present a picture that is literally too good to be true. At the first tantrum or tiff, the bloom comes off the rose. No child is perfect, nor can you expect a new stepparent not to make a few mistakes. In an atmosphere of heightened expectations, misunderstandings are bound to occur. For example, knowing that Diane often spends her first half hour home recapping her day, Ron might have quietly let her in on the kids' big surprise. Before Rebecca and Henry arrived for the weekend, they might have reached some compromises, such as where toys could and could not be left in the house and how they would approach the issues that really matter to them (how the phone is answered) and those that do not (how Henry hangs up his bath towel). Ideally, Ron and Diane together would have discussed these points with the children in a family meeting (see page 400).

How CHILDREN MAY FEEL ABOUT STEPFAMILIES

No matter how good your child's relationship with his stepparent or step- and half siblings, a stepfamily is a study in things that are not really what they seem. In steps, children may see a new person or group of people who threaten to splinter his already-divided loyalties. Children are often dismayingly quick to point out that your new spouse is not his "real" mother or father, or that the other kids aren't his "real" siblings. Stepparents, understandably, grow weary of trying to win the affection and respect another parent already claims. And biological parents can be emotionally squeezed by their perpetual place in the middle.

That said, remember: A successful stepfamily is not only a worthy goal but an attainable one. To achieve it, however, parents must be in touch with their children and give them the time and the space to find themselves in their new family. All too often, parents are so intent on making everything perfect right away that anything a child says or does—even if it was something they would have said or done to a biological parent or sibling—gets blown out of proportion. Nowhere else in your child's life is she made to feel so acutely that other people's (namely your) happiness depends on her. This is a terrible burden for any child to bear. The bond you share with your child is probably one of the only forms of unqualified love, and it is forever. The breakup of your last marriage did not sever it; the birth of your new marriage shouldn't either.

This can be hard for remarried parents, caught up as they often are in the excitement of their new relationship, concerned about their new spouse's feelings, and sometimes unconsciously skipping the pages to the "happily ever after." It's crucial that you learn to see the new family as your child sees it and to understand that, for various reasons, your child may not believe he has the same stake in this new enterprise that you do. Think back to what it took for you and your ex to conquer normal birth-sibling rivalry, for example: the time, the energy, the talks, the fights, the screaming, the crying. Now, when your child is confronted with a new step- or half sibling, his feelings are similar but stronger, sharpened by his past experience and misguided, often-unconscious beliefs: "When Daddy sees how unhappy I am with Laura, he'll go back to

Mommy." "Mommy and Roy are so happy with their new baby. I'll bet if I had been a better baby, Mommy and Daddy would still be together." "Dad always said I was his only special girl, but how can I be when now he has Eve's two girls, too?" Only by addressing the real issue can you reassure your child of your love and help her see her new family in a positive light.

BE SURE YOUR CHILD UNDERSTANDS THAT . . .

✔ *You know how odd it might seem for him to see you with someone else.* "I know it must seem strange for you to see me with someone other than your mother/father."

✔ *Your new partner and he will have a specific relationship.* "Jane and I are getting married, and that will make her your stepmom (and her children your stepsiblings). But she will never try or be able to take your mother's place."

"Richard is/is not able to discipline you about homework/manners/school problems/arguing in the house. He will not punish you until he discusses the situation with me. I will decide what punishment Is appropriate."

"Whether you like the fact that I am remarrying or not, you have to behave appropriately toward Jane, as you would to anyone."

"I have talked to Richard, and we have agreed that he cannot criticize your father or anyone else in our family, or hit you, or lock you in your room. He can, however, give you a time-out and ask you to help with chores around the house after you've done your homework."

✔ *You know he might feel uncomfortable around the new person, and you will try to help.* "Do you have ideas how we can help you to feel more comfortable with Jane around?"

✔ *You know he might be worried about how the new relationship will affect your relationship with him.* "Let's talk about what you and I can do to keep our special rela-

tionship strong. What can we do alone that will give us a good feeling?"

✔ *You do not expect your child's relationship with the new family members to blossom overnight.* "I know that your stepparent and your stepsiblings are not like your mom/dad and your brothers/sisters. I know that the love you have for your family is very special, and those people are very special. No one could ever take their place, and no one will try to. I do hope, though, that over time you and Jane/Richard and her/his children will learn to be friends."

✔ *It can be hard to adjust to new rules, routines, and traditions.* "Jane/Richard and her/his children used to have their own home, just like we did, with their own rules and routines. Some of them were very different than ours, which isn't really good or bad, just something we have to adjust to. Now that we're all together, we'll work together to try to understand each other and come up with new ways to do things that work for us."

✔ *You understand that he may be angry at you or your ex and taking it out on a new stepfamily member.* "I know you're not happy with this situation, and it may take some time for you to adjust. Maybe your anger toward Jane/Richard/your stepsiblings is really anger toward me and your mom/dad for divorcing and getting you in this situation to start with. I am willing to talk to you about that if you want to."

STEPFAMILIES END THE DREAM OF RECONCILIATION

Once most children learn that a parent is seriously involved with someone, it becomes easier for them to understand that their parents will not reconcile. This does not mean that they accept it, however, and for many the dream of you two getting back together still flickers, however faintly. Your remarriage essentially ends that dream forever. Many children experience this as a loss and may mourn this vanished possibility. They may also hold the new stepparent responsible for you and your ex not getting back together again. This is a particularly difficult situation if you and your new spouse began your relationship in infidelity. (See page 378.)

KIDS DON'T SEE STEPPARENTS AS "REAL" PARENTS

Write four things that will change with divorce.
1. Getting married
2. My mom having a boyfriend
3. Having a different person in the house
4. Calling someone else Dad
—Girl, ten

Reading these points, you're probably thinking, Well, obviously . . . Without thinking, though, we often send kids the message that their stepparent is in some way their parent, too, and should be treated accordingly. All relationships are not created equal, and children know this. That's why they often resist the efforts of a biological parent to make this new family "just like a real family." Sometimes parents mistakenly assume that if everyone involved just "acts like a member of a real family," the rest will take care of itself. Others feel it's only fair that a new spouse who assumes many parental responsibilities for a stepchild (supporting the new family, staying home to take care of the children, for instance) receives some parental consideration: being called Mom or Dad, having the authority to make rules for and to discipline the child, and so on.

A dad displaced. An eight-year-old girl's "family after parents are divorced" provides a revealing example of placement. From left to right, she's drawn herself frowning, a smiling mom and stepdad, and a frowning "first dad." Beyond the most obvious interpretation—that Mom and her stepdad are coming between the artist and her first dad—we can see other things. First, by placing Mom and her stepdad literally in the way, she tells us they are obstacles, something she must "go through" to get to her father. Second, she and her first dad are united by—and distinguished from Mom and her stepdad in—their sadness. Finally, she is the largest figure, and the only figure whose feet are firmly planted on the ground.

In some families, this approach may work very well, but it's not unusual for it to backfire just because of how your child feels about things. She has probably come out of the divorce feeling her loyalty is already divided between you and your ex. Just as your child may worry that by loving you she will hurt her other parent, so she may feel that even by being nice or appearing to like your new spouse, she is "betraying" your ex in another way. It's one thing to feel you've hurt a parent by loving someone you already love, someone they themselves loved once; it's quite another to feel you're inflicting the same hurt for the sake of someone who until recently was a total stranger.

Sometimes when a parent makes a child feel that she should love a stepparent the same way she loves her parent, it can make her feel you're pushing her away. Your bond with your child is special, created through birth or choice. To suggest to your child that, simply by virtue of falling in love with you, your new spouse deserves to be thought of and loved in the same way cheapens the true meaning of parenthood. Again, this is not what most parents have in mind when they encourage the "parentification" of a stepparent's role, but this is how children may see it. As his parent, neither you nor your ex is "replaceable." The love he feels extends back farther than he can remember and is built on years of devotion, care, and love. That's something no one can possibly re-create, no matter how good their intentions.

Giving your child and his new stepparent time to find their own relationship turns down the pressure on everyone. Your child is less likely to feel he is betraying his other parent if his affection toward his stepparent is freely given rather than demanded.

STEP- AND HALF SIBLINGS MAKE YOU "SOMEONE ELSE'S PARENT," TOO

> Dear Dad,
> I know you have your own life, and you have another daughter. And you and June are together, and you have your own responsibilities. But I want you to know I still love you.
> —Teenage girl

If your spouse brings to the family children from a previous marriage, your becoming a stepparent may be problematic for your child. If the stepchild is close to your child's age, it sets the stage for sibling rivalry untempered by blood bonds or the gradual relationship building that occurs naturally with siblings (who usually begin their relationship while one of them is a cute, lovable, nonspeaking, and powerless baby). Children for whom divorce brought feelings of parental rejection may have an especially hard time having to share you. If you are a conscientious stepparent trying hard to forge a relationship with your stepchild, you may seem to your child to be favoring that child over him. This is a common problem for divorced fathers, since they are more likely to live with a new spouse's children from a previous marriage than are divorced mothers. It's not unusual for a child to feel that simply by living with his stepsiblings, you are giving them more of your time and your love than he is getting.

THE STEPFAMILY HOME IS NOT THE SAME AS YOUR KIDS' OTHER HOME

It would be impossible, not to mention unfair to your new spouse, to create a home exactly like the one you shared with your ex or that either of you have maintained since breaking up. There are bound to be large and small differences in rules, traditions, routines, and even mundane everyday matters (such as mealtimes and bedtimes, where things are kept, what level of untidiness is acceptable). Generally speaking, kids can benefit by learning to adapt to some differences in rules, as long as those rules are consistent within the household and apply to all family members of roughly the same age. So, for example, not only would you expect your eight-year-old to make her own bed every morning she is with you and your new spouse, but ideally, you would have her nine-year-old stepsibling make his, too. At the same time, the eight-year-old who gets good grades and finishes her homework promptly should be permitted an hour of television after dinner even if her stepsibling has to spend that hour finishing his homework.

STEPCOUSINS, STEPGRANDPARENTS, STEPAUNTS, STEPUNCLES: WHO ARE THESE PEOPLE?

Name four things that will change with the divorce.
 1. *I would get a stepfather.*
 2. *I would move to another state.*
 3. *I would get a new last name.*
 4. *I would get new relatives.*
 —Boy, nine

If meeting and getting to know a new extended family are overwhelming and stressful for newlyweds (who happily choose to join a bigger family), imagine what it's like for a child. There's one child and five, ten, twenty, fifty of "them." Where once there were two sets of grandparents, there may now be four (if any of them have divorced and remarried, even five

FAMILY NECKLACE

Collect a variety of beads. These are widely available in fabric and craft stores, hobby stores, toy stores, and specialty bead stores. You can also make your own beads from Fimo-type modeling material (at art-supply stores). The average household is a treasure trove of potential "found" beads: ornate buttons, large dried seeds and beans, nuts (the hardware type), and Mom's old costume jewelry.

Beads come in an amazing array of colors, textures, and materials: clay, glass, brass, silver, cloisonné, semiprecious stone, agate, shell, ceramic, wood, anodized aluminum, dried resins (cinnabar, amber), and so on. A good bead store will have samples from all over the world.

Have your child choose different beads to represent different family members. These might be their birthstones, or the colors of their birthstones, or simply beads with character or some characteristic reminiscent of the person. Your child might choose beads whose origin or material has special meaning, such as Venetian glass for her Italian grandmother or African trade beads or Japanese cloisonné. You can discuss with your child why each one was chosen, and you may learn something about how she views each person. The child should not be pressured to include everyone if she doesn't want to; she may include deceased relatives, pets, and even special friends, if she so chooses. She can also add to the Family Necklace as family additions occur.

She can string the beads in any order she wishes (use a fairly sturdy material, either nylon fishing line or Tiger Tail–type wire, available at craft and bead stores). However, you might suggest she arrange the beads beginning with her bead in the middle and working through each side of the family on either side. A typical arrangement might begin as shown in the illustration for an only child with half siblings on father's side and stepsiblings on mother's. (Note: Each number represents a family member's position; there could be any number of beads.)

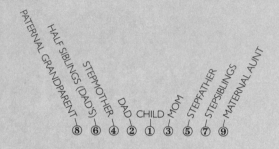

The beads can be made into a necklace or bracelet. It needn't be ornate (a few beads on a leather string, appropriate for a boy, will suffice).

PURPOSE: After divorce, family can become confusing for blended families. This necklace helps a child identify who is in her family and how family members are related to her. Furthermore, by wearing the jewelry, the child can gain the sense of having family with her all the time and feel herself part of a large family.

or six); five cousins can become twenty cousins, with aunts and uncles multiplying all around. Keeping names, faces, and relationships straight is hard enough, let alone actually getting to know them personally.

Some children may feel they already have grandparents, aunts, uncles, cousins, et cetera, and feel some divided loyalty between them and the new cast members. Extended stepfamily members may not be sensitive about how they allude to your child, your divorce, or the new step-family. Mary Sue, now thirty-five, vividly recalls the first big holiday dinner with her stepmother's family:

> All her family did all day was tell me what a great mother she'd be—just like, even better than a 'real' mother (which I already had, thank you)—and how she loved me just like her 'real' daughter. At the same time, it was hard to ignore that they showed more interest in her daughter than in me. I just remember thinking they were rude and pushy. It was like my feelings didn't matter, like I had no history, no past, no life that didn't begin the day my dad married Helene. I felt no one was interested in me, only in my stepmother and stepsister. I left that day feeling like I could never fit into that family, that I would always be viewed as a guest. My anger about this never really went away, and I can't say I ever had more than a polite relationship with any of them for the next twenty years.

Mary Sue's father and stepmother were obligated to make this transition easier for her. Rather than an introduction to the family en masse, small gatherings spread out over several months would have given her and her new relatives opportunities to really talk and get to know one another. Mary Sue described herself feeling like a "guest" rather than a real member of the family. Ironically, her hurt feelings might have been avoided if she had been treated with the respect and courtesy a guest deserves. Someone, preferably her stepmother, since it was her family, should have stayed at Mary Sue's side, introduced her to the rest of the family, and kept the focus of conversation on her.

LOSS OF IDENTITY AND YOUR CHILD'S SPECIAL PLACE IN THE FAMILY

Your child's self-conception—the story she tells herself about who she is—is constantly being rewritten. She probably thinks of herself as you and your ex's daughter, somebody's sister, grandchild, niece, cousin, friend, student, and so on. Your divorce added other items to her personal inventory, and so will your remarriage. Suddenly to be so-and-so's stepdaughter, stepsibling, half sibling, or step-whatever (fill in the blank) calls for other revisions. To a degree most adults don't always appreciate, simply the act of referring to someone as "my stepbrother" or "my step-dad" can prompt curious questions from friends, questions your child may not care to answer.

Whatever your child's place or role within her biological family, it will probably change somewhat now. When both spouses bring children into a marriage, all of them change "job descriptions," but these are more than mere descriptions; they are an important part of your child's self-identity. Every first family has only one eldest; one youngest; one first, second, third, or only middle. Other distinctions of honor—such as being the only girl or the only boy, or the "caboose" baby—make kids feel special and unique.

FAMILY MEETINGS

As parents, we often lament that our children never come to us for advice or to discuss what's on their mind. Mentally review last week's schedule, though, and you'd probably be hard-pressed to come up with five or ten quiet moments you could call your own. Is it any wonder that in real life so many of those special Hallmark moments totally elude us?

It's a common problem, but an easy one to solve. By instituting regularly scheduled family meetings, you stake claim to a block of time dedicated to nothing but talking and listening. Family meetings can help family members discuss and deal with problems, resolve conflicts, and simply get to know one another better. Every family runs its own meetings as it sees fit, but family meetings usually work best for everyone if you agree to some ground rules. You might designate one particular night as meeting night and agree that everyone's participation is mandatory (although no one will be forced to speak if they don't want to). Many families find it helpful to exclude the youngest children, who cannot talk and may be disruptive. Family members can take turns leading the meetings and setting the agenda. At the very least, everyone must agree that no one can make mean comments or embarrass anyone else during the meeting. Even when discussions get a little heated, the family meeting should be regarded by all as a safe place.

Family meetings can concern everything from planning the next family outing, announcing changes in family policy on matters such as chores and allowances, sharing important news, resolving conflicts, or simply talking about how the week went. For the communication to work best, parents should do more than simply chair the meeting. Talk about what's on your mind, too: "I've been having a real battle with my boss over a new filing system. I can't seem to make him change his mind. What do you think I should do?" You may not get the answers you need, but your kids will delight in this turn of the tables and benefit from practicing their problem-solving skills.

It takes a while for each family to find its stride, but when the family meeting really works, the positive effect spreads throughout the week. Knowing there is a special time and place to express feelings, raise issues, and complain makes it easier to "hold that thought" until later. Of course, major problems should be addressed immediately, but discussing them days later in the meeting, when tempers have cooled, offers opportunities for reconsideration and further discussion. Even habitual complainers ease off a bit, knowing they will have a more attentive audience at the meeting.

And remember: Family meetings are for sharing good news, too. Not every meeting has to be a recap of the past week's conflicts. Start off by asking each person to tell about the good things that happened to him or her that week, what each would like to do for the next family birthday party, or what movie to rent that night.

SUGGESTION BOX

Decorate a shoebox with your child and place it in a central location (the kitchen, for example) with a notepad and a pencil next to it. Family members can write (anonymously, if desired) suggestions to be discussed at the next family meeting.

PURPOSE: This can help a child feel that her concerns and thoughts will be addressed. It tells her that her input is important and serves as an outlet for her ideas on improving family life.

OUR FAMILY TIMES

Encourage everyone in your family to put together a monthly newsletter or newspaper. Each family member has her own "department": humor, school happenings, family calendar, illustrations, book review, recipes—whatever you like. It can be as simple or as elaborate as you wish as you long as you remember to keep it fun.

PURPOSE: Family projects like this provide countless opportunities for learning about teamwork, cooperation, and the pride of accomplishment. This can be especially helpful for blended families. Years later, the family newsletter can provide a fascinating contemporaneous picture of your new family and how it grew.

Children also strike their own identities by having accomplishments and claiming interests their siblings do not. That's why it is rare to find a family of three children in which all three excel in the same area. Typically, one is the athlete, another the scholar, another the easygoing social butterfly. Siblings who are close together in age, say eighteen months or less, very often grow up to have quite different interests, outlooks, and personalities. It is almost as though they purposely define themselves as different from each other.

When two families merge, children often feel they have lost some of what makes them special. They may have lost their familiar place in the birth order (your only child now has siblings, your eldest is younger than your spouse's eldest, your youngest older than her youngest, and so on) and in those attributes that were formerly exclusively theirs. Twelve-year-old Cerise had straight A's in math and science and was taking a high-school-level physics course that summer. She enjoyed being the family's academic star until her father married Elaine, whose sixteen-year-old son, Matt, was already a college sophomore at MIT. Four-year-old Sean had been an only child, his every accomplishment the focus of attention. Then his mother married Victor, whose three-year-old identical-twin girls, Lola and Lily, drew comments from strangers wherever they went. Gavin's daughter Andrea was the baby of the family until he married a woman with two children younger than his daughter. And six-year-old John practically worshiped his all-knowing eleven-year-old brother, Tony, until his mother married a man whose teenage son, Ricky, drove a car and was even "cooler." In one way or another, all of these kids will experience a period of displacement before they settle into their new roles.

Even when step- and half siblings get along well and benefit from their new sibling relationships, as many of them do, there's still a period of adjustment as each child finds his place in the new family. During this time, you can help as a parent by anticipating the changes in your new family and how they will impact your child. Some, like those pertaining to birth order, are fairly obvious. Others may not be so clear, and parents should be on the lookout for signs of depression, sudden changes in friends, interests, or academic performance, and anger directed at a particular family member.

KIDS FEAR THAT THEY MAY CAUSE THIS MARRIAGE TO END

Children who have witnessed divorce have probably seen their parents sad, angry, frightened, and vulnerable. Because kids depend on us to be strong and to protect them, the realization that we can be hurt is sobering and even terrifying for them. As we know, children are more comfortable assuming responsibility for something they have no control over than to accept that they have no control. So when Rebecca overhears her father's angry words with Diane, she can't help but believe she is to blame. After all, if she weren't there, they wouldn't be fighting, would they?

Deep inside, children really do want to see their parents happy, even if it is not with each other. Whatever their problems with the stepparent, most would not wish him or her to disappear, if only for their parent's sake. For this reason, even normally expressive children may try to protect a parent by keeping problems about the stepparent or stepfamily to themselves. These problems can range from basic household rules to keeping secret a stepparent's or stepsibling's inappropriate behavior, even sexual abuse. As always, communication is critical.

How PARENTS CAN HELP CHILDREN MAKE THE TRANSITION

When a stepparent isn't "real." Children are often acutely aware that step- and half relatives are not "real" relatives. In this eight-year-old girl's family portrait, everyone is happy, yet she still needs to point out that the man is not her "real" dad.

• *Let your child know that your special relationship with him will not change.* Set aside special private time that's exclusively for the two of you, and use that time to listen to your child. Children who feel free to talk it out are less likely to act it out. If your child is old enough, ask, "What are some of the things you like or don't like about the new situation?" and really listen without automatically jumping to the defense of your new family.

• *Let your child know that it's okay to talk about his other parent, that the "other part of his life" is not off-limits in your home.* When children are told or feel that they cannot discuss their other parent, what they did in the other parent's home, or how they feel about their other parent with you or their new stepparent, they can feel tremendous pain and rejection. While it is not acceptable or healthy for your child to act as a spy or messenger between your homes, she should not be discouraged from talking about your ex in a healthy way. Whether it's telling your new spouse about how her mom made chocolate-chip cookies or asking you why you don't play catch with him like his dad does, remind yourself that these are not necessarily criticisms or challenges. For a moment, imagine spending half your life among people with whom you could not discuss one of your parents. Remember how much both you and your ex mean to your child, and respect your child's right to continue having both of you in his life, regardless of whose home he's in.

• *Let your child know that he will always be special.* Even if he's not the only athlete in the family now or the eldest in the new blended family, he's still a wonderful, unique individual. Acknowledge and help him deal with his losses, but be sure to point out the positive side, too: "It's true that you're no longer the baby of our family, but now you get to be somebody's big brother. And I know how much you've probably wanted to boss somebody else around for a change."

• *Give all the relationships in your new family time to develop naturally.* One adult child of divorce told me, "When my two sisters and I moved in with our father and stepmother, my father bent over backward to make us all like each other. At first, it was a disaster. But after a while, we began getting to know our stepmother, and whatever bonds we forged happened naturally, while she taught my sisters to knit and me to do bookkeeping or told us stories about her own life over cups of homemade espresso and Italian pastries. Those were the 'unplannable' things—ones that did not include my father—that made our family take root."

PROTECT YOUR NEW MARRIAGE

I do not like my mom getting married again.
I am afraid that my mom will get married again and will not love me.
I hope that when my mom probably gets married, it is to a good father.
—Girl, nine

Not again. *This eight-year-old girl illustrates her sadness over her parents' divorce. When children witness marital conflict between a parent and a stepparent, these feelings are renewed.*

Newly married couples need time to establish their relationship, and those in stepfamilies should anticipate some additional stress. You can safeguard your relationship while at the same time improving parent- and stepparent-child relationships by observing some simple guidelines (which, by the way, are similar to those outlined previously to help parents isolate children from conflict).

• *Keep your personal business between you and your new spouse private.* Often remarried parents make the mistake of sharing with their kids, especially teens, the kind of information they would never disclose if their spouse were their child's biological parent.

• *Be clear with your ex about your child's relationship with her new stepparent.* When you tell your ex about your remarriage, don't wait to be asked about your new spouse's parental role. Think through and then address the issues that you know would concern you if it were your ex remarrying. Before Ron and Diane married, Ron might have said to Rebecca and Henry's mother, "I've had a nice conversation with the kids, and they know that, while Diane will be involved in lots of decisions about our new household, she is not replacing you. Diane is clear that the kids will address her by her first name [or, for younger children, another term that is not "Mom," "Mommy," "Mother," "Dad," "Daddy," "Father," perhaps a foreign-language equivalent]. Diane also understands that you and I will continue to make the decisions we see fit regarding the children, as we always have, and that whatever discussions we have will be between you and me. She will not be relaying messages to you, except in an emergency." If you have a poor relationship with your ex and don't feel you can have such a discussion, at least write a letter stating that your child will not be calling your new spouse Mom or Dad, if that's the case, and that your new spouse will not take your ex's place in making decisions about your child. This does not mean that you won't be taking your new spouse's thoughts into account, only that the final discussion—and decision—about your child will always lie with you and your ex.

• *Discuss and deal with divorce-related child issues privately.* Discuss your differences in private, not in the heat of a disagreement in front of the child. Pick and choose your battles, but once you agree on an issue, present a united front whenever possible.

• *Don't make your new spouse the messenger between your ex and you or your child.* As much as possible, keep your current spouse out of the loop. In one study, stepfamily members cited problems with the new spouse's ex as among the top stressors in their new family.[10]

• *Do not blame your new spouse for problems in the home or suggest that your child will make things better for you by keeping your new spouse happy.* Your problems with your new spouse are yours and should not be shared with your children. Asking your child to essentially rescue you—by behaving in a certain way, for instance, or doing something your spouse wants him to do—is inappropriate and potentially harmful. By making your new spouse the villain, you set back her relationship with your child and give your child permission to be angry at her for putting you in a position to be rescued.

If you must ask your child to change his behavior or do something, accept ownership of your request. Timothy told his fourteen-year-old son, Paul, "Please, Lena's on my case because she thinks you're rude when you don't say hello. I couldn't care less about it—you're a big boy, you can make your own decisions—but she's driving me crazy with it. Do me a favor, just give her a quick hi so she'll get off my back." Timothy may feel he's made a compelling, persuasive case, but Paul probably sees the matter quite differently, thanks in large part to his dad. By blaming

Lena, expressing her concerns in a way that makes her sound whiny and unjustified, and then portraying himself as the victim of his new wife's bullying, Timothy has succeeded only in giving Paul reasons not to like his stepmother. He should not be surprised tomorrow when Paul slams the front door harder and behaves even more rudely.

Timothy could have expressed the same point without alluding to his problems with his wife, thereby presenting a united front and forcing Paul to focus on the real issue of his behavior: "I believe it's disrespectful to both Lena and me when you come in after school and go to your room without saying hello. Everyone in this family deserves to be treated courteously, and that kind of rudeness is unacceptable. If you are angry or upset about something, you can talk it over with me, or your mom, or anyone you like. Or we can deal with it in a family meeting this week. But taking it out on Lena this way is not acceptable."

• *When you and your child discuss your spouse, be open to your child's feelings and thoughts but remain neutral toward your spouse and supportive of his relationship with your child.* Don't overlook the possibility that your child may come to the new family with unrealistic expectations of his new stepparent or stepsiblings. For example, after Timothy told Paul he expected him to behave more courteously, the boy replied, "Well, maybe I would be more polite if she ever noticed me. You know, Mom always goes to my soccer games because she knows it's important to me. Lena hasn't been to one yet this season, and that's why I'm mad at her."

Everything Paul said was true; Lena did not share Paul's mother's enthusiasm for his sports endeavors. Here, it is Timothy's responsibility to help his son learn to deal with the new situation. "Paul, I hear you saying that you wish Lena would be more like Mom in that way, and I understand why you feel as you do. It's nice to know someone's cheering you from the sidelines, and I guess that even though I'm there when your mom is not, you'd like to see Lena there, too. In a family, each of us needs time for our own interests. Usually on your game days, Lena is doing her volunteer work at the hospital, and you know how important that is to her. Maybe we can think of other ways you two can spend time together that you both would enjoy."

"Well, I guess there's that science-fiction festival next week. I really want to go, but it's all midnight shows and I know you don't like sci-fi. Do you think Lena would go with me? They're showing one of her favorites—*The Day the Earth Stood Still*."

"Ask her. I'll bet she'll be thrilled," Timothy answered. "I'm very proud of you for coming up with a good solution here."

• *Don't set up your new spouse to compete with your ex.* Avoid making implicit ("Isn't this the nicest bedroom you ever had?") or explicit ("Boy, no one's ever bought you as nice a present as your stepdad") comparisons between your child's other parent and your current spouse. All you're doing is begging your child to take exception and suffer the pain of your indirect criticism of someone she loves.

OF HOMES AND HEARTS

THINGS 2 (OR MORE) DO

FAMILY NOBILITY

Create a family crest or family flag. Use cardboard or fabric; paint T-shirts with special fabric markers or paints (available at most fabric, craft, and hobby stores, among other places). Use the symbol on holiday cards, stationery, and computer creations.

VARIATION: Create a secret family handshake or special greeting (such as a line from a favorite film that has special meaning to you).

PURPOSE: This activity helps focus on the positive definition of ourselves in this new family and creates unity. Kids love to be part of a club or team, and this allows them to create something of that nature. Pay attention to what symbols they use to define this new family. Discuss what their crest, logo, or pictures mean to them.

Whether your child resides primarily in or is an occasional visitor to the stepfamily home, it's important that he feel that, wherever he is, he is welcome and he belongs. This seems so obvious, but we adults tend to focus on the big picture ("Of course, she knows this is her home, too") and often overlook the little things that children never seem to miss. For example, few would argue that Diane has every right to expect everyone to help keep her new home as she wants it. But that doesn't address the very real feelings of rejection little Rebecca experienced as she watched her and her brother's toys being whisked into a basket.

If stepfamilies are about anything, it's compromise. Surely, there was room for some in this instance, perhaps allowing toys out in one of the common rooms, insisting they all be put away at bedtime, or limiting the number of toys that could be out at once. It doesn't sound like a big deal, but the sense of not belonging that children often have is made up of many little things like this, things parents and stepparents may overlook. One man I know who spent summers with his stepfamily as a young boy still vividly recalls the disorientation of never knowing where everything in the kitchen was kept, being afraid to ask, and then being reprimanded for putting things away in the wrong places. Another stepchild, now a grown woman, recalls how uncomfortable she felt around her stepfamily because they didn't say grace at dinner, as her family did.

Home is where the heart is, but it's also a physical place where your child should be able to leave her mark. Displaying photos, artwork, crafts, mementos, awards, greeting cards, and other meaningful items tells your child that she is on your mind when she's not there. More important, it shows her that she has a place, literally, in your home. While it would be unwise to cater to your child's every whim and preference, stocking the kitchen with a few of her favorite foods, laying in a supply of her favorite bubble bath and art supplies, and keeping a collection of games and toys that are exclusively hers (and cannot be used by other children when she's not around) also let her know that she belongs. Inviting her friends and other relatives to visit in your home, encouraging her to talk about her life B.D. (before divorce), and involving her in family decisions are all ways of breaking down the barriers stepfamilies unconsciously demand members erect between the past and the present.

FINALLY

> Musical she is not
> At times, she's fun
> Rather than TV, she plays football.
> Today and every day, she teaches me a new sign
> Hearing is hard, because she's deaf,
> But a stepsister she is to me.
> —Boy, twelve

There's no question about it: Stepfamilies have more of everything. We tend to focus on their challenges and problems; in fact, one leading stepfamily organization publishes a long list of the dozens of ways in which stepfamilies are different from other families. Yet if we define a family as a group of people who love, care for, and support each other, a stepfamily can be as "real" as any other type. In the context of a new family, you can put into practice the lessons you—and your children—have learned from divorce. And there is a lot to be said for step-relationships, unrestricted as they are by set ideas about what's "correct." In stepsiblings, even stepparents, children can find new best friends, mentors, people whom they can look up to, and people who can look up to them. In rare instances, some stepsiblings even end up marrying each other. The sense of belonging that we know is so crucial to a child—the sense that divorce so often betrays—can be found in your new family.

Q *Dear Gary,*
This is the second marriage for me and the third for my soon-to-be ex. In a few weeks we will be announcing to our son, his two daughters, and my older son from my previous marriage that we will be separating. All we fight about is the three stepkids, and they know it. I love my husband, and I'm tempted to tell the kids that they're the reason we're breaking up. Maybe then they would shape up, and we could save this marriage. What do you think?

A The responsibility for saving your marriage rests exclusively with you and your husband. Dragging the kids into it is inappropriate and unfair. Imagine how they will feel if you two break up even if they do "shape up." While your collective children may do things that the two of you argue about, the fact is that you have chosen to argue about these things rather than either avoiding these problems or learning to deal with them in a more constructive manner. Your situation reminds me of people who say, "Money was the reason we divorced." Money was not the problem; the problem was how they chose to deal with their differences over money.

If you still love your husband and really want to save this marriage, you should enlist a counselor who can help you learn to better cope with your situation. If your marriage is stronger, the two of you can learn how to best affect change in your stepkids, if it's needed.

Q *Dear Gary,*
My seventeen-year-old stepson lives with us, and my teenage daughter, who lives out of state, spends most of each summer here. When I suggested to my wife that we not leave James and Christy home alone overnight or that they should both wear bathrobes over their sleepwear (which consists of boxer shorts for James and baby-doll pajamas for my daughter), she says I'm being silly and accuses me of "not trusting" the kids. They are good kids, but I was a boy once myself. Am I overreacting?

A Kudos to you for not tempting fate. They are not brother and sis-ter, and caution is definitely warranted. It is not a matter of trust; you wouldn't let one of them walk around like that if the other had a friend sleeping over. Remember: Your love for your new spouse does not automatically eliminate whatever interest your respective children would have in each other had they met under any other circumstances.

Given this, it is wise and prudent for parents in step- and blended families to establish clear, firm rules on matters of proper attire, nudity, privacy, and so on, from the start. What may be okay in a biological family (your preschooler coming into the bathroom while you're showering to get something, siblings running around in their underwear, older children "wrestling," for instance) may not be okay in your new family.

Your wife wants yours magically to be a "family" where every-one blends together and feels like brother and sister, but she must accept that cannot happen to the extent that she desires it. Help your wife see that it's in everyone's best interest—especially your children's—to honestly acknowledge and respect their normal teenage impulses. You two need to support each other in helping your teens avoid a mistake that could have serious consequences. Trust your instincts.

Q *Dear Gary,*
My new husband and I are expecting our first child together, a girl. Obviously, we're thrilled, and my seven-year-old son can't wait to be a big brother. The problem is my ex-mother-in-law. Every time Nathan refers to his "new little sister," she pointedly corrects him by saying, "You mean 'new little half sister.'" She even told him the baby would never be his "real" sister, since they have different fathers. Her son abandoned us, pays no child support, and hasn't seen or called Nathan in three years. Frankly, I'm tempted to cut off all con-tact with my ex's family, except that Grandma is Nathan's only living grand-parent. What should I do?

A I am assuming that Nathan has a good relationship with his grand-mother, aside from these little derogatory remarks. If she is con-stantly hurting Nathan's feelings, it is hard to see it as a beneficial relationship, and you should consider greatly limiting it.

However, often grandparents say things that even young grandchildren can be taught to take with a grain of salt. Discuss the comments with Nathan and explain that Grandma is upset with her own son and is expressing it in the wrong way. If he can get past that and still enjoy Grandma, so can you. At seven, Nathan is smart enough to understand that people say stupid things sometimes and to begin to understand why.

If, on the other hand, Grandma's comments are hurting Nathan, discuss it with her. Give her the chance to clean up her act or make amends (an apology to Nathan would be ideal) before you cut off contact. Even then, keep in mind that people do change. It's possible that once your daughter is born and Grandma sees how much Nathan loves her, the comments will cease. Perhaps sharply curtailing his contact with her for the next few months, and explaining to Grandma why, might solve the problem without Nathan's totally losing her.

Q *Dear Gary,*
My ex-husband and his fiancée plan to have all their children participate in their wedding ceremony. Our ten-year-old daughter assumed she would be the lead junior bridesmaid. She's since learned that her thirteen-year-old future stepsister is to have that honor, and she will be one of several "junior bridesmaids" instead. My daughter is crushed but refuses to say anything to her father (she already fears that he might love the other girl more, since she lives with him), and she has sworn me to secrecy. Meanwhile, she's been ranting about "that brat." I see a fierce and ugly rivalry brewing if something isn't done quickly. Any ideas?

A It has already brewed, and it's ready to be poured. Try your very best to convince your daughter to discuss the matter with her father. If she feels she can't face him alone, offer to accompany her or to talk to her father on her behalf. New stepfamily members often encounter discrepancies in their respective beliefs about custom and tradition. For instance, one family opens Christmas gifts on the eve, the other in the morning; one believes black should be worn only for funerals, the other thinks black is okay even for weddings; one celebrates every religious holiday on the calendar, the other sticks to the biggies. It could very well be a simple misunderstanding (perhaps your ex's fiancée just assumed that tradition dictates that the oldest girl leads) and a quick intervention will make a big difference.

As you convince your daughter to share her feelings with her dad, explain to her that if she truly wants a relationship with her dad, she has to work at it as well. It isn't always easy to be close to somebody, and it takes great effort at times. Discuss with her the jealousy she has and reassure her that it is totally understandable. Be sympathetic to the entire situation and how "stepfamily-hood"—while statistically common—is a big adjustment for most children.

This should be a good lesson for her in working on relationships. You could even tell her how you personally have learned from your mistakes in the marriage that you need to communicate your feelings to someone you love. The person you love deserves that so they can work it out with you. If you do speak to her father (whether in her presence or not), do not criticize—"How could you do that?"—since that would betray your daughter's trust and severely damage her relationship with him. He is likely to become upset with her for telling you instead of him. Either approach this with a genuine heart to help your daughter and her father or let it go.

Q *Dear Gary,*
Next month I'm marrying Sid, and we're creating a big, beautiful blended family: his three children from a previous marriage and my thirteen-year-old twins. Of course, I'll be taking Sid's last name and just assumed the twins' surname would stay the same. His children use both parents' last names, hyphenated. Last night, though, one of my girls confided that it would be "embarrassing" to her to have to explain why "everybody in our family has a different last name." My other daughter, who likes to think she's joining the Brady Bunch, disagrees. She hasn't seen her father in five years. She adores Sid and would love to take Sid's last name, too, so she and her stepsiblings could "really be a family." Now I'm beginning to wonder if I should keep my current name (the twins' surname), revert to my maiden name, or change the twins' names to Sid's. None of these solutions really appeals to me, but it seems that whichever way I go, there will be problems. Help.

A This is not a decision to be taken lightly or made solely to accommodate social norms (for example, because it would be simpler for your new family socially if everyone shared the same name). Your name is an inextricable part of who you are. Whatever decision you and your child make, keep your eye on the issue's two core components: the legal aspects of changing a child's surname (for which you should consult your attorney) and the emotional issues behind your children's feelings about the subject. Whatever decision you and your child come to, be sure to discuss it from a point of view that considers your child's emotions. Also bear in mind that your ex may very well have a strong opinion in the matter as well, which, depending on the circumstances, will warrant consideration. You should also avoid changing the surname of a child who is old enough to refuse it.

First ask yourself, Is a name change warranted? Here you must consider your child's father's feelings about the change and your child's current relationship with him. If, for example, your children have had little or no contact with their father for five years, despite your doing everything humanly possible to get him involved, the change to Sid's name might be a positive move. Another possibility you might consider is allowing your children to hyphenate their last name, combining their father's surname and Sid's.

Second, the emotional issues. A child who wants to change her name may be seeking a new identity. While this may be a healthy impulse, children need to mourn the loss of identity and love they felt in the past. Discuss the issue. If your child says, "No, it doesn't bother me," realize that she is defending her feelings. After all, if your daughter had a great relationship with her biological father, changing her name probably wouldn't even be an issue. If your child does decide to change her name, treat this decision seriously. You might say, "Look, it has to be upsetting, and we haven't really talked about it. I'm not saying you have to cry about it for the next month, but at least understand that it can be very sad that your father doesn't see or talk to you as much as he should." Help your child to see that even when we move forward to happier things, change itself is often occasion for sadness.

Epilogue

The Changing Family

When Divorce Procedures are Through,
It's sunshine up ahead!

Happier days ahead. *For some children, as for this sixteen-year-old girl, divorce brings comfort. It is up to you as a parent to help your child find the "sunshine up ahead."*

A friend of mine can never begin reading someone's life story without first flipping to the last pages and reading the very end. As she explains, "When I know how it all ends, what I learn as I read makes more sense." Unfortunately, none of us ever gets the chance to flip ahead and skim forward to see how it all turns out for our kids. And perhaps that's for the best, because it helps us focus on what's happening right now. But, of course, what parents wouldn't love to peek ahead, to find out if they were doing the right thing!

We cannot change the past, but we can do much to form the future, even if we do so without a clear view of the end result. If the countless studies on children of divorce don't always succeed in telling concerned parents exactly what to do, they have at least given us some clear ideas on what not to do. While invaluable, those studies cannot possibly take into account the things parents do every day that defy quantification: simply listening, letting your child know you understand, being there with a hug or a smile.

Throughout the book, I've provided examples and guidelines for dealing with the most common problems divorced parents face. I hope this has given you a new way of looking at your child and how she experiences divorce. We all know what the problems are, and in most cases, we can see—if we are honest—where they took root and how they fed on lack of communication, thoughtlessness, and misunderstanding. Every word you've read here grew from my fervent belief that children are far more fragile and yet far more capable than we realize. Yes, they often hold the answers to the problems that regularly baffle us, but they need our support, encouragement, love, and protection, too. If nothing else, I hope you will finish this book with a greater respect for the wondrous, unique person your child is today. Becoming a parent confers upon you the highest honor and the greatest responsibility in the world: the chance to love a child, to guide and nurture her, and to stand beside her. To be there for your child is not an obligation but a blessing.

STORY TIME

Create a story about an imaginary family. Each day a different person (parent or child) adds another bit to the story. This is a very flexible activity: You can do it sitting around the kitchen table all at once, or you can start it on the computer and have each person type in his or her additions each day.

PURPOSE: This activity helps build your child's imagination while letting you hear the story she is weaving around family. Notice how your child develops characters and their relationships.

I've said this before, but it bears repeating, especially on those days when you feel you're not a good parent or there is nothing you can do. Remember: We help our children move on not by ignoring their pain but by helping them express it; not by diminishing their problems or handing them our adult take on them but by helping them find their own solutions. Most important, we admit where there may be no solution, and we work with our children to seek resolution. No one knows your child as well as you do; no one is in a better position to help than you are.

Think of the sandcastles children build so carefully. Filling pails with water and sand, they create these monuments, then watch as they're washed away. They pause, then start the process all over again. Some castles will topple, others will stand, but what matters is that the children built them, crude but magical testaments to the optimism, resilience, and tenacity that all children possess and that any parent can teach her child to use in learning to grow with—not in spite of—divorce.

trolled study. Their sole purpose is to help children express their feelings about themselves, their families, and their lives in the wake of divorce. Despite that, in perusing another group of a thousand randomly selected workbooks from which we drew over half of the children's drawings and most of the excerpts from the children's writings, we noticed some interesting patterns. For example, even though it is almost always preferable for children to be told of the impending separation/divorce by both parents, only about 20 percent of kids between eleven and seventeen were. Disturbingly, 21 percent of fourteen- to seventeen-year-olds and 26 percent of eleven- to fourteen-year-olds claim they were never "told," but described learning of the divorce by "figuring it out" or "overhearing" fights and conversations. For 5 percent in both these groups the "announcement" was one parent walking out.

Since Sandcastles group leaders are encouraged to direct each group as they see fit, there is a wide variation in which workbook questions are answered and which workbook activities are followed. Much also depends on the children's ages. The program is designed to be developmentally appropriate for each of the four age groups, and the workbook for each group is different in terms of content, how similar exercises/questions are worded, and so on.

Although children at six and seven years of age (the youngest Sandcastles participants) are given opportunities to write in their workbooks, most draw. Our early plans to survey their workbooks were quickly dashed when we saw that the fill-in statement "I do not like . . ." prompted a wide range of responses, from "when Daddy leaves" to "eating broccoli," "watching sports on TV," and "when my brother hits me." The fact that unpopular vegetables and hostile siblings were mentioned almost as often as divorce-related subjects led us to conclude that we could derive no meaningful statistical picture from this age group, even though their drawings are among the most eloquent.

Nine- to eleven-year-olds draw more than they write, but children between eleven and fourteen write much more than they draw. The workbooks of teenagers in the fourteen- to seventeen-year-old group typically are returned with the largest percentage of blank pages. Teenagers are the least interested in drawing and the most adept at expressing themselves in writing, yet they tend to prefer talking, and group leaders tend to encourage discussion rather than workbook activities.

The following questions represent only a small portion of the workbook. Most of the written activities, such as "Write a poem about

Appendix 1

The Sandcastles Survey

Much of what you've read in this book is based on what I've learned from running the Sandcastles Program. To date, over ten thousand children in Dade County, Florida, have participated in the Sandcastles Program, as have approximately twenty thousand more across the country, and in Canada and Panama. Each child who participates in the Program receives a workbook during the course of the Program. In this, the child indicates only his or her age and sex on the cover page. Inside the workbook, children are asked to draw pictures and provide written answers to questions. The children are told that they may write or draw anything they wish; that these workbooks are to be returned to the group leader before their parents join the session in the last half hour; and that they are anonymous. Virtually all of these workbooks are then forwarded to me personally, and while it would be impossible for me to read each one, I have perused thousands and found them a source of insight and inspiration. Writing in their private, totally anonymous workbooks, children often reveal the fears and questions they dare not voice.

As you read these results, it's important to bear in mind that this is an informal survey of over five hundred randomly selected, anonymous workbooks. These workbooks were not designed for use in a strictly con-

your family," "Write a letter to your mother/father," and "List three wishes," are impossible to translate into statistics. Many of the seemingly straightforward questions, such as "I hope that . . . ," or "I'm afraid that . . . ," prompt such a wide variety of answers that it's impossible to discern any pattern of statistical significance. For these reasons, we've chosen to concentrate on a few questions whose answers offer insight into how children experience divorce.

The Numbers. These simple statistics were based on the responses taken from randomly selected, anonymous completed workbooks. In each group, approximately one third were completed by boys, one third by girls, and the remaining third from workbooks on which no gender was indicated. The number of workbooks varied by age group, most significantly the eight- to ten-year-old group since so few children answered most or all of the questions. Only a minority of Sandcastles participants of any age answered all of the questions used in this survey. Since this is not a strictly designed study, there was no observer on hand during the actual program sessions, so it's impossible to speculate why that is the case (lack of time, other activities, no interest). Again, the workbooks are a means of expression.

These answers are based on:

Age	Workbooks	Material from
8 to 10	218	page 7
11 to 13	158	pages 3–4
14 to 17	179	pages 3–4

Percentages are rounded off to the nearest tenth, which is why some percentage totals are slightly greater or less than 100. Percentages are calculated by counting only responses. So, for example, if in 179 workbooks a particular question is answered in 154 of them, the percentages are based on 154, not 179. Unlike other surveys, we cannot explain or speculate the reasons behind a nonresponse, so we have excluded them all. In most cases, any answer that receives three or more responses is included. Other responses are identified as "other."

THE RESULTS
EIGHT- TO TEN-YEAR-OLDS
TOTAL NUMBER OF WORKBOOKS: 218

Note that these are responses to "fill in the blanks," so there is a wider range of responses that may not involve divorce-related issues.

"I AM HAPPY WHEN . . ."		
RESPONSE	NUMBER	PERCENTAGE
Parents are together	34	22.4
Am with/see/visit father	26	17
Other	25	16
Parents get along/don't fight	23	15.1
I'm with both parents	16	10.5
Mother/father/family is happy	9	5.9
Parents separated/divorced	4	2.6
With mother	3	2
Totals	152	99.4

"I AM SAD WHEN . . ."

RESPONSE	NUMBER	PERCENTAGE
Parents fight	58	35.2
Parents divorce/separate	34	20.6
Other	20	12.1
Can't talk to/see/be with father	13	7.9
Without parents	7	4.2
I get hurt	6	3.6
Mother/father/family is sad	6	3.6
I get hit	4	2.4
Don't see mother	3	1.8
I feel bad	3	1.8
I'm alone	3	1.8
I don't see mother or father	3	1.8
Totals	165	99.8

"I CRY WHEN . . ."

RESPONSE	NUMBER	PERCENTAGE
Parents fight	38	30.4
I'm sad/mad/unhappy	20	16
Other	17	13.6
I get hit [by parent]	11	8.8
I get hurt	11	8.8
Parents separated/divorced	8	6.4
Mother cries	5	4
I think of divorce	4	3.2
Parents are apart	3	2.4
People die	2	1.6
I'm angry	2	1.6
Parents get hurt	2	1.6
I miss parents	2	1.6
Totals	125	100

"I DO NOT UNDERSTAND . . ."

RESPONSE	NUMBER	PERCENTAGE
Why parents separated/divorced/about the divorce/divorce	84	55.6
Other	28	19.2
Why parents fight	22	14.6
Why parents got together/why people marry then break up	6	4
Totals	151	100

"I WISH I COULD TELL PARENTS . . ."

RESPONSE	NUMBER	PERCENTAGE
Don't divorce/don't separate	58	43.6
I love them	36	27.1
Other	19	14.3
Don't fight	8	6
I feel bad/sad	4	3
Why?	2	1.5
How I feel	2	1.5
To be friends	2	1.5
I'm scared	2	1.5
Totals	133	101.5

ELEVEN- TO THIRTEEN-YEAR-OLDS
TOTAL NUMBER OF WORKBOOKS: 158

"HOW WERE YOU TOLD [ABOUT THE DIVORCE]?"		
RESPONSE	NUMBER	PERCENTAGE
by mother alone	43	28.7
figured it out/guessed/overheard	39	26
by mother and father together	31	20.7
by father alone	17	11.3
response unclear	12	8
one parent left the house	5	3.3
don't know/recall	2	1.3
by a judge	1	.7
Totals	150	100

"WHO DID YOU TELL FIRST?"

RESPONSE	NUMBER	PERCENTAGE
friend	49	35
no one	40	28.6
sibling	16	11.4
cousin	7	5
grandparent	7	5
a parent	5	3.6
aunt/uncle	4	2.9
teacher/counselor/coach	4	2.9
don't recall	2	1.4
other identified person	3	2.1
boyfriend/girlfriend	1	.7
police	1	.7
stepsibling	1	.7
Totals	140	100

"WERE YOU UPSET AT ONE PARENT MORE THAN THE OTHER [AND IF SO, WHY]?"

RESPONSE	NUMBER	PERCENTAGE
no/not angry at either	80	58.8
father	32	23.5
mother	15	11
both	5	3.7
one, not identified	3	2.2
stepfather	1	.7
Totals	136	99.9

"DO YOU WISH THAT YOUR PARENTS WOULD STAY TOGETHER?"

RESPONSE	NUMBER	PERCENTAGE
yes	77	59.7
no	35	27.1
ambivalent ("don't know"/"sometimes yes, sometimes no")	17	13.2
Totals	129	100

"DID YOUR PARENTS ARGUE A LOT?"

RESPONSE	NUMBER	PERCENTAGE
yes	87	70.2
no	30	24.2
not sure/don't remember	7	5.6
Totals	124	100

"DO THEY STILL ARGUE?"

RESPONSE	NUMBER	PERCENTAGE
no	82	67.2
yes	39	32
not sure	1	.8
Totals	122	100

FOURTEEN- TO SEVENTEEN-YEAR-OLDS
TOTAL NUMBER OF WORKBOOKS: 179

"HOW WERE YOU TOLD [ABOUT THE DIVORCE]?"		
RESPONSE	NUMBER	PERCENTAGE
by mother alone	51	28.7
figured it out/guessed/overheard	38	21.3
by mother and father together	37	20.8
unclear	16	9
by father alone	14	7.9
don't know/recall	10	5.6
one parent left the house	5	3.3
by both, separately	3	1.7
by sibling or relative	3	1.7
by family friend	1	.6
Totals	178	99.5

"WHO DID YOU TELL FIRST?"		
RESPONSE	NUMBER	PERCENTAGE
friend	64	38.6
no one	50	30.1
boyfriend/girlfriend	10	6
sibling	10	6
don't recall	9	5.4
cousin	6	3.6
grandparent	5	2.4
other relative	4	2.4
parent	3	1.8
teacher/counselor/coach	3	1.8
other identified person	2	1.2
Totals	166	99.9

"WERE YOU UPSET AT ONE PARENT MORE THAN THE OTHER [AND IF SO, WHY]?"

RESPONSE	NUMBER	PERCENTAGE
no/not angry at either	98	58.3
father	44	26.2
mother	12	7.1
both	8	4.8
one, not identified	5	3
stepfather	1	.6
Totals	174	100

"DO YOU WISH THAT YOUR PARENTS WOULD STAY TOGETHER?"

RESPONSE	NUMBER	PERCENTAGE
no	83	50.6
yes	58	35.4
ambivalent ("don't know"/"sometimes yes, sometimes no")	23	14
Totals	164	100

"DID YOUR PARENTS ARGUE A LOT?"

RESPONSE	NUMBER	PERCENTAGE
yes	124	74.3
no	39	23.4
not sure/don't remember	4	2.4
Totals	167	100.1

"DO THEY STILL ARGUE?"

RESPONSE	NUMBER	PERCENTAGE
no	92	59.7
yes	58	37.7
not sure	4	2.6
Totals	154	100

Appendix 2

Sample Authorization for Emergency
Treatment of Minors

SAMPLE AUTHORIZATION FOR EMERGENCY TREATMENT OF MINORS

Name of minor:_____

Date of birth: _____

List medications the child takes regularly:_____

_____

List prior surgeries and serious illnesses, with dates:_____

_____

List known allergies to medication:_____

_____

I/We, being the parent(s) or legal guardian(s) of the above-named minor, do hereby appoint:

Name   Address   Telephone

_____

_____

to act in my/our behalf in authorizing emergency medical, dental, surgical care, and hospitalization for the above-named minor during the period of my/our absence, from (date) _____ to (date) _____.

This document shall be presented to a physician, dentist, or appropriate hospital representative at such time as emergency medical, dental, surgical care, or hospitalization may be required.

_____

Parent/guardian signature   Address   Phone

_____

Parent/guardian print name   Relationship to minor

_____

Notary public signature   Date   (Notary public stamp)

_____

Insurance company ID or contract or group number

_____

Family or primary-care physician   Phone   Hospital

ATTACH PHOTOCOPIES OF FRONT AND BACK OF EACH HEALTH INSURANCE CARD.

Notes

INTRODUCTION   Parenting After Divorce

1. Steven Garasky, "The Effects of Family Structure on Educational Attainment," *American Journal of Economics and Sociology* 54, January 1, 1995, pp. 88+; David Hamburg, "The New Family," *Current,* July 1, 1993, pp. 4+; Barbara Ehrenreich, "In Defense of Splitting Up," *Time,* April 8, 1996, p. 1 (electronic version); Elizabeth Gleick, "Hell Hath No Fury," *Time,* October 7, 1996, p. 2 (electronic version).
2. Garasky, "Effects of Family Structure"; David Hamburg, "The American Family Transformed," *Society* 30, February 1, 1993, pp. 60+.
3. For example, the U.S. divorce rate per 1,000 population: 1950, 2.6; 1960, 2.2; 1970, 3.5; 1980, 5.2; 1992, 4.8. U.S. National Center for Health Statistics, Vital Statistics of the United States, "No. 90: Live Births, Deaths, Marriages, and Divorces," *Statistical Abstract of the United States,* 1994. See also David Popenoe, *Life Without Father: Compelling New Evidence That Fatherhood and Marriage Are Indispensable for the Good of Children and Society* (New York: Free Press, 1996), p. 27.

CHAPTER 6   The Season of Change:
            Understanding Your Nine- to Twelve-Year-Old

1. Michael D. Resnick, Peter S. Bearman, Robert William Blum, Karl E. Bauman, et al., "Protecting Adolescents from Harm: Findings from the National Longitudinal Study on Adolescent Health," *The Journal of the American Medical Association* 278, September 10, 1997, pp. 823–832.
2. Susan Gilbert, "Youth Study Elevates Family's Role," *The New York Times,* September 10, 1997.

CHAPTER 7   The Quest for Independence:
            Understanding Your Thirteen- to Seventeen-Year-Old

1. Susan Mitchell, "The Next Baby Boom," *American Demographics* 17, October 1, 1995, pp. 22+.

CHAPTER 12   Hello, Goodbye: Custody and Visitation

1. Susan Mitchell, "The Next Baby Boom"; Sonia Nazario, "The Second Wives' Crusade," *Los Angeles Times,* December 3, 1995, pp. 20+.

CHAPTER 13   One Heart, Two Homes: Parenting the Child of Divorce

1. Text derived from Current Population Survey, 1994. "Children under 18 Years Living with Father Only, by Marital Status of Father," and "Children under 18 Years Living with Mother Only, by Marital Status of Mother": (1,077 × 1,000 fathers) + (5,799 × 1,000 mothers) = 6,876,000 divorced parents.
2. James A. Levine and Todd L. Pittinsky, *Working Fathers: New Strategies for Balancing Work and Family* (New York: Addison-Wesley, 1997), pp. 24–25.

CHAPTER 14   Our New Life: Dealing with Divorce-Related Change

1. Gleick, "Hell Hath No Fury."
2. National Public Radio, transcript, "Divorce in America, part 2," from *Morning Edition,* June 22, 1996.
3. NPR, "Divorce in America."

CHAPTER 15   "There's Someone I Want You to Meet": Your New Significant Other

1. Popenoe, *Life Without Father,* p. 66.
2. Barbara Dafoe Whitehead, "Dan Quayle Was Right," *Atlantic Monthly,* April 1993 (electronic version).

CHAPTER 16   More Than "Another Chance": The Stepfamily

1. E. M. Hetherington, cited in Judith Studer, "When Parents Divorce: Assisting Teens Adjust Through a Group Approach," *Guidance & Counseling* 11, June 1, 1996, pp. 33+.
2. Ibid.
3. Virginia Rutter, "Lessons from Stepfamilies," *Psychology Today* 27, May 1, 1994, pp. 30+.
4. Keith Goldschmidt, "America's Stepfamilies: Here They Are at a Glance," Gannett News Service, September 1, 1994.
5. Richard Whitmire, "Stepfamilies' Problems Greater Than Traditional Families," *USA Today,* September 1, 1994.
6. Goldschmidt, "America's Stepfamilies."
7. "Some Worse Off When Parent Marries Again," *USA Today,* January 4, 1996.
8. Rutter, "Lessons."
9. Ibid.
10. Lyn Rhoden, "Stepfamilies in Therapy: Insights from SAA [the Stepfamily Association of America]," *Stepfamilies* 14, April 1, 1994, pp. 5+.

Recommended Reading

BASIC PARENTING SKILLS

Dinkmeyer, Don, and Gary D. McKay. *The Parent's Handbook: Systematic Training for Effective Parenting (S.T.E.P.).* Circle Pines, Minn.: American Guidance Service, 1982.

Faber, Adele, and Elaine Mazlish. *How to Talk So Your Children Will Listen and Listen So Your Children Will Talk.* New York: Avon, 1982.

Ginnot, Haim. *Between Parent and Child: New Solutions to Old Problems.* New York: Macmillan, 1965.

Gordon, Thomas. *Parent Effectiveness Training (P.E.T.).* New York: P. H. Wyden, 1970.

RECOMMENDED BOOKS ON DIVORCE FOR CHILDREN

Banks, Ann. *When Your Parents Get a Divorce: A Kid's Journal.* New York: Puffin Books, 1990. Ages 7 to 10.

Berman, Clair. *What Am I Doing in a Stepfamily?* Secaucus, N.J.: Lyle Stuart, 1982. Ages 5 to 10.

Boegehold, Betty. *Daddy Doesn't Live Here Anymore: A Book About Divorce.* Racine, Wisc.: Western Publishing, 1985. Ages 4 to 8.

Brown, Laurene Krasny, and Marc Brown. *Dinosaurs Divorce: A Guide for Changing Families.* Boston: Little, Brown, 1986. Ages 5 to 10.

Cragin Herzig, Allison. *Shadows on the Pond.* Boston: Little, Brown, 1985. Ages 12 and up.

Krementz, Jill. *How It Feels When Parents Divorce.* New York: Knopf, 1988. Ages 8 and up.

Lansky, Vicki. *It's Not Your Fault, Koko Bear.* Minnetonka, Minnesota: Book Peddlers, 1997. Ages 3 to 7.

McGuire, Paula. *Putting It Together: Teenagers Talk About Family Breakups.* New York: Delacorte, 1987.

Pfeffer, Sarah Beth. *Dear Dad, Dear Laurie.* New York: Scholastic, 1990. Ages 8 to 12.

Rogers, Fred. *Let's Talk About It: Divorce.* New York: G. P. Putnam's Sons, 1996. Ages 3 to 6.

Rosenberg, Maxine B. *Living with a Single Parent.* New York: Bradbury Press, 1992. Ages 8 to 13.

Vigna, Judith. *Mommy and Me by Ourselves Again.* Niles, Ill.: A. Whitman, 1987. Ages 4 to 8.

Index

ABOUT THE AUTHORS

M. GARY NEUMAN is a Florida-state-licensed mental health counselor, a Florida Supreme Court–certified family mediator, a rabbi, and the creator of the nationally recognized Sandcastles Program for children of divorce. Since he first introduced the one-time, three-and-a-half-hour support-group program in 1995, it has been mandated in over a dozen U.S. cities, including Miami, Pittsburgh, and Minneapolis, and is operating on a voluntary basis in several more, as well as in Panama and Canada. As a result, he and the Sandcastles Program have received national coverage, on National Public Radio, *Dateline, Good Morning America, The NBC Nightly News, CBS Weekend News,* and *Today,* and been written about in numerous publications, including *Time* and *Parenting.* In 1996 his monthly national syndicated column "Changing Families" won a Parenting Publications of America Award of Excellence. He tours the country, speaking about marital and family issues, including the unrecognized needs of children and divorce. He also conducts in-person training seminars for leaders of Sandcastles programs nationwide. Neuman maintains a private practice in Miami, Florida, where he sees adults, children, and families. He lives with his wife and five children in Miami Beach, Florida.

PATRICIA ROMANOWSKI is the coauthor of sixteen books, including *We Don't Die, Love Beyond Life,* Mary Wilson's *Dreamgirl: My Life as a Supreme,* and La Toya Jackson's *La Toya: Growing Up in the Jackson Family.* She is coauthor of singer Teddy Pendergrass's forthcoming autobiography *Truly Blessed: The Teddy Pendergrass Story.* She lives on Long Island with her husband, author Philip Bashe, and their son, Justin.

ABOUT THE SANDCASTLES PROGRAM

The Sandcastles Program is a one-session support group experience for children ages six to seventeen (see the box on page 8 for more details). The program consists of a leader's manual, which outlines the innovative activities used in the groups, children's workbooks, and a video.

The Sandcastles Program operates throughout the United States, Canada, and Panama. If you would like more information on Sandcastles seminars, please write to:

The Sandcastles Program
M. Gary Neuman, LMHC
Post Office Box 402691
Miami Beach, FL 33140-0691
Web address: www.sandcastlesprogram.com